ONE WEEK LOAN

Longman Critical Readers

General Editor:

VICTORIAN WOMEN POETS

Edited and Introduced by

TESS COSSLETT

LONGMAN
LONDON AND NEW YORK

Addison Wesley Longman Limited
Edinburgh Gate,
Harlow, Essex CM20 2JE,
United Kingdom
and Associated Companies throughout the world

*Published in the United States of America
by Addison Wesley Longman Inc., New York*

First published 1996

ISBN 0 582 276497 PPR
ISBN 0 582 276500 CSD

British Library Cataloguing in Publication Data

A catalogue record for this book is available from the British Library

Library of Congress Cataloging-in-Publication Data

Victorian women poets / edited and introduced by Tess Cosslett.
    p. cm.
  Includes bibliographical references and index.
  ISBN 0-582-27649-7 (PPR). — ISBN 0-582-27650-0 (CSD)
  1. English poetry—19th century—History and criticism. 2. Women
and literature—Great Britain—History—19th century. 3. English
poetry—Women authors—History and criticism. 4. Great Britain—
History—Victoria, 1837-1901. I. Cosslett, Tess.
PR595.W6V5 1996
821'.8099287—dc20   96–23025
                                                               CIP

Transferred to digital print on demand 2001
Printed and bound by Antony Rowe Ltd, Eastbourne

Contents

General Editors' Preface

The outlines of contemporary critical theory are now often taught as a standard feature of a degree in literary studies. The development of particular theories has seen a thorough transformation of literary criticism. For example, Marxist and Foucauldian theories have revolutionised Shakespeare studies, and 'deconstruction' has led to a complete reassessment of Romantic poetry. Feminist criticism has left scarcely any period of literature unaffected by its searching critiques. Teachers of literary studies can no longer fall back on a standardised, received, methodology.

Lecturers and teachers are now urgently looking for guidance in a rapidly changing critical environment. They need help in understanding the latest revisions in literary theory, and especially in grasping the practical effects of the new theories in the form of theoretically sensitised new readings. A number of volumes in the series anthologise important essays on particular theories. However, in order to grasp the full implications and possible uses of particular theories it is essential to see them put to work. This series provides substantial volumes of new readings, presented in an accessible form and with a significant amount of editorial guidance.

Each volume includes a substantial introduction which explores the theoretical issues and conflicts embodied in the essays selected and locates the areas of disagreement between positions. The pluralism of theories has to be put on the agenda of literary studies. We can no longer pretend that we all tacitly accept the same practices in literary studies. Neither is a *laissez-faire* attitude any longer tenable. Literature departments need to go beyond the mere toleration of theoretical differences: it is not enough merely to agree to differ; they need actually to 'stage' the differences openly. The volumes in this series all attempt to dramatise the differences, not necessarily with a view to resolving them but in order to foreground the choices presented by different theories or to argue for a particular route through the impasses the differences present.

The theory 'revolution' has had real effects. It has loosened the grip of traditional empiricist and romantic assumptions about language and literature. It is not always clear what is being proposed as the new agenda for literary studies, and indeed the very notion of 'literature' is questioned by the post-structuralist strain in theory. However, the uncertainties and obscurities of contemporary theories appear much less worrying when we see what the best critics have been able to do with them in practice. This series aims to disseminate the best of recent criticism and to show that it is possible to re-read the canonical texts of literature in new and challenging ways.

RAMAN SELDEN AND STAN SMITH

The Publishers and fellow Series Editor regret to record that Raman Selden died after a short illness in May 1991 at the age of fifty-three. Ray Selden was a fine scholar and a lovely man. All those he has worked with will remember him with much affection and respect.

Acknowledgements

We are grateful to the following for permission to reproduce copyright material:

the author, Mary Wilson Carpenter for her article ' "Eat me, drink me, love me": The Consumable Female Body in Christina Rossetti's *Goblin Market*' from *Victorian Poetry*, 29 (1991); Gordon & Breach Publishers for the article 'The archetypal feminine in Emily Bronte's poetry' by Christine Gallant from *Women's* Studies, 7 (1980); Indiana University Press for the article 'Face to Face: Elizabeth Barrett Browning's *Aurora Leigh* in Nineteenth-Century Poetry' by Dolores Rosenblum from *Victorian Studies*, 26 (1983); the author, Cora Kaplan for her Introduction to *Elizabeth Barrett Browning, Her Novel in Verse: Aurora Leigh and other Poems*, first published by the Women's Press, 1978, 34 Great Sutton Street, London EC1V 0DX; Macmillan Press Ltd and Cornell University Press for the essay 'Defiled Text and Political Poetry' from *Intellectual Women and Victorian Patriarchy* by Deirdre David. Copyright © Deirdre David 1987; the author, Dorothy Mermin for her essay 'Heroic Sisterhood in *Goblin Market*' from *Victorian Poetry*, 21 (1983); the University of North Carolina Press for the essay 'Intertextuality: Dante, Petrarch and Christina Rossetti' from *Christina Rossetti in Context* by Antony H Harrison. Copyright © 1988 by the University of North Carolina Press; Pinter Publishers, a Cassell imprint for the essay ' "What language can utter the feeling": Identity in the Poetry of Emily Bronte' by Kathryn Burlinson from *Subjectivity and Literature from the Romantics to the Present Day* (ed.) Philip Shaw and Peter Stockwell (1991); Prentice Hall/Harvester Wheatsheaf for the essay 'Christina Rossetti – Diary of a Feminist Reading' by Isobel Armstrong from *Women Reading Women's Writting* (ed.) Sue Roe (1987) and extracts form 'Michael Field' from *Victorian Women Poets* by Angela Leighton (1992); Princeton University Press for the essay 'Emily Bronte' from *Women Writers and Poetic Identity* by Margaret Homans. Copyright © 1980 by P.U.P; Routledge and the authors for the essays 'A Music of

Acknowledgements

thine own' from *Victorian Poetry* by Isobel Armstrong © Isobel
Armstrong and 'A printing woman who has lost her place' from *Affairs
of the Hearth* by Rod Edmond © Rod Edmond; Yale University Press for
extracts from the essay 'The Aesthetics of Renunciation' from *The
Madwoman in the Attic* by Sandra Gilbert and Susan Gubar (1979).
Copyright © Yale University.

We have unfortunately been unable to trace the copyright holder of the
article ' "Men sell not such in any town": exchange in *Goblin Market*' by
Terrence Holt from *Victorian Poetry*, 28 (1990) and would appreciate any
information which would enable us to do so.

Introduction

Having been asked to lecture on Victorian Women Poets on our first-year course, I recently bought a copy of the course textbook, the *Norton Anthology of Poetry*.[1] I was disappointed, but not really surprised, to find that it contained only five poems by Emily Brontë, three by Elizabeth Barrett Browning, and eight by Christina Rossetti. Other Victorian women poets, such as Augusta Webster or Michael Field, were not represented at all. The Anthology also did not reproduce any selections from Barrett Browning's and Rossetti's brilliant narrative poems, *Aurora Leigh* and *Goblin Market*, though excerpts from longer poems by men – Wordsworth's *Prelude*, Tennyson's *In Memoriam* – were included. The more recent *Norton Anthology of English Literature* is slightly more generous, containing at least *Goblin Market*, and a short selection from *Aurora Leigh*.[2] The point I am making here, is that these poets are barely yet part of the canon of 'great' English literature, despite the fact that in their lifetimes Rossetti and Barrett Browning at least were widely read and highly regarded as accomplished and important poets. There are two possible explanations for their subsequent neglect: one is the general disfavour that things Victorian fell into in the earlier part of this century. Great Victorian reputations were gleefully deflated by the Modernists. Yet Tennyson and Browning have at least partially recovered from this critical fashion – not *as* important as the Romantics or the Modernists, but still there. The second explanation brings in the question of *gender* – the fact that these were *women* poets. Jan Montefiore has written convincingly about the way in which women, however famous in their day, get left out when literary history comes to be written.[3] The illusion is given that there were no women poets, no women novelists – each generation of women has to start again. The historical recovery of lost women – writers, artists, scientists, feminists – has been a major project of the recent feminist movement. The term 'herstory' has even been coined to describe this new, woman-centred narrative of the past, as opposed to the male-centred '*his*-story' that has been prevalent.

1

In literary studies, this 'herstorical' impetus has taken the form of challenges to the male-dominated canon of English Literature, and pressure for the inclusion of neglected women writers, and/or the establishment of a rival 'women's tradition' of writing. The 'rediscovery' by feminist critics in the late 1970s of Emily Brontë, Barrett Browning and Rossetti as Victorian women poets was part of this process, which is still going on. While the discovery of a host of neglected women novelists was one of the earliest developments in feminist criticism, a similar discovery of even more women poets is a more recent phenomenon, a further development of the original impulse that brought Brontë, Barrett Browning and Rossetti to critical attention. This development raises for me, as editor of this book, the question, '*which* Victorian women poets?' There are now more than three to choose from. Given that the more recent 'discoveries' have as yet attracted relatively little criticism, I have dealt with this problem by including two essays which cover a number of relatively little-known poets: an extract from Isobel Armstrong's *Victorian Poetry*, on the Romantic precursors of the Victorian women poets, and part of the chapter on 'Michael Field', from Angela Leighton's recent *Victorian Women Poets* (which also includes chapters on L.E.L., Felicia Hemans, Augusta Webster, Alice Meynell and Charlotte Mew). I have chosen the chapter on 'Michael Field' (the pseudonym of two women poets) because it shows the influence of lesbian criticism in making available a lesbian reading of their poetry.

The relative uncanonicity of all the Victorian women poets has had an interesting effect on the critical writing about them, producing particularly sympathetic, protective and inclusive approaches. Whereas a canonical author such as George Eliot or D.H. Lawrence (the subjects of previous volumes in this series) emerges in the 1960s with established New Critical and/or Leavisite readings attached, which are then attacked from various clearly defined theoretical positions (feminist, Marxist, deconstructionist, psychoanalytic), these newly arrived writers attract a less iconoclastic and more mixed kind of writing. In the first place, there is no point in demolishing their authority or undermining their meanings when neither of these are as yet established – this may account for a shortage of deconstructionist criticism here. The feminist move to disinter these poets is celebratory and respectful, of women's writing and women writers, and the reverberations from this impulse can still be felt.

They have surely contributed to a second characteristic of this criticism that I have mentioned: its inclusiveness, and unwillingness to be pigeonholed as belonging to any one particular theoretical school, while using the resources of many. There is often a mixture of a prevailing feminism, a historical and biographical approach, linking the writer to social and political issues, *and* a clever post-structuralist reading of individual poems. The critic is claiming the importance of these writers in as many ways as possible, and filling as many gaps in our knowledge as possible. There is a refreshing sense of the critics enjoying and promoting these writers, rather than putting them through a theoretical mill. This desire for as inclusive a criticism as possible, not limited to one theoretical school, is articulated in Isobel Armstrong's essay 'Christina Rossetti: Diary of a Feminist Reading', and in Leighton's *Victorian Women Poets*; and even a seminal essay like Cora Kaplan's Introduction to the Women's Press edition of *Aurora Leigh*, often cited for its Marxist-feminist approach, also includes reference to French feminist theories of women's language, and Anglo-American theories of a women's tradition in writing. As Leighton puts it:

> To interpret the text only in terms of its politics or ideology is to risk becoming doggedly literal-minded. But to interpret the text only as a 'free play of signifiers', as a matter of endlessly intertextual styles, is to lose the specific, evaluative reasons for selecting some texts rather than others.
>
> . . . Between the biographical–historical matter of my chapters and the formalist–aesthetic interpretations of the poems there is a tension which is itself, implicitly, the literary argument of this book.[4]

So it would not, I think, be helpful to group my selections, or this Introduction, by different critical schools or approaches. Instead, the sections on Brontë, Barrett Browning and Rossetti each start with a 'classic' feminist reading: Margaret Homans on Emily Brontë in *Women Writers and Poetic Identity*; Cora Kaplan's Introduction to *Aurora Leigh*; and Gilbert and Gubar on Rossetti in *The Madwoman in the Attic*. These three pieces already cover a broad spectrum of psychoanalytic, historicist and Marxist approaches. From here on, there is a general movement towards more complex and sophisticated readings, but in some ways the terms of the debate have been set. The questions critics circle around are:

(1) 'Aesthetic' versus 'social–political' readings (sometimes cast as psychoanalytic or post-structuralist versus Marxist-feminist). There are also attempts to bring these two approaches together.
(2) How 'feminist' are these writers? Or are they colluding with patriarchal ideology? Are they victims or rebels? More sophisticated theories of language and of ideology enable later critics to bypass these dualistic questions, and read the poetry as subtly subversive, or in contradictory relationships with different

ideologies/discourses. Different meanings of 'feminist' also
complicate the picture.
(3)   Is there a 'women's tradition', and how do these poets relate to it?
There is a movement here between reference to an essentialised
women's poetry or women's language, and a more specific and
situated concept of a particular nineteenth-century or Romantic
feminine tradition, within and against which these women write.
Other critics see them silenced by or revising a male tradition.

The answers to this last question affect how one views the practice of
grouping these writers together on the basis of gender, as *women* poets
– as indeed this book does. Political and/or aesthetic reasons are
advanced or implied by different critics for doing so.

The next three sections of the Introduction take these three questions,
and follow their ramifications in the critical extracts I have chosen.

'Inner' and 'outer' readings

In an essay on Christina Rossetti and Emily Dickinson (not reproduced
here), Cora Kaplan describes a particular kind of lyric both these poets
write, whose 'indefinite' and multiple meanings resist being bound into
any single biographical, political or psychoanalytic interpretation.[5] She
links this indefiniteness to the inwardness of the poems, their lack of
social reference. As we shall see in the next section, she poses this
inwardness as a problem for would-be feminist interpretations. Though
Kaplan is only talking about a certain kind of lyric, and insists that
other poems by these poets have more definable meanings, she has
identified a problem with the critical–theoretical interpretation of poetry
in general. Unlike the novel in general (especially in the Victorian
period), the 'meaning' of poetry is less easy to pin down, to fit into any
one theoretical framework. Kaplan is writing before interpretations
involving 'multiplicity' as a good in itself became fashionable – but the
feminist goals of social–political critique and celebration of neglected
women writers still sit uneasily with this sort of postmodern approach.

Isobel Armstrong, in her *Diary of a Feminist Reading*, worries more
productively about similar issues: in her case, the opposition is
between the 'aesthetic' or 'formal', and the 'theoretical' or 'feminist'.
For her, the aesthetic qualities of Rossetti's poetry are, and have been
since her childhood, a source of delight. Her wonderfully tentative
essay explores how that delight could be linked to various theoretical
approaches, without forcing the poetry into a particular theoretical
mould. She deliberately takes on a poem without overt 'female' content

('Winter Rain') to experiment with feminist versions of Lacanian and Derridean readings. In her confrontation with official feminist literary criticism in the person of Elaine Showalter, the disagreement between them is over form versus content. Armstrong wants to integrate language and politics, not abandoning the formalist training of her New Critical background as irretrievably 'male', despite its blindness to Rossetti's qualities. Armstrong's recent book, *Victorian Poetry* (from which Chapter 15 comes), carries this project further – in the Introduction, she sees both Marxist readings, which ignore multiple meanings, and deconstructionist readings, which ignore social context, as inadequate.

Attempts to reconcile these oppositions of inward and outward, aesthetic and social–political, figure in much of the criticism in this book. Christine Gallant sees the very inwardness and lack of social reference in Emily Brontë's poetry as an implied criticism of Brontë's social world: the Jungian archetypal feminine of the poetry criticises conventional Victorian femininity. Angela Leighton makes a similar point about Michael Field's poetry: its very remoteness from the ideologies of the 'real world' offers a challenge to those ideologies.

A more complex interrelation between the aesthetic and the political is offered by Margaret Homans, in the Introduction to *Women Writers and Poetic Identity* (her chapter on Brontë is reproduced here). She points out that the tradition of Romantic lyric poetry, like the lyrics Kaplan points to, minimises any connection to 'practical experience'. A 'thematic' approach therefore will not be productive for a feminist critic. Instead, it is the textual relationship of women's poetry to the conventions of this male tradition that Homans analyses, hoping to 'synthesise a literary criticism that is both textual and feminist'. She sees Gilbert and Gubar as sharing in this enterprise – their *Madwoman in the Attic* (from which Chapter 8 comes) uses textual analysis to display not an overt, social–political message, but a hidden feminist rage embodied in transgressive 'madwoman' figures, as a response to the 'angelic' women of male-authored texts, and the social–political context in which women are discouraged from writing. Dual, if not multiple, meanings are allowed for by their approach.

That the social–political meanings of women's poetry can be located in their relation to and reworkings of a dominant male tradition is also argued by Anthony Harrison, who insists that Rossetti's parodic reworkings of the love sonnet tradition in the *Monna Innominata* series work to critique social reality. He rejects definitions of intertextuality that remove it from any social reference. The combination of intertextual readings with social–political interpretations in Kaplan's Introduction to *Aurora Leigh* prefigures Harrison's approach, even though sophisticated theories of intertextuality were not available to her.

Harrison also makes the point that Victorian social behaviour was conditioned to some extent by literary paradigms. The Lacanian theories of language and Foucauldian theories of discourse deployed by Terence Holt and Mary Wilson Carpenter in their articles on Rossetti minimise even more the distinction between the inner and outer, linguistic and social. The post-structuralist frameworks they use are based on the assumption that it is language that constructs reality: everything is 'text'. So Carpenter can describe the Victorian Church as a 'social text', part of the 'social and discursive matrix' in which Rossetti's *Goblin Market* was written, and Holt sees the poem's protagonists caught in analogous webs of language and power relations. Rod Edmond, writing on *Aurora Leigh*, and using theories of ideology taken from Gramsci and Williams, also finds it easy to link 'literary product' to 'social practice', insisting that the poem must be seen in its Victorian context as a 'cultural event'. He also makes allowance for different interpretations of the text, not by an 'internal' analysis, but by looking 'outward' at its reception and translation in different historical moments.

Edmond also questions most previous interpretations of *Aurora Leigh* for their exclusively 'inward', psychoanalytic focus: 'These critics all see the poem as Aurora's inner quest . . . , rather than as an exploration of the problem of how to live authentically outside family structures and in pursuit of her vocation. . . . The poem's metaphorical language has a social as well as psychological reference.'[6] A lot of this criticism, like Dolores Rosenblum's essay (Chapter 5), has centred on the text's deployment of the 'mother' image. But Deirdre David, like Edmond making use of Gramsci, does an 'outward' social–political reading that produces a surprisingly conservative Barrett Browning. Kathryn Burlinson's reading of Brontë, on the other hand, by concentrating on the issue of 'subjectivity', appears completely to elide the social, though all such readings carry an implicit attack on the individualist and unitary humanist notions of identity that are supposed to underpin capitalist and patriarchal societies.

In all these approaches, inward, outward, or combining the two, very few critics allow for the problem of multiple interpretations which Kaplan raises in her essay on Rossetti and Dickinson. It is a problem which the reader of this collection, presented with a multitude of different interpretations, cannot avoid. The reader may want to choose some interpretations and reject others; or to take refuge in a postmodern concept of the ultimate indeterminacy of meaning. I would have liked, had space permitted, to have included in this collection Leighton's chapter on Rossetti, from her book *Victorian Women Poets* (from which the 'Michael Field' chapter reproduced here comes), in which she applies such a theory of indeterminacy to *Goblin Market*, reading it as subversively undermining all fixed meanings that might be expected from a Victorian moral tale: though even here the textual indeterminacy implicitly bears a subversive political meaning.

How feminist are these poems?

Nearly all the critics represented here refer to or write within feminism. Perhaps only Burlinson's article on Bronte appears oblivious to it. But they are often using the term with different meanings, and with different ideas as to what constitutes a feminist reading of a literary text. Some are concerned to find an overt feminist message in the texts, or dismayed at not finding one. Others find hidden feminist meanings beneath a patriarchal surface; or they find subversive reworkings or parodies of patriarchal conventions, social or textual. Some read the Victorian women poets as female victims of male-centred social or textual or psychic structures, and others look for evidence of resistance, overt or covert.

The divisions into 'inner' and 'outer' readings that I discussed in the last section cut across these different reading strategies. Kaplan, in her essay on Rossetti and Dickinson, sees their 'inward' lyrics as a problem for feminists, for two reasons. First, because they exclude social–political reference, which is what she assumes feminists are looking for – an overt critique of patriarchal society. Instead, she finds the poetry accepting of patriarchal constraints. Secondly, the psychoanalytic readings that seem appropriate to this 'inward' poetry work to confirm women's passivity and masochism: she sees a difficult contradiction for feminism here, 'between progressive social struggle and the recalcitrant female psyche'. The only way out seems to be to regard women's writing as an instructive 'record of oppression', as well as an expression of feminist defiance. This negative conclusion is developed, with much greater theoretical sophistication, by Holt – psychoanalysis for him shows not just women's lack of agency, but everyone's, caught in the traps of a monolithic male-centred language system: phallogocentrism.

Other writers, however, find different ingenious ways around Kaplan's dilemma. Gilbert and Gubar, as we have seen, use a psychoanalytic model to discover a repressed feminist rage beneath the conformist surface of their texts. Yet their approach still casts the Victorian women poets as victims of oppression, their poetry dependent on an 'aesthetics of renunciation'. Other critics find less depressing meanings in psychoanalysis, either by turning to non-Freudian variants (Jung, in Gallant; object relations, in Rosenblum), or by discovering alternative versions of Freudian or Lacanian formulations in the poetry itself. This second approach has the advantage of dismantling the hierarchical relationship between theory and text, by which the theory 'explains' the text – here, the texts talk back, on an equal footing with the theorists. Thus Armstrong, in her *Diary of a Feminist Reading*, suggests that Rossetti's 'Winter Rain' revises Lacan, seeming to 'go round behind Lacanian determinism'. Of course Rossetti cannot be aware of Lacan, the 'revision' takes place in the mind of the critic or reader who knows both psychoanalytic theory and Rossetti's poetry, and who takes both to be addressing the same problems. Likewise, Rosenblum reads the images of the mother's face in *Aurora Leigh* to be revising both a male Romantic tradition and Lacanian ideas of mother-lack. In a very similar move, Carpenter reads Rossetti as revising Lacan's construction of the 'mirror stage'.

French feminist revisions of Lacan might be expected to offer these critics another way round depressive or oppressive psychoanalytic readings, but these theorists generally get short shrift here. To simplify greatly, it is possible to construct from the work of Cixous, Irigaray and Kristeva a theory that women can write in a separate female language, irrational, poetic, 'semiotic', outside the oppressive 'phallogocentric' system of the patriarchal 'symbolic order'. Armstrong finds Kristeva's theory of the semiotic briefly useful in interpreting Rossetti, but has reservations. Kaplan, writing on *Aurora Leigh*, concedes that the text could be voicing the revolutionary women's language of Cixous and Irigaray, but counters this by pointing to its social–political limitations. Shirley Foster in an essay entitled 'Speaking beyond Patriarchy' (not reproduced here) argues that far from using a special women's language, Rossetti and Dickinson use and subvert the language of patriarchy, taking on a patriarchal voice in order to undermine or parody it.[7] The idea of parodying a male tradition figures largely in Harrison's intertextual study of Rossetti's *Monna Innominata*. It is another way of attributing subversive agency to these poets – they are not, as Homans claimed, the victims of a male tradition, but subtly undermine it from within. Kaplan's problem with their lack of overt protest, their seemingly conventional attitudes, disappears once we read irony or parody into their poems. The rather condescending or pitying tones of critics towards the Victorian women poets as unconscious victims also disappears as the artistry and skill of their language is recognised, the precision of their intertextual references and revisions.

While some critics thus find feminist agency in psychoanalytic and textual readings, others use the social–political to find an anti-feminist meaning. This is notably so in the case of David (Chapter 6), who employs a Gramscian model of the traditional intellectual to produce a conservative, anti-feminist Barrett Browning by an 'outward', social–political reading. Gilbert and Gubar too imply that the outward, overt

message of *Aurora Leigh* is conservative – Aurora 'capitulates' to
Romney at the end. The concentration of many critics on 'inner',
psychoanalytic readings of *Aurora Leigh* could be a reaction to this
'overt' conservative interpretation: if they read Romney, and Marian
Erle, as aspects of Aurora's psyche, as Rosenblum does, they can come
up with more feminist-friendly readings than if Romney is a
representation of the oppressive male, or Marian Erle of a working-class
woman. Edmond solves this problem differently, by a richer, more
complex social–political reading that locates *Aurora Leigh*'s feminism in
an historical context.

The different feminist reading strategies outlined here are also
complicated by different assumptions as to what 'feminism' is.
Contemporary feminists have moved towards an increasing recognition
of differences within feminism – both the differences introduced by
taking account of class, race and sexual orientation as categories of
oppression alongside gender, and differences of political strategy. These
latter have been usefully categorised by Alison Jagger, as liberal
feminism, radical feminism and socialist feminism.[8] Liberal feminists
are individualists who seek to gain equality with men within the
existing system. Radical feminists are often separatists, who celebrate
female community, feminine qualities and the female body. Socialist
feminists want to ally feminism and Marxism, a critique of patriarchy
and a critique of capitalism. These categories are often useful in
understanding the arguments of the critics. For instance, Kaplan
writing on *Aurora Leigh* takes a radical feminist delight in Barrett
Browning's use of imagery based on woman's body; but as a socialist
feminist she disapproves of Browning's liberal feminist individualism
and blindness to class prejudice. Gallant's celebration of an ahistorical
archetypal feminine in Brontë's poetry puts her into the radical feminist
camp – though the individualism of Brontë's hero-Queen, A.G.A., is
more like liberal feminism. The discovery of images of female
community in *Goblin Market* or *Aurora Leigh* by Mermin, Carpenter and
Rosenblum, has a radical feminist impulse, while David's demolition of
Barrett Browning is partly based on a socialist-feminist distaste for her
class attitudes.

A slightly different categorisation of the different 'stages' of feminism
by Julia Kristeva, as explained by Toril Moi, is also useful:

(1) Women demand equal access to the symbolic order. Liberal
    feminism. Equality.
(2) Women reject the male symbolic order in the name of difference.
    Radical feminism. Femininity extolled.
(3) (This is Kristeva's own position.) Women reject the dichotomy
    between masculine and feminine as metaphysical.[9]

The various subversive or parodic readings of Rossetti would fall into the third stage here, as would some of Leighton's lesbian reading of Michael Field. Historicised readings, like those of Carpenter and Edmond, also relativise the meanings of masculine and feminine: these terms can have different meanings in different cultural contexts, they are not fixed. Edmond argues (in a part of his chapter on *Aurora Leigh* not reproduced here) that the imagery of masculinity and femininity in the poem works not to reconcile these opposites, but to undermine the way the Victorians constructed them.

Edmond's chapter also brings in another complication: what 'feminism' could mean in a Victorian context. While some critics look back to find echoes of contemporary feminisms, others, like Edmond, reconstruct the Victorian feminist context, seeing Barrett Browning as part of a 'new', mid-century feminism that had detached itself from socialism. At the same time, he can make a link between some of Barrett Browning's words and the contemporary Greenham Common women: as he says, texts can take on new ideological meanings in a new context. Edmond's reconstruction of the Victorian context, and of an active Victorian feminism, is connected to a general rethinking by Victorianist feminist critics. While earlier critics tended to present Victorian women (as writers and as represented in texts) in the role of victims, subsequent writers have increasingly stressed their agency. They were not the passive objects of a monolithic ideology, but could use different and contradictory ideologies for their own purposes. Carpenter's article is a good example of this approach, in her discovery of a subversive, proto-feminist, resistant discourse in the Anglican sisterhoods – a move prefigured by Mermin in her less theorised article.

While these critics pay attention to differences of historical context, and questions of class difference are noted by Kaplan (on *Aurora Leigh*) and David, what of other differences of race and sexual orientation? Considerations of race make a brief, surprising appearance in David's chapter in Barrett Browning's political poetry – while the poems on European social problems are tainted by a classist distancing, in her poem on slavery in America, 'The Runaway Slave at Pilgrim's Point', the poet for once allows herself to take the viewpoint of the oppressed, and to articulate a revolutionary anger. Race also appears in Carpenter's article, in the form of a critique of imperialism, a critique that *Goblin Market* shares in, while another Rossetti poem, 'In the Round Tower at Jhansi', does not. Challenges to imperialism and to gender roles, are seen to go together in the one poem, while the other supports the status quo in gender and colonial relations. Lesbian interpretations figure in Carpenter and in Leighton. Carpenter finds the homoeroticism of *Goblin Market* obvious, important, and ignored in previous readings. Leighton, profiting by Christine White's article ' "Poets and lovers evermore" ', is able to give a full-scale lesbian reading of Michael Field's work.[10] Lesbian readings of pre-1920s women's writing were to some extent retarded by the influential argument of Lillian Faderman that most close woman-to-woman relationships in the past were examples of 'romantic friendship', an acceptable and popular mode of relationship between women, not of lesbian sexual relations, which would have been (largely) unthinkable.[11] White argues persuasively that Michael Field's poems are evidence of a lesbian erotic relationship, not merely of romantic friendship. This allows Leighton not just to reclaim Michael Field as lesbian, but to argue that the lesbianism of the poetry puts it in a different tradition from the rest of Victorian women's poetry, involving the expression of a happy, pagan eroticism denied to heterosexual Victorian women poets.

Is there a women's tradition?

How to place these poets in a literary tradition is a question that occupies most of the critics selected here. The rediscovery of more women poets, and especially the construction of a Romantic feminine poetic tradition around figures such as Felicia Hemans and Laetitia Landon has provided a literary 'home' for the Victorian women poets that was not available to earlier critics. Consequently, they often placed the poets in relation to a male poetic tradition, or in relation to female novelists of the nineteenth century. These 'placings' are of course still possible and still deployed. As well as deciding which tradition to place the poets in, critics have to decide how these poets relate to that tradition, what the mechanics of a literary tradition are. Here, other theoretical assumptions play a part: the tradition can be read as a Freudian family drama, an intertextual matrix, a sustaining female community. It is also important to ask why these critics are invoking a tradition: is it in order to explain why women haven't written poetry, or have failed in what they wrote? Or is it to show the sources of their strength? Or to demonstrate their powerful revisions? Or to provide a rationale for grouping them together as 'women poets'?

Both Gilbert and Gubar, and Homans, make the idea of a tradition central to their arguments, and both see Victorian women poets in relation to a male tradition. Gilbert and Gubar make use of and revise the Freudian model of poetic tradition proposed by Harold Bloom in his book *The Anxiety of Influence*.[12] Bloom sees 'strong' poets (all male) in Oedipal conflict with their predecessors, sons battling with fathers for possession of the mother, the poetic 'muse'. Gilbert and Gubar insert the woman writer into this tradition, and see her as doubly anxious, having to deal not only with strong male predecessors, but with those predecessors' demeaning and silencing portrayals of women, and their implication that to write is in itself a male activity. In this Oedipal drama, women are castrated – as Gilbert and Gubar famously ask, 'If the pen is a metaphorical penis, with what organ can females generate texts?'[13] The repressed rage produced by this situation, and by their efforts to appear as 'good', angelic women, can be found in the mad or monstrous doubles who inhabit nineteenth-century women's texts. While this theory places women in relation to a male tradition, it also works to create a female tradition of oppressed, enraged, repressed women writers. *Jane Eyre* is Gilbert and Gubar's paradigmatic text – other works such as *Goblin Market* and *Aurora Leigh* may appear to fit the theory less exactly. As Armstrong says in her extract on *Predecessors*, a notion of tradition founded on the idea of women's oppression risks making all poems come out the same.

Gilbert and Gubar do situate their tradition historically in the nineteenth century, but both their psychoanalytic model, and some incautious remarks about the recovery of an almost archetypal 'woman writer', give it also an ahistorical, essentialist slant. Homans, in the Introduction to *Women Writers and Poetic Identity*, is more cautious and careful in the historical location of her tradition, differentiating it from what she interprets as the essentialist ideas of the French feminists: 'nothing in literature is simply or inherently feminine. . . . Nature is not inherently Mother Nature but only where Milton and Wordsworth and their readers agree to see it that way.'[14] Like Gilbert and Gubar, she locates the women poets in relation to a masculine tradition, and the ways that tradition gendered the poet as male, and his material, Nature, as female. In this she sees a dilemma for potential female poets, which either silences them (Dorothy Wordsworth), or creates difficulties for their poetry. Like Gilbert and Gubar's approach, this sets up a tradition of disabled, victimised female poets, without even the resistant feature of Gilbert and Gubar's feminist rage.

Both Gilbert and Gubar and Homans are using their notions of tradition in part to explain the dearth of nineteenth-century women poets – Gilbert and Gubar see women poets in an even worse difficulty than women novelists. The rediscovery and promotion of a Romantic women's poetic tradition, culminating in the figures of Hemans and Landon, appears to have made that argument redundant for the moment – the fault lies with subsequent literary historians and canon-makers, not with nineteenth-century conditions. Germaine Greer has, however, recently revived the idea of women poets as disabled by their position in society.[15] Even where they wrote voluminously – her example here is Landon – the quality of what they produced was vitiated by their lack of education, and by praise of the wrong sort.

But Greer's judgements are heavily biased by a pervasive and implicit anti-Romanticism, and she appears to have little acquaintance with or use for critical theory and the ways feminist critics have deployed it.

Anne Mellor and Marlon Ross have been instrumental in recreating the feminine Romantic tradition: interestingly, Mellor places Emily Brontë in the masculine Romantic tradition – but as her argument is based on *Wuthering Heights*, I have not included it here.[16] Mellor links the feminine Romantic poets to Burke's category of the 'beautiful', while the masculine poets belong to his category of the 'sublime'. For Armstrong, the feminine Romantic tradition both sustains and constricts subsequent women poets. Leighton sees the achievements of Victorian women poets as consisting in their arguments with and challenges to this tradition. In her view, Michael Field triumphantly eludes the tradition altogether, but at the expense of some of the creative tensions in the work of heterosexual women poets. Michael Field's poetry is seen to belong more in the French tradition, or in a lost lesbian tradition going back to Sappho.

The recreation of a Romantic feminine tradition does not, however, invalidate criticism that points to interactions between women poets and a masculine tradition. David's argument that Barrett Browning, 'possessing no sustaining female poetic tradition', instead turned to a male tradition to give herself poetic authority, does look outdated. But it is still useful to investigate, as David does, Barrett Browning's use of and relation to male authority figures such as Carlyle. Even more so, Harrison's complicated intertextual argument about *Monna Innominata*'s relation to Dante, to the love-sonnet tradition, and to male contemporary writers in the same tradition, is very much to the point. In both these cases, the male tradition is not something that overwhelms or silences these poets, but something from which they pick and choose, revise or appropriate – in the one case, in order to filch authority, in the other, in order to subvert. Subversive revisions of a Romantic male tradition are found by Rosenblum in *Aurora Leigh*, and by Armstrong in Rossetti's poem about the wind. Kaplan and Edmond both point to *Aurora Leigh*'s 'unmannerly' intrusion into and appropriation of the male stronghold of the epic. Both these writers also emphasise the importance of the female novelistic tradition to Barrett Browning. Kaplan in particular looks at revisions of Madame de Staël's *Corinne*, and George Sand's novels, as well as of contemporary male-authored social-problem novels such as Kingsley's *Alton Locke*. Edmond points to similarities and differences with and from contemporary women novelists such as George Eliot or Mrs Gaskell. A new departure is Burlinson's confident placing of Brontë in a conventionally periodised male literary tradition – Romantic, Victorian, modernist – which Brontë neither revises nor is oppressed by, but rather anticipates. Burlinson's approach perhaps relates to Mellor's placing of Brontë as 'masculine' in terms of the Romantic tradition.

Why, then, group these poets together on the basis of gender, as 'women poets'? Leighton's and Armstrong's arguments for a recognised and distinct feminine nineteenth-century tradition are justification enough. The danger is, however, that these poets as a group will be seen as 'equivalent' to any one male poet: Armstrong's book on *Victorian Poetry* has separate chapters on Tennyson and Browning, but only one on the women poets. Similarly, I was asked to provide two lectures for our first-year course, one on 'Victorian women poets', and one on 'Tennyson', rather than on 'Victorian male poets'. But there are also other valid reasons for grouping these poets together. The argument of common oppression is still relevant, so long as it doesn't make them all come out the same, or cast them as pathetic victims. Contemporary feminists can learn much from these poets about the historical position and difficulties of women as writers in the nineteenth century, and the strategies by which these difficulties were overcome. As a group, these writers also make a common challenge to the canon, revealing the gender-biases of literary history. Still another reason is celebratory – these are good poets, and politically useful for silencing those internal and external voices that say 'Women can't write, women can't paint.'[17]

In the next four sections, I shall discuss briefly my selections, poet by poet, highlighting the particular focuses of debate in each case.

Emily Brontë

There is relatively little criticism on Brontë's poetry, as opposed to other Victorian women poets, especially Rossetti. I have reflected this imbalance in the amount of critical attention by choosing three extracts for this section, four on Barrett Browning, six on Rossetti, and two on other poets. Why has Brontë's poetry been neglected by critics? Partly, it has been overshadowed by *Wuthering Heights*, on which there is a vast critical output. But there are also other possible reasons, which can be inferred from the first two of the extracts reproduced here, by Homans and Gallant, both from 1980. These seem to promise a renewal of interest in Brontë's poetry, as, along with other women poets, she is taken up by enthusiastic feminist critics. But both Homans's and Gallant's approaches can be seen to lead to dead ends. The point of Homans's argument is to show the difficulties, even impossibilities, of writing Romantic poetry as a woman. She sees Dorothy Wordsworth as totally silenced as a poet by the gender structure of Romantic poetry. Brontë is a less hopeless case, but even she is menaced by the powerful male muses called up by her poetry: forces that take away her female poetic agency. The structure of Homans's chapter on Brontë is to demonstrate these difficulties in the poetry, and then (at the end of the chapter, not reproduced here) to show the difficulties overcome in the more objective genre of the novel, *Wuthering Heights*. This argument reinscribes the idea that the poetry is a comparative failure, as opposed to the triumph of *Wuthering Heights*. It seems to have taken feminist criticism a while to recover from Homans's rather negative placing of the Romantic women poets – for instance, only recently are we getting a positive re-evaluation of Dorothy Wordsworth's poetry;[18] and the only other major study of Brontë's poetry still puts it in the context of 'male muses'.[19]

Homans partly achieves her effect by concentrating on the non-Gondal poems. The Gondal poems, with their mythical super-heroine A.G.A., would seem to lend themselves to a more celebratory feminist reading. This is indeed what we find in Gallant's article, where A.G.A. is celebrated as an incarnation of the Jungian archetypal feminine. Brontë's fantasy world of Gondal, peopled by mythic heroes and heroines, lends itself superbly to Jungian readings. But the problem here is that Jungian readings have become deeply unfashionable in feminist, and indeed other, academic literary criticism. Nowadays, it is hard to escape from the Freudian/Lacanian orthodoxies. This is regrettable, especially as approaches derived from Jung still feature strongly in popular and radical feminism – witness the huge success of Clarissa Pinkola Estés' *Women Who Run With the Wolves*.[20] In the late 1970s and early 1980s, Jung's ideas provided fertile ground for feminist interpretations – Annis Pratt's *Archetypal Patterns in Women's Fiction* is a good example of this trend; but it is hardly respectable now, in the stampede away from anything apparently tainted with essentialism (that is, ascribing the 'feminine' to anything inherently fixed, or 'archetypal', as opposed to socially constructed).[21] The essentialism of the French feminists is routinely attacked, but they are still taken seriously: Jung has the added burden of a masculinist bias to his theories. So have Freud and Lacan, of course, but they can be claimed as social constructionists, showing the processes by which gender is acquired. Gallant's article, if a little naïve, nevertheless shows how there can be a strong feminist appropriation of Jung too: the 'archetypal feminine' she discovers in the poems is quite different from, and critical of, the socially constructed Victorian feminine that constricted Brontë's life. There are a few encouraging signs that Jung is being revalued and revised by feminist critics, the archetypes being made more historicised and less fixed, but his fall from favour could explain the lack of interest in poetry which is so blatantly dealing in myths and archetypes.[22]

The third essay in my selection, by Burlinson, shows a very recent and quite different application of Lacanian theories to Brontë's representation of subjectivity. This move rescues Brontë from the traps of Romanticism where Homans left her, and places her instead as a forerunner of Modernism. But Burlinson's approach is still problematic for a feminist criticism of Brontë's poetry, in that it aligns Brontë with other *male* writers of the Victorian and Modernist periods. Another article that I might have included had there been more space, is Emma Francis's 'Is Emily Brontë a Woman?' from the same collection as Burlinson, which pertinently raises the problem that Brontë's poetry poses for feminist attempts at appropriation, the poetry always escaping categorisation according to gender, period and genre.[23]

Elizabeth Barrett Browning

Criticism on Barrett Browning tends to focus on her long narrative poem, *Aurora Leigh*, though I have also included a chapter from Deidre David's book which discusses some of her political poetry. *Aurora Leigh* at first sight seems a gift to feminist criticism – the story of a woman's successful struggle to become an independent poet, full of 'women's' imagery. Its publication by the Women's Press confirmed its status as feminist classic. The poem fitted into the preoccupation with the woman writer, and a women's culture, in early feminist criticism – Elaine Showalter having declared in a famous essay that 'gynocriticism', or the study of women's writing, was the proper task of feminist literary studies.[24] But from the beginning there were also worries about the poem's lack of what we would now call 'political correctness'. These centred on two areas: the rather stereotyped portrayal of the working classes (all grotesquely evil, apart from the saintly Marian Erle); and Aurora's eventual 'capitulation' in marriage to her cousin Romney Leigh, whose first marriage proposal she refuses so forcefully in Book II, arguing for the greater importance of her poetic vocation. That Romney had been symbolically blinded by the end, and that his socialist schemes proved mistaken, only increased feminist and socialist unease with the conclusion.

Kaplan's comprehensive Introduction to the Virago edition raises these doubts, especially those about class relations in the poem, while also celebrating its female imagery, and energetic reworkings of contemporary texts by men and women. Kaplan's piece is a good example of what I have called an 'inclusive' style of criticism, taking up various approaches, weighing pros and cons. It is interesting that more recent debates about differences between women – class, race, sexual orientation – tend to imply that these differences make any feminism impossible. Yet Kaplan is quite clear about the classist limitation of *Aurora Leigh*, while also being quite clear about its feminist strengths.

Gilbert and Gubar's section on *Aurora Leigh* in *The Madwoman in the Attic* (not reproduced here) finds the poem's feminism limited not by its depiction of the working class, but by the marriage ending.[25] They read Aurora as embracing an ethic of service, learnt first from the sufferings of Marian Erle. Romney's blinding does not diminish his patriarchal hold over Aurora at the end. Yet beneath this conventional ending, they read a hidden rebelliousness, in Aurora's large projects for her art, tactfully put into Romney's mouth. Thus the poem fits neatly into the double meanings they assign to all Victorian women's texts: a conformist surface and a hidden rage. The 'incorrectness' of the ending is explained away as a necessary conformity forced on women writers by Victorian patriarchy. It must be said, however, that in the case of *Aurora Leigh* there seems no particular reason to regard one of the two meanings as 'surface' and one as 'hidden': both are openly stated, rather than one being hidden away in the imagery or symbolism.

Rosenblum's article evades the limitations seen by Kaplan, Gilbert and Gubar by concentrating on a particular aspect of the 'woman's figure' in the poem – its deployment of images of the mother's face. In doing so, she becomes part of a debate on the poem's imagery and the figure of the mother, pursued in a number of books and articles by different critics (none of these are reproduced here). Virginia Steinmetz, for instance, sees images of 'mother-lack', rather than the reassuring reciprocating face Rosenblum finds.[26] Barbara Charlesworth Gelpi, on the other hand, sees the imagery working towards an androgynous combination of masculine and feminine qualities;[27] while Leighton, in her book on Barrett Browning, sees the poem's presiding image as the father, its main project being a working out of Barrett Browning's problematic relationship with her own father.[28] Sandra Gilbert reasserts a movement from paternal to maternal imagery, which she links to the plot's movement from England to Italy, 'fatherland' to 'motherland'.[29] Rosenblum's concentration on the mother's face produces a triumphalist reading, in which Barrett Browning solves the problems that male Romantic writers and contemporary Lacanian psychoanalysis set for female subjectivity. The mother's face, with its answering gaze, confirms a strong female subjectivity. More recent parlance, drawing on the language of feminist film criticism, might see this figure as offering women an escape from the imprisoning and defining 'male gaze'.

David's book on *Intellectual Women and Victorian Patriarchy* (from which Chapter 6 comes) restores the political dimension to Barrett Browning's poetry, and in her chapter on *Aurora Leigh* (not reproduced here) she picks up on the disquieting features noted by Kaplan and Gilbert and Gubar to produce a politically conservative, anti-feminist reading. In her chapter on Barrett Browning's other political poetry, she stresses Barrett Browning's dependence on Carlyle in her political thought, and her antipathy to socialism. In Gramscian terms, Barrett Browning is a 'traditional intellectual', harking back to an idealised past, and speaking from a transcendent, classless position. But, as a woman, she does not have the authority to speak from this position, and has to invoke male authority. This reading fits into David's overall thesis that Victorian women intellectuals were compromised by their divided roles, as women and as intellectuals, trying to claim authority in a patriarchal culture.

Anyone who has studied Victorian literature will not be surprised that attacks on the middle classes, and exposés of working-class suffering, came mostly from the Right, not the Left. Putting Barrett Browning's politics back into her Victorian context, Rod Edmond shows that in Victorian terms it is still possible to read her as a feminist. In his reading, she is not a Gramscian traditional intellectual, but a mouthpiece of an 'emergent' ideology, in Raymond Williams's terms. Her attitudes to class and to marriage are not a failure to be sufficiently feminist, nor a smokescreen for a hidden feminist agenda; instead, they are the historical concomitants of a particular kind of Victorian feminism. Setting *Aurora Leigh* in the context of contemporary legal changes, novels and art-works, Edmond reads it as a 'cultural event' in its own time. That its more radical messages were concealed or lost sight of is not due to Barrett Browning's cautiousness or compromise – it is due to the dominant ideology assimilating and muting its emergent potential. This renewed attention to *Aurora Leigh*'s historical context balances the somewhat essentialist concern with 'female' imagery, and the ahistorical demands that it conform to our notions of feminism. On the other hand, Edmond himself points out that the poem's reclamation as a 'feminist classic' is part of our historical moment, a new reading now available.

Christina Rossetti

There is more criticism of Rossetti than of any other Victorian woman poet. Early feminist critics judged her hostile to feminist readings, as someone who submitted to and upheld Victorian gender conventions, but more recently critics have increasingly revelled in the complexities, hidden meanings and ironies of her verse. Its very evasiveness and opacity is perhaps congenial to a postmodern temperament. Much of the criticism of Rossetti is focused on *Goblin Market*, which seems endlessly susceptible to new interpretations. But some critics are interested in her lyric poetry; and her sonnet sequence, *Monna Innominata*, has recently attracted attention for its complicated revisionary relationship with the love-sonnet tradition. There is also some criticism of her religious poetry, but this does not usually show the influence of critical theory.

Kaplan's article on Rossetti and Dickinson, discussed above, raises Rossetti's poetry as a problem for feminist interpretation. As well as the 'indefinite' lyrics, Kaplan discusses and finds unsatisfactory some proto-feminist interpretations of *Goblin Market* by Maureen Duffy and Ellen Moers. Simultaneously (1979), Gilbert and Gubar provide a powerful feminist reading of the poem. Though they may be straining to fit it into their 'madwoman' model, their interpretation has the virtue of stressing Laura's importance as desirous, transgressive woman, and the repressive undertones of its conclusion. To read the poem as being about writing, rather than the obvious sexual meaning, is a challenging revision, and their two-layered, surface and repressed, reading begins to show up some of the poem's complexity and contradictions.

As Kaplan suggested, Gilbert and Gubar read the poem as evidence of women's oppression. Their interpretation is opposed by Mermin's triumphalist reading – she sees the poem as not being about 'bitter repression', but as 'a fantasy of feminine freedom and self-sufficiency'. In her interpretation, Lizzie, not Laura, becomes the feminist heroine, rescuing her sister from sexual dependence on men. The ending is not a repressive return to Victorian domesticity, but a fantasy of an all-female community.

The opposition between these two interpretations, Gilbert and Gubar's and Mermin's, structures much of the following debate about *Goblin Market*. It is re-enacted with greater theoretical sophistication by Holt and Carpenter's articles. Holt follows the 'negative' line of Gilbert and Gubar, seeing the possibility of escape to somewhere 'outside' the system as undercut by the very language in which it is put. Like Gilbert and Gubar, he posits a monolithic patriarchal ideology, from which these women cannot escape, backing it up with Foucauldian theories of discourse and Lacanian theories of language and the symbolic order. He also develops the Marxist implication of the 'market' in the poem, its use of metaphors of commodity and exchange.

Carpenter, on the other hand, once more reads liberation into the female community at the end of the poem. Using a more complex theory of ideology and discourses, she is able to find a way round

Holt's oppressive reading. Taking up Mermin's comment about Rossetti's involvement with the Anglican sisterhoods, she does some detailed reading of the discourse of the Oxford movement, discovering there unexpected possibilities of feminist resistance. She strengthens her 'separatist' reading by emphasising the poem's homoeroticism, and complicates her reading of its 'market' imagery by introducing a post-colonialist critique of imperialism. White women figure as both consumers and objects of exchange in this economy. Rather than dividing the debate on *Goblin Market* into Laura versus Lizzie as feminist heroine, she divides it differently into those who see only Laura learning something in the poem, and those (like Carpenter) who see Lizzie as also changed by her experiences, by learning to 'look' and intervene in a system she wanted to ignore. If both women are changed, the ending is not a reimposition of an oppressive order, nor an untenable fantasy. Carpenter's reading of 'In the Round Tower at Jhansi', however, reconfirms that Rossetti's poetry can be implicated in the oppressive ideologies of its time. 'Rossetti' as a poet is complex and multiple.

Isobel Armstrong's article (dated 1987, so placed after Mermin in my selection) cuts across these debates, picking up Kaplan's worries about the resistant 'aesthetic' qualities of Rossetti's verse. Her tentative applications of Lacan, Derrida and Kristeva to a Rossetti poem leave the impression that the poem is always richer, deeper and more evasive than any one theoretical reading, while it engages in productive debate with the theorists. Choosing a poem without overt 'female' content, she is not concerned like other critics to claim or dispute a feminist message. Its 'feminism' lies in some deeper interrogation of male-centred structures.

Harrison's chapter (placed chronologically after Armstrong and before Holt) also works on the aesthetic qualities of Rossetti's poetry – the *Monna Innominata* sonnet sequence in this case. Using theories of intertextuality and parody, he charts its engagement with and revision of Dante and the love-sonnet tradition. Rossetti, as a woman, speaks from the position of the usually silent love-object, and thus exposes the bankruptcy of the whole tradition. In this way, gender is central to his argument, and the social critique he reads into Rossetti's parodic revisions has an implied feminist meaning. It was hard to decide between Harrison's chapter and William Whitla's equally brilliant and complex reading of this same sequence.[30] Whitla in particular provides a clever deconstructive reading of Rossetti's 'Preface' to the sonnets. The sophistication of these critiques, and their engagement with Rossetti's own sophistication, her multi-layered meanings, indicates how far Rossetti criticism has come since Kaplan's rather baffled incomprehension.

Other poets

Previously minor or forgotten nineteenth-century women poets are still being discovered and brought into prominence. The extract from Armstrong's book, on 'Precursors', discusses the ways in which such poets might be seen as part of a 'tradition'. She rejects the notion of a tradition based on female oppression, or female experience. Instead, she concentrates on the contemporary meanings of 'feminine' and 'poetess', in order to show that a nineteenth-century feminine poetic tradition existed and was recognised. Constricting as the nineteenth-century definitions of the 'feminine' in poetry were, ironically they secured an unprecedented respect and attention for the poetesses, and supplied them with a set of conventions within and against which to write. Armstrong is aware of a possible classist bias in the reconstruction of this feminine poetic tradition, and discusses several working-class women poets, before defining the tradition as largely middle-class. She focuses on Laetitia Landon and Felicia Hemans, two poets of the Romantic period, in order to show the feminine poetic tradition out of which the Victorian women poets came. As she says, the Victorian women poets looked back to these women as their precursors, and she is concerned to reconstruct what their poetry meant to later writers.

Leighton's book on the *Victorian Women Poets* similarly begins with chapters on Landon and Hemans, implying that they form a continuum with the later, strictly speaking 'Victorian' women poets, and help to explain the tradition with which the later poets have to contend. Armstrong sees Landon and Hemans as part of a tradition of feminine affective or expressive poetry; similarly, Leighton sees them as writing 'from the heart'. Anne Mellor's book on *Romanticism and Gender* also characterises Landon and Hemans as part of a sentimental feminine Romantic tradition, while the male Romantic poets take on the 'sublime'.[31] The construction of a feminine Romantic tradition is a major move away from a criticism which, like Homans, sees Romantic and Victorian women poets in solitary combat with an overwhelming, inimical and wholly male poetic tradition.

Leighton's chapter on the later Michael Field reveals a different, Sapphic, tradition, in which she places them. Their lesbian poetry thus evades the tensions the heterosexual women poets encounter in dealing with the 'feminine' tradition. They are able to write freely about desire, and to revel in a pagan relationship with Nature. Leighton relates their lack of embarrassment or guilt to a historical context that allowed their love to flourish without labelling it as abnormal or wrong. Without the growth of lesbian criticism, such a reading would have been invisible a few years ago, just as the burgeoning of feminist criticism brought Brontë, Barrett Browning and Rossetti back into notice, as women poets.

Leighton's reading of Michael Field demolishes the idea that there were no lesbian poets before this century, just as some of Armstrong's readings show that there were working-class women poets. And the continuing rediscovery of many women poets also lays to rest ideas of women's silencing or absence as poets in the nineteenth century.

In providing this survey of recent criticism on Victorian women poets, I have wanted to avoid a simple narrative of progress. It is sometimes assumed that critical approaches necessarily follow a forward, developmental path, as structuralism is followed by post-structuralism, modernism by postmodernism, even feminism by post-feminism. The whole structure of the academic institution, of course, fosters this progressive model, with the pressure to publish and to correct the 'failings' of one's predecessors. In criticism of the Victorian women poets, I see no such inevitable progress. Delighted feminist critics fall upon these neglected women poets in the late 1970s and early 1980s, exploiting the openness of the field to produce radically new, exciting feminist readings. It is these 'founding' readings that I still find the most perceptive, most daring, in their uses of different critical approaches to a feminist end. Later critics refine upon, shore up, circle round, the debates set up by these earlier critics. Of course, it may be that I am only taking part in another feature of the academic publishing institution – after a decent interval, one's reviled predecessors can be rediscovered and revived (as has happened to the Victorian women poets themselves). In so far as there has been progress, I would see it in the discovery and promotion of more women poets, rendering obsolete theories devised to explain their absence or failure; and in the more precisely researched historicised readings of critics like Edmond and Carpenter, enabled by new theories of discourse and ideology. And yet I still admire the more emotive, sometimes essentialist, enthusiasms of earlier critics.

These poets raise awkward questions of value and quality for any criticism that would ignore these issues – *not* in that they are without value and quality ('greatness'), and are being promoted for political/ interested reasons; quite the reverse: they are poets whose value and quality are highly appreciated by a group of readers who find them both enjoyable and empowering. I should like to refer you here once again to Armstrong's essay on Rossetti, which begins with her nine-year-old sense of 'That's it' on first reading Rossetti's 'Who Has Seen the Wind', takes us through the revelations made and the hesitations aroused by 'applying' various theoretical approaches to Rossetti's poetry, and ends with a call for a complex 'gendered account of pleasure'.

Notes

1. 3rd edn (New York and London: W.W. Norton and Co., 1983).
2. 6th edn (New York and London: W.W. Norton and Co., 1993).
3. JAN MONTEFIORE, *Feminism and Poetry* (London and New York: Pandora, 1987), pp. 20–5.
4. p. 7.
5. CORA KAPLAN, 'The Indefinite Disclosed: Christina Rossetti and Emily Dickinson', in *Women Writing and Writing About Women*, ed. Mary Jacobus (London: Croom Helm, 1979), pp. 61–79.
6. p. 157.
7. SHIRLEY FOSTER, 'Speaking Beyond Patriarchy: The Female Voice in Emily Dickinson and Christina Rossetti', in *The Body and the Text: Hélène Cixous, Reading and Teaching*, ed. Helen Wilcox, Keith McWatters, Ann Thompson and Linda R. Williams (New York and London: Harvester Wheatsheaf, 1990), pp. 66–77.
8. ALISON M. JAGGAR, *Feminist Politics and Human Nature* (Totowa, New Jersey: Rowman and Allanhead, 1983).
9. TORIL MOI, *Sexual/Textual Politics: Feminist Literary Theory* (London and New York: Routledge, 1985), p. 12.
10. CHRISTINE WHITE, ' "Poets and lovers evermore": Interpreting Female Love in the Poetry and Journals of Michael Field', *Textual Practice*, 4 (1990): 197–212.
11. LILLIAN FADERMAN, *Surpassing the Love of Men: Romantic Friendship and Love between Women from the Renaissance to the Present* (1981; London: Women's Press, 1985).
12. HAROLD BLOOM, *The Anxiety of Influence* (New York and Oxford: Oxford University Press, 1973).
13. p. 7.
14. pp. 3–4.
15. GERMAINE GREER, *Slip-Shod Sibyls: Recognition, Rejection and the Woman Poet* (London: Viking, 1995).
16. ANNE K. MELLOR, *Romanticism and Gender* (New York and London: Routledge, 1993); MARLON B. ROSS, *The Contours of Masculine Desire* (New York and Oxford: Oxford University Press, 1989).
17. VIRGINIA WOOLF, *To the Lighthouse* (1938; London: Dent, 1964), p. 56.
18. See e.g. MELLOR, *Romanticism and Gender*, pp. 144–69.
19. IRENE TAYLOR, *Holy Ghosts: The Male Muses of Emily and Charlotte Brontë* (New York and Oxford: Columbia University Press, 1990).
20. CLARISSA PINKOLA ESTÉS, *Women Who Run With the Wolves: Contacting the Power of the Wild Woman* (London: Rider, 1992).
21. ANNIS PRATT, *Archetypal Patterns in Women's Fiction* (Brighton: Harvester Press, 1982).
22. See *Jungian Literary Criticism*, ed. Richard P. Sugg (Evanston, Illinois: Northwestern University Press, 1992), and ANNIS PRATT, *Dancing with Goddesses: Archetypes, Poetry, and Empowerment* (Bloomington Indiana: Indiana University Press, 1994).
23. EMMA FRANCIS, 'Is Emily Brontë a Woman?: Femininity, Feminism and the Paranoid Critical Subject', in *Subjectivity and Literature from the Romantics to the Present Day*, ed. Philip Shaw and Peter Stockwell (London and New York: Pinter Publishers, 1991), pp. 28–40.
24. ELAINE SHOWALTER, 'Feminist Criticism in the Wilderness' in *Writing and*

Sexual Difference, ed. Elizabeth Abel (Chicago: Chicago University Press, 1982), pp. 9–35.

25. pp. 575–80.
26. VIRGINIA V. STEINMETZ, 'Images of "Mother-Want" in Elizabeth Barrett Browning's *Aurora Leigh*', *Victorian Poetry*, 21 (1983): 351–67.
27. BARBARA CHARLESWORTH GELPI, '*Aurora Leigh*: The Vocation of the Woman Poet', *Victorian Poetry*, 19 (1981): 35–48.
28. ANGELA LEIGHTON, *Elizabeth Barrett Browning* (Hemel Hempstead: Harvester Wheatsheaf, 1986).
29. SANDRA GILBERT, 'From *Patria* to *Matria*: Elizabeth Barrett Browning's Risorgimento', *PMLA* (*Publications of the Modern Language Association of America*), 99 (1984): 194–209.
30. WILLIAM WHITLA, 'Questioning the Convention: Christina Rossetti's Sonnet Sequence *Monna Innominata*', in *The Achievement of Christina Rossetti*, ed. David Kent (Ithaca and London: Cornell University Press, 1987), pp. 82–131.
31. MELLOR, *Romanticism and Gender*, pp. 107–43.

Part One
Emily Brontë

1 Emily Brontë*

MARGARET HOMANS

Margaret Homans's chapter on Emily Brontë should be read in the context of her overall argument about the position of the woman writer in the Romantic poetic tradition. She takes this tradition to be masculine: only later do critics begin to unearth a feminine Romantic tradition. Her opening remarks refer back to her previous chapter on Dorothy Wordsworth: William embodies the intimidating male poetic genius central to a tradition in which women figure only as the 'nature' upon which that genius works. The case of Brontë takes the argument a step further: the 'male muses' in her poetry are imaginative embodiments of the same genius figure. As Homans points out, gender reversal is never symmetrical: a male muse is not as tractable as a female one, and operates to undermine and silence Brontë's female poetic subjectivity. What was new and exciting about Homans's argument was her location of gender difference in the actual form and assumptions of a particular historical tradition, not in any essential male or female qualities in the poets themselves. The feminist point of her argument is to explain and excuse the failure and absence of women poets in the Romantic tradition. In reading Brontë's poetry as failure, however, Homans is perhaps over-influenced by the terms of the very tradition she sets out to expose.

To be told by her own brother that she is like nature, and implicitly or explicitly that she cannot have her own subjectivity, would seem to be the most compelling of reasons for a woman to feel dislocated from the poetic tradition in which these opinions originate. To receive these views personally as a sister and not just generically as a woman prevents Dorothy Wordsworth even from wishing to seek a way around

---

* Reprinted from Margaret Homans, *Women Writers and Poetic Identity* (Princeton: Princeton University Press, 1980), pp. 104–22.

them. And yet it appears that Dorothy's difficulties as a poet result not just from her unique personal situation, because although Emily Brontë proceeds much further toward the establishment of authentic poetic identity, her poems just as much as Dorothy's reveal that the sources of poetic power are not felt to be within the self. Brontë is troubled by the apparent otherness of her mind's powers, which she imagines as a series of masculine visitants who bring visionary experience to her. As the alien centers of imaginative power, they repeat, in a general way, Dorothy's implicit picture of her brother as a center of an imaginative power that is never hers. The major and obvious difference between these two configurations is that Brontë's masculine figures for poetic power are invented and contained within her poems, where William Wordsworth has his own irreducible existence, and that consequently they do share their power with the poet, if grudgingly, rather than keeping it perpetually apart.

Brontë's masculine visitants are comparable to a masculine poet's muse. The development of a masculine muse by a woman poet should not logically be surprising, but the phenomenon is new with Brontë (and recurs in Dickinson) and represents a first step toward the internalization of poetic power. There is no such thing, however, as a simple reversal of roles; unlike the usual situation in which a female muse's power exists to be overcome, the poet's ability to master her muse is in this case genuinely in question. Instead of invoking a visitant's aid and then proceeding with a poem on a chosen subject, Brontë often makes her entire poem an extended invocation. Many of her poems dwell on the masculine figures of alien power, elevating them from the status of agency to that of the major subject. This arrest itself suggests that she is not confident of having obtained the visitants' support, and the content of these poems is a continuous effort to wrest the visitants' power away from them and make it her own. It is not inherent in the concept of a masculine muse that he should take and keep more power than does the traditionally feminine muse, but in Brontë's poems he does.

Two comments about the poet's character by those who knew her suggest a biographical analogy for what the poems reveal. These comments share the assumption, hardly questionable in the nineteenth century, that power is synonymous with masculinity, in regard both to character and to accomplishment. Her French teacher in Brussels, M. Héger, said that 'she should have been a man – a great navigator',[1] and Charlotte Brontë writes that under a simple exterior 'lay a secret power and fire that might have informed the brain and kindled the veins of a hero'.[2] What is interesting here is not that Emily's strength of character should be considered manly, but that both these observers should compare this quality in her character to the character of a man of action, a hero or a navigator, rather than to that of a great author, even though Charlotte's words were written to accompany an edition of *Wuthering Heights*. This circumstance suggests that this sternness was not, or at least did not seem to be, fully integrated into Brontë's character, but stood apart. An inflexibility of will seemed to have her in its power, and to harm her more than it helped.

We can never know how far this lack of integration existed in Brontë's own character, but when Charlotte turns to discussing the novel itself, in the preface to her edition of *Wuthering Heights*, she continues in the same vein:

> Whether it is right or advisable to create beings like Heathcliff, I do not know: I scarcely think it is. But this I know, the writer who possesses the creative gift owns something of which he is not always master – something that at times strangely wills and works for itself. ... Be the work grim or glorious, dread or divine, you have little choice left but quiescent adoption.
>
> (*WH*, p. 12)

Possessed by a power not her own, the writer is 'the nominal artist' and deserves neither praise nor blame. In the guise of defender, Charlotte does her sister considerable injustice, if she means that Emily was literally not in control of what she wrote. But as a conscious artist Emily does create a myth of imaginative possession. The account in Charlotte's preface is a literalization of figurative events in Emily's poems on the imagination, and although she betrays herself to be an insensitive reader of her sister's work, there is a certain truth in her misinterpretation.[3]

Brontë makes those visionary visitants an overt, even a major, subject of her poetry, but she also identifies another alien power of poetry that, perhaps because it is a more profound threat to her own identity, is less willingly acknowledged and therefore less apparent than the visionary power. This power belongs to nature, who inspires and endeavors to control the poet's speech in much the same manner as the visionary visitants. Nature is sometimes, though not always, characterized as feminine. For Dorothy to be identified by her brother with nature is to be silenced, because nature's language is not human; here, even though nature is a speaking object, the result is the same forfeiting of subjectivity that Dorothy experiences. As in Dorothy's 'A Winter's Ramble in Grasmere Vale', Brontë portrays nature speaking in place of or in competition with the poet's own speech, and the poet must silence or turn away from nature in order to speak in her own right. Both Brontë's ambition and her success are greater in this regard than Dorothy's, but in her eagerness to defend against this alternate power of poetry, the poet overvalues and distorts the visionary experience offered by male figures without, however, decreasing her sense of its foreignness. Cutting herself off from one source of poetic identity, and not quite believing in the other, she finds nowhere a settled identity. The poet defends herself from the danger of becoming a feminine object by aligning her poetic self with the stage in feminine development in which the mother is rejected in favor of a turn toward masculine objects, but that turn cannot become an identity. Only in the novel, where she is free to displace the traditional feminine character of nature, can she return to what the reader senses is a more authentic belief.

What is of interest here is not so much the sexual identity of the mind presented in the poems, but the question of whether the poet can claim poetic identity at all, or whether the right to that identity is lodged in external powers, be they masculine or feminine. But the Brontës were also aware of the problem of sexual identity as it is represented textually. Charlotte shared a general cultural prejudice against 'the poetry women generally write' (*WH*, p. 4), and all three sisters must have defined themselves against this paradigm, consciously or not. In Charlotte's account of their choice of the sexually ambiguous pseudonyms, Currer, Ellis, and Acton, she says that they did not want to declare themselves women, because of a tendency among critics to condescend to 'authoresses', 'without at that time suspecting that our mode of writing and thinking was not what is called "feminine"' (*WH*, p. 4). Contemporary reviewers of *Wuthering Heights* spoke of Ellis Bell's 'power' and 'mastery'. If Charlotte means that later on they did come to understand that their writing was not 'what is called "feminine"', it is not clear whether she welcomed this distinction, thinking of 'the poetry women generally write', or whether this distinction was an affront to her sense of identity and integrity as a woman. They did not want to abdicate their proper identity and assume 'Christian names positively masculine', yet they could hardly wish, in the world in which they lived, to be grouped with authoresses.[4]

The pseudonyms were 'veils', and perhaps insignificant in themselves, but it is impossible to imagine that the sisters could have questioned such a fundamental aspect of self-presentation without having felt, previously or at the time, a less trivial uncertainty about their sexual identity as writers. These considerations are as relevant to the poet's textual sense of identity as to her manner of presenting her works to the public, because the sense of literary identity is established through reading and through the poet's sense of her place in literary tradition. The choice to be named 'Ellis', assuming that Emily participated in the decision, must represent the poet's wish not to have, as a writer, a determinate sexual identity. This wish may result partly from the desire not to be judged on the basis of gender, but sexual identification is problematic also because the two origins of poetry that she perceives as being available to her are sexually defined, and she can consider neither to be identifiable with the self. Feminine nature and forms of the masculine Word present her with a choice she does not wish to make. The arrangement of this choice is of course her own, but it may express her frustration at the sexual restriction of so many aspects of literary tradition and practice. Brontë's separation from the two sources of her power may be, then, the result not of any fragmentation of her own sense of identity, but of her uneasiness about their sexual orientation. She may not be able to, but also perhaps does not wish to, claim identification with either one.[5]

The history of the poet's negotiations for poetic identity is traced in a sequence of poems that forms the core of Brontë's canon. In 1844 Brontë made two books of transcriptions, for which she selected poems written at different periods in her life. She copied these poems into two notebooks, in a book-like printing and format that indicates that these were the poems that she considered to be her best. One notebook is a collection of poems about Gondal, the fictive land that in her adolescence she had invented and peopled, and whose sagas she continued to elaborate up to the year of her death. The other notebook, considered here, bears no title but consists largely of poems that are either explicitly or implicitly about imaginative experience. Of the poems that she published in the 1846 *Poems by Currer, Ellis, and Acton Bell*, five were chosen from the Gondal notebook and fifteen from the non-Gondal group. In making these transcriptions, Brontë retained many of the dates on which the poems were written, though arranging the poems in a new sequence that is roughly but not entirely chronological. The apparent care with which the poems were chosen and arranged indicates that, in the non-Gondal notebook, she is consciously developing a myth of the imagination; consequently this reading follows her arrangement of the poems rather than the chronological sequence.[6]

The pattern of borrowing an identity began very early, in the make-believe world of the Brontë children's 'Young Men's Play', in which Emily represented the polar explorer, Sir Edward Parry.[7] In subsequent 'plays' (the precursors of Gondal), in which the children invented nations and populations engendering lengthy prose tales and then poetry, the mobile adoption of fictive roles proliferates. In a child this borrowing is by itself unremarkable, and for an adult poet it is part of the procedure of any fictional writing to adopt various personae, but Brontë retains this pattern of supplanting identity even when it begins to produce sinister effects. It has been argued that in the conventional heroic posing of the Gondal poems (the first was written in 1836, when

the poet was seventeen) she is concealing or suppressing her own
identity, to the detriment of the poems, because she has difficulty
representing her own genuine powers.[8] The figures she creates in the
Gondal poems are often borrowed from gothic or Byronic sources,[9] and
these borrowed personae are often themselves possessed by passions
that they do not control, as for example in these lines from a poem of
1837:

> The burning tears that would keep welling,
> The groans that mocked at every tear
> That burst from out their dreary dwelling
> . . . .
> Sometimes a curse, sometimes a prayer
> Would quiver on my parchèd tongue.
>
> (P 15)

In other early poems, the speaker is bound by 'a tyrant spell', possessed
in dreams by 'the shadows of the dead', and in many places
overwhelmed by despair and by harrowing memories.

The possession of these early poems is emotional rather than creative,
but when Brontë turns from the melodrama of Gondal to poems about
her own mind, she retains the language of possession. The visionary
visitant of later poems takes many forms, but he is always masculine,
and he is threatening as well as inspiring, dangerous as well as
beloved.[10] He is threatening more because, being external, he can
withdraw her poetic powers at will than because of any dangerous
content in the visions he brings. Her ambivalence toward these figures
produces an unstable relationship with them. The poet early succeeds
in exerting a measure of control over this figure, but this control
succeeds not in harnessing the visitant's power but only
counterproductively in suppressing it, and later the visitant's power
returns in a sinister form.

A poem of 1840 invokes a visitation from 'thee', using the language of
romantic love augmented by devotional speech:

> My worn heart throbs so wildly
> 'Twill break for thee.
> . . . .
> Will not mine angel comfort?
> Mine idol hear?
>
> (P 138, A 11)

The first three stanzas place the speaker at the mercy of this figure, but
the last appears to fulfill its own wishes: 'O I shall surely win thee, /

Beloved, again!' 'Mine angel' here is at least fictively external to the poet, but subsequent poems trace the internalization of this figure. The next poem, addressed to 'O Dream', records the passing of a Wordsworthian gleam at the end of childhood. Though this figure has entity enough to have an 'angel brow', the darkening vision is the result of dissociating the dream from external lights. Depriving this figure of its illusory otherness decreases its powers:

> The sun-beam and the storm,
> The summer-eve divine,
> The silent night of solemn calm,
> The full moon's cloudless shine,
>
> Were once entwined with thee,
> But now with weary pain,
> Lost vision! 'tis enough for me –
> Thou canst not shine again.
>
> (P 86, A 12)

Whereas the discovery that this figure was not external but a function of the self might be expected to increase the poet's feeling of her own power, she experiences only loss. Turning from the light vanishing 'from off thine angel brow' to the loss of 'every joy that lit my brow', the next poem presents a further stage in this internalization that merely contracts the vision to a relic of his former power and makes the self a mortuary without any compensatory gain in power.

> The barren mountain-side lies bare;
> And sunshine and awaking morn
> Paint no more golden visions there.
>
> Yet, ever in my grateful breast,
> Thy darling shade shall cherished be;
> For God alone doth know how blest
> My early years have been in thee!
>
> (P 135, A 13)

She internalizes this visionary faculty only as it diminishes because, like Dorothy Wordsworth, she cannot believe that any poetic power could be at once internal and powerful.

The issue of visionary power is closed for four years and the next eight poems in the copybook take up different themes. The next poem on this subject, 'My Comforter' (P 168, A 22), addresses a revived but very differently characterized figure. Having accepted the discovery of earlier poems that if visionary power is internal it must be weak, the poet now embraces rather than lamenting its triviality. Condescending to her comforter, she tells it that it has 'not taught / A feeling strange or new; / Thou hast but roused a latent thought', and she guards from it the secret of the occasion for which she is being soothed: 'What my soul bore my soul alone / Within itself may tell.' The speaker's hollow gain is that she is in the position of power now in this relationship, and she reduces her 'idol' to a 'sweet thing' that calms but could not comprehend. The next two poems, though separated in composition by a year, are paired in the manuscript because they both involve a figure named 'Fancy' who is, like this comforter, clearly a subordinate. The subject of the poem is the 'Dark world' of actuality, and the speaker simply conjures a substitutive dream though the agency of this servile 'Fancy . . . my Fairy love!' A fantasy of perfect and happy worlds in heaven is introduced by a fiat: 'And this shall be my dream to-night – / I'll think . . .' (P 157, A 23). Acknowledged as a fantasy, this easy day-dream is hardly efficacious in any way. In assuming the powers of the figure she once pleadingly invoked and worshipped, she finds that its powers vanish. Its powers resided in its defiance and in her desire. Like Dorothy in 'Holiday at Gwerndwffnant', 'Irregular Verses', and the Cottage poems, she identifies her own poetry with fancy while readily admitting to its inferiority. As before, she does not conceive of a poetic power that would be both her own and powerful. The titling of the next poem in the notebook sequence, 'To Imagination' (P 174, A 25), represents an effort to ennoble this faculty by association with the term that Coleridge reserves for the mind's highest powers. Indeed, it is here not quite so servile as before: it is a 'benignant power' with a 'kind voice', a 'solacer of human cares', and 'my true friend'. But the poem still turns on a simplistic opposition between the hopeless 'world without' that includes 'Nature's sad reality' and 'Truth', and the escapist 'world within', comprising dreams and Fancy, which is the province of what she calls 'Imagination'. If not the fancy itself, it purveys a fanciful 'phantom bliss' that the speaker mistrusts even while she welcomes it. What is significant here is that the poet recognizes that the moments of greatest power occur when this imagination voids the distinction between the 'world within' and the 'world without' to refer to a real but also desirable world elsewhere. She makes a continuity between fantasy and possibility:

> But thou art ever there to bring
> The hovering visions back and breathe
> New glories o'er the blighted spring
> And call a lovelier life from death,
> And whisper with a voice divine
> Of real worlds as bright as thine.

She increases the power of her imagination by associating it with 'real worlds', but the cost of that gain in power is that voice returns to a source outside the self.

The poem transcribed next, written six weeks later, returns to a suspiciously harsh opposition between real worlds and reason, which must be renounced, and a 'God of Visions', who, unlike her imagination, seems to require complete devotion. She calls it a 'radiant angel', an honorific term that has dropped out of her vocabulary since the early poems. Shunning 'the common paths that others run', she

> gave my spirit to adore
> Thee, ever present, phantom thing –
> My slave, my comrade, and my King!
>
> (P 176, A 26)

The next two verses explicate the last line. This passage is the main source for the myth of possession, as it is for comparisons between Brontë and Dickinson, who also addresses a power that is at once master and slave. Her accounts of 'slave' and 'comrade', though told with greater energy than before, are familiar, but when she turns to 'my King' she is scarcely convincing:

> And yet, a king – though prudence well
> Have taught thy subject to rebel.
>
> And am I wrong to worship where
> Faith cannot doubt nor Hope despair
> Since my own soul can grant my prayer?

There is no apparent reason for inflating this figure into a king, since at the same time she so overtly makes it a part of herself and easily governable. Her insistence on intimacy must be concealing some unexplained alienation, of which the term 'king' is the trace.

The account of the speaker's turn from reason to visions in this poem is framed by two opening stanzas and two closing lines that set the poem in a court of law. The poem's occasion is the speaker's invocation to her 'radiant angel' to come to her defense against 'Stern Reason''s judgment. Reason 'is mocking at my overthrow', as if the speaker had suffered or gone mad because of her preference. Her invocation is desperate:

> O thy sweet tongue must plead for me
> And tell why I have chosen thee!

> Stern Reason is to judgement come
> Arrayed in all her forms of gloom:
> Wilt thou my advocate be dumb?
> No, radiant angel, speak and say
> Why I did cast the world away.

The subsequent stanzas seem to do what the speaker is asking her God of Visions to do, in that they explain her choice, but that she closes with the same invocation with which she began indicates that this defense has been inadequate:

> Speak, God of Visions, plead for me
> And tell why I have chosen thee!

That implied inadequacy expresses powerlessness or subjugation far more vividly than does her guarded declaration that he is her king. If 'my own soul can grant my prayer', the poem logically ought not to end with the implication that her God of Visions has not spoken and will not speak for her. The God is a tongue or a voice, and an advocate is one who speaks for someone else. That the speaker thus displaces her powers of speech indicates that language is alien to her. Her soul may be synonymous with her God of Visions, but without certainty of her power over language visions are of no use for poetry and she is alienated from her own poethood. That language is an alien power may account for the reduction of visionary power from 'mine idol' to 'sweet thing', coincident with its internalization. Mastering and containing the power undoes it, and yet to see it again as external threatens the poet's existence as a poet.

The next poem, 'Enough of Thought, Philosopher', carries the implications of the danger of the externality of poetic power one step further by considering the possibility that there is not much difference between a sought-after 'Spirit' (another imaginary visitant) and oblivious death. The Spirit represents a power to unify warring factions within human personality and to make their combined strength 'far more fair / Than the divided sources were' (P 181, A 27). But the 'lifeless rest' the speaker seeks when she abandons her futile search for this Spirit performs much the same function, if ingloriously:

> O let me die, that power and will
> Their cruel strife may close,
> And vanquished Good, victorious Ill
> Be lost in one repose.

This verse and the one preceding it were substituted for an original conclusion that characterizes death simply as 'eternal sleep' rather than as the closure of strife, so that the parallel between death and the imaginative Spirit is not accidental, but the product of purposeful revision. That death mimics the Spirit here undermines imaginative efficacy. The speaker has imagined this Spirit and has created a compelling visual image of his powers of unification (the Spirit supervises the confluence of three rivers and kindles the 'inky sea' where they meet 'with sudden blaze' so that 'the glad deep sparkled wide and bright – / White as the sun'). But only its mimicker and antagonist, ironically, can fulfill the Spirit's promise.

'Enough of Thought, Philosopher', dated 3 February 1845, is the last of the poems in the non-Gondal notebook to consider as overt subject-matter the topic of imaginative power. The poet does return to this subject, but as part of the Gondal sequence, suggesting that although the poet no longer wished to treat this difficult subject, and perhaps repressed it, it must have been an unfinished issue of considerable importance to have found another way to surface out of place. Rather than resolving the problem of her mastery over her God of Visions, this poem allows her to express her fears more freely because more indirectly. The poem in question is the one that begins 'Silent is the House – all are laid asleep', dated 9 October 1845. The passage on imagination is the first three stanzas, which exist in an uneasy relation to the rest of the poem, a narrative. Both Emily and Charlotte Brontë recognized this uneasiness, as the poem is printed only in excerpts in both the 1846 *Poems* and the group of poems published by Charlotte in her 1850 edition of *Wuthering Heights*, Emily selected parts of the narrative for the 1846 edition, and Charlotte printed just the three stanzas about imagination, with a two-stanza conclusion of her own, under the title of 'The Visionary'. The 'I' in the first three stanzas of the original poem is apparently the same as the 'I' of the poems on imagination in the non-Gondal notebook, while in the rest of the poem the speaker is a dramatic character named Julian.

> Silent is the House – all are laid asleep;
> One, alone, looks out o'er the snow wreaths deep;
> Watching every cloud, dreading every breeze
> That whirls the 'wildering drifts and bends the groaning trees.
>
> Cheerful is the hearth, soft the matted floor;
> Not one shivering gust creeps through pane or door;
> The little lamp burns straight, its rays shoot strong and far;
> I trim it well to be the Wanderer's guiding-star.

Frown, my haughty sire; chide, my angry dame;
Set your slaves to spy, threaten me with shame:
But neither sire nor dame, nor prying serf shall know
What angel nightly tracks that waste of winter snow.

In the dungeon crypts idly did I stray,
Reckless of the lives wasting there away;
'Draw the ponderous bars; open, Warder stern!'
He dare not say me nay – the hinges harshly turn.

(P 190)

It is possible that the poet is identifying that Wanderer by moving,
without indicating any transition, into an imaginative tale, as if the
discovery of a topic for verse signaled the Wanderer's arrival. The 'I'
idly straying in dungeon crypts would be the mind searching for an
adventure to recount, taking on the persona of Julian only in the next
line.[11]

Once his friend, Rochelle is now Julian's 'conquered foe', incarcerated
in his dungeons. Julian visits the prison 'reckless of the lives wasting
there away', and finds Rochelle beautiful and sanctified by her hope for
liberty through a quick death. Falling instantly in love, he decides to
free her, but not until after some deliberations that confirm the implicit
obnoxiousness of his idle stroll through his own dungeons. Having
forgotten that he must have incarcerated her for a reason, he worries
that if he frees her she will not return his love, whereas if he keeps her
in prison she will remain subject to him. Though he calls it 'selfish
love' and makes his decision 'short strife', that he must elaborate his
decision at all is appalling in a dramatic hero, given the romantic terms
of the tale. Having freed her, he takes her home and nurses her back
to health, self-righteously accruing a greater heroism by his devotion to
her and his sacrifice of the opportunity to go to war, for which he is
much scorned by his kin. Rochelle drops out of the tale once she has
been rescued, so that it is quite startling when Julian thinks to refer to
her at the end, even though she is now merely the object of his self-
serving sacrifice and the ground for his self-praise.

Another hand than mine my rightful banner held
And gathered my renown on Freedom's crimson field;
Yet I had no desire the glorious prize to gain –
It needed braver nerve to face the world's disdain.

And by the patient strength that could that world defy,
By suffering, with calm mind, contempt and calumny;
By never-doubting love, unswerving constancy,
Rochelle, I earned at last an equal love from thee!

This self-serving character who, unsought, frees Rochelle from her dungeon invites comparison with the liberator she does seek, who is described earlier in the poem. 'A messenger of Hope', she tells Julian scornfully, visits her at twilight, and when he comes, 'visions rise and change which kill me with desire'. She describes the advent of these visions as if they were visions of poetic inspiration. First 'a soundless calm descends' in which she seems to forget her imprisonment,

'– unuttered harmony
That I could never dream till earth was lost to me.

'Then dawns the Invisible, the Unseen its truth reveals;
My outward sense is gone, my inward essence feels –
Its wings are almost free, its home, its harbour found;
Measuring the gulf it stoops and dares the final bound!'

Her 'messenger of Hope' is a vision of death, but the vision is described with Wordsworth's language for imaginative experience: '. . . we are laid asleep / In body, and become a living soul'. This allusion equates imaginative experience with death. There is no room in the narrative for finding this equation faulty, since the life Julian offers is so unappealing and so distastefully achieved. Rochelle's vision includes a soaring bird as the traditional image of the soul's escape; Julian uses a bird as his metaphor for capturing her. He fears that she will fly away, in the passage on his decision between 'ruth and selfish love':

Then like a tender child whose hand did just enfold,
Safe in its eager grasp, a bird it wept to hold,
When pierced with one wild glance from the
    troubled hazel eye,
It gushes into tears and lets its treasure fly. . . .

When she does not fly away upon release, it is because she is a 'wounded dove'. During her recovery, 'Death gazed greedily / And only Hope remained a faithful friend to me.' This possessive 'to me' opposes Rochelle's claim to a different hope, who came 'every night to me'.

That Rochelle's vision of death is valued more highly than her human liberator, and that it appears to be so similar to imaginative experience, would seem to make that vision analogous to the Wanderer of the first three stanzas. Both the messenger of hope and the Wanderer are imaginary visitants. Rochelle's 'My outward sense is gone, my inward essence feels' is quite like the poet's situation:

Silent is the House – all are laid asleep;
One, alone, looks out o'er the snow wreaths deep.

Rochelle's loss of self-consciousness is curiously paralleled by the use of 'one' instead of 'I' here, and by the trance of quietness in the poet's room. Furthermore, Julian, himself unimaginative, is associated with loss of voice. Rochelle seems delighted when the jailor's departure makes it possible for Julian to free her, but for this knowledge we are dependent on Julian's own untrustworthy reading of her expression, because she never speaks again after finishing her inspired description of the vision of death. Life with Julian is to be mute, but the vision of death inspires speech. Many commentators, reading Rochelle's vision as an extreme expression of mystical experience, identify that mystical experience as having been Brontë's own, and locate the passage as the culmination of a sequence of poems including those on imagination discussed above, thereby tacitly identifying mystical and imaginative experience.[12]

But the analogy between Rochelle's vision and the Wanderer cannot be made into an identity, because the poet is trying to avoid her suspicion that the Wanderer, as a muse-like bringer of poetry, is also a messenger of death. It cannot be that only the expectation of death is inspiring. Rochelle is entirely passive, and her desire fails, while the first three stanzas present an active self whose wish is efficacious: the Wanderer arrives. And what he brings is in itself efficacious. By relegating the fear of death, and passivity in relation to the control of voice, to the narrated story, the poet can exorcize these difficulties from the contemplation of her own imagination. Displacement fosters the belief that they are not her own. Still, the poet does not dispel her own intimation that imagination is the intuition and expectation of death. By setting the scene in winter the poet balances two possibilities. The snowy scene may exist to demonstrate the Wanderer's dependence on her: without the brightness and steadiness of her lamp's rays, the Wanderer would be lost in the snow, as Lockwood is lost in the snow at the beginning of *Wuthering Heights*. The poet makes that 'wildering' and threatening landscape safe and intelligible, so that whatever the Wanderer brings – the story – depends on the poet's primary powers of clarification. But because he crosses a 'waste of winter snow' the Wanderer may come from regions of death, like the messenger of hope. The room is warm and still because 'not one shivering gust creeps through pane or door', suggesting a resistance to the visitor's entrance as well as a welcome.

The third stanza, though part of the prefatory material on the poet's own experience, disrupts the tone that the first two verses establish. Their apparent calm and confidence is broken by its defensive anger:

Frown, my haughty sire; chide, my angry dame;
Set your slaves to spy, threaten me with shame:
But neither sire nor dame, nor prying serf shall know
What angel nightly tracks that waste of winter snow.

The source of this sudden defensiveness is uncertain. Nothing in the first two stanzas seems to provoke it, yet suddenly the poet's world is populated by suspicious and ill-intentioned people. The line 'Silent is the House – all are laid asleep' may refer to these people, whose silence would now be revealed to have been the result of suppression. The defense is against the inference that the Wanderer is a human lover, whether sire and dame are the house's inhabitants or the poem's readers. The poet may be disturbed at the unintentionally erotic implications of her myth. However, neither of these interpretations accounts for the abruptness of the tonal shift and for the energy of the poet's distress. There must be a quantity of pent-up anxiety that finds partial expression in these lines, as if redirected from its original goal. If the rest of the poem exhibits any potential source of anxiety, it is the association of the imagination with death, and it may be that the delusion of persecution in stanza 3 is a redirection of the poet's fears of her own imaginative experience. Those fears may have chosen this particular course with a certain design. Even though the poet's intention seems to be to discourage the view that the Wanderer is a human lover, it is she who first plants the suggestion in the reader's mind. It may be that she raises the erotic possibility as a screen to hide an even more threatening fatality. By invoking the presence of sire, dame, and serfs, no matter how nasty they are, she wakes the dead. 'Laid asleep', they represented the proximity of death and imaginative experience; frowning and chiding, they sever that connection.

The Wanderer does not actually bring death in the same way that Rochelle's messenger promises. It is because he may choose to give or withhold language that he is associated with death, because the withholding of language is death to the poetic vocation. The plea to 'speak for me' in the poem addressed to the God of Visions (P 176, A 26) betrays the dangers of alien control of language. That plea reappears in the messenger's envoicing of Rochelle, in Julian's domineering way of speaking for her, and in the Wanderer's provision of a story to the hitherto silent poet. Feminine figures rely on masculine figures for their speech, and the poet herself defers to the Wanderer and then to Julian as his chosen speaker. The poet has no rebuttal for Julian's deceptively cheerful interpretation of the final state of events. The poem never returns to her, as if she had set in motion a self-sufficient machine.

Notes

1. Quoted in ELIZABETH GASKELL, *The Life of Charlotte Brontë* (1857; Harmondsworth, Middlesex: Penguin, 1975), p. 230.
2. From the 'Biographical Notice of Ellis and Acton Bell', written for her 1850 edition of *Wuthering Heights* and *Agnes Grey*. All quotations from *Wuthering Heights* and Charlotte's prefatory material are from *Wuthering Heights*, ed. William M. Sale (New York: Norton, 1963), cited hereafter as *WH* with page numbers.
3. For accounts of Charlotte's misunderstanding of her sister's work, and the real harm it may have done, see PHILIP HENDERSON, Intro., *Emily Brontë: Poems Selected with an Introduction* (London: Lawson and Dunn, 1947), pp. ix–xii; and ROBIN GROVE, '"It Would Not Do": Emily Brontë as Poet', in *The Art of Emily Brontë*, ed. Anne Smith (London: Vision Press, 1976), pp. 34–9.
4. CAROL OHMANN discusses the way critics trivialized *Wuthering Heights* once its author's identity had been revealed, in 'Emily Brontë in the Hands of Male Critics', *College English*, 32 (1971): 906–13.
5. C. DAY LEWIS argues, on the biographical level, that Brontë was unconsciously frustrated at not being a man, and that her dissatisfaction with the world was a projection of this frustration. See 'The Poetry of Emily Brontë', *Brontë Society Transactions*, 13 (1957): 94–7.
6. All quotations from Brontë's poetry are from *The Complete Poems of Emily Jane Brontë*, ed. C.W. Hatfield (New York: Columbia University Press, 1941), cited as P followed by the poem number assigned by Hatfield. In this edition, each of the poems in the non-Gondal notebook bears a number according to its position in the notebook (A 1–A 31); these numbers, where applicable, will be cited as well as Hatfield's numbers, which are assigned chronologically.
7. FANNIE E. RATCHFORD, *The Brontës' Web of Childhood* (New York: Columbia University Press, 1941), p. 12.
8. GROVE, in Smith (ed.), pp. 42–6. ROSALIND MILES, in an essay in the same collection, 'A Baby God: The Creative Dynamism of Emily Brontë's Poetry', pp. 68–73, searching for autobiographical information, laments the absence of an authorial self.
9. A number of readers have noted the use of Byronic themes and stances in Brontë's poetry, for example HELEN BROWN, 'The Influence of Byron on Emily Brontë', *Modern Language Review*, 34 (1939), 374–81; DOROTHY J. COOPER, 'The Romantics and Emily Brontë', *Brontë Society Transactions*, 12 (1952): 106–12; ALAN LOXTERMAN, '*Wuthering Heights* as Romantic Poem and Victorian Novel', in *A Festschrift for Prof. Marguerite Roberts*, ed. Frieda E. Penninger (Richmond, Va.: University of Richmond, 1976), pp. 91–2. Cooper also cites parallels between Brontë's poetry and gothic novels.
10. J. HILLIS MILLER discusses her ambivalent relation to her imagination in *The Disappearance of God: Five Nineteenth-Century Writers* (Cambridge: The Belknap Press of Harvard University Press, 1963), pp. 158–9; CHARLES MORGAN also sketches a theory of ambiguously received possession, in *Reflections in a Mirror* (London: Macmillan, 1944), pp. 142–5. My purpose is to expand and elaborate these suggestions.
11. JONATHAN WORDSWORTH has suggested that the 'I' is Julian throughout, and that the first three stanzas are the present-time frame for a recollection. If the figure at the window is Julian, then the Wanderer would be his beloved, Rochelle, in human or ghostly form. This reading would account for the

erotic implications of the third stanza, but the voice in the first three stanzas differs too much from the voice we learn to recognize as Julian's for this reading to make sense. See 'Wordsworth and the Poetry of Emily Brontë', *Brontë Society Transactions*, 16 (1972): 85–100.

12. See, among others: MARGARET WILLY, 'Emily Brontë: Poet and Mystic', *English*, 6 (1946): 117–22; MURIEL A. DOBSON, 'Was Emily Brontë a Mystic?', *Brontë Society Transactions*, 11 (1948): 166–75; JACQUES BLONDEL, *Emily Brontë: Expérience spirituelle et création poétique* (Paris: Presses Universitaires de France, 1955), pp. 192–218.

2 The Archetypal Feminine in Emily Brontë's Poetry*

CHRISTINE GALLANT

Christine Gallant's article shows how a different choice of poems, and a different critical approach, can produce a completely different feminist reading of Brontë's poems. Where Homans, in the previous extract, sees failure, Gallant sees triumph. Gallant's context is the celebratory one of a special edition of *Women's Studies*, on 'The Triumph of the Woman Poet'. Gallant's Jungian approach to Brontë, published in the same year as Homans's book, could be seen as the kind of essentialist reading Homans was trying to get away from. I have decided, however, not to encourage such a simplistic narrative of progress by putting Gallant first. Her project is to rescue Brontë's poetry from neglect, and gender-blind or male-biased misreadings, arguing instead for the relevance of a 'feminine' reading. In doing so, she distinguishes sharply between the socially constructed Victorian 'feminine', and the unchanging, Jungian archetypal 'feminine', which belongs to the realm of mythology and the great world religions. The biographical slant of the article is used to suggest that Brontë rejected the one in her outward social life and embraced the other in the secret inner world of her poetry. While it could be argued whether the archetypal is unchanging, or socially and textually constructed, Gallant's approach shows how an identification with nature need not lead to silence, but can give rise to a strong feminine voice, and the creation of a powerful mythology. Here Jung's ideas give more scope for female agency than the identification of the female with absence and lack in Freud or Lacan.

Although to many critics Emily Brontë has seemed a writer largely unaffected either by her sex or her culture, her poetry was significantly shaped by her experience of what it was to be a woman in nineteenth-century England. She has been called 'the Sphinx of literature'[1] by her

---

* Reprinted from *Women's Studies*, 7, nos 1–2 (1980): 79–90.

partisans, who, in comparing her to that mythic female so intimately involved with the maternal drama unfolding for Oedipus, have commented more appropriately than they realize. Reclusive, desiring only to return home when she was sent to Roe Head at seventeen and to Brussels at twenty-four, writing poetry she did not show even to her family,[2] Brontë seems a completely internalized poet. When her sister Charlotte discovered her poems by accident and insisted that they be published, it took several weeks to overcome the poet's violent resistance to the idea. Nor was this Brontë very eager to capitalize on the subsequent publication of her poetry; indeed, she was contemptuous of it when it appeared.

Her indifference to literary fame has almost been matched by the critics' inattention to her poetry. Most criticism has focused on *Wuthering Heights*, and a good deal of what has been written about the poems discusses them only in relation to that book. Edith Sitwell summarizes one considerable body of critical opinion when she says of Brontë's poetry in general and 'Cold in the earth' in particular, 'I do not care for it, nor do I think the emotions expressed in it are genuine.'[3] L.P. Hartfield, writing for the sympathetic audience of *The Brontë Society Transactions*, defends the poetry as 'genuine' (whatever that undefined word means) but then damns it unintentionally by calling the emotions which inform it those 'of a rather weak, fearful, clinging, mood- and nerve-ridden personality'.[4] (Perhaps coincidentally, Hartfield calls Brontë 'Emily' throughout his article.)

Here we might think that we are again in the presence of the male-defined 'typical woman poet' (which would explain the comparative critical silence about her poetry) except that when we look at the actual poems we find them concentrated, economical in language, and direct in diction. And surely if *Wuthering Heights* is admitted to be one of the great British novels of the nineteenth century, it seems myopic to ignore the profusion of poetry which its author has left us. There is an authentic and haunting power to a number of poems which lifts them above their usual designation as 'minor poetry of a major novelist'. The private myth of Gondal underlying this poetry, seemingly so arbitrarily created in Brontë's childhood and so stubbornly maintained through adulthood, actually is solidly within the traditions of the great chthonic world religions: hers is a matriarchal mythology.

The textual history of her poetry is rather a complex one. In 1844 Brontë began to copy her poems into two small notebooks. In the one she wrote those few pieces she considered personal and in the other those connected with the mythic history of the land of Gondal, thus making it quite clear that there *was* a distinction between them in her own mind. The existence of the small wine-red notebook entitled 'Gondal Poems' was not widely known to Brontë scholars until it was presented to the British Museum in 1933 by the descendants of Mr George Smith of Smith, Elder and Company, Charlotte's publishers. Until this discovery, the general assumption had been that many of the Gondal poems were personal outpourings of feeling, traceable to piquantly unknown events in Brontë's life. Now, however, it became clear that these poems were fictional. C.W. Hatfield incorporated the titles and dates found in this notebook into his edition of the poetry, which remains the most reliable.

Emily Brontë began writing Gondal poems when she was eight, and in the ensuing years, nearly all of her greatest poetry was generated by her private mythology. These poems tend to be allusive and cryptic, but it is possible to gather from them the main outlines of a narrative: the two Pacific islands of Gondal and Gaaldine experience continual civil war, with their inhabitants always fierce, passionate and patriotic in this strife. Chief among them are Queen Augusta of Almeda ('A.G.A.') and King Julius Brenzaida of Angora, who is finally assassinated.

It has proved hard for scholars to resist discussing all of Brontë's poetry together, and there are two bodies of critical interpretation. One, represented most prominently by Fanny Ratchford, perhaps the authoritative expert on the saga of Gondal, holds that all of Brontë's poetry relates to some aspect of the Gondal plot-sequence.[5] The other argues that she assumed a mythic persona in order to write more freely of her own emotions and her own concerns. Most commentators belonging to this latter group think that basic to the poetry is a growing disillusionment with Nature, an increasing desire for annihilation of identity.[6]

But what if we accept Brontë's own division of her poems into those which capture the private moment and those which advance the myth? Although not more than a handful of the poems may truly be termed 'personal', the distinctions between the two groups of works are significant. Each explores reality in a psychologically complementary way. The one searches for meaning in the individual self, and the other seeks the archetypal experience of the Feminine which, as C.G. Jung suggests, is associated with all that is emotional, maternal and chthonic.[7] We have an immediate apprehension of the events in Brontë's own life in her 'personal' poems, but we enter the unchanging world of the archetype in the Gondal poems. Brontë evidently preferred to remain in that latter world for the most part, continuing her exploration of what it is to be – in Jung's sense – Feminine.

It is apparent that the creation of these Gondal poems was an overriding concern, for Brontë began writing them in very early childhood and zealously kept on doing so until her death. One can only speculate about the reason for this continuing affirmation of the archetypal Feminine, but a possible explanation is that by so doing she resisted the experience of the contemporary womanhood which others around her were obliged to undergo.

Her early life was accompanied by family strain and tragedy. Shortly after she was born, her family moved to the country parish of Haworth where her father had been newly appointed clergyman: four years later, her mother died of cancer. Miss Elizabeth Branwell, the eldest sister of the Brontës' mother, came to reign. What scanty evidence is left about the mother's character indicates that she was sprightly, sweet-tempered, and idealistic in her views that poverty could be of great advantage in attaining spiritual perfection. Miss Branwell, however, was all that the stereotypical maiden lady of that period is supposed to have been: authoritarian and repressive, with Victorian society's standard idea of 'womanly' and 'correct' behavior. Her strictness and severity drove out the two female servants who had accompanied the Brontës in their move to Haworth. She taught the small children reading and ciphering, and later (the girls only, naturally) sewing in every branch, with long hours of practice. Emily's sisters Anne and Charlotte showed the more insidious effects of so-called 'feminine' behavior. They fell passively and hopelessly in love: Anne with her father's friendly but superficial curate who died of cholera, and Charlotte with M. Heger of Brussels, who was married and uninterested.

Whether or not their sister drew her own conclusions from these experiences must remain conjecture, but certainly Emily Bronte increasingly shut out as many elements that her society would have called 'feminine' as she could. After her two disastrous bouts with outside schools, she remained home to run the house: baking, cooking, cleaning for her father and aunt. This might be considered 'woman's work' but it was hard physical labor that bred total independence from others and their routines. The poet gave her life its form, visiting no one and uncommunicative to those who came to see others in her family, reading as she kneaded the bread, rambling around the moors with her huge mastiff 'Keeper' when she wished, staying up at night to write poetry.

Although the Gondal poems spanned thirteen years or so, one really cannot speak of their 'development' for they are remarkably consistent. One comes across poems widely separated in time (considering Brontë's brief life): the famous elegies, 'There should be no despair' (1839) and 'Cold in the earth' (1845); the poems, 'Fall, leaves, fall' (1838) and 'The linnet in the rocky dells' (1844), similar in theme and poetic power. There is a recurring situation and emotional tone in all of them. Again and again, Brontë constructs the histories of Gondal's dominant and passionate women, tracing the fortunes of the beautiful and tempestuous Queen Augusta who had a long succession of discarded lovers. It is a mythic world emphatically excluding the real world known then by women. Nearly all of the poems are interior monologues, and usually the speaker is either a woman or a lover remembering a woman. This person is at some key dramatic point in the story – imprisonment in a dungeon, treacherous betrayal by one of the warring Gondal factions, impending death – and is recalling the central emotion of his or her life. Gondal poems are usually poems of the past.

As poems of the past, they do not seek a present emotion but rather evoke one already known. Over and over the Gondal poems seek to make possible the *experience* of emotion and inner psychological consistency (love, patriotic loyalty, stoical 'endurance') in the face of external dissociation (separation from Nature through imprisonment, betrayal, treason, death). The best of the Gondal poems derive their power from the effect they produce of having distilled emotion, rendering it in its essential form. The outlines of the emotion being recalled are almost inhuman in their lack of any qualification or modification, which may be why some commentators call them false or 'mood- and nerve-ridden'. But such criticism misses the point. What Brontë is really writing about is the preservation of feeling in the face of inevitable extinction; more importantly, the preservation of the *capacity* to feel.

The central image of 'There should be no despair' is that of the heart pouring out pulses of feeling, with life thus being maintained. All of the poem's images from Nature show this effusion as 'the nightly stars are burning', the 'evening sheds its silent dew', and 'the sunshine gilds the morning'. The nostalgia of loss provokes the experience, which coincidentally explains the necessity of writing such poems again and again: the initial emotion 'around your heart' will then remain a present reality. Thus the weeping 'must be so', and Nature is caught in this perpetual experience as 'winds sigh as you are sighing' and 'Winter pours its grief in snow'.

'Cold in the earth' is both a more complex and a more famous poem; it has been called 'one of the great love poems in the language'.[8] The great question of this poem is whether the speaker (Rosina) has lost her love for the assassinated King Julius Brenzaida in the 'fifteen wild Decembers' since he died. Increasingly in the course of the poem, she moves from the present to the past. The 'divinest anguish' which she expresses at the end of her lament comes to be quite indistinguishable from the 'life's bliss' she used to know with Julius. By the impassioned conclusion of the poem, she is thoroughly controlled by the past and her ultimate rejection of the present rewards her with the emotion uncorrupted by 'the empty world'.

The consistently heightened rhetoric and extremity of mood of all these Gondal poems, and 'Cold in the earth' especially, at once tell us that we are in the presence of something archetypal for Brontë. The dominating presence of female figures has already been remarked. Jung could have been writing of them when he said of the Great Mother archetype that its 'essential aspects [are] . . . her orgiastic emotionality and her Stygian depths'.[9] Nearly all of Gondal's women act very much like the Great Mothers of world mythologies whose realm is the underworld, and whose subservient male consorts always head for death after the consummation. Most of the best Gondal poems are 'infernal' poems. Queen Augusta's love usually has distinctly chthonic overtones. Frequently her lovers call on her from the brink of the grave. Typical of this theme, though not of Brontë's finest work, is number 61 entitled 'A.G.A.':

> Call Death – yes, Death, he is thine own!
> The grave must close those limbs around,
> And hush, forever hush the tone
> I loved above all earthly sound.
> Well, pass away with the other flowers:
> Too dark for them, too dark for thee
> Are the hours to come, the joyless hours,
> That Time is treasuring up for me.

While Rosina remained in the 'empty world' above for fifteen years after Julius's death, she also knew 'a burning wish to hasten down to that tomb already more than mine'. Her poem as a whole could be Persephone's epithalamion to Pluto after their separation.

Not only do female figures dominate the myth of Gondal, but Nature too seems almost a separate character. In fact, sometimes in Brontë's early poems, the poet loses interest once the natural setting has been described and lets her work trail off in unfinished lines. Archetypally, Nature has always had a maternal role: it is the maw which devours the dead, and the womb which produces life from the seemingly lifeless seeds placed within it. In these Gondal poems, Brontë assumes the mythic attitude that is traditionally bound up with the worship of nature-goddesses: dissolution and death are the grounds for life – in Brontë, the life of the emotion – and the very cycles of Nature maintain life.

So in 'There should be no despair for you' the movement of Nature is towards the decay of Winter (a state similar to the despair of the speaker) 'where Autumn's leaves [were] lying' and also towards new life which is about to 'revive'. As the speaker reminds us of the snow and leaves, 'from their fate your fate cannot be parted'. And in 'Cold in the earth' it is just those details of Nature, which would supposedly have dissolved both the outlines of emotion and, literally enough, the dead lover, that have in fact maintained them. Julius is 'cold in the earth . . . cold in the dreary grave', and thus evidently still a presence for Rosina. His 'noble heart' is covered with 'heath and fernleaves', but it is so 'for ever, ever more'. So if Rosina is able to say, 'All my life's bliss is in the grave with thee', then that 'bliss' does still exist, as the entire poem bears witness.

Like so many other of her poems set firmly in the Gondal sequence, 'Fall, leaves, fall' has been read biographically by many as proof of a growing death-wish by Brontë.[10] I would argue that Brontë does not attempt here an annihilation of self but rather an affirmation of self. As the poem proceeds, the speaker, Augusta, approaches her own realm, the underworld.

Downward movement characterizes the poem. The leaves 'fall', the flowers shed their petals and 'die', the leaves 'flutter from the autumn tree', the 'wreaths of snow' descend upon the rosebushes. The mood of the speaker changes too as she first feels 'bliss', then breaks into a 'Smile', and finally 'sing[s]'. Given the obvious identification between herself and Nature in the poem, she too must be descending, joyously, into the nether regions with song. Those 'wreaths of snow' suggest the formalized funeral wreath, and indeed in the next line night itself has decayed and the speaker, singing, has entered into a 'drearier day' which is more than an overcast winter morning but rather the beginning of a new state of self. By the end of the poem we are in the chthonic world of the Earth-Mother, with a correspondence established finally between the downward cycle of Nature in the poem and the speaker's own psychological experience.

'The linnet in the rocky dells' is a variation on this same theme. It remains at one remove from Augusta since it is the lament of a prison-guard ('E.W.') for her death, and so it lacks the barely concealed sinister quality of 'Fall, leaves, fall' where we are brought into the very presence of the speaker. This poem too has been taken to express Brontë's desire for fusion with Nature, or, alternately, her desire for death.[11] But I think that instead the 'Lady' at last assumes her true identity in the course of the poem, at home in 'the land of Death'. There is the underlying metaphor of Augusta as the mother who 'nourishes' her children through her body's decay: the bee draws honey from 'the heather-bells that hide my lady fair', 'the wild deer' feed from the enriched grass growing 'above her breast', 'the wild birds raise their brood' presumably better sheltered by the foliage which flourishes above her grave. Ultimately, the 'Lady' escapes to the underworld, like

Rosina and Augusta, as she becomes 'the Dweller in the land of Death'. She is 'changed and careless' – a fine grisly touch – and one with Nature at the end.

It is tempting to consider 'No coward soul is mine' as the culmination of Brontë's poetry, and so it has been read by many. At last Brontë is ready to die since 'what thou art may never be destroyed'. Biography seems to help us here, for in fact she caught cold at her brother's funeral, refused to see any doctors, and died of 'inflammation of the lungs' – she who had ranged the moors in all weathers for most of her life and who had never been seriously ill save for the (significantly) psychosomatic illness that brought her home from Roe Head. Furthermore, Brontë had stopped writing poetry about a year before 'No coward soul is mine', and before that time she had been writing at least a poem a month (and usually many more). She left one more poetic fragment. But she did not die for two more years, so the unfinished state of that fragment seems to mean that she simply lost interest in writing any poetry after 'No coward soul is mine'.

Literature, however, proceeds out of the quickness of life; and how can a poet write a poem thinking: 'This is my final credo and completes all that I will ever have to say in the future'? Also, there are troubling elements in this last complete poem, and the experience of reading it is unsettling. It appears to be a luminous statement of religious faith in an eternal God, a denial of all the ambiguous elements of 'the world's storm-troubled sphere'. But one must ask: where have those 'storms' which 'trouble' the world and the 'thousand creeds that move men's hearts' come from, if not from God? Or do they come from some Gnostic Demi-Urge? Such determined tenacity of belief as Brontë shows can tell us as much about the believer as about what is believed. It can be turned against the part of the self that does still doubt, and be a sign that one is trying to strengthen oneself in a new role about which one actually has uncertainties. The tone of this poem seems so resolutely unshaken, yet again and again Brontë brings up the spectre of the world which her 'Faith' has destroyed. Fully half the poem is spent denying the substantiality of 'the world's storm-troubled sphere' which she has supposedly transcended.

There are further things to be noted about it in the context of the Gondal poems. It is not part of the Gondal saga in any way yet it has the same extremity of expression, the same fixed emotion (here, faith) as have those poems. Since Brontë is addressing God, it may seem quite natural for her to declare what is in effect an undying love; however, we should not ignore the strong similarity to, say, Rosina's statement of emotional fidelity through the years to Julius Brenzaida. I find it very significant that after composing this rousing declaration of faith in

'Almighty ever-present God', Brontë goes back to Gondal in her *real* last poem, ignored by her critics – 'Why seek to know what date, what clime'.

It is an interior monologue by a soldier of Gondal fighting in yet another civil war, joying only in killing until his own son is placed in danger by the enemy and he at last feels the parent's love for his 'heart's own darling'. His son is spared; he adopts his dead enemy's daughter who 'was full of anguish wild' until finally 'one moonless night [he] let her go' – and at that precise point, Brontë abandons the whole thing. Again, the central theme is the attempt to regain the ability to feel; again, the male speaker is obviously going to feel endless remorse towards this passionate little female who 'hated [him] like we hate hell'. There is again the extreme designation: the speaker's group are 'foot-kissers of triumphant crime', and 'crushers of helpless misery'. Brontë's half-hearted revision of the poem only bothers with the opening stanzas describing a Nature again very like the devouring Great Mother. It is August when the crops are ordinarily harvested, usually the time when such goddesses have been worshipped. Here, the metaphor is explicit, for when the 'ripe sheaves' of 'corn' are gathered, they are 'threshed out and kneaded-up with gore . . . with furious toil of hoofs and feet' in the war.

Thus apparently end the last lines of poetry that Brontë ever wrote. Whether 'No coward soul is mine' does give us her unswerving faith in the 'God within [her] breast', or whether (as I think) it expresses rather her desire for a unity as yet unrealized, still it is an area of human experience which she evidently does not wish to pursue. Rather than trying to transcend 'the world's storm-troubled sphere' by 'holding . . . fast by [God's] infinity', she leaves that 'sphere' by entering again into Gondal and its archetypal world of the Feminine which by now should be so familiar to her. And it must be emphasized that if the collective world of the archetype may be a great source of creative vitality for a person, it may also be one of great danger (as Jung warns again and again). One may come to identify with the archetype, and lose one's individuality. Dissociation is the ultimate result. This is certainly not to say that Brontë had come to that state, and in any case, she died too soon to say what *would* have happened to her poetry had she lived on into old age. However, it seems that Brontë by this time had explored the archetypal Feminine with all its dark splendor as fully in her poetry as she could.

And yet, as a woman of great talent (some would say genius) who was forced by historical circumstances inward to the only adventure open to her – the exploration of her own psyche – what else could she have done? Her personal world seems to have increasingly closed in upon itself as the years went by, partly of her own choosing and partly not at all through her own will. She was the female offspring of a poor but respectable family living in a remote part of England. She was never trained in any way, even to be a competent teacher or governess (although she briefly tried to gain such preparation at school), for what money the family had went into the short-lived artistic education of her dilettante brother Branwell. The possibility of marriage would seem to have been closed to her as surely as the possibility of her successfully earning her living. In the social context of nineteenth-century England, she was decidedly 'unfeminine', with her proud reserve, her plain speaking, her constant desire for solitude. It is with real pain that one reads of the dismissal of Brontë's magnificence in these recollections of her by a fellow-boarder at Brussels: 'I simply disliked her from the start; her tallish, ungainly, ill-dressed figure contrasting so strongly with Charlotte's small, neat, trim figure ... always answering our jokes with "I wish to be as God made me".'[12]

Charlotte apparently slipped one of her own poems ('Often rebuked, yet always back returning') into the 1850 *Selections from Poems by Ellis Bell* to serve as an apologetic explanation of Ellis who seemed in 'his' poems to be so much involved with 'idle dreams of things that cannot be' (l. 4). But the concluding lines express her sister's poetic explorations better than Charlotte could ever have realized, epitomizing Emily Brontë's search for the chthonic Feminine within herself:

The earth that wakes *one* human heart to feeling
Can centre both the worlds of Heaven and Hell.

Notes

1. L.P. HARTFIELD, 'Emily Brontë in Gondal and Gaaldine', *Brontë Society Transactions*, XIV, no. 5 (1965): 4.
2. Anne Brontë wrote in 1841, 'She [Emily] is writing some poetry, too. I wonder what it is about?' C.W. Hatfield (ed.), *The Complete Poems of Emily Jane Brontë* (New York: Columbia University Press, 1941), p. 234.
3. HARTFIELD, p. 4.
4. Ibid., p. 4.
5. FANNIE E. RATCHFORD, *Gondal's Queen: A Novel In Verse by Emily Jane Bronte* (Austin, Texas: University of Texas Press, 1955), p. 29.
6. See DENIS DONOGHUE, 'Emily Brontë: On the Latitude of Interpretation' in *Harvard English Studies*, I (1970): 108; and LAWRENCE J. STARZYK, 'Emily Brontë: Poetry In A Mingled Tone', *Criticism*, 14 (1972): 120.
7. This has offended many feminists who dislike Jung's idea that there are fixed sexual characteristics, but it should be pointed out that archetypes are quite neutral in value and certainly not behavioral roles to be followed. [*Chthonic*: dwelling in the earth or the underworld. In this context it refers

to myths about Earth Goddesses, and to the traditional association of the feminine with Nature.]

8. WINIFRED GÉRIN, *Emily Brontë: A Biography* (Oxford: Clarendon Press, 1971), p. 173.
9. C.G. JUNG, *Archetypes and the Collective Unconscious*, trans. R.F.C. Hull (Princeton: Princeton University Press, 1969), p. 82.
10. DONOGHUE, p. 115; STARZYK, p. 130.
11. GÉRIN, p. 253.
12. Ibid., p. 130.

3 'What Language Can Utter the Feeling': Identity in the Poetry of Emily Brontë*

Kathryn Burlinson

While in the previous chapters Homans sees Brontë's poetic subjectivity challenged and even suppressed by the strong voice of male poetic genius, and Gallant sees her adopting the strong voice of the feminine archetype, Burlinson finds multiple and dispersed subjectivities in the different and not always clearly distinguished voices of the poems. The absence of the transcendent Romantic poetic self is, for Burlinson, not a problem or a failure: rather, Brontë's exploration of multiple subjectivities and of the limits of representation places her in a Victorian poetic tradition, and even as an antecedent of modernism. Brontë's gender becomes unimportant in this argument – it is her historical placing within a mainstream tradition that is significant. A splitting of the 'self' is already implicit in Homans's and Gallant's arguments – poet and muse, social self and archetype. Burlinson's post-structuralist position enables her to celebrate a recognition of the fragmentation of subjectivity: the unitary self is a delusion. Brontë's dispersed subjectivity anticipates what is often thought of as a postmodern position, in which psychoanalysis has undermined the coherence of the self, and deconstruction has unmasked the impossibilities of representation, language being a shifting system of signifiers without a fixed signified. Burlinson, however, locates these 'postmodern' (she does not use this term herself) insights at the end of Romanticism, and the beginnings of modernism. She thus rescues Brontë from the position of belated Romantic, and recreates her as a precursor of contemporary debates. Her Brontë is neither as historically bounded as Homans's, nor as ahistorical as Gallant's.

'No coward soul is mine' proclaims the speaker of Emily Brontë's 1846 lyric which takes this line as its title; 'No trembler in the world's

* Reprinted from PHILIP SHAW and PETER STOCKWELL (eds), *Subjectivity and Literature from the Romantics to the Present Day* (London and New York: Pinter Publishers, 1991), pp. 41–8.

storm-troubled sphere'.[1] Such courageous assertions accord with the popular conception of Emily Brontë as wild girl of the moors, unafraid to separate fighting dogs with her bare hands, battling against elements and elegance alike. Brontë myths have notoriously overshadowed Brontë texts, yet in Emily Brontë's poetry there are instances where poetic voices wilfully speak out against convention and constraint, giving some credence to the literary myth-makers. In 'Often rebuked, yet always back returning' (H: 255),[2] the speaker naïvely yet proudly defies religious, historical and literary tradition, asserting independence of spirit and refusing guidance outside the self:

> I'll walk, but not in old heroic traces,
> And not in paths of high morality,
> And not among the half-distinguished faces
> The clouded forms of long-past history.

(stanza 1)

> I'll walk where mine own nature would be leading:
> It vexes me to choose another guide . . .

(stanza 4)

Yet alongside such unequivocal affirmations run other, far less assured, figurations of the self; figurations that problematize the issue of 'mine own nature' and propose a model of identity that is unstable, divided and temporally indeterminate. The making of the self is a constant preoccupation in Brontë's lyric verse, as it is in *Wuthering Heights* (Brontë 1967). Leo Bersani's observation on the novel that 'the question is not so much what to be as how to be' might equally be applied to the poetry (Bersani 1978: 190).

In this focus on subjectivity, Brontë may be seen to have much in common with her romantic forefathers, and certainly Wordsworthian and Byronic ideologies of the self are noticeable in her work. But Brontë also exhibits a post-romantic (and Victorian) preoccupation with the legacy of romanticism, where doubts about the self and its potentiality underpin poetic articulation.[3] Transcendent subjectivity may still be desired in Brontë's writing, but the impossibility of this project is repeatedly figured. There is a troubled recognition that the high romantic dream of obliterating the distinction between subject and object necessarily defeats itself, for the negation of difference is also the negation of the self. As Catherine Belsey (1986: 68) has put it, 'the obliteration of the object implies the fading of the subject' for the self ceases to be when it has no other against which to define itself. A similar recognition occurs in 'I'm happiest when most away' of 1838

(H: 220), where imaginative apprehension of a state outside the constraints of self-consciousness simultaneously anticipates the dissolution of the self. Union with 'infinite immensity' only takes place 'When I am not and none beside'.

Historically situated between the political and aesthetic idealism of romanticism and the emergence and consolidation of Victorian cultural identity,[4] Brontë's poetic texts are the site of a struggle in which self-representation is fraught with doubt and difficulty. A number of lyrics discussed here focus on locating the self in language and in time; others explicitly address self-division and yearn for its cessation. One such is 'Enough of Thought, Philosopher' of 1845 (H: 220), a dialogue in which one speaker challenges the 'sad refrain' of a 'Philosopher', whose recurrent 'musings' on quotidian existence, as Stevie Davies (1983: 86) has observed, amount to an unqualified death-wish:

> O for the time when I shall sleep
> Without identity,
> And never care how rain may steep
> Or snow may cover me!
>
> No promised Heaven, these wild Desires
> Could all or half fulfil;
> No threatened Hell, with quenchless fires,
> Subdue this quenchless will!
>
> (stanzas 2 and 3)

The next stanza establishes the link between the philosopher's death-drive and the experience of self-division, as the self is split into conflicting forces. Sacrilegiously, the philosopher claims that 'Three Gods within this little frame / Are warring night and day'. This blasphemous parallel to the Holy Trinity goes beyond a simple dualism of the self, and proposes a model of identity which denies unity within. Though the lyric's other speaker then recalls a vision in which a 'Spirit' unified three divergent streams (or selves), the philosopher's search for such an experience of subjective totality is described as 'an endless search and always wrong!' Scepticism about the existence of a unifying agent blends with yearning for such a possibility, as the philosopher replies to the first speaker:

> – And even for that Spirit, Seer,
> I've watched and searched my lifetime long;
> Sought Him in Heaven, Hell, Earth and Air,
> An endless search and always wrong!

Had I but seen his glorious eye
Once light the clouds that 'wilder me,
I ne'er had raised this coward cry
To cease to think and cease to be.

(stanzas 10 and 11)

The philosopher cannot find the 'Spirit' or 'Word' which might assure stability, and this produces a despair which is seen to find relief only in release from self-consciousness. Only in death may the warring selves make peace, as all is finally 'lost in one repose'.

'Enough of Thought, Philosopher' is one among a number of Brontë's poems which use dialogue as a way of writing about divisions in the self. But Brontë does not always allow her speakers to remain as distinct as they appear in this poem; not, for example, in the lyric 'In the earth, the earth, thou shalt be laid' (H: 190). Here the stances adopted by the two speakers dissolve, towards the end of the lyric, into a complex interfusion in which absolute positions are difficult to distinguish. The lyric may be read as an internal dialogue that contemplates romantic perspectives on death. Its significance in relation to Brontë's model of identity lies in its inability to maintain stability, even between the seemingly opposed inner voices.

The poem begins with the first speaker gloomily predicting the mortal fate of the other, perceiving the grave as morbid and repellent: 'In the earth, the earth, thou shalt be laid, / A grey stone standing over thee; / Black mould beneath thee spread / And black mould to cover thee.' The second voice then expresses a romantic ideal of death as ultimate mergence with nature: 'Well, there is rest there, / So fast come thy prophecy; / The time when my sunny hair / Shall with grass roots twinèd be.' An opposition is thus established between the two points of view, with the borderline between life and death appearing more questionable for the second speaker than for the first. Nature's process of absorption and reclamation is simultaneously a process which the second speaker wishes to surrender to, and one that s/he looks forward to being actively involved in.

The first speaker then protests: 'But cold, cold is that resting place / . . . All who loved thy living face / Will shrink from its gloom and thee.' Yet here the first speaker adopts the discourse of the second in speaking of the grave as a 'resting place'. Although this is a clichéd euphemism, it nonetheless implies some ongoing possibility of consciousness or sentience after death. The oppositions between the two voices, and between life/death begin to be problematized. This kind of impinging of one voice upon another continues through the next stanza, as the second speaker replies: '. . . *here* the world is chill, / And sworn friends fall from me; / But *there*, they'll own me still / And prize my memory.'

It is the second speaker that now insists on division and separation, but s/he inverts the other's perspective in attributing 'chill' to the living world and constancy in relationships to the grave.

In the lyric's penultimate stanza, only one voice remains, and it appears to be that of the first speaker, lamenting the death of the other: 'Farewell, then, all that love, / All that deep sympathy.' The lyric's last stanza, however, ends with the following couplet: 'One heart broke only there – / *That* heart was worthy thee!' This is an odd and equivocal ending, for 'There' appears to refer to the grave, yet hearts conventionally break in the living, not the dead. There is an ambiguity about *which* heart is being referred to, and this raises the question as to who is actually speaking. The assertion in the penultimate stanza is similarly disorienting, as the speaker seems simultaneously to posit absolute truths about the indifference of the universe: '... heaven laughs above / Earth never misses thee', and to undermine these certainties by seeming to speak from a position in which such things are not knowable – i.e. from this side of death.

The lyric, ultimately, refuses to settle on a stable point of reference. And it illustrates the difficulty of locating any final point of certainty with the self, as internal dialogue becomes increasingly scrambled and confused.

Uncertainty, self-doubt, and self-diffusive energies may be found not only in Brontë's lyric verse but also in the Gondal poems, where the persona of a particular character acts as a mask behind which explorations of identity take place. 'Rosina Alcona to Julius Brenzaida' (H: 222) is concerned with memory; not only the memory of an other but the remembrance of the self's past selves, and in A.G.A. (H: 54–5) it is the multiple shadows and spectres of the unconscious mind which preoccupy the lyric. Often, it is through temporal shifts in Brontë's texts that the flux of subjectivity is registered, as the lyrics slide and skip between different temporal locations. A fairly minor example of this tendency can be seen in 'I am the only being whose doom' of 1837 (H: 36). What is also interesting here is the way in which the text disrupts the reader's position, refusing us the satisfaction of stability at the lyric's end.

In the first part of this poem, the 'I' reflects upon itself, writing itself in negative formulations and speaking of its own insignificance to others:

I am the only being whose doom
No tongue would ask, no eye would mourn;
I never caused a thought of gloom,
A smile of joy, since I was born.

(stanza 1)

A special responsibility is placed upon the reader here for the utterance is dependent upon an addressee, yet the 'I' claims to have no relation with any textual 'other'. But we are not able simply to identify with the speaker's plight. For at the end of the poem, she likens herself to all who are 'hollow, servile, insincere' and confesses to her own 'corruption'. This final stanza confirms what the reader may have felt in stanzas 3 and 4, where the speaker admits, and then immediately denies, the desire for love. Stanza 3 confesses that:

> There have been times I cannot hide,
> There have been times when this was drear,
> When my sad soul forgot its pride
> And longed for one to love me here.
>
> (stanza 3)

Though the speaker is looking back in time, we are told that she 'cannot' hide her past desire 'for one to love me here'. The present tense of 'cannot' locates the utterance in this temporal dimension, yet the next stanza banishes not only past feelings but their present acknowledgement:

> But those were in the early glow
> Of feelings since subdued by care;
> And they have died so long ago,
> I hardly now believe they were.
>
> (stanza 4)

We cannot share the speaker's tendency to disbelieve, following so recent an admission. The voice of this lyric refuses to speak logically and sequentially about itself, finally throwing all its utterances into question in the final stanza. We cannot force coherence on the text; rather it forces us to accept an unstable, shifting and untrustworthy self.

If lyrics such as 'I am the only being whose doom' force an acceptance of inconsistencies and contradictions in respect of subjectivity, other Brontë poems explore the connected problem of the relationship between ourselves and our language. One such is 'Loud without the wind was roaring' of 1838 (H: 90). This will be quoted in full.

> 1. Loud without the wind was roaring
>   Through the waned autumnal sky;
>   Drenching wet, the cold rain pouring
>   Spoke of storming winters nigh.

2. All too like that dreary eve
   Sighed within repining grief;
   Sighed at first, but sighed not long –
   Sweet – How softly sweet it came!
   Wild words of an ancient song,
   Undefined, without a name.

3. 'It was spring, for the skylark was singing.'
   Those words, they awakened a spell –
   They unlocked a deep fountain whose springing
   Nor Absence nor Distance can quell.

4. In the gloom of a cloudy November,
   They uttered the music of May;
   They kindled the perishing ember
   Into fervour that could not decay.

5. Awaken on all my dear moorlands
   The wind in its glory and pride!
   O call me from valleys and highlands
   To walk by the hill-river's side!

6. It is swelled with the first snowy weather;
   The rocks they are icy and hoar
   And darker waves round the long heather
   And the fern-leaves are sunny no more.

7. There are no yellow-stars on the mountain,
   The blue-bells have long died away
   From the brink of the moss-bedded fountain,
   From the side of the wintery brae –

8. But lovelier than corn-fields all waving
   In emerald and scarlet and gold
   Are the slopes where the north-wind is raving,
   And the glens where I wandered of old.

9. 'It was morning; the bright sun was beaming.'
   How sweetly that brought back to me
   The time when nor labour nor dreaming
   Broke the sleep of the happy and free.

10. But blithely we rose as the dusk heaven
    Was melting to amber and blue;
    And swift were the wings to our feet given
    While we traversed the meadows of dew,

11. For the moors, for the moors where the short grass
    Like velvet beneath us should lie!
    For the moors, for the moors where each high pass
    Rose sunny against the clear sky!

12. For the moors where the linnet was trilling
    Its song on the old granite stone;
    Where the lark – the wild skylark was filling
    Every breast with delight like its own.

13. What language can utter the feeling
    That rose when, in exile afar,
    On the brow of a lonely hill kneeling
    I saw the brown heath growing there.

14. It was scattered and stunted, and told me
    That soon even that would be gone;
    Its whispered, 'The grim walls enfold me;
    I have bloomed in my last summer's sun.'

15. But not the loved music whose waking
    Makes the soul of the Swiss die away
    Has a spell more adored and heart-breaking
    Than in its half-blighted bells lay.

16. The spirit that bent 'neath its power,
    How it longed, how it burned to be free!
    If I could have wept in that hour
    Those tears had been heaven to me.

17. Well, well, the sad minutes are moving
    Though loaded with trouble and pain;
    And sometime the loved and the loving
    Shall meet on the mountains again.

This text is ostensibly concerned with the speaker's recollections of the natural world. The lyric also raises questions, however, about writing and representation, for example in stanza 13, as the speaker asks 'What language can utter the feeling / That rose when, in exile afar, / On the brow of a lonely hill kneeling / I saw the brown heath growing there.'

This is a question that the text yearns to answer, to this end deploying a range of linguistic strategies throughout the poem, all of which seek, in one way or another, to 'utter the feeling' and establish relation. The question is also, and crucially, concerned with the problem of matching past experience – 'I saw the brown heath growing there' – with present expression. Re-presentation in writing, in respect of nature, the self and time, is a central problem with which the lyric struggles. Stanza 14 describes the heath's communication with the speaker: 'It was scattered and stunted, and told me / That soon even that would be gone; / Its whispered, "The grim walls enfold me; / I have bloomed in my last summer's sun."' The problem here of course is that words are re-presenting nature, that nature is seen to speak in words. The existence of any 'pre-linguistic', unmediated contact between the speaker and the natural world is lost in the recollection, as words stand in for nature in its absence. Nature's figuration within poetic/linguistic convention is stressed at the very start of the lyric, as the pouring rain of the first stanza '*Spoke* of stormy winters nigh' (my italics). Further the relation between human and natural realms is baldly exposed as relying on the adoption of simile or metaphor in the opening of stanza 2: 'All too like that dreary eve / Sighed within repining grief'.

Language as agency is also stressed as the 'words' of a remembered 'song' awaken 'a spell' in the third stanza, unlocking a 'deep fountain' or spontaneous linguistic overflowing which promises to overcome 'Absence' and 'Distance'. But this is a promise that remains unfulfilled, as all that is generated is more language – language which assures that temporal and spatial division is maintained.

As the lyric progresses, the speaker's attempt to recover personal experience is overriden (or re-covered) by the constant production of new texts. In the ninth stanza, the remembered song generates another temporal and linguistic frame – 'that brought back to me' – which then evokes another text – 'The time when nor labour nor dreaming / Broke the sleep of the happy and free'. The pre-lapsarian tone of these lines suddenly gives way to a romance mode as a lovers' narrative is introduced at the beginning of stanza 10: 'But blithely we rose'. The lovers, however, do not reach their destination, though they begin a journey, for by the time we reach stanza 13 it is only the 'I' which remains, and an 'exile[d]' 'I' at that: the affirmation of relation between self and other, which fades, then shifts to an affirmation of relation between self and nature, which is immediately problematized in 'What language can utter the feeling'.

One of the effects of this production of new texts is to render it difficult to locate the speaker in time. The lyric operates within at least three temporal dimensions, three 'layers' of memory, but there is (once again) no fixed point from which the 'I' speaks.

The 'Wild words of an ancient song / Undefined, without a name', come to the speaker as if in a moment of inspiration in the lyric's second stanza, and appear in different guises in the quoted lines of stanzas 3 and 9. We do not learn the origin of this song though it evokes origin in itself, speaking of beginnings – 'spring' and 'morning' – and of an ancient time before linguistic definition – 'Undefined, without a name'. This appears to echo Rousseau's idea that song preceded speech,[5] yet although the lyric strives to recover the 'sweet' moment of hearing the song, this proves as impossible as it would be to discover the original Word, *writing*'s mythical inspiration. The quoted lines of stanzas 3 and 9 are of course *remembered*, and do not necessarily correspond to the 'ancient song' itself.

If it is the original Word that is desired, the paradox highlighted in this lyric is that writing moves onwards in its attempt to recapture. The lyric chases nature yet reveals the impossibility of capturing it in its own time, as language continually imposes *its* terms and *its* time. 'Loud without the wind was roaring' ends with the poem registering the onward march of time in the movement of a line: 'Well, well, the sad minutes are moving' as it looks forward to the next time – 'sometime' – when, it is promised, a union will take place.

'Loud without the wind was roaring', like the other poems discussed here, illustrates Brontë's interrogation of identity and representation – themes pursued also in *Wuthering Heights*. Brontë's poetry has often been devalued beside the achievement of her novel, but this perspective appears fit for review. The poetry does, however, demand an aesthetics which can allow for fractures and fragmentations, uncertainties and contradictions. In 1976 Robin Grove sounded slightly alarmed when he suggested that in Brontë's verse 'No "self" worth speaking of is, really, engaged' (Grove 1976: 44). Yet by 1983, Stevie Davies was confidently asserting the 'continuous and irascible self-division' in Brontë's poetry (Davies 1983: 86). I will go further in suggesting that Brontë's explorations of identity and her questioning of the stable subject may be relevant to the discussion not only of romantic and Victorian verse, but also of modernist writing. If the instability of subjectivity is seen as a primary preoccupation of modernism, it is clearly not confined therein. To adopt a teleological perspective is of course problematic, but we might nonetheless feel prompted to rewrite the biographical comment made by Brontë's tutor M. Héger: 'She should have been a man – a great navigator' (Gaskell 1975: 230), since from the perspective of the twentieth century, her own navigations appear to have been right on course.

Notes

1. All references to Brontë's poems are to *The Complete Poems of Emily Jane Brontë*, edited by C.W. Hatfield (New York, Columbia University Press: 1941); hereafter referred to as H followed by page number, e.g. 'No coward soul is mine' (H: 243).
2. Hatfield disputes Emily's authorship of this poem, but this has subsequently been contested and it is generally agreed that the poem is Emily's.
3. For a discussion of this tendency in the work of Robert Browning, see AIDAN DAY's critical commentary in *Browning: Selected Poetry and Prose* (London: Routledge, 1991). It might also be argued here that Shelley's verse is troubled by similar preoccupations.
4. Although there is much disagreement about precisely what constitutes the Victorian period, I am taking Victoria's accession to the throne in 1837 as its beginning. The bulk of Brontë's poetry was written between 1838 and 1845.
5. See ROUSSEAU's *Essay on the Origin of Language* (1967), trans. John H. Moran, and DERRIDA's critique in *Of Grammatology* (1974: 165–268), trans. Gayatri Spivak (Baltimore: Johns Hopkins University Press).

References

BELSEY, C. (1986), 'The Romantic Construction of the Unconscious', in Barker et al., (eds), *Literature, Politics and Theory* (London: Methuen), pp. 57–76.

BERSANI, L. (1978), *A Future For Astyanax* (London: Marion Boyars Ltd).

BRONTË, E. (1967), *Wuthering Heights* (ed. David Daiches) (Harmondsworth: Penguin).

DAVIES, S. (1983), *Emily Brontë: The Artist As A Free Woman* (Manchester: Carcanet).

DAY, A. (ed.) (1991), *Browning: Selected Poetry and Prose* (London: Routledge).

DERRIDA, J. (1974), *Of Grammatology* (trans. Gayatri Spivak) (Baltimore: Johns Hopkins University Press).

GASKELL, E. (1975), *The Life Of Charlotte Brontë* (Harmondsworth: Penguin).

GROVE, R. (1976), '"It Would Not Do": Emily Brontë as Poet', in Smith, A. (ed.) (1976), *The Art Of Emily Brontë* (London: Vision Press), pp. 33–67.

HATFIELD, C.W. (ed.) (1941), *The Complete Poems of Emily Jane Brontë* (New York: Columbia University Press).

HOMANS, M. (1980), *Women Writers and Poetic Identity* (Princeton: Princeton University Press).

ROUSSEAU, J. (1967), *Essay On The Origin Of Language* (trans. John H. Moran) (New York: F. Ungar).

Part Two
Elizabeth Barrett Browning

4 Introduction to *Aurora Leigh**

CORA KAPLAN

Kaplan's wide-ranging Introduction to *Aurora Leigh* sets the scene for
many of the future debates about Barrett Browning's poetry. Kaplan
establishes the poem's feminist credentials by pointing immediately to
its female imagery – the 'woman's figure'. Her later reading of this
imagery as the return of a revolutionary, hitherto suppressed women's
language echoes the ideas of French feminist writers such as Hélène
Cixous. At the same time, she avoids the essentialism and ahistoricity
of such a reading by putting the poem in context as a contribution to
the Victorian 'woman question', and also relating it to liberal and radical variants of her contemporary feminism. As a socialist feminist
herself, this brings up her main objection to the poem: its treatment of
the working class, and its failure to attack capitalism as well as patriarchy. Nevertheless, she is not arguing for any narrow 'politically
correct' dismissal of the poem, but for complex, multiple readings from
different historical perspectives. Within the Victorian context, she points
out the transgressive nature of the poem's form and content. Her celebration of its energetic 'patchwork' nature perhaps reflects a reaction
against New Critical ideas of organic form. Her examination of the
Victorian critical response to the poem demonstrates the taboos it was
breaking, as well as testifying to its contemporary importance: Barrett
Browning's subsequent exclusion from the canon also exercises her.
The extract ends as Kaplan begins to demonstrate in more detail the
way in which the poem appropriates and transforms other nineteenth-
century texts: it exists in a historically particular discursive context.

> Never flinch,
> But still, unscrupulously epic, catch
> Upon the burning lava of a song
> The full-veined, heaving, double breasted Age:

* Reprinted from ELIZABETH BARRETT BROWNING, *Aurora Leigh*, ed. Cora Kaplan
(London: The Women's Press, 1978), pp. 5–17.

With this 'woman's figure' the doubled female voice of *Aurora Leigh*, its woman–poet–author and woman–poet–heroine, defines the poet's task. The age is Victoria's, but Elizabeth Barrett Browning calls back a looser Elizabethan speech to extend her image from matriarch to nursing mother, 'the paps from which we all have sucked'. Milk and Lava pour from the poem in twin streams; *Aurora Leigh* (1857) produces the fullest and most violent exposition of the 'woman question' in mid-Victorian literature. In her discussion about self-determination Barrett Browning remembers and revises the work of other great women writers from Mme de Staël to George Sand and integrates the debate on gender relations, into which most eminent Victorians were drawn in the forties and fifties, with other political and cultural issues of those years. *Aurora Leigh* is a collage of Romantic and Victorian texts reworked from a woman's perspective. Gender difference, class warfare, the relation of art to politics: these three subjects as they were argued by the English and Continental intelligentsia are all engaged as intersecting issues in the poem. The longest poem of the decade, it is, to use another 'woman's figure', a vast quilt, made up of other garments, the pattern dazzling because, not in spite, of its irregularities.

'Fate has not been kind to Mrs Browning as a writer. Nobody reads her, nobody discusses her, nobody troubles to put her in her place.' Virginia Woolf's comment is almost as true today as in 1932. Elizabeth Barrett Browning's 'place' among eminent Victorians was so well assured in her lifetime that she was a prominent candidate for poet laureate when Wordsworth died at mid-century. It is empty today. The chairs have been moved up to hide her absence from that otherwise meticulously reconstructed feast Victorian studies have served up to us in the past twenty years. Her excision from the retrospective canon of great Victorian poets began relatively recently with the twentieth-century revision of literary taste, although women writers like Woolf never cut her out of *their* list. *Aurora Leigh*, Barrett Browning's 'art-novel' or 'novel–poem', was widely noticed and enjoyed an immediate and continuing popularity for at least a generation following its publication in 1857. It ran through thirteen editions in England by 1873 and was still read and republished up until the turn of the century. Conceived as early as 1845, just at the point of her meeting with Robert Browning, she saw it ambitiously if somewhat vaguely as a 'sort of novel–poem . . . running into the midst of our conventions, and rushing into drawing rooms and the like "where angels fear to tread"; and so, meeting face to face and without mask the Humanity of the age and speaking the truth of it out plainly. That is my intention.' The intention lay fallow during the intense and artistically productive years of her early married life, but in 1853 she started to write it in great bursts – towards the end, some three years later, at the rate of thirty or forty lines a day – writing, revising and producing fair copy, sometimes simultaneously. Her dedication of the poem to her loved and admired friend John Kenyon shows how much she staked on 'the most mature of my works, and the one into which my highest convictions upon Life and Art have entered'. To a correspondent in 1856 she wrote, 'I mean that when you have read my new book, you put away all my other poems ... and know me only by the new.' The hectic composition and self-assurance are reflected in the finished poem whose 'Speed, energy, forthrightness and complete self-confidence', says Woolf, make us 'read to the end enthralled'.

Aurora Leigh comes between two very explicitly political books: *Casa Guidi Windows* (1851) and *Poems Before Congress* (1860), verse which deals much more directly than *Aurora Leigh* with the revolutionary issues of 1848 and after. Elizabeth Barrett was a lyric poet with an interest in political and social questions; \ Elizabeth Barrett Browning was primarily a political poet whose subjects were slavery, suppressed nationality (Italy), the plight of the poor and the position of women. |

Aurora Leigh is Barrett Browning's fullest exploration of this last subject. In 1845, when the poem was forming in her mind, she did not directly relate it to the woman question, but saw the success of an earlier poem, 'Lady Geraldine's Courtship', about the love of a titled woman for a poor poet, as encouragement 'to go on, and touch this real everyday life of our age, and hold it with my two hands. I want to write a poem of a new class, in a measure – a Don Juan, without the mockery and impurity. ...' 'Lady Geraldine' touched on a subject central to most women novelists of the time: the ability of women to choose their own partners without the approval of kin or society. *Aurora Leigh* includes this as a sub-theme only; its more modern preoccupation is whether marriage itself is a good thing, especially for women with a vocation. Elizabeth Barrett Browning, justifying her elopement to Mary Russell Mitford, explains, 'It never was high up in my ideal, even before my illness brought myself so far down. A happy marriage was the happiest condition, I believed vaguely – but *where were the happy marriages*?' Novels which concerned themselves only with happy marriages, Jane Austen's for example, struck her with their 'narrowness – the want of all aspiration towards, or instinct of the possibility of *enlargement* of any kind'. Yet she was equally dubious about the political implications of the woman question. Again to Miss Mitford she wrote, 'I am *not*, as you are perhaps aware, a very strong partisan of the Rights-of-woman-side of the argument – at least I have not been, since I was twelve years old. I believe that, considering men and women in the mass, there *is* an *inequality* of intellect, and that is proved by the very state of things of which gifted women complain; and more than proved by the manner in which their complaint is

71

received by their own sisterhood.' She thought the feminist views of her friends Anna Jameson or Harriet Martineau too advanced for ordinary middle-class women to take in, and this prejudice 'proved' female inferiority. The conscious snobbery of this view is mitigated by her contradictory belief that 'the difference between men and women arose from the inferiority of education of the latter', and her strong defence of women as writers and reformers. But her chief sympathies were reserved for women who wrote: *'You*, who are a woman and man in one, judge if it isn't a hard and difficult process for a woman to get forgiven for her strength by her grace . . . every woman of letters knows it is hard.'

Aurora Leigh expresses this equivocal view of the woman question. The story of a young poet, the daughter of an English father and Italian mother, it is about the development of a woman writer. Aurora is brought up alone in Italy by her widower father. He dies when she is thirteen and she is sent back to England to live with his sister, a maiden lady, in the English countryside. The aunt tries to educate her as a perfect English lady, but the young woman resists and secretly constructs a syllabus of her own from her father's stored library. At twenty she receives a proposal from her cousin Romney, heir to the Leigh fortunes, who asks her to abandon poetry and join him in a life given over to social and political reform. She refuses, eloquently defending poetry and women's right to determine their own careers. Her aunt is furious; the marriage was blessed, even arranged, so that Aurora would inherit her share of the family fortune. The aunt dies with an unopened bequest from Romney in her hands. Aurora is left only £300 (she refuses Romney's money) and heads for London and a garret where she slowly builds herself a reputation as a writer. Romney pursues his own career, rescuing, in the course of his good works, a poor girl, Marian Erle, who has run away from her brutal and drunken parents. He sets her up as a seamstress in London and eventually decides to marry her, not for love but as a gesture towards the breakdown of class barriers. Aurora, who has seen little of her cousin in her years in London, is informed of this imminent marriage by Lady Waldemar, an aristocrat passionately in love with Romney. Lady Waldemar wishes Aurora to intervene in the marriage, but after meeting Marian, Aurora gives it her blessing. On the wedding day rich and poor gather for the ceremony. Marian stands her bridegroom up, explaining in a letter that she does not really love him. Distressed, Romney returns to his utopian projects. Aurora finishes a major book and goes to the Continent to rest. There she glimpses and pursues Marian, whom she discovers with an illegitimate son. It appears that Marian had been persuaded against the marriage by Lady Waldemar, betrayed by her servant and raped and abandoned in France. Aurora persuades Marian to accompany her to Italy. In Florence the two women live in relative happiness and self-sufficiency with the child. Through a series of rather clumsy plot manipulations Aurora learns that Romney has been ill and is convinced he is married to Lady Waldemar to whom she has written an outraged letter. He arrives soon after, unwed, and ready to atone for Marian's misfortunes by marrying her. Marian will have none of it! She sees her early love for Romney as an unequal infatuation and her commitment to her child as excluding marriage which might produce legitimate siblings. Aurora learns that Romney has been blinded during a riot where local peasants and his London down-and-outs combine in the sacking and burning of Leigh Hall. He has given up his socialism and philanthropic schemes. There is a mutual confession of love. Romney accepts Aurora's 'art' as a higher good than politics and asks her to speak for them both in the future. Aurora, Marian and Lady Waldemar form the triptych through which Barrett Browning speaks her views on the woman question.

In the opening of Book V of *Aurora Leigh* there is a long discursive section on the poet's vocation where the author dismisses the lyric mode – ballad, pastoral and Barrett Browning's own favourite, the sonnet – as static forms: the poet 'can stand / Like Atlas in the sonnet and support / His own heavens pregnant with dynastic stars; / But then he must stand still, nor take a step.' The move into epic poetry chipped at her reputation in establishment circles, but enhanced her popularity. It was a venture into a male stronghold; epic and dramatic verse are associated with the Classicists and with Shakespeare, Milton, Shelley and Tennyson, and later, Browning. In 1893 the influential critic Edmund Gosse wrote that women have achieved nothing 'in the great solid branches of poetry in epic, in tragedy, in didactic and philosophical verse. . . . The reason is apparently that the artistic nature is not strongly developed in her.' This typical retrospective judgment may be a clue to *Aurora Leigh*'s modern oblivion, and one reason why such an important and diverse poet as Barrett Browning is now known almost exclusively as the author of *Sonnets from the Portuguese* (1850), her brilliant series of love lyrics to her husband. Twentieth-century male poet-critics echo Gosse's belief that women's voice in poetry, as in life, should be confined to the lyric. How can one account then for a sustained narrative poem that is both didactic and philosophical as well as passionate and female, an unmannerly intervention in the 'high' patriarchal discourse of bourgeois culture? *Aurora Leigh* makes few apologies for this rude eruption into the after-dinner subjects that go with the port and cigars. Barrett Browning knew less about 'this live throbbing age, / That brawls, cheats, maddens, calculates, aspires' than Mrs Gaskell. But it is the latter, in *Mary Barton*, who intervenes with the authorial voice to offer a timid sop to male expertise: 'I am not sure if I can express myself in the technical terms of either masters or workmen. . . .'

The taboo, it is stronger than prejudice, against women's entry into public discourse as speakers or writers, was in grave danger of being definitively broken in the mid-nineteenth century as more and more educated, literate women entered the arena as imaginative writers, social critics and reformers. The oppression of women within the dominant class was in no way as materially brutal as the oppression of women of the working class, but it had its own rationale and articulation. The mid-century saw the development of a liberal 'separate but equal' argument which sometimes tangled with, sometimes included the definition of women's sphere and the development of the cult of true womanhood. The publicity given on the woman question hardly dented the continued elaboration of mores and manners which ensured that daughters were marriageable, i.e. virgins. Patriarchal dominance involved the suppression of women's speech outside the home and a rigorous censorship of what she could read or write. All the major women writers were both vulnerable to and sensitive about charges of 'coarseness'. The Brontë sisters, Sand and Barrett Browning were labelled coarse by their critics, and, occasionally, by other women. Sexual impurity, even in thought, was *the* unforgivable sin, the social lever through which Victorian culture controlled its females, and kept them from an alliance with their looser-lived working-class sisters.

The debates on the woman question which took up so many pages of leading British periodicals between 1830 and 1860 should not be seen as marginal to a male-dominated ruling class, increasingly threatened from below by an organising proletariat. Caught between this and the need to accommodate a limited demand for equity from informed women of their own class, they were equally committed to the absolute necessity of maintaining social control over females, and its corollary, the sexual division of labour. To get a sense of the space and importance given to the issue, one only has to leaf through the major quarterlies for a given year. The winter 1857 issue of the *North British Review* had both a substantial review of *Aurora Leigh* and a long review article dealing with eight books, titled 'The Employment of Women', which ranges from an abrupt dismissal of Margaret Fuller's *Woman in the Nineteenth Century* for its romantic obscurity, to a serious discussion of Anna Jameson's *The Communion of Labour*, a work which argued that middle-class women should be 'employed' in ameliorating the condition of the female poor. In support of Mrs Jameson the article quotes both Tennyson's *The Princess* and *Aurora Leigh*.

The right to write was closely connected with every wider choice that women might wish to make. In an age characterised by the importance of the popular press as the place of ideological production and the spread of female literacy, it was of prime importance to warn women off questioning traditional sexual morality. |Public writing and public speech, closely allied, were both real and symbolic acts of self-determination for women. |Barrett Browning uses the phrase 'I write' four times in the first two stanzas of Book I, emphasising the connection between the first-person narrative and the 'act' of women's speech; between the expression of woman's feelings and thoughts and the legitimate professional exercise of that expression. Barrett Browning makes the link between women's intervention into political debate and her role as imaginative writer quite clear in her defence of Harriet Beecher Stowe's *Uncle Tom's Cabin*. She rejoices in Stowe's success as 'a woman and a human being' and pushes the message home to her timid female correspondent:

> Oh, and is it possible that you think a woman has no business with questions like the question of slavery? Then she had better use a pen no more. She had better subside into slavery and concubinage herself I think as in the times of old, shut herself up with the Penelopes in the 'women's apartment', and take no rank among thinkers and speakers.

Writing is a skilled task learned at the expense of 'Long green days / Worn bare of grass and sunshine, – long calm nights / From which the silken sleeps were fretted out ... with no amateur's / Irreverent haste and busy idleness / I set myself to art!' *Aurora Leigh* enters, however tentatively, into debates on *all* the forbidden subjects. In the first-person epic voice of a major poet, it breaks a very specific silence, almost a gentlemen's agreement between women authors and the arbiters of high culture in Victorian England, that allowed women to write if only they would shut up about it.

Barrett Browning makes the condition of the poem's very existence the fact that its protagonist is a woman and a poet. |Aurora's biography is a detailed account both of the socialisation of women and the making of a poet. | Her rejection of her cousin's proposal is directly related to her sense of her own vocation. Books III and IV are full of the trivia of a young writer's daily life. Book V, the poem's centrepiece, begins as a long digression on the poet's task. Having established Aurora as artist so firmly in the first half of the poem, she can afford to let Books VI–IX take up the narrative line and extend the discussion of female autonomy to her working-class character, Marian Erle, and Marian's scheming opposite, Lady Waldemar. Aurora has a vocation and a recognised status, and can be identified by more than her sexual or emotional relationships within the poem. The female voice, simultaneously the author's and Aurora's, speaks with authority on just those questions about politics and high culture from which women were generally excluded. *Aurora Leigh*'s other subject, the relationship between art and political change, is reformulated by the fact that, in the poem, the poet is female and the political reformer male. The poetic and all it stands for in *Aurora Leigh* – inspiration, Christian love, individual expression – becomes feminised as a consequence. The mechanical dogmas of utopian socialism, Romney's 'formulas', are straw theories with little chance against this warm wind. Abstract political discourse yields, at the end of the work, to poetry.

So much we can find in *Aurora Leigh* without situating the poem too precisely in the historical moment of its production. Read in the 1970s, it does at first seem to be, as Ellen Moers has said, '*the* feminist poem', radical in its celebration of the centrality of female experience. In spite of its conventional happy ending it is possible to see it as contributing to a feminist theory of art which argues that women's language, precisely because it has been suppressed by patriarchal societies, re-enters discourse with a shattering revolutionary force, speaking all that is repressed and forbidden in human experience. Certainly Elizabeth Barrett Browning saw herself as part of a submerged literary tradition of female writers. Physically she compared herself to Sappho, 'little and black'; Mme de Staël was her romantic precursor, George Sand her contemporary idol. No woman poet in English after Emily Dickinson and before Sylvia Plath rang such extreme changes on the 'woman's figure', but women's writing, both prose and poetry, is now a rich cultural resource. Its relation to political change in the situation of women is no less problematic for us than it was for Barrett Browning and her contemporaries. We have only to look at the sections of the poem which are crude and alienating, the vicious picture of the rural and urban poor, to see that there are painful contradictions in a liberal feminist position on art or politics.

Both liberal and radical feminism insist that patriarchal domination is *the* problem of human cultures. It tends to ignore or diminish the importance of class conflict, race and the operations of capital, and to make small distinction between the oppressions of middle-class women and working-class or Third World women. The strains in *Aurora Leigh* which prefigure modern radical feminism are not only the heroine's relation to art, but also the way in which Barrett Browning manipulates her working-class figure, Marian Erle. Marian is given the most brutal early history of any figure in the poem – drunken ignorant parents, a mother who 'sells' her to the first male buyer – but she enters the world of our genteel protagonists literate and unsullied. Taken up by Romney as a symbolic cause – his marriage to her is intended as a sort of virtuous miscegenation between the classes – she is betrayed, raped and abandoned in a series of villainies which suggest that sisterhood is a frail concept at best. When Aurora finds and rescues her in Book VII, a genuine alliance of female sympathy is formed between women of different classes who have the added complication of loving the same man.

But this sisterhood is bought in the narrative at the expense of a representation of the poor as a lumpen motley of thieves, drunkards, rapists and childbeaters, except for Marian, whose embourgeoisement in terms of language and understanding occurs at embarrassing speed. Only children (innocents) and prostitutes (exploited by men) escape with full sympathy. What is really missing is any adequate attempt at analysis of the intersecting oppressions of capitalism and patriarchy. Elizabeth Barrett Browning has as her particular political target in the poem the Christian Socialism adapted from Fourier and Owen and practised by F.D. Maurice, Charles Kingsley and others, but since she has no answer to the misery of the poor except her own brand of Christian love – and poetry – her solutions to class conflict are even less adequate than theirs. Inevitably a theory which identifies the radical practice of art with the achievement of radical social change, or asserts the unity of female experience without examining the forms taken by that experience in different social groups, will emerge with a theory of art and politics unconnected with material reality and deeply élitist. This is true of the book read in her time and ours.

Aurora Leigh is more than a single text. It is different as it is read and understood at each separate point in history, as it is inserted into historically particular ideological structures. There is a danger in either blaming the poem for its political incoherence by relegating those debates to history or in praising it only for the euphoria with which it ruptures and transforms female language. Works of art should not be attacked because they do not conform to notions of political correctness, but they must be understood in relation to the seductive ideologies and political possibilities both of the times in which they were written and the times in which they are read. Otherwise Barrett Browning's belief that the 'artist's part is both to do and to be' stands in place of, not on behalf of, political transformation.

When *Aurora Leigh* was published in 1857, its author was one of the leading literary figures in England, her reputation ensuring extended notices in the periodical and newspaper press. Ruskin called it 'the first perfect poetical expression of the Age', and there were delighted responses from Swinburne, D.G. and William Rossetti, Walter Savage Landor and many other writers, critics and artists. Reviews in the major quarterlies were considerably less favourable. Most could not cope with the transitions from high to common language, 'wilfully alternated passages of sorry prose with bursts of splendid poetry', the ambitious scope of the subject matter and the obscure and violent imagery. The overriding technique of the reviewers was to quote passages 'of great beauty' next to lines they disliked. They wanted the plot to be either more realistic or more allegorical – either *Jane Eyre* or Tennyson's *Princess*, not both at once. A few radical critics, especially the *Westminster Review*, objected to her castration of Romney's socialist projects; a few conservative reviewers thought that the conventions 'which are society's unwritten laws, are condemned in too sweeping and unexamining a style'. The *National Review* found the imagery 'savage':

> Burning lava and a woman's breast! and concentrated in the latter the fullest ideas of life. It is absolute pain to read it. No man could have written it; for independently of its cruelty, there is a tinge in it of a sort of forward familiarity, with which Mrs Browning sometimes, and never without uneasiness to her readers, touches upon things which the instinct of the other sex prevents them, when undebased, from approaching without reverence and tenderness.

Several reviewers object to Aurora as being 'not a genuine woman', alternately cold and intellectual, and morbidly preoccupied with the 'misappreciation of woman by man'. *Blackwoods'* declared, 'We must maintain that woman was created to be dependent on the man, and not in the primary sense his lady and his mistress. The extreme independence of Aurora detracts from the feminine charm, and mars the interest which we otherwise might have felt in so intellectual a heroine.' The *Dublin University Review* is even more explicit:

> Indeed in the effort to stand, not only on a pedestal beside man, but actually to occupy his place, we see Mrs Browning commit grave errors. . . . She is occasionally coarse in expression and unfeminine in thought; and utters what, if they be even truths, are so conveyed that we would hesitate to present them to the eye of the readers of her own sex. . . . The days when such a woman as Aphra Behn can hope to be palatable to the female sex are gone forever.

The *North American Review* was more enlightened about the poem's feminism:

> When we transfer Mrs Browning from the ranks of female poets to those of the poets of England, we would not be understood to separate her from the first class. Mrs Browning's poems are, in all respects, the utterance of a woman – of a woman of great learning, rich experience, and powerful genius, uniting to her woman's nature

the strength which is sometimes thought peculiar to a man. She is
like the Amazon in the midst of battle ... [and has] ... attained to
such a height of poetic excellence, not in spite of her woman's nature,
but by means of it.

What is remarkable about even the most negative and chauvinist
reviews is that they acknowledge the great power of the poem,
recognise its importance in contemporary literature and place its author
in the first rank of poets.

While the greatest part of these long reviews is given over to
summary of the plot interspersed by quotation, there are occasional
acute analyses of what it means to be a woman writer. *The National
Review* said:

She gives no voice to the world around her. It is herself she is
pressed to utter. And this is not only the unconscious but the direct
and conscious aim of her striving. ... She is never the passive subject
of that sort of inspiration by which some *men* [my italics] almost
unconsciously render back the impressions of things around them;
what comes from her is part of her. It is the song of her own soul
she 'struggles to outbear' and she grasps the outer world to make it
yield her a language.

In this respect the critic may be confusing what is characteristically
female in Barrett Browning's verse – the need to transform a
metaphorical tradition and political perspective formed and dominated
by the male voice – with the personal or individual elements in the
poem. The critic who notes her popularity with women is close to the
mark when writing that she 'speaks what is struggling for utterance in
their own hearts and they find in her poems the revelation of
themselves'.

What the critical reception indicates is how fully the poem, with all
its dissonant and outrageous elements, was taken to the heart of
Victorian culture. Everybody in polite society read it, even the Queen,
and Barrett Browning was delighted by reports that it had corrupted
women of sixty and been banned by horrified parents. The ways in
which the poem is challenged and embraced is a comment on the
contradictory presence of women writers on the woman question in
mid-Victorian culture. It is as if they appear so prominently in the
discourses of the ruling class in direct relation to their continued
powerlessness in its social and political structures.

Aurora Leigh is a dense and complex text. Deliberately discursive and
philosophical, the reflective sections of the poem state very clearly
Barrett Browning's position on women's relation to self-determination,

art, love, politics. The self-conscious didacticism of the poem includes some of its best 'poetic' passages: Aurora's description of her aunt; her bitter diatribe on female education; her definition of modern poetry. But these sections are complemented by a less visible polemic built into the poem's structure and narrative. The plot borrows elements from so many other literary sources, and reworks them in a semi-parodic and sometimes semi-conscious fashion, that one can find a cutting commentary on the literary and political culture through an analysis of the 'sources' of the plot alone. The narrative, often criticised for its lack of realism or simple credibility, is an elaborate collage of typical themes and motifs of the novels and long poems of the 1840s and 1850s. Years of ill-health, during which Elizabeth Barrett saw few people outside the Barrett household, had reinforced an early indiscriminate addiction to print, a habit that persisted through her married life. Characterising her life as secluded even before her illness, she thought that living less in society than in books and poetry was 'a disadvantage to her art'. She compared herself in her late thirties to a 'blind poet' who would willingly exchange 'some of this lumbering, ponderous, helpless knowledge of books, for some experience of life and man'. She lived with peculiar intensity through the written word, her own and other people's. Books substituted for the variety and pattern of social experience which make a novelist. Many social events in *Aurora Leigh*, as well as many of the social types, are drawn more from fiction than from life, but released through poetic licence from the demands of a realistic mode of representation. In the bed-sitting-room at Wimpole Street, and in the sequence of apartments in France and Italy after 1846, the Victorian world as represented in the social novel is reduced to a sort of essence and reconstituted in *Aurora Leigh* as a different brew altogether. Several times removed from the 'real', it is neither a distorted reflection of Victorian life nor a lifeless imitation of other literature, but a living critical commentary on both, full of its own ideological idiosyncrasies.

Victorian readers already familiar with Tennyson, Clough, Kingsley, the Brontës, Gaskell and Sand would have caught echoes that we are too far away to hear. Barrett Browning played very self-consciously too on earlier, romantic sources. The growth of the poet in Books I and II takes us very naturally back to Wordsworth, and large parts of the poem play with themes and characters from a novel that every literate lady of Elizabeth Barrett's generation loved, Mme de Staël's *Corinne, or Italy* (1807). The narrative of *Aurora Leigh* is a critical revaluation of its multiple sources in which didactic asides are interleaved with the story, much as de Staël leavened her romance with long sections on Italian manners, culture and art.

Crucially, the seemingly fragmented, discursive poem (two thousand lines longer than *Paradise Lost*, as one reviewer noted sourly) is tightened and held by a rope of female imagery. One reviewer at least appreciated the 'command of imagery' which gave a 'vital continuity, through the whole of this immensely long work'. Approved and taboo subjects are slyly intertwined so that menstruation, childbirth, suckling, child-rearing, rape and prostitution, are all braided together in the metaphorical language. The mother–child relationship – Aurora and her mother, Aurora and her father, Marian and her son – receives special emphasis. Suckling becomes a multi-purpose symbol of nurturing and growth. It links the narrative themes of Aurora's development as a poet and Marian's rehabilitation, to the philosophical and aesthetic themes: the relationship of art to its 'age'. Mothering and writing are identified as the process of 'stringing pretty words that make no sense / And kissing full sense into empty words'.

The force of the 'woman's figure' is an argument for the genre Barrett Browning has chosen. The social and domestic novel that operated under the constraints of realism, as realism was defined in the middle of the nineteenth century, had little room for the rhetorical excesses acceptable in the female gothic novel written half a century earlier, and in the romance *Corinne*. After Jane Austen's reaction against the emotional and romantic in women's writing, heightened language became a dangerous tool for women novelists. Sneaked in as explosive interjections in Charlotte Brontë's novels, they immediately brought upon her the accusation of coarseness. More liberty was given to poets. Felicia Hemans, one of the most popular women poets in England before Elizabeth Barrett replaced her in the public eye, was rarely criticised for her passionate expression. Her love-crossed heroines could weep or commit suicide with impunity, while Brontë's Lucy Snow or Jane Eyre were reproved for a private howl at bedtime.

Most of the charges of coarseness are directed at any indication that women had a self-centred, independent sexuality. In Charlotte Brontë's novels, women are characteristically made to repress these feelings. Elizabeth Barrett's inhibitions are reflected in her comment on Sand's 'disgusting tendency . . . towards representing the passion of love under its physical aspects'. Even Aurora resists and denies her passion for Romney lest he suppress or divert her sense of vocation. As a result, Aurora's sexuality is displaced into her poetry, projected on to landscapes, the Age, art, through the 'woman's figure'. Love denied is rerouted through language. Comparing England, where her mind and spirit mature, to Italy which represents the body and passion, she describes England as a series of negations of the sexualised Italian panorama:

        ... Not my headlong leaps
    Of waters that cry out for joy or fear ...
                    Not indeed
    My multitudinous mountains, sitting in
    The magic circle with the mutual touch
    Electric panting from their full deep hearts
    Beneath the influent heavens and waiting for
    Communion and commission. Italy
    Is one thing, England one.

This is straight out of *Corinne*, protected from censure by being
suggestive, half-completed metaphor. Breasts, one is tempted to add,
are one thing in verse, another in prose.

Aurora Leigh should be read as an overlapping sequence of dialogues
with other texts, other writers. None of these debates are finished,
some pursue contradictory arguments. The poem tries to make an
overarching ideological statement by enlarging the personal to
encompass the political, but the individual history interior to the poem
– its 'novel' – cannot answer the questions which the work as a whole
puts to discourses outside it. What is true of *Aurora Leigh* is, of course,
true of all writing. The pauses and awkward jumps in the text, the
sense that the speaker has turned abruptly from one discussion to
another, has omitted some vital point or has clammed up just as the
argument gets interesting – those moments should claim our attention
as powerfully as the seeming integration of structure and symbol. The
text's unity is that adult voice that does not permit interruption as it
tells us how things should be: its unintegrated remarks and pointed
silences remind us that the 'knowledge' of any one age is constantly
open to rupture and revision. If we follow Elizabeth Barrett Browning
through a select few of the debates in which she engaged we can
understand the ways she could and could not meet 'face to face and
without mask the Humanity of the age', and speak 'the truth of it out
plainly'.

5 Face to Face: Elizabeth Barrett Browning's *Aurora Leigh* and Nineteenth-Century Poetry*

Dolores Rosenblum

Rosenblum's study of the female face in *Aurora Leigh* takes up an aspect of the 'woman's figure' that Kaplan pointed to in the poem. Rosenblum is not interested in the questions of class that trouble Kaplan, but her interest in imagery is not ahistorical. On the one hand, she deploys various psychoanalytic theories; but on the other she places Barrett Browning's use of the iconic female face in a Romantic tradition of visionary encounters. The tradition she describes is recognisably the same as Homans's (Chapter 1) – one in which women's faces are silent and unresponsive, 'others' who confirm the selfhood of male poets. Rosenblum, however, shows Barrett Browning questioning and re-vising this tradition (as Kaplan shows her revising the plots of other contemporary texts), to produce in Marian Erle a fully living maternal face that confirms the woman poet's selfhood and vocation. Rosenblum rejects the Lacanian idea of language as based on mother-lack, and makes use instead of Winnicot's object-relations psychology to argue for the responsive mother's face as vital to cognition and creativity (but see Carpenter's note 39, Chapter 13). While Rosenblum then uses Browning and Rossetti as a partial contrast to Barrett Browning, in that the responsive face they are looking for is ultimately the face of Christ, Carpenter sees Rossetti also deploying an inter-female gaze as a subver-sion of Lacanian ideas.

Two-thirds of the way through her verse novel on the growth of a poet, *Aurora Leigh*, Elizabeth Barrett Browning describes a recognition scene between her heroine and a woman presumed dead. Aurora's recognition of this beloved face and her subsequent recovery of the living woman mark a crucial stage in her development, confirming her parallel achievements of self-integration and commitment to her poetic vocation. The face that the poet-heroine recognizes – and that

* Reprinted from *Victorian Studies*, 26 (1983): 321–38.

recognizes her – is a mother's face, belonging to a woman who has survived a sexual fall, and hence a social death, to bear a child, create a new society of two, and tell her story. The poet who imagines this recognition and the persona who finds the living woman symbolically recover their mothers, lost not only through death, but also through the repudiation of the mother that is the 'natural' course of a daughter's development.[1] Both poet and persona discover a new myth of origins, a mother-presence to substitute for the mother-lack as a source for poetic inspiration.[2]

Although this recognition-scene belongs in part to a novelistic tradition, it is more deeply linked with Romantic visionary aesthetics.[3] In resuscitating the dead and outcast mother, Barrett Browning, the poet who has declared her aim to meet 'face to face' the 'Humanity' of the age,[4] succeeds in humanizing the silent, iconic female face that looms over so much nineteenth-century poetry, from John Keats to Dante Gabriel Rossetti and Algernon Charles Swinburne.[5] For the Romantic poet the female face is often the means to visionary experience, a gateway standing at the beginning or the end of the romantic quest for self. On the one hand, it may be as distant as the enigmatic mask of Keats's Moneta, whose face the poet longs to penetrate, as if it were a veil, to see the 'things the hollow brain / Behind enwomb[s]'.[6] On the other, it may be as familiar as Dorothy Wordsworth's face, a mirror in which the poet hopes to see 'what [he] was once'.[7] Whether sibylline or erotic, distant or intimate, for the visionary poet the female figure, like nature, is freighted with crucial doubts and expectations: she is the beloved, sister, or muse in whom he seeks confirmation of his identity and vocation. Her iconic face, at times a species of natural vista, at times a triumph of art, comes to 'haunt' the nineteenth-century poet precisely because it can be made to stand for everything – except female selfhood. Much as he longs for a living face, what he projects is a dead mask. Its power resides not in its capacity to originate meaning, but in its ability to appear and disappear – or to be summoned and dismissed – in the poet's serious game of mastering himself and 'reality'.

One way of seeing the female face in nineteenth-century poetry is as picture or statue, something that does not change, that has material permanence, and that may be owned by the poet-speaker. Thus in Lord Byron's 'To Mary on receiving her picture',[8] the literal icon becomes a means of controlling anticipated loss, the one thing that will last through time to meet his 'fond expiring gaze', while in 'The Dream', the living beloved's face is fossilized as an eidetic image: 'There was but one beloved face on earth, / And that was shining on him: he had look'd / Upon it *till it could not pass away*' (ll. 48–50; my italics). According to the Romantic aesthetic, if he is to go on writing poetry, he must choose the 'world' over the 'home', and the fixed icon over the living face.

Women are also pictures in Robert Browning's work, such as 'My Last Duchess', 'A Likeness', or 'A Face'. But in poems like these the appropriation of living beauty in art is qualified by an ironic play of emphasis, shifting from the collector, to the voyeur, to the readers themselves. As we shall see later, Browning's deconstructive irony ultimately leads away from the reified female face. But Browning's complex awareness seems an isolated instance in the progress of female iconicization in the nineteenth century. Dante Gabriel Rossetti, for instance, sees women not only as pictures, but as a species of ghost as well, apparitions that exert a paralysing influence on the gazer. His images in painting and poetry of dreamy, cataleptically absent women have come to stand for the extreme of female iconicization. One of the most striking faces in nineteenth-century poetry is not that of a beautiful woman, but a spectre in a mirror, called 'Might-have-been', or 'No-more', or 'too late', who watches 'sleepless with cold commemorative eyes'.[9] The face is the gazer's own, of course, the opposite of the apperceptive face, and a version of the cold mother who witnesses the self's defeats. Yet all the poems which enshrine Elizabeth Siddal's face are also about this haunting. All ask Saturn's question about the gazer's 'strong identity', which has always fled. 'Mirrored' and 'absorbed' by her eyes, the poet achieves an existence at once planetary and embryonic, 'light-circled in a heaven of deep-drawn rays' (*The House of Life*, XXVI). But Siddal's face, picture and ghost, haunts not so much because she symbolizes the poet's yearning and regret, as because she symbolizes absence itself. 'What of her glass without her?' he asks, and invokes the terror of a mirror without an image (*The House of Life*, LIII). The woman in his art is an unchanging icon demonstrating various impossibilities, including that of her own existence.

It is not my aim, however, to berate the nineteenth-century male poets for inventing a series of beautiful heads – mirrors, icons, monoliths, pictures, ghosts, mandalas – and investing them with so much meaning, yet so limited a range of expression. At his most human, the poet wants the kind of recognition Byron imagines in this stanza from the 'Epistle to Augusta':

> The world is all before me; I but ask
> Of Nature that with which she will comply –
> It is but in her summer's sun to bask,
> To mingle with the quiet of her sky,
> To see her *gentle face without a mask*,
> And never gaze on it with apathy.
> She was my early friend, and now shall be
> My sister – till I look again on thee.

> (XI, my italics)

Here, because it is modelled on Augusta's, Nature's face seems alive and, because Byron has projected the maternal, mirroring face on nature, the actual woman's face escapes reification. This inhuman face is most human-like, a mother/sister face both women and men might imagine as a source for intersubjective recognition. It seems difficult, however, for the male poet to sustain this vision of a 'gentle face without a mask'. Operating within a system of iconography and an aesthetic that perpetuates the conception of woman as sign and as other, poets like Byron and Dante Gabriel Rossetti, no matter how much they long for the living face, remain as much captive of the mask as the female figure who wears it. Within that system, the female face as an image of ideal beauty becomes static and mute, capable perhaps of fantastic transformations, but unchanging and inexpressive in any human sense.

But what can this reification mean for the woman poet who attempts to gaze at the visionary face? Inheriting a literary tradition in which the seeing self is usually male, the seen other female, what stance can Elizabeth Barrett Browning take toward the face that above all means *in silence?* In the next part of this essay I suggest that the prototype for the iconic female face is the maternal face, and speculate on how the reification of the maternal face poses special problems for the woman poet. In my treatment of *Aurora Leigh* I show how Barrett Browning reclaims an expressive mother/sister face by confronting falsifying masks and by breaking down the silent iconicity of the female face. Finally, I compare Barrett Browning's stance toward female iconicity with that of Robert Browning and Christina Rossetti, both of whom, unalike as they are, find the authentic human face to be the face of the suffering Christ. Only Barrett Browning claims the beautiful female face as a mirror which does not falsify female subjectivity. In order to do so she must recover – or reinvent – the mother-face with which her male predecessors and contemporaries were obsessed.

1

'Face to face' is both a common locution in the nineteenth century and a resonant echo of the Pauline text. Precisely in its combination of banality and profundity the wish to see face to face suggests primal wishes, primal experiences. The origins of such wishes are not mysterious, and yet they turn up in surprising ways. Charles Lamb's 'The Old Familiar Faces', for instance, records the most commonplace – and comfortable – regret for old companions. The suppressed first stanza, however, tells us that the first loss is like no other, that every face reminds him of the one lost face: 'Where are they gone, the old familiar faces? / I had a mother, but she died, and left me, / Died prematurely in a day of horrors –'.[10] More obliquely William Morris's

'A Garden by the Sea' records a deeply regressive wish to 'seek within the jaws of death / An entrance to the happy place, / To seek the unforgotten face'.[11] Both poets, then, more or less directly express longing for the lost mother-face, and both seem to be struggling to recall – or repress – very early experiences.

We can begin to account for the intensity of Lamb's and Morris's nostalgia for what appears to be a maternal face by glancing at contemporary cognitive psychology and object-relations psychoanalytic theory, both of which assign primary importance to the face-to-face encounter in human development. In psychologist Jerome Kagan's view, the infant's cognitive development, as well as such affective experiences as fear at unusual stimuli and separation anxiety, proceed from its attempts to deal with discrepancies from an early established schema of the human face. As might be expected, the infant's development of the schema derives from direct and vocal face-to-face interaction between mother and infant.[12] In other words, it is the face of the primary caretaker, whether a mother or a mother-surrogate, that becomes the infant's first cognitive scheme. In a parallel vein, the British psychoanalyst D.W. Winnicot, following Jacques Lacan, postulates that the mother's face is a mirror in which the infant recognizes itself: in her face the infant sees itself being seen. If the mother's face is unresponsive, then it becomes an object of perception, rather than 'apperception', and the interchange of looks is no longer 'creative'.[13] Is it possible for this mirror-face, whether responsive or unresponsive, to be perceived as an independent subject by the gazer who superimposes it on live women or imaginary ones? The feminist theorist Dorothy Dinnerstein would say not, although she too acknowledges the importance of the face-to-face encounter, invoking the power of the mother's gaze as well as her touch. In the early exchange between 'the first "you" and the nascent "I" ', the self is born. But for Dinnerstein the 'you' is also an 'it': our interaction with the mother's face as mirror interferes with our perception of her as an independent subject, and is responsible for what she calls woman's 'anomalous image', alternately idealized and debased.[14]

It is at this point that we can begin to see what is at stake in the poetic representations of the female face for women and for women poets. If it is the mother's face that the infant fixates on and that carries such a charge of cognitive and affective experience, likely it is her face in its benign and adversarial aspects that haunts the nineteenth-century poet. It is, however, a face that is quintessentially other: an object of vision, a mute icon, a silent mirror. As mesmerized as the male poet by the beloved face, the woman poet looks and finds in such images only her own reification. Identifying with the gazer, she sees herself being seen, but not in the benign, apperceptive way in which the infant ideally experiences itself as seen by the mother. Identifying with the mother, on the other hand, she sees herself being seen as an object, as a parody of the benignly mirroring maternal face. It is this image of self as 'sight', as a mute sign to be read by others,[15] that Barrett Browning struggles to overthrow in her re-creations of the face-to-face encounter. As well as the mother's responsive expression and warm touch, it is her speech that fosters the child's development: s/he learns to generate the 'mother-tongue' while looking into the beloved face. In *Aurora Leigh*, Barrett Browning confronts the distorting projections – pictures and ghosts – before which women and men fall silent, replacing them with the schema of the apperceptive maternal face that women can reclaim as an authentic face, as they recover an authentic language.

2

When in the Sixth Book, the orphaned poet encounters the long-lost Marian Erle, who was betrayed first by her mother, then by Lady Waldemar in concert with her maid, and who is herself now a mother, a mythic recognition takes place.[16] Aurora looks at the living face of one who has been dead, vanished from the earth after ostensibly fleeing from an impossible, class-crossing marriage with Romney Leigh, and the 'dead' woman recognizes her. The finding of Marian confirms Aurora's previous discovery of a living poetics that revives her 'dead' art: Marian embodies the 'more intimate Humanity' (V, 100), the 'full-veined, heaving, double-breasted Age' (V, 216) that Aurora has already invented as her true poetic subject. Aurora can now go on to fulfill her womanly nature, for the recovery of the maternal face that returns her gaze enables her to reinstate the mother within herself. Now she can make the bridge between art and life, give and receive love.

Before her meeting with Marian, Aurora has known only mask-like women's faces on which she projects her fantasies of mothers, and which press upon her in mute influence. The first of these is her own dead mother's. As a motherless child, Aurora gazes fixedly at her mother's portrait, struggling to establish the schema that will allow her to assimilate other faces, and to develop her own picture of the world. But the portrait is a death-mask, painted from the corpse, a grotesque collage of death and sexuality, a white face looming above a red brocade dress. What Aurora discovers in gazing at this portrait is the multiplicity of female masks. Everything she had 'heard or read or dreamed' mixed with that face:

> . . . which did not therefore change,
> But kept the mystic level of all forms,
> Hates, fears, and admirations, was by turns

Ghost, fiend, and angel, fairy, witch, and sprite,
A dauntless Muse who eyes a dreadful Fate,
A loving Psyche who loses sight of Love,
A still Medusa with mild milky brows
All curdled and all clothed upon with snakes
Whose slime falls fast as sweat will; or anon
Our Lady of the Passion, stabbed with swords
Where the Babe sucked; or Lamia in her first
Moonlighted pallor, ere she shrunk and blinked
And shuddering wriggled down to the unclean,
Or my own mother. . . .

(I, 151–64)

As Aurora herself points out, the woman in the portrait does not
change, but rather shifts: she is always the same and always all things.
This face provides no answering look; it is a phantasmagoria of all the
projections of female identity that Aurora must master or be
overwhelmed by. Aurora's vision implies, as Sandra Gilbert and Susan
Gubar point out, that 'not only is she herself fated to inhabit male-
defined masks and costumes, as her mother did, but that male-defined
masks and costumes inevitably inhabit *her*, altering her vision'.[17]
Aurora's success in developing her poet-self depends on her efforts to
tear herself away from this transfixing face and to resist it when it turns
up in another guise.

One of these guises is the face of the witch stepmother, at the hands
of whom the fairy-tale heroine undergoes an initiation. The surrogate
mother in Aurora's case is her aunt, her father's sister, who hates
Aurora's dead Italian mother for causing her brother to forfeit his
inheritance (through a clause in the entail forbidding marriage to a
foreigner). When the orphaned Aurora presents herself to the aunt, she
is subjected to a painful scrutiny, combining reproach and threatened
retribution in a way that suggests an angry mother. With 'two grey-
steel naked-bladed eyes' the aunt searches Aurora's face, which is a
happy combination of father's brow and mother's smile, to find the tell-
tale signs of 'intermarriage': 'My mother in my face' (I, 327–8).
Aurora's face betrays a sexual secret, as well as a tainted lineage. The
underlying secret is a variation on the Oedipal triangle: the aunt is
perceived by Aurora as a mother who is angry because Aurora has had
a sexual alliance with the father, albeit phantasmal, and symbolized by
the sexual 'mother' in her face. Fortunately for Aurora, the split
between the Oedipal mother and the 'good' mother of infancy can be
absolute, as it is for the fairy-tale heroine; she can virtually kill off her
aunt/mother and repudiate her system of values without much internal
conflict.

Like a mother, her aunt is her chief educator into womanhood, that is, into marriageability. The growing Aurora is set to acquiring the useless accomplishments of a woman of her class, shedding her 'sweet Tuscan words' – her mother-tongue – for her father's language of 'the collects and the catechism, / The creeds, from Athanasius back to Nice' (I, 387–93). From the father's orthodoxies she moves on to his intellectual empire: 'the royal genealogies / Of Oviedo, the internal laws / Of the Burmese empire, – by how many feet / Mount Chimborazo outsoars Teneriffe' (I, 407–10), collections of facts that are useless precisely because they measure, without ordering, fabular patriarchal imperialism. As consorts of colonial rulers, Englishwomen are trained to be 'models to the universe' (I, 446); like colonial subjects, however, their essential characteristic is their 'potential faculty in everything / Of abdicating power in it' (I, 441–2). But Aurora resists this father-sponsored, mother-mediated education by a familiar Romantic stratagem. Like Marian Erle later in the poem, she discovers a powerful nurturance in Nature:

> I had relations in the Unseen, and drew
> The elemental nutriment and heat
> From nature, as earth feels the sun at nights,
> Or as a babe sucks surely in the dark.

> (I, 473–6)

Deprived of her true mother-face, even her true mother-tongue, Aurora withdraws to a dark and covert alliance with an elemental mother which will allow her to preserve her 'inner life with all its ample room / For heart and lungs, for will and intellect / Inviolable by conventions' (I, 478–80). And in a garret room she discovers, like a mouse among the 'giant fossils' of her past, boxes of books 'in her father's name', the books of the poets, the only useful knowledge she can take from his world (I, 833–45). These are her true patrimony, and without them she cannot make her way out into the larger world, but they are still 'fossils', enormous and dead; as 'mouse' she chews and digests, in the process undermining that monolithic literary inheritance which she must ultimately reject.

As Aurora grows towards marriageable age, fairy-tale and romantic nature myth modulate into a novelistic conflict of codes. Although Aurora has escaped what appear to be a wicked stepmother's designs on her life, she still has to deal with the 'realistic' consequences of her aunt's value system. When the grown Aurora refuses her cousin Romney's marriage offer, the aunt, who sees only the economic necessity of the match, subjects Aurora to another intense and coercive scrutiny. If verbal bullying will not work, then she will use silent looks to read Aurora's mind and break her resolve. Servants, neighbours,

even the dog, 'watch' her to see if her will is slackening. In just such
ways parents or their surrogates coerce the rebellious child into
internalizing parental expectations. And in just such ways, perhaps,
mothers, in collusion with paternal authority, coerce rebellious
daughters into internalizing the patriarchal value system.

When the aunt dies, that look is fixed in a death-mask that Aurora
contemplates in much the same way that she contemplated her mother's
portrait. Looking at the dead woman, sitting upright in her chair,
Aurora sees 'the dumb derision of that grey, peaked face' (II, 928), and
meditates on its absolute fixity. From now on she is free to marry or
not, but she is not free of the mask-like female face. She must still
confront false and terrifying faces, the chief of these being the face of
the beautiful Lady Waldemar, who takes the aunt's place both as witch-
mother (bewitching rather than grim) and as death-mask (deadly and
object-like rather than dead).

Lady Waldemar is not only instrumental in the degradation of Marian
Erle: she also represents the social order that victimizes the Marian
Erles of this world: she is one of the fine ladies who tries on a dress
and looks at herself in the mirror, not noticing the pale worn
seamstresses behind her (IV, 251–60). She also influences with her look,
much as Aurora's aunt did. Marian wonders:

> *Did* she speak,
> . . . or did she only sign?
> Or did she put a word into her face
> And look, and so impress you with the word?
>
> (VI, 963–6)

Her emanations are hurtful, like the 'morning sun' (VI, 1008); she is the
other who overwhelms the self: 'Leaning on my face / Her heavy agate
eyes which crushed my will' (VI, 1076–77). Ultimately she is a picture-
or statue-woman. Watching two men staring at Lady Waldemar's
picturesque – and provocative – beauty, Aurora discovers how she
herself is a woman observed. If Lady Waldemar is a 'Venus Meretrix',
Aurora is also a statue, a 'Pallas' with a face 'intensely calm and sad',
and other men have been watching and choosing her (V, 766, 799).
Lady Waldemar is an aspect of the mother-portrait that Aurora must
engage with in a private and mortal struggle. She is the snow-queen,
and also Lamia; finally, she is a hag in a hood, 'preserved / From such
a light as [Aurora] could hold to her face / To flare its ugly wrinkles
out to shame' (VII, 685–7).

When Aurora first meets Marian Erle, she is struck by her 'ineffable'
face. It is, however, an imperfect face:[18] changeful, because it can look
'white or brown', with too much hair, dimples that go better with fuller

cheeks, and an overlarge mouth, 'though the milky little teeth /
Dissolved it to so infantine a smile' (III, 798–823). Although Marian
Erle's face will become the focus for Aurora's recognition of herself in
the maternal face, at this point she has the vulnerable appeal of a child,
and stands for the motherless child in Aurora. Aurora hears Marian's
story of betrayal by her mother (who would have sold her to a man),
recognizes her nobility in suffering, and gives her blessing to the
marriage between Marian and Romney. Aurora tells Romney that
'among the gallery portraits of our Leighs / We shall not find a sweeter
signory / Than this pure forehead's' (IV, 297–9). This marriage, then,
would parallel the marriage between Aurora's father and the Italian girl
whose face one day in church 'flashed like a cymbal on his face' (I, 87).
But this ideological marriage does not take place, and Aurora cannot
recover her parents in this way. Marian's disappearance and the violent
disruption of the wedding, coupled with Romney's scepticism about her
art's 'use', triggers a new stage in Aurora's growth as a poet. She
rejects her previous facile and derivative work, and invokes the figure
of the corpse of Earth resurrected by Christ, a powerful female figure
who sounds like a new myth of the mother in the poet: 'The body of
our body, the green earth, / Indubitably human like this flesh' (V, 117–
18). Having imagined this mythic figure, Aurora is able to formulate
her credo of the artist's 'double vision' that sees both near and far, to
complete her modern epic, and to return to Italy, her mother country.

At the ill-fated wedding, the crowd was bestial, 'an ugly crest / Of
faces' (IV, 569–70), and Aurora could see salvation only in Romney's
'masterful pale face' (IV, 850), a mastery that failed, since he could not
control the crowd, and it was Lord Howe who saved her. In Paris,
where she has stopped *en route* to Italy, she walks in the crowd and can
bear 'to look into the swarthiest face of things' (VI, 148). Earlier she has
realized that nature must not be idealized as a cold pastoral. Now she
realizes that nature includes everything and is contained in everything,
even 'the hungry beggar-boy / (Who stares unseen against our absent
eyes)' and who contains 'both flowers and firmaments' (VI, 186–94). As
Aurora continues walking through the streets of Paris, struggling to
construct a 'larger metaphysics' and a 'completer poetry' that would be
more adequate to daily needs than Romney's social programmes, at the
moment that she asserts the power of the word, she is struck by a
recognition:

> What face is that?
> What a face, what a look, what a likeness! Full on mine
> The sudden blow of it came down . . .
> . . . .
> It was as if a meditative man

Were dreaming out a summer afternoon
And watching gnats a-prick upon a pond,
When something floats up suddenly, out there,
Turns over . . . a dead face, known once alive . . .
So old, so new. . . .

(VI, 231–40)

So the dead face surfaces, and everything that has been denied
surfaces,[19] not as horror, but as a liberating recovery of the truth.
Aurora cannot reject her vision as a phantom. Memory yields a true
likeness: 'That face persists, / It floats up, it turns over in my mind, /
As like to Marian as one dead is like / The same alive' (VI, 308–11).
Saying that the dead person looks like the living person emphasizes the
irrevocability of the separation: the two are alike but not identical.
This vision allows Aurora to acknowledge that her mother is dead, that
she persists in memory, but not in phantasmal projections. It also
allows her to enact a symbolic resurrection of both the mother and the
mothered child in herself. As she remembers, 'those eyes, / . . . saw me
too, / As I saw them' (VI, 325–7). But memory must go all the way:
Aurora, starting to write to Romney, realizes that she saw not only a
face, but also a thing clasped under a shawl – a child. So the sexual
secret surfaces, like the dead face, as mythic truth rather than horrific
mystery. Having recognized the maternal face, and having been
recognized, Aurora goes on to find Marian through the agency of living
speech: as Marian asks after a spray of flowers in 'stranger's French'
(VI, 347), Aurora hears the mother-tongue (now English) underlying the
foreign language. In Marian's narrative of her betrayal, rape, and the
birth that is actually the source of her deliverance, Aurora will discover
nothing less than a myth of her own origins.

A woman who has been betrayed by her mother, and oppressed and
brutalized by the patriarchal culture, but who has given birth as a
virgin, in that she cannot in any way be said to have 'known' the man
who raped her, Marian is a symbol for the birth of self.[20] As a child,
Marian, like Aurora, had found her parent in nature in a blind,
mystical-sensuous fusion. Her own sight blackened by looking at the
sky, she felt 'some grand blind Love came down, / And groped her out,
and clasped her with a kiss' (III, 893–4). That androgynous parent,
'skyey father and mother both in one' (III, 899) sustained Marian in a
brutalized life, while she escaped conventional feminization. Now, with
the birth of her child, it is as though instead of a rape, Marian had
sustained a divine impregnation by her own self-created and self-
creating parent. Her relation with the child replicates her relation with
the androgynous parent: the child gazes on *her* skyey face ('accepting
it / In change for heaven itself . . .': VI, 588–9), while she, Madonna and

Psyche, gazes on him. Implicitly, she discovers the same universe that Aurora 'saw' in the beggar-boy, thus confirming Aurora's poetic vision. Conventional Freudian theory would suggest that the child fulfills the persistent female wish for a penis, transformed into a wish for a child by the father.[21] I would suggest that the child fulfills an even stronger need to replace 'fathering' and patriarchal vistas by the mother-vision that sees the 'flowers and firmaments' within, the self immanent in the face-to-face encounter. The underlying wish may indeed be the wish to have a child by the mother,[22] except that the child is a reborn, humanized self. For a time Aurora, Marian and the child will form a holy family, and a small matrilineal community: the child will not miss a father, 'since two mothers shall / Make that up to him' (VII, 124–5).

But Aurora's quest is not yet over. She must integrate the other 'parent' as well. As her feelings for Romney surface, Aurora experiences a terrible weakness and weariness, followed by an explosion of self-hatred. She excoriates all women:

> Poor mixed rags
> Forsooth we're made of, like those other dolls
> That lean with pretty faces into fairs.
> It seems as if I had a man in me,
> Despising such a woman.

(VII, 210–14)

This 'man' has been with her all along, however, as the critical viewer observing the self-observed. It is only now, when she is on the way to reinstating the strength-giving mother in her, that she can perhaps afford to acknowledge the male critic in her, and find ways to deal with 'him'.

Aurora Leigh's new poetry begets a new portrait. In the Seventh Book, while Aurora is living with Marian in Italy and at once recovering her past and laying it to rest, she receives a letter from a male friend, a painter, telling her of her book's critical success and of his new marriage and new portrait. He has married the woman whose compelling eyes had found their way into his portraits of Danaë, and, having changed his style and left 'mythologies', has painted 'the whole sweet face' that 'looks upon his soul / Like a face on water, to beget itself' (VII, 593–4). If he has executed the painting, Kate Ward has conceived it, while Aurora's writing has begotten the new Kate, who insisted on having herself painted in a cloak like Aurora's, and with Aurora's books in her hand. Kate is thus a mirror for Aurora, even though Aurora cannot yet stop despising herself.

The book is Aurora's symbolic child, the parallel to Marian's child, and as word, as 'truth', it has a productive influence in the world, as

opposed to the coercive influence of phantasmal projections and shifting
faces. Having been sent into the world to bring the twofold natural–
spiritual truth to everyman, it is no longer 'hers'. She is no longer
defined by her vocation, or rather, she no longer needs the book in
order to create a self. Ultimately, however, the 'man' inside her cannot
stop criticizing until she unites with her cousin, her brother-self, in a
symbolic – and real – marriage.[23]

In all her other books Romney had seen Aurora herself, like a moon
in a pond, but in this last book he has seen something 'separate from
herself / Beyond her' (VIII, 606–7). But the Romney who has this new
vision of Aurora's art is actually blind. Sight thus becomes divided
along Christian–Platonic lines of sight and insight. Romney Leigh is
blinded in order to symbolize the failure of his materialist vision, and to
effect his removal from the world of appearances, so that Aurora can
never be to him an icon of female beauty or female virtue, a moon and
her reflection. Nor need she look to him for a reflection of her worth.
The 'spiritual' woman who has acknowledged her 'natural' needs can
now marry the 'natural' man who has acquired 'spiritual' insight. The
last lines of the poem show Romney in something of the attitude of the
resigned, iconic woman, raising his head to gaze mutely toward the
heavenly city, while Aurora looks on him and, like a mother
interpreting the world to a child, names his unarticulated vision:
'"Jasper first", I said; / "And second, sapphire; third, chalcedony; / The
rest in order: – last, an amethyst"' (IX, 962–4).

Looking into the mirror face of a mother–sister marks Aurora's
discovery of an integrated self and a poetics. The triumph of the
woman as she 'is' rather than 'seems' in a series of mask-like projections
involves a resuscitation of a 'dead' woman, dead either by her
conversion into a sign or by her exclusion from the world of
signification altogether. In reviving the dead woman Barrett Browning
sets out to revive a dead sign system. Her response to a tradition that
denies female subjectivity in order to erect female symbols is to
reappropriate those symbols and make them 'live' differently: the
beautiful mother-face belongs to a 'fallen' woman, the mother of an
illegitimate child, and to a woman-poet, the mother of poems.

3

Barrett Browning is not entirely alone in her enterprise: not
surprisingly, Robert Browning's confrontations with female iconicity
parallel hers, and both Browning and Christina Rossetti suggest that
there is an important model for a humanized version of the beloved
face within the Christian tradition. As I have mentioned earlier, Robert
Browning, perhaps alone of nineteenth-century male poets, adopts an
ironic stance toward the iconic female face. Both more casually and

more seriously than any Romantic poet, he demonstrates how the ideal beloved is an obsessive illusion that only embeds the seeker more deeply within his solipsism. In 'Numpholeptos' the ideal beloved looks backward to Keats's 'Belle Dame' and forward to Swinburne's implacable Sphinx in 'A Leave-Taking'. This poem records a complex interplay between the speaker's disenchantment with the emptiness of the female enigma – 'No more seeking love / At end of toil, and finding, calm above / My passion, the old statuesque regard, / The sad petrific smile!' – and his obsessive need to renew the 'crimson-quest', ever hopeful that it may 'deepen to a sunrise, not decay / To that cold sad sweet smile'.[24] The irony deepens in the fascinating rhyming narrative 'Beatricé Signorini', which can be read as the culmination of Browning's poems about painting. Its titular subject is a passionate and misused woman, the painter's wife; its quester is a painter who goes to school to an actual historical figure, Artemisia Gentileschi. Artemisia is the impossible ideal beloved not because she is a cold reflection, but because she refuses to be assimilated to the schema. She is 'resolute to care / Nowise beyond the plain sufficiency / of fact that *she is she and I am I*' (p. 997, my italics). The central symbol of the poem is a decentered portrait, a wreath of flowers, scrupulously painted by Artemisia, surrounding a blank upon which the painter is to inscribe his version of the fair face. The ideal face he paints in is, of course, Artemisia's. The painter thus thinks he has captured in art (and captured the art of) the woman he could neither subdue nor abdicate to in life. Beatricé, the wife, 'reads' only the flowers, a message from woman to woman, and in a startling operatic gesture, she slashes away the face in the center, defacing the painter's vision and effacing the betrayal of women in and by art.

Both the betrayal and the significance of 'defacement' as a humanizing of the visionary ideal, are present as themes in the poetry of Christina Rossetti, who was as concerned as the rest of her Victorian contemporaries with the ambiguities of the human mask, and who longed as intensely as Barrett Browning for the confrontation face to face. In two poems which can be read as pendants, 'In An Artist's Studio' and 'The Descent From the Cross', Christina Rossetti suggests that the authentic face of the ideal beloved may be the human face of suffering. In the first poem she unmasks as the authentic face the worn, changing face of Elizabeth Siddal, Dante Gabriel's model for his reductive and obsessive images of the 'one face' that 'haunts his dream'.[25] In the second, she contemplates the model for all unmaskings, the suffering face of the crucified Christ. In a stunning allusion to Marlowe's Helen, Rossetti asks: 'Is this the Face that thrills with awe / Seraphs who veil their face above?' (p. 254). She concludes that this disfigured face, the transformation of the 'face without a flaw', is the ultimate face of Love. Here Rossetti seems to be saying that if we are to gaze steadfastly at the face of the beloved we must be prepared to see the face of suffering and death as well.

It is at this focal point, the contemplation of Christ's face, that Barrett Browning, Christina Rossetti and Robert Browning converge in their common mistrust of idealized and unvarying images. Against the fixity that signals Romantic transcendence, Robert Browning opposes a peculiarly plastic immanence, characterizing the human face as 'evidence / O' the soul at work inside, and, all the more intense, / So much the more grotesque' (*Fifine at The Fair*, XCVI, p. 726). In the Epilogue to *Dramatis Personae* he makes clear that the model for this plasticity is Christ's face, 'that one Face' that 'far from vanish [sic] rather grows, / Or decomposes but to recompose' (p. 414). Each human face illustrates this constancy through flux, even through 'grotesque' transformations.

Christ's face of suffering and mortal change is the literal focal point of Barrett Browning's early epic, *The Seraphim*. As the seraphs gaze upon the scene of Christ's death, His human face of suffering turns out to be a more awesome sight than Heaven's splendors, and seraphic vision is limited, for this sight can be appreciated fully only by human gazers who see a face like their own, and a face that looks back. In demoting seraphic vision, Elizabeth Barrett Browning – like both Robert Browning and Christina Rossetti – seems to reject the Romantic visionary mode, stressing instead the humanized inter-subjective vision 'face to face'. Unlike either of these poets, however, Barrett Browning is unwilling to give up the fair face as an idealized projection. Her aim is to reclaim that face as informed by woman's living purposes. When Barrett Browning removes the mask or topples the image, what emerges – as in 'Lord Walter's Wife' – is the same beautiful face as the face of the treacherous suitor's Lilith-like projections. The woman is not betrayed, but the suitor is deluded; his projections are false, but her beauty is true. She claims her own face and speaks in her own voice:

> There! Look me full in the face! – in the face.
>   Understand, if you can,
> That the eyes of such women as I am are clean as
>   the palm of a man.
>
> (*Works*, VI, p. 9)

Barrett Browning's achievement in *Aurora Leigh* is to suggest how such a face, the beautiful face of the mother–sister–beloved, can be a 'mirror' without the sacrifice of female subjectivity. Possibly the 'It-ness' that Dinnerstein describes as inherent in male images of women is not an inevitable consequence of the earliest encounter between infant and mother-as-mirror. The falsifying projections may represent subsequent failures of vision, with the face that is looked 'at' rather than 'into', as Winnicot puts it (Winnicot, p. 28), becoming the mirror that reflects only Narcissus or the mask that falsifies the self. In *Aurora Leigh*, Barrett Browning comes closer than any previous poet to showing how, within an image-system that revolves around a distant beloved, and ultimately around mother-absence, the living female face in its presence – beautiful, but not deathly still – can be a subject for poetry.

Notes

1. See *The Standard Edition of the Complete Psychological Works of Sigmund Freud*, trans. and ed. James Strachey and Anna Freud, 24 vols (London: Hogarth Press and Institute of Psycho-Analysis, 1964), XXII p. 119, for Freud's description of the female child's change of her erotogenic zone and her object. A more recent, feminist view of this change is presented by CLARA THOMPSON, who interprets the daughter's rejection of the mother as a rationally based rejection of the mother's actual cultural powerlessness. See 'Penis Envy in Women', in *Psychoanalysis and Women*, ed. Jean B. Miller (New York: Brunner, Mazel, 1973), pp. 43–7.
2. It is Jacques Lacan's theory that the discovery of absence or lack motivates speech. Lacan bases this hypothesis on Freud's interpretation of the child's game of 'Fort–Da', in which the child makes a symbolic object appear and disappear. In Lacan's view, the lack of this object stimulates the desire to reunite with it, and language flows from the effort to fill the gap. To the extent that object stands for the mother, it is the inaccessibility and distance associated with her – rather than her presence – that ostensibly motivates language; see LACAN's *Ecrits: A Selection*, trans. Alan Sheridan (London: Tavistock, 1977), pp. 103–12.
3. The most obvious link is Elizabeth Gaskell's *Ruth*, from which Barrett Browning derived Marian Erle's story. The novel contains a chapter entitled 'Recognition' in which the seduced woman encounters her seducer after she has borne her child and established herself as a governess. Gaskell's adherence to a novelistic code calling for the reunion of 'lovers' highlights the significance of Barrett Browning's departure in having the key recognition occur between women. In any case, however, the kind of recognition Barrett Browning imagines seems closer in tone to the Romantic visionary encounter between seeker and quest-object than the novelistic encounter between characters, although it can be seen as a revision of both sets of conventions.
4. *The Letters of Robert Browning and Elizabeth Barrett Barrett*, 1845–1846, ed. Elvan Kintner, 2 vols (Cambridge, Massachusetts: Harvard University Press, 1969), I, p. 31.
5. It is impossible in a paper of this scope to exemplify the range of female types apostrophized by the Romantic and Victorian poets. The tradition of the complimentary portrait extends back in English poetry at least as far as Sidney, where the female beloved is already firmly 'other', and already an emblem of transcendence. What I am suggesting, however, is that in

nineteenth-century poetry the scale of the beautiful face enlarges, at times literally – witness Keats's Thea, his Moneta and Mnemosyne, even Cynthia – and the iconic or talismanic power intensifies. As the century wears on, the Victorian preoccupation with death combines with the worship of beauty to produce images of female powerlessness that paradoxically have great iconic power. In 'The Lady of Shalott', for instance, Tennyson needs the image of a dead woman enshrined as a kind of art object – 'She has a lovely face' is Lancelot's epitaph for her – in order to engage crucial aesthetic issues (ALFRED LORD TENNYSON, *The Poems of Tennyson*, ed. Christopher Ricks: London, Longman, 1969).

6. JOHN KEATS, *The Fall of Hyperion*, in *The Poetical Works of Keats*, ed. H.W. Garrod (London: Oxford University Press, 1908), I, pp. 276–77.

7. WILLIAM WORDSWORTH, 'Tintern Abbey', in *The Poetical Works of Wordsworth*, ed. Thomas Hutchinson, rev. Ernest de Selincourt (London: Oxford University Press, 1936, 1950).

8. LORD BYRON, *Poetical Works*, ed. Frederick Page, 3rd edn: corrected by John Jump (London: Oxford University Press, 1970). Subsequent references are to this edition, and line or stanza numbers are cited in the text.

9. DANTE GABRIEL ROSSETTI, *The House of Life*, in *The Works of Dante Gabriel Rossetti*, ed. William M. Rossetti (London: Ellis, 1911), XCVII. Subsequent references are to this edition, and sonnet numbers are cited in the text.

10. CHARLES LAMB, *The Works of Charles and Mary Lamb*, ed. Thomas Hutchinson (London: Oxford University Press, 1924), p. 547.

11. WILLIAM MORRIS, *The Collected Works of William Morris*, 24 vols (London: Longman's Green, 1910–15), IX, p. 149.

12. JEROME KAGAN, *Change and Continuity in Infancy* (New York: Wiley, 1971), pp. 7, 31.

13. D.W. WINNICOT, 'Mirror-role of Mother and Family in Child Development', in *The Predicament of the Family*, ed. Peter Lomas (New York: International Universities Press, 1967), pp. 26–33.

14. DOROTHY DINNERSTEIN, *The Mermaid and the Minotaur. Sexual Arrangements and Human Malaise* (New York: Harper & Row, 1976), pp. 104, 111, 170.

15. This experience of self as visual object has been treated by SIMONE DE BEAUVOIR in *The Second Sex*, where she stresses the adolescent girl's transformation of face into mask (trans. and ed. H.M. Parshley (New York: Knopf, 1952), p. 335). De Beauvoir's argument seems to be echoed by the art critic John Berger. In *Ways of Seeing* BERGER describes women as split between a surveyor-self, who is 'male', and a surveyed-self, who is 'female'. Because a woman cannot 'act', she exemplifies how she is to be treated: 'She turns herself into an object – and most particularly an object of vision: a sight' (Harmondsworth: Penguin, 1977: p. 47).

16. The maid is a woman 'not a monster', with 'both her breasts / made right to suckle babes'; ELIZABETH BARRETT BROWNING, *The Complete Works of Elizabeth Barrett Browning*, ed. Charlotte Porter and Helen Clarke, 6 vols (1900; repr. New York: AMS Press, 1973), VI, ll. 1183–4. Subsequent references are to this edition, and volume and line numbers are cited in the text.

17. SANDRA M. GILBERT and SUSAN GUBAR, *The Madwoman in the Attic: The Woman Writer and the Nineteenth-Century Literary Imagination* (New Haven and London: Yale University Press, 1979), p. 19.

18. The particularity of the description of Marian's face, following the poetic epithet 'Ineffable', suggests that Barrett Browning, in order to stress Marian's deviation from supposedly aristocratic norms, is resorting to novelistic

conventions. In this instance, Barrett Browning again differs interestingly from Gaskell, whose Ruth is classically beautiful. See MICHAEL IRWIN, *Picturing: Description and Illusion in the Nineteenth-Century Novel* (London: Allen & Unwin, 1979) for commentary on novelistic portraiture. In general, however, her face-to-face encounters owe more to poetic models, in which the face is more of a typificatory schema than a diversified instance. For an interesting discussion of physiognomy and narrative conventions, see JEANNE FAHNESTOCK, 'The Heroine of Irregular Features: Physiognomy and Conventions of Heroine Description', *Victorian Studies*, 24 (1981): 325–50.

19. In *Mrs Browning: A Poet's Work and Its Setting* (London: Faber & Faber, 1962, p. 98), ALETHEA HAYTER makes the connection between Barrett Browning's brother's death and this image. What is remarkable is that the image is made to stand for the recovery of a lost connection, as if Barrett Browning is working through her ambivalent feelings about her brother and her guilt over his death in the course of this poem. Since the 'dead' face is Marian's, however, it seems likely that Barrett Browning is also exploring her feelings about her mother's death.

20. In her otherwise insightful analysis of *Aurora Leigh*, Sandra Gilbert underestimates the power of the encounter between Aurora and Marian Erle, implying that it takes Aurora in the direction of compromise. Gilbert claims that in linking up with Romney, Aurora becomes 'a modest bride of Apollo who labors for her glorious blind master . . . in an "unwearied" trance of self-abnegation'. As she herself realizes, this is not the whole story: the ending does grant the power of vision and speech to Aurora; see GILBERT and GUBAR, pp. 575–80. I would claim that the encounter with Marian Erle does more than teach Aurora 'service', and the superiority of 'love' over 'art'. Rather, Marian Erle confirms the integrated self to which Aurora has been struggling to give birth.

21. See 'Some Psychical Consequences of the Anatomical Distinction between the Sexes', in FREUD, XIX, p. 256.

22. See 'Female Sexuality', in FREUD, XXI, p. 239.

23. In a recent essay, Barbara Charlesworth Gelpi correctly points out that Aurora is related to Romney as the 'brother of her soul'. GELPI, whose argument mine parallels, shows how Aurora's growth depends on a reconciliation between 'masculine' activity and 'feminine' spiritual insight. See 'Aurora Leigh: The Vocation of the Woman Poet', *Victorian Poetry*, 19 (1981): 35–48.

24. ROBERT BROWNING, *The Poetical Works of Robert Browning*, ed. G. Robert Stange (Boston: Houghton Mifflin Company, 1974), pp. 813, 814. Subsequent references are to this edition, and page numbers are cited in the text.

25. CHRISTINA ROSSETTI, *The Poetical Works of Christina Georgina Rossetti*, ed. William Michael Rossetti (London: Macmillan, 1911), p. 330. Subsequent references are to this edition, and page numbers are cited in the text.

6 Defiled Text and Political Poetry*

DEIRDRE DAVID

David's extract takes up the political criticism levelled at Barrett Browning by Kaplan in Chapter 4, and explores it further in the context of both *Aurora Leigh* and Barrett Browning's other political poetry. Rather than seeing Barrett Browning's attitude to the working classes as an excusable blot on an otherwise laudable feminist poem, David presents the poet's conservative political stance as central to her position as a 'traditional' intellectual. By using Gramsci's formulation here, David signals that her criticism is coming from a socialist direction. Barrett Browning's criticisms of middle-class attitudes, industrial expansion, and working conditions are aligned with those of the right-wing Carlyle. Contrary to Kaplan's assumption, Barrett Browning does critique capitalism, but from a conservative direction. While David's argument is important in ensuring that we do not too easily appropriate Barrett Browning to our contemporary progressive politics, her own charac terisation of Barrett Browning's politics as 'conservative' perhaps also too neatly puts a contemporary label on to a complex and shifting set of Victorian attitudes. Victorian social criticism came for the most part from 'conservative' thinkers such as Carlyle and Ruskin, who were acknowledged by, and in Ruskin's case profoundly influenced, socialist thinkers. Towards the end of the extract, David investigates the contradictions involved in Barrett Browning as a woman deriving her authority from a male tradition – her gender position weakens her power to speak out strongly and angrily. Moreover, in David's reading, her conservative stance compromises her feminism.

A poem that begins with the admonition from Ecclesiastes, 'Of writing many books there is no end', *Aurora Leigh* is pervaded by metaphors of

* Reprinted from Deirdre David, *Intellectual Women and Victorian Patriarchy* (London: Macmillan, 1987), pp. 128–42.

writing, the most notable being that employed by Aurora in likening man's soul to a multiply inscribed text. Refuting enlightenment beliefs in the soul as 'clear white paper', she imagines it as:

A palimpsest, a prophet's holograph,
Defiled, erased and covered by a monk's –
The apocalypse, by a Longus! poring on
Which obscene text, we may discern perhaps
Some fair, fine trace of what was written once,
Some upstroke of an alpha and omega
Expressing the old scripture.

(I, 826–32)

Richly invested with Barrett Browning's philosophical and political values, the lines signalise her recurrent preoccupation with the traditional Christian myth of lost unity. Man's soul is likened to a scripture which once possessed its own perfect form and its own internal coherence: as Christ declares in Revelation 1: 8, 'I am Alpha and Omega, the beginning and the ending', so man, in an ideal correspondence to this unity, once possessed a unified soul/text. But the soul/text which once resembled the holograph inscribed by a prophet, who was, in his turn, inspired by the original inscriber of all things, has been defiled by later writers: man's original soul/text has been debased from its primary meaning and transformed from oracular revelation to pastoral romance (the apocalypse inscribed by a Longus). Associating herself with the biblical prophetic tradition, proclaiming herself as God's new interpreter and inscriber of the ideal world which will replace that sundered by the social cleft, Barrett Browning instructs man in discovering traces of the original text in the degenerate palimpsest. If soul, text, and form have been debased through inscribed interpretation, erasure and deformation, so, too, the alpha and omega of Victorian life has become obscured by the inscriptions of materialism, commercial individualism, and socialist politics. In a much less ambiguous prophetic stance than that adopted by Harriet Martineau at Niagara Falls, Aurora Leigh performs the ideal mission of the poet as Barrett Browning described it in her Preface to 'A Vision of Poets' – she reclaims the oracular function of poetry and destroys the 'evil' of a 'social incrustation over a great idea'. Empowered by vocation to reveal the connections between God, man, culture and society which have been obscured in a secular world, the ideal poet is made a woman poet in *Aurora Leigh*. Moreover, she is a political poet whose ideas echo the conservative thought of Barrett Browning, an intellectual we may associate with the traditional function as Gramsci describes it.

Barrett Browning's political thought frequently resembles that aspect of Carlyle's which excoriates mercantilism and mechanisation. In her *Contributions towards an Essay on Carlyle*, taken from letters to R.H. Horne written during 1843, Carlyle is, as one might expect, the antithesis of Martineau's intellectual inspiration, Jeremy Bentham; he speaks a 'soul-language', is the figurative opener of a long closed, bricked-up, 'encrusted' window in the 'blind wall of his century' (6, pp. 312–21). To peer through the window opened by the force of Carlyle's swirling, vital prose is to see, if one is Elizabeth Barrett Browning, not very far back in the century. It is to have a vision of the Romantic revolutionary spirit embodied and mythologized in the figures of Byron and Shelley, to glimpse the heroic energy of Napoleon, and to diminish the material achievements of the English middle class. 'When we drive out, from the cloud of steam, majestical white horses, / Are we greater than the first men who led black ones by the mane?' asks the lowly poet in 'Lady Geraldine's Courtship' (2, ll. 207–8). According to Barrett Browning's politics, clearly not: her poet observes that if man touches the ocean floor, strikes the star, or wraps 'the globe intensely with one hot electric breath', he is only displaying technological power which is within his tether and of his making. 'Materialist / The age's name is', declares Romney to Aurora as they debate the proper ways to remedy the evils of that age. To understand the full significance of these evils in *Aurora Leigh* and the conservative weight of their remedies, it is necessary to examine the antagonism to English middle-class values expressed in Barrett Browning's other political poetry.

Much of this poetry is more overtly concerned with Italy than it is with England. An impassioned partisan of Italian nationalism, Barrett Browning mourns and celebrates Italian history in 'Casa Guidi Windows', published in 1857, and in a collection, *Poems Before Congress*, published in 1860 and greeted by *Blackwood's Magazine* with the following affronted declaration: 'We are strongly of opinion that, for the peace and welfare of society, it is a good and wholesome rule that women should not interfere with politics' (*Blackwood's Magazine*, 87: 490). However, the two-part 'Casa Guidi Windows', an impressionistic meditation on Italian culture and politics viewed from the fenestrated seclusion of Barrett Browning's intense readings, contains strong criticism of the British commercialism celebrated at the Crystal Palace in 1851 and of England's failure to support Italian aspirations. To all sympathisers with the Italian cause, unity had seemed likely in 1848; but conflict between different revolutionary factions had debilitated the struggle and the restoration of Austrian military rule served to darken all hopes of Italian nationhood by the end of 1849. Europe after the events of 1848 is painted by Barrett Browning as a 'Fair-going world', bent upon exhibiting glories of trade and trophies of imperialism, and deaf to the cries of people suffering under domestic and foreign tyranny. England displays the signs of imperial might – the corals, diamonds, porcelains, intricate glassware and models of the steamships that make her the queen of 'liberal' trading nations – but where is the 'light of teaching' for the poor, asks Barrett Browning, where is the 'help for women sobbing out of sight / Because men made the laws?' And England is not singular in her indifference:

> No remedy, my England, for such woes?
> No outlet, Austria, for the scourged and bound,
> No entrance for the exiled? no repose,
> Russia, for knouted Poles worked underground,
> And gentle ladies bleached among the snows?
> No mercy for the slave America?
>
> (3, Part 2, ll. 641–6)

In a manner suggestive of Gramsci's definitions of traditional intellectual activity, she scathingly attributes England's 'woes' to contemporary spineless liberal politics and to rampant mid nineteenth-century mercantilism. According to Gramsci, the traditional intellectual believes (or wants to believe) in the existence of an 'historical continuity uninterrupted even by the most complicated and radical changes in political and social forms'. This structure of feeling impels such intellectuals to 'put themselves forward as autonomous and independent of the dominant social group' ('The Intellectuals', pp. 5–7). Barrett Browning's politics are defined by a self-sustained myth of transcendent poetic practice and by strong antagonism to the dominant middle class. In the Preface to *Poems Before Congress*, she sarcastically imagines an English politican who would say, 'This is good for your trade; this is necessary for your domination . . . [but] it will profit nothing to the general humanity; therefore away with it! – it is not for you or for me' (3, p. 315). In general, her politics express a yearning for a utopian society in which economic development and better ways of existence for 'humanity' have little to do with each other: the relationship, for example, between Victorian commercial expansion and improved living conditions escapes her idealistic polarisation of trade and the social good. That the industrial revolution produced intense and far-reaching misery is beyond question, but the threat and visibility of that misery generated a surveillance and consolidation of the working classes which produced certain improvements, however minimal, in the working and living conditions of those who suffered.

To be sure, Barrett Browning's attacks upon English politics are voiced from her adopted Italian perspective, but she had consistently practised a poetry of social criticism from the time she was the secluded English 'poetess' of 1838.[1] 'The Soul's Travelling', her first flight into such poetry, bears a suitably uplifting motto from Synesius, the late fourth-century Christian Neoplatonist: 'Now, to spread one's intellectual wings'. The poem is characterised by that irregularity of form and carefully constructed appearance of inspired and spontaneous verse which reveals its origins in Barrett Browning's most intensely 'Spasmodic' period: dwelling in the city, a cacophonous place from which he imaginatively travels to the quiet of the country, the speaker/ poet catalogues the noises of a teeming town – a town noticeably Hogarthian in its anticipation of the carnivalesque church scene in *Aurora Leigh*:[2]

> The champ of the steeds on the silver bit,
> As they whirl the rich man's chariot by;
> The beggar's whine as he looks at it, –
> But it goes too fast for charity; . . .
> The gin-door's oath, that hollowly chinks
> Guilt upon grief, and wrong upon hate;
> The cabman's cry to get out of the way;
> The dustman's call down the area-grate;
> The young maid's jest, and the old wife's scold;
>
> (2: ll. 15–33)

In an ironic turn at the end of the stanza, all the dissonant noises of champing steeds, whining beggars, of drunken oaths which 'chink' as glasses and coins chink together, of dustmen's calls down area-grates which 'grate' upon the reader, are drowned out by the ringing bells and blaring trumpets greeting the Queen's coronation. In desperation the poet imaginatively flies from the Blakeian town to find 'a grassy niche / Hollowed in a seaside hill', where the only sound is 'Distance-softened noise made more old / Than Nereid's singing, the tide spent / Joining soft issues with the shore / In harmony of discontent'. Paradoxically, this unpeopled spot offers 'a harmony of discontent' because the poet still feels that which makes the 'city's moan', and the poem concludes with the recognition that all travelling of the poetic imagination from city streets to unspoiled nature is necessarily futile. All men and all poets must fly to God's throne where 'the archangel, raising / Unto Thy face his full ecstatic gazing, / Forgets the rush and rapture of his wings!' Expressly critical of degraded city life full of shriek and moan, the poem argues that the poet possesses a special gift of escape from dissonance through his imagination, and finally suggests that both city dissonance and country harmony can only be, must be, transcended in a flight to God. The glory of this flight lies in a falling away of self-consciousness from the archangel and from the poet: as the angel forgets 'the rush and rapture of his wings', so the poet loses awareness of his power which has lifted him to God's glory.

105

In this early poem, Barrett Browning foreshadows the dedication of Aurora's poetic power to the building of a New Jerusalem. But before her union with Romney and before her understanding that 'Art's a service', Aurora lives in a London as disturbing as that evoked in 'The Soul's Travelling'. Enshrouded literally and symbolically by a fog which is more strangely comforting than it is threatening, and feeling 'serene and unafraid of solitude', she writes inferior poetry.

There, in a proverbial garret whose windows reveal the chimney pots of a tangled city rather than the stately turrets of Romney's country house that Aurora viewed from her green chamber, she sees:

Fog only, the great tawny weltering fog,
Involve the passive city, strangle it
Alive, and draw it off into the void,
Spires, bridges, streets, and squares, as if a sponge
Had wiped out London, – or as noon and night
Had clapped together and utterly struck out
The intermediate time, undoing themselves
In the act. Your city poets see such things
Not despicable.

(III, 179–87)

Here she is surprised by 'a sudden sense of vision and of tune' and writes poetry that implicitly fills the absence created by the shrouding fog, a creeping, deadly force which seems to kill the city, to 'strangle' it and 'draw it off into the void'. Somewhat schematically in terms of Aurora Leigh's aesthetic values (and those of Barrett Browning) this poetry is, of course, commercially successful but inspired by no belief in the mission of the poet. According to Aurora, 'I did some excellent things indifferently, / Some bad things excellently. Both were praised, / The latter loudest' (III, 205–7). In the lengthy aesthetic meditations of Book V which, among other things, question the rigid imposition of form upon content, Aurora distills her views in these terms: 'Inward evermore / To outward, – so in life, and so in art / Which still is life' (V, 227–9). The London poetry produced by the 'city poet' has originated in an 'outward' world, which though sometimes shrouded by fog, is the materialistic world feeding and applauding a skill ungoverned by transcendent vision; at the end of the 'novel–poem' figuring an epic quest and thereby defying governing rules of appropriate form, Aurora Leigh's poetry is properly directed by an 'inward' vision which will build a new city, and, one might add, a new poetics itself which reconciles the early Spasmodic inspiration of 'A Soul's Travelling' with politics and society.

Whether writing poetry about Italian history, English politics, or poetry itself, Barrett Browning tends to form her arguments in terms of confinement and liberation. Until she left England as Mrs Robert Browning, Elizabeth Barrett was literally confined to a domestic space she described as a prison, guarded by closed doors against which she wanted to dash herself 'with a passionate impatience of the needless captivity'. She writes of talking exclusively by post and gloomily likens herself to someone incarcerated in a dungeon driven to scrawling mottoes on a wall. The image of the closed door is elaborated in her letters after her marriage: she speaks of the time before she left England as one in which all the doors of her life were closed to her, shutting her in 'as in a prison'. Before one marvellous door stood Browning, who, after much dedicated persuasion, released her from the obsessive grip of a father who had forbidden *any* of his children to marry. A month after her marriage, she observed that had she asked her father's permission, it would have been like 'placing a knife in his hand' (*The Letters of Elizabeth Barrett Browning (L. EBB)*, 1, pp. 275, 293). It is hardly surprising that a father whose pathological will was unyielding, who refused permission for Barrett Browning to travel to Italy in the autumn of 1845 (a journey urged upon her by her doctors and her friends) causes his daughter to cast him in the role of knife-wielding patriarch. Yet that father who brandishes the symbolic knife (which in *Aurora Leigh* also cleaves the social body) was consistently, if ambiguously, defended by his daughter. She declared to Browning that 'the evil is in the system' which sanctions paternal enforcement of filial submission by that 'most dishonouring of necessities, the necessity of living'. In terms of her career as a political intellectual, the most significant connection she makes between the patriarchal 'system' and society is to be found in her association of domestic and socialistic tyranny.

Conceding in 1848 that the cooperation of individuals and families designed to organise more economically 'the means of life' may be beneficial, she is vehemently opposed to such spontaneous small-scale cooperation becoming a 'government scheme': 'All such patriarchal planning in a government issues naturally into absolutism, and is adapted to states of society more or less barbaric' (*L. EBB*, 1, p. 359). Socialism was thoroughly repugnant to her, a political system that stifled individualism and called forth in her writings a language suffused with fervent emotionalism. 'I love liberty so intensely that I hate Socialism. I hold it to be the most desecrating and dishonouring to humanity of all creeds. I would rather (for me) live under the absolutism of Nicholas of Russia than in a Fourier machine, with my individuality sucked out of me by a social air-pump' (*L. EBB*, 1, p. 452). Preferring the absolutism of tyranny to the dehumanisation of socialism, and speaking from an essentialist perspective, she mythologises, even literalises, individuality as an essence that can be forcibly extracted from the human body, while at the same time she implicitly likens this explicitly political individualism to the familial individualism of rebellious children held under the knife of patriarchy. Her intense loathing of socialism is further revealed in her reactions to the death of Margaret Fuller Ossoli. She flatly declared that 'it was better for her to go' as 'only God and a few friends can be expected to distinguish between the pure personality of a woman and her professed opinions', opinions Barrett Browning felt were 'deeply coloured by those blood colours of Socialistic views' (*L. EBB*, 1, p. 460). Deeply sympathetic to Margaret Fuller as a wife and mother, finding in her life many parallels to her own exile from a mother country, she found Fuller's politics that much more repulsive.

In a telling image from *Aurora Leigh*, Barrett Browning indicts socialism in Lord Howe's misguided support of Romney's social programmes. According to Aurora, Lord Howe is:

A born aristocrat, bred radical,
And educated Socialist, who still
Goes floating, on traditions of his kind,
Across the theoretic flood from France,
Though, like a drenched Noah on a rotten deck,
Scarce safer for his place there.

(IV, 710–15)

He floats on French socialist theory, but unlike Romney, his detachment keeps him from getting wet. Vincent Carrington, Romney's painter friend, describes Lord Howe as standing 'high upon the brink of theories, / Observes the swimmers and cries "Very fine," / But keeps dry linen equally, – unlike / That gallant breaster, Romney!' (III, 115–18). Heroic swimmer as he is, however, Romney is finally defeated by the sea of engulfing theory (even if he is blinded by fire), by that wave of socialist doctrine formed by Louis Blanc and Fourier and which crossed the channel in the 1830s. Romney's literal blinding seems to be a punishment for his political blindness. Unable to see the folly of his utopian socialism, he loses his sight in a fire at the Phalanstery he establishes at his country estate. If Brontë punishes Rochester for his vaunting masculinity, as some critics believe, then Barrett Browning certainly punishes Romney for his politics.

As a political conservative favouring the values of the land-owning classes in England, as a conservative poet lamenting the 'defilement' of a once heroic culture, Barrett Browning speaks as a Gramscian traditional intellectual and abhors the liberalism and mercantilism of the swelling middle classes. In her two powerful poems attacking the exploitation of children she holds mercantile greed accountable for their suffering. 'The Cry of the Children', the poem written after reading the full report investigating employment of children in mines and factories, emphasises the sounds of the factory machinery that drown out the sobs of child-workers. She employs droning, monotonous rhyme and metre to make the reader experience the dreadful and dizzying effects of the factory. The seventh stanza is evocative of the concrete imagery deployed in *Aurora Leigh*:

> For all day the wheels are droning, turning;
> Their wind comes in our faces,
> Till our hearts turn, our heads with pulses burning,
> And the walls turn in their places:
> Turns the sky in the high window, blank and reeling,
> Turns the long light that drops adown the wall,
> Turn the black flies that crawl along the ceiling:
> All are turning, all the day, and we with all.
> And all day the iron wheels are droning,
> And sometimes we could pray,
> 'O ye wheels' (breaking out in a mad moaning),
> 'Stop! be silent for to-day!'

(3, ll. 78–88)

The unrelenting assonance, the repetition of 'turning' whereby the turning of the machinery makes the children's hearts turn, the walls turn, the sky turn, the flies turn, the sense of all movement generated by that droning movement of 'iron wheels' so that industrial manufacture determines and perverts natural movements of the human body, of the sky, and of insects – all this strongly anticipates Dickens's image of the mad, melancholy elephants in *Hard Times*. There, in Bounderby's factory, the piston of the steam-engine works 'monotonously up and down like the head of an elephant in a state of melancholy madness'. Dickens makes the movement of machinery become the movement of perverted nature. Barrett Browning, however, converts nature into a movement that resembles the machine and thereby more directly (if less imaginatively) indicts the factory system and those who profit from it. The poem concludes with an accusing lament from the children: how long, they cry, 'Oh cruel nation, / Will you stand, to move the world on a child's heart' (ll. 152–3). With the pun upon stand, the poem interrogates British mercantilism: how long will it stand, endure, a commercial power that stands, rests upon, depends upon, exploitation, and how long will it figuratively stand with its crushing weight upon the heart of a child? The cry in this poem seems to issue from the centre of Blake's 'London', where the speaker hears 'mind-forg'd manacles' in every cry of every man and every infant.

In the second of her poems of social protest dealing with children, 'A Song for the Ragged Schools of London', written in 1854 for a charity bazaar organised by her sister, Barrett Browning relies upon the familiar association of the Roman and British empires in order to make the song a monitory one. Listening in Rome to hymns of praise for Britain's imperial power, her rich natural resources, her morally correct middle class, the speaker advises, 'Lordly English, think it o'er, / Caesar's doing is undone!' England should remember that she already has 'ruins worse than Rome's' in her 'pauper men and women':

Women leering through the gas
(Just such bosoms used to nurse you),
Men, turned wolves by famine – pass!
Those can speak themselves, and curse you
But these others – children small,
Spilt like blots about the city,
Quay, and street, and palace-wall –
Take them up into your pity!

(3, ll. 40–7)

Characteristically defying the patriarchal injunction that women writers avoid discussion of sexuality, she insists that the English see their mothers' breasts in those of the prostitutes, and in an ironic allusion to the myth of the founders of Rome (Romulus and Remus who were suckled by wolves), the British poor, the detritus of Empire, have become wolves. 'Pass', instructs the speaker, for these women and men will curse you, but the children cannot, and they are imagined by Barrett Browning as blots upon the gilded façade of British imperial power and as literal disfigurations of the urban scene. These children again seem to inhabit a Blakeian city, but where Blake's brilliant imagination could make the speaker of 'London' *hear* how 'the hapless Soldier's sigh / Runs in blood down Palace walls', Barrett Browning more literally sees the children as visual blots on those walls enclosing the centres of empire.

In these two poems of social criticism informed by Barrett Browning's political opposition to the English mercantile middle class and by her strong belief that this class 'defiles' a potentially shining and heroic world, the speaker undertakes to voice the suffering of those unable to articulate their own misery. When the children do speak in 'The Cry of the Children', it is in the context of an interrogation of English power, in a poetic frame which deploys the rhetoric of accusation: 'Do ye hear the children weeping, O my brothers' begins the first stanza; 'Do you question the young children' begins the second; and the closing stanza of the poem contains the children's question as to 'how long' they must suffer. The second poem is a barely mediated request from the famous poet-mother to her sisters on behalf of the poor children of London: 'Our own babes cry in them all.' Both poems plead for liberation from miserable confinement: that the poet must speak for the oppressed intensifies the actual conditions of oppression which make the suffering voiceless. But at the same time that voice of civilised outrage tends to temper the misery being described simply by virtue of the fact that the suffering must be mediated by a voice of privilege. The most stirring of Barrett Browning's poems of social protest is the one in which the speaker is empowered by her hatred of her oppressor to articulate her own rage. Speaking in the language of brutal literalness that frequently characterises *Aurora Leigh*, she is the pursued figure of 'The Runaway Slave at Pilgrim's Point'.

In September 1833 Barrett Browning professed herself profoundly 'glad' that the recent Parliamentary Bill freeing the West Indian slaves had passed, despite the exacerbation of financial difficulties for her father caused by the legislation.[3] Her anti-slavery poem was written for a Boston bazaar held in 1848 and is a savagely ironic interrogation of the freedom proclaimed by white pilgrims arriving in New England. So fiercely hateful is the tone of the poem, so proudly adamant is its anger, that in a first reading it comes as a shock to realise in the ninth stanza that the speaker is female: a slave who narrates the story of having strangled the child she has borne from rape by her white masters (the poem implies she has been raped by more than one man). She mocks the disjunction between the American myth of freedom and the reality of her experience by literally and figuratively taking a stand:

I stand on the mark beside the shore
Of the first white pilgrim's bended knee,
Where exile turned to ancestor,
And God was thanked for liberty.

(3, ll. 1–4)

She then bends her knee on the spot that marks, 'stands' for liberty in the way that she 'stands' for oppression, and addresses the poem to the 'pilgrim-souls' whose presence she feels in this place. She kneels to curse the land blessed in the name of freedom, to curse the patriarchal line of oppressors, for she is triply oppressed as slave, as black, and as woman. The slave she loved has been dragged from her ('I crawled to touch / His blood marks in the dust') and the hated child she carried on her breast is 'an amulet that hung too slack'. The child's whiteness is unbearable, and the genuine horror of the poem lies in the mother's hatred of her infant. She sees her master's hated look in the child's innocent eyes, the white man's struggles for political liberty in the

moans of her baby as he struggles to free himself from the shawl with
which she has bound him. In a violently ironic reversal of the master–
slave relationship, the black female slave becomes the oppressor of a
white male infant, and the irony is intensified by the reader's awareness
of the only power such a figure *can* exercise to brutally pervert the
nurturing relationship between mother and baby. Finally obliterating
his mocking difference from her and thus reconciling herself to him, she
strangles the infant and buries him in the forest: 'Earth, 'twixt me and
my baby, strewed, – / All, changed to black earth, – nothing white, – /
A dark child in the dark!' (ll. 184–6).

Raped, flogged, a cursing, bleeding figure who finally jumps from the
rock in a dreadful parody of the liberation achieved by white pilgrims
as they stepped on to this same rock, she is Barrett Browning's
wounded woman taken to the extremes of figuration. Leaping, she
cries 'I am floated along, as if I should die / Of liberty's exquisite pain.'
Lacking the racial status and class meaning that makes Marian Erle
appealing to Romney Leigh, and lacking an Aurora Leigh to nurture
and enfold her into a matriarchal household, she possesses the one
thing that Barrett Browning could not, or would not, give Marian – a
cursing, authentic voice empowered by rage.[4] If her later poem 'A
Curse for a Nation' (1859) is any guide, Barrett Browning was reluctant
to voice directly a woman's curse, to repeat in her own poetic persona
the indictments of slavery so chillingly articulated in the earlier stanzas.
Half-knowingly, it seems, she anticipates the dictum that was
Blackwood's Magazine's response to the poem: 'To bless and not to curse
is woman's function' (87: 494).

The poet-speaker resists instructions from an angel to write a
'Nation's curse' for America, claiming that she is bound in gratitude
and love to that country and deeply grieved for her own:

> . . . 'Evermore
> My heart is sore
> For my own land's sins: for little feet
> Of children bleeding along the street:
>
> 'For parked-up honours that gainsay
> The right of way:
> For almsgiving through a door that is
> Not open enough for two friends to kiss:'

$$(3, \text{ll. } 17\text{–}24)$$

The prologue concludes with the poet's acquiescence in the angel's
judgment that 'A curse from the depths of womanhood / Is very salt,
and bitter, and good', and in having the poet speaker agree to write this

curse, Barrett Browning places her in an ambiguous position, a figure burdened with contending imperatives suggestive of those imposed upon women poets in a male-dominated culture. The angel issues a stern instruction, 'Write! Write a Nation's curse for me / And send it over the Western Sea.' The poet falters, three times refusing to write the poem, until overmastered by the logic of the angel. When she declares 'To curse, choose men. / For I, a woman, have only known / How the heart melts and tears run down', he responds that her curse will be that much more effective coming from her womanhood: 'So thus I wrote, and mourned indeed, / What all may read, / And thus, as was enjoined on me, / I send it over the Western sea' (ll. 49–52).

The elaborate apology *for* the poem serves both to intensify the criticism articulated *in* the poem and to reveal an important ambiguity in Barrett Browning's career as woman poet engaged by politics: that is to say, the force of the curse and the immensity of the evil cursed are emphasised by a woman's inadequacy to the cursing task, and the American nation must be in a pretty bad way if a woman's curse is needed. The woman is not powerful enough to deliver the appropriate curse and yet *too* powerful to be doing such a thing. It seems to me that important questions relating to the definition of a woman's poetic voice in the Victorian period, to Barrett Browning's affiliation with a male poetic tradition, and to her chosen ratification of conservative political thought, are raised by this poem. Possessing no sustaining female poetic tradition, from where does the Victorian woman poet derive her authority to speak? What are the suitable subjects for poetry written by women? Does the Victorian woman poet possess the intellectual strength to perform strong political criticism? Enacting a scene of male authority and female obedience which recalls Harriet Martineau's subaltern status, Barrett Browning's female poet can perform a male function when 'enjoined' to do so by a male voice.

Somewhat ironically, then, a recurrent emphasis of the political poetry written by a woman poet 'authorised' by a male voice and affiliated with male poetic practice is a plea for liberation. Slaves must be freed from oppression, children from exploitation, nations from foreign domination, and society from the injurious, materialistic, middle-class ideologies that have created the 'social cleft' and 'defiled' a once heroic culture. What then of women, whether they be poets 'authorised' by male angels or transformed by Barrett Browning into metaphors of imprisonment? If, in a certain sense, English society is symbolically raped, if the Italian motherland is brutally penetrated and exploited by Austrian imperial forces, if raped working-class women symbolise careless exploitation of the poor, how do we characterise Barrett Browning's sexual politics? How does she view woman's actual experience when she is not employing it as metaphor? It would seem

113

that conservative politics not only led her to excoriate the middle class for its materialism; she also believed that most women are intellectually inferior to most men and that woman's art must be made the attendant of patriarchy.

Notes

1. Elizabeth Barrett and Robert Browning were impelled to live abroad after their marriage. For a number of reasons, their life together would have been unmanageable in England. With Barrett Browning's limited private income which, until it was supplemented with a hundred pounds annuity from Frederic Kenyon on the birth of her son, constituted the Brownings' principal financial support, it was cheaper to live in Italy. It was also better for Barrett Browning's health. And lastly, her father having forbidden any of his children to marry, it was probably easier for his daughter to bear his absolute rejection from a distance, a rejection which lasted until Edward Barrett's death.

2. The most extensive discussion of the influence of the early Victorian Spasmodics upon Barrett Browning is that of Jerome Buckley. BUCKLEY suggests that *Aurora Leigh* 'throbbed with a Spasmodic faith in the poet's mission', and that until the end of her life Barrett Browning 'retained the highly emotional attitude towards aesthetic and religious problems which characterized the work of the many younger Spasmodics' (*The Victorian Temper*, pp. 61–2).

3. The Moulton Barrett family fortunes, founded in the eighteenth century, were based on the possession of Jamaican estates. Barrett Browning's father's maternal grandfather was the original patriarch, the owner of extensive plantation and slave holdings; her mother's family owned sugar plantations and a shipping company which plied the West Indian trade.

4. While GARDINER TAPLIN may be correct in judging the poem 'too blunt and shocking to have any enduring artistic worth' (*The Life of Elizabeth Barrett Browning*, p. 194), its very violence contributes to Barrett Browning's dramatisation of what was, in actuality, a commonplace event. As Barbara Omolade has pointed out, the sexual exploitation of black female slaves by white male owners was an 'accepted burden of the slave community'. OMOLADE's carefully documented essay, an historical collage of events, personal accounts documenting the black woman's subjugation, testifies to Barrett Browning's dramatic distortion of what was established practice – male sexual domination and exploitation ('Hearts of Darkness', in Ann Snitow et al. (eds), *Powers of Desire: The Politics of Sexuality*, pp. 350–67).

References

BARRETT BROWNING, ELIZABETH, *The Letters of Elizabeth Barrett Browning*, ed. with biographical additions by Frederic G. Kenyon, 2 vols (London: Macmillan, 1897) (abbreviated in the text as *L. EBB*).

BARRETT BROWNING, ELIZABETH, *The Complete Works of Mrs Elizabeth Barrett Browning*, ed. Charlotte Porter and Helen A. Clarke, 6 vols (New York: George D. Sproul, 1901) (all references to the work of Elizabeth Barrett Browning are to this edition; citations are by volume and page or line number(s), except in the case of *Aurora Leigh* where citations are by book and line number(s) and book numbers are indicated by roman numerals).

BUCKLEY, JEROME H., *The Victorian Temper: A Study in Literary Culture* (New York: Vintage Books, 1951).

GRAMSCI, ANTONIO, 'The Intellectuals', in *Selections from the Prison Notebooks of Antonio Gramsci*, ed. and trans. Quintin Hoare and Geoffrey Nowell Smith (New York: International Publishers, 1971).

SNITOW, ANN, CHRISTINE STANSELL and SHARON THOMSON (eds), *Powers of Desire: The Politics of Sexuality* (New York: Monthly Review Press, 1983).

TAPLIN, GARDINER B., *The Life of Elizabeth Barrett Browning* (New Haven, Conn.: Yale University Press, 1957).

7 'A Printing Woman Who Has Lost her Place': Elizabeth Barrett Browning's *Aurora Leigh**

ROD EDMOND

Edmond, like David in the previous chapter, wants to place Barrett
Browning in the social and political context of her time. But rather than
fixing the poet's ideological position, he is interested in the ways in
which the text is taken up, received, replied to, 'translated', so that it
takes part in a wider social debate. He makes use of both Raymond
Williams's and Terry Eagleton's ideas about the ways in which texts
contribute to emergent ideological formations. The particular formation
he is interested in is the 'woman question', in its legal and political as
well as artistic manifestations. Society is a web of competing discourses
in which texts participate: the historical context is not mere background,
but part of this web. Like Kaplan (Chapter 4), Edmond is also interested
in *Aurora Leigh*'s relation to and revision of other texts – unlike David,
who places Barrett Browning in a male poetic tradition, he sees her as
part of a newly emergent tradition of women writers. The ideological
project the text participates in is the formation of a female public
discourse. But this project is always under threat, and Edmond traces
Aurora Leigh's twentieth-century neglect to its successful assimilation and
appropriation by a conservative establishment. Instead of compromising *Aurora Leigh*'s feminist credentials by pointing to its conservatism,
as David does, he identifies its particular form of Victorian middle-class
anti-socialist feminism; at the same time, new 'translations' into com-
temporary feminist discourses are as valid as its Victorian meanings.
The meaning of the text is multiple and always contested.

There was, however, more at issue in the gestation of *Aurora Leigh* than
the claims of the present over the past. Barrett Browning was intensely
conscious of herself as a woman writer, and this, too, impelled the

* Reprinted from ROD EDMOND, *Affairs of the Hearth* (London and New York:
Routledge, 1988), pp. 133–41, 165–7.

search for new forms. In *Aurora Leigh* she tried to resuscitate the almost lost form of epic:

> Never flinch,
> But still, unscrupulously epic, catch
> Upon the burning lava of a song
> The full-veined, heaving, double-breasted Age
>
> (V, 214–17)

The striking female image of the Victorian age all but obscures that word 'unscrupulously'. A little earlier in Book V Aurora has asked whether it is possible to write an epic in this 'pewter age' which seems so unheroic. Milton had asked a similar question in writing his epic – whether 'an age too late ... / ... damp my intended wing' (*Paradise Lost*, IX, 44–5). But although *Paradise Lost* challenges and rejects many epic conventions, Milton could never be described as 'unscrupulous', and his Christian epic rests upon the sacred source of biblical narrative which ensures its superiority to classical epic. Barrett Browning's epic, on the other hand, really is unscrupulous. It is contemporary and its sources are profane and female. These sources have been well documented, and comprehensive accounts have been given of the influence of Madame de Staël's *Corinne*, George Sand's *Consuelo*, Elizabeth Gaskell's *Ruth*, and *Jane Eyre*, to name but a few.[1] But these writers were novelists. Barrett Browning extended their work into territory long occupied by male writers. Cora Kaplan has described this venture into epic and dramatic verse as an 'unmannerly intervention in the "high" patriarchal discourse of bourgeois culture'.[2] 'Unmannerly' teams well with 'unscrupulous'. *Aurora Leigh* isn't an epic in any conventionally recognizable sense of the term, and the preoccupation of contemporary reviewers with the poem's form – what was it? what gave it unity? was it unified? – was understandable, even if their discussion of these questions was laboured and sometimes obtuse. Barrett Browning appropriated the term 'epic' and redefined it, using it polemically to emphasize the significance of contemporary life and the centrality of women and women's writing. It was less a venture into a male stronghold than the construction of her own out of new materials, with the ancient name of epic then placed defiantly over the entrance.

Aurora Leigh also, however, questioned and reworked Tennyson and Clough's treatment of the woman question. Barrett Browning wrote bitingly of *The Princess*: 'What woman will tell the great poet that Mary Wolstonecraft [sic] herself never dreamt of setting up collegiate states, proctordom & the rest ... which is a worn-out plaything in the hands of one sex already & need not be *transferred* in order to be proved ridiculous?'[3] Aurora Leigh's refusal to abandon her vocation implicitly

117

criticized the terms of Ida's marriage in *The Princess*, and Clough's treatment of the cross-class marriage theme in *The Bothie* is interrogated. I shall return to these points later in the chapter. But *Aurora Leigh*'s mainspring was the work of contemporary and near-contemporary women writers. By the middle of the nineteenth century this constituted a visible tradition which *Aurora Leigh* drew on and contributed to. G.H. Lewes acknowledged this tradition when in 1852 he surveyed many of those texts which were to be sources for *Aurora Leigh* and recognized both their literary and broader significance: 'The appearance of Woman in the field of literature is a significant fact. It is the correlate of her position in society.'[4] Most reviewers also placed *Aurora Leigh* in this broad context, although Coventry Patmore in the *North British Review* seemed unaware of it and complained that as Barrett Browning was almost the only modern example of a woman poet, the story of *Aurora Leigh* was uninteresting from its very singularity.[5] Other reviewers, however, granted the work a certain representative character without necessarily welcoming it: 'The extreme independence of Aurora detracts from the feminine charm . . . she is made to resemble too closely some of the female portraits of George Sand, which were never to our liking.'[6]

The more interesting criticisms of *Aurora Leigh* concentrated on the problem of its form – was it a poem? – and the associated question of its engagement with contemporary issues. The *Blackwoods'* reviewer was categorical:

> It is not the province of the poet to depict things as they are, but so to refine and purify as to purge out the grosser matter; and this he cannot do if he attempts to give a faithful picture of his own times. . . . All poetical characters, all poetical situations, must be idealized. The language is not that of common life, which belongs essentially to the domain of prose. Therein lies the distinction between a novel and a poem.[7]

This reviewer then quoted lines from the poem which he had laid out as prose, and asked, rhetorically, whether this was poetry? The *Westminster Review* did precisely the same thing and criticized the poem for lapsing into coarseness, attributing this to an attempt by Barrett Browning 'to prove her manhood'.[8] The poet and painter William Bell Scott also noted Barrett Browning's 'manly manner'.[9] Barrett Browning herself hated the concept of 'manly': 'I am not very fond of praising men by calling them *manly*. I hate and detest a masculine man'.[10] What is most striking about these reviews is the way in which the question of language and form repeatedly raised that of gender, and then extended further to the position of women and other extra-literary areas of ideological and social practice. To understand more fully why this should have been, it is necessary to have some sense of the social and political context in which *Aurora Leigh* was produced and read.

The work was written and read against the background of widespread public debate over the related questions of married women's property rights, divorce, custody, and women and work. In the public mind these issues were also linked with prostitution, another burning issue of the 1850s. The Marriage and Divorce Bill was submitted to Parliament in 1854 as a measure narrowly concerned with the jurisdiction of the ecclesiastical courts and Parliament over divorce, but over the next three years it broadened into a debate about the legal status of married women and about the marital relationship itself. This began when Caroline Norton, whose fight for the custody of her children had prompted the 1839 Infants' Custody Act, took up the case for the protection of the property of divorced, separated or deserted wives. Far more radical, however, was Barbara Leigh Smith's demand for the right of all married women to own property and have an independent legal existence. This was a direct attack on the common-law doctrine of spousal unity, or coverture, whereby a married woman had no legal identity apart from her husband. A petitioning campaign for a married woman's property law followed, and Parliament was forced to consider this question and the related issue of equalization of the grounds for divorce. The 1857 Divorce Act, however, confirmed the sexual double-standard whereby a woman could be divorced for adultery but could divorce her husband only if his adultery was aggravated by incest, bigamy, or extreme cruelty. It also forestalled a Married Woman's Property Bill which would have abolished the doctrine of spousal unity with respect to married women's property. The 1857 Act dealt only with the property rights of separated and deserted wives, where the marriage was for all practical purposes at an end. Marriage itself remained intact, and the Divorce Act simply gave legal recognition to *de facto* marital breakdown. It was the demand for married women's property rights which had been the really significant issue. This was based on the assumption that marriage involved two separate individuals, and was perceived by most members of both Houses as posing a fundamental threat to the unity of the family.[11]

This fear for the family also surfaced in parliamentary debates on the frequent attempts to remove the ban on marriage with deceased wife's sister. One such bill was debated and defeated in 1856 while Parliament was also considering divorce and married women's property, and the issues became intertwined. The main argument for reform was the need for widowers to find mothers for their children, and the bill did not attract feminist support. Opponents of reform, however, expressed fears about sullying the purity of the English home, thereby tangling the issue with that of divorce and married women's property rights. Both measures were felt to threaten the family.[12] At least one novel was written on this subject, Mrs Frewin's *The Inheritance of Evil, or The Consequences of Marrying a Deceased Wife's Sister* (1849).[13]

It was also during the 1850s that the question of women and work became the subject of widespread public debate. Educational and professional opportunities for women were slowly and unevenly beginning to open up. There was also growing middle-class concern about the fate of its single women, whose numbers were felt to be increasing as male emigration stepped up, and the rising material expectations and cost of middle-class marriage meant that men were marrying later than previously.[14] Barbara Leigh Smith's pamphlet 'Women and Work' (1856) discussed employment for middle-class women and was widely debated and criticized. The organizers of the married women's property petitioning campaign established the *Englishwoman's Journal* in 1857, and this became the centre for organizations such as the Association for the Promotion of the Employment of Women founded in the late 1850s.[15]

The reviewer of a number of books on the woman question in the *North British Review* in 1857 announced that the employment of women was one of the great matters of the age. Young women, the reviewer argued, were raised only to become dependants: 'We bring them up with the assumption that they may marry; and that then there will be an end of them. They will be absorbed into the man, and become "non-existent".' The use of 'non-existent' refers to an earlier *North British Review* article on the Marriage and Divorce Bill and is aimed at the doctrine of spousal unity. The reviewer then went on to argue that the lack of jobs for poorer women was a major cause of the rapid growth of prostitution.[16] It was in 1857 that William Acton's classic account of prostitution in London and other large cities appeared, and there had been a spate of writing and painting on the subject since the 1840s. Thomas Hood's poem 'The Bridge of Sighs' (1844), on the recovery of the body of a prostitute from the Thames, was enormously influential. D.G. Rossetti's 'Jenny', begun in 1847, and Meredith's 'London by Lamplight' in *Poems 1851*, were other notable poetic treatments of this subject, and we have already seen it touched on in *The Bothie*. Gaskell had tracked and developed the twin themes of the fallen woman and prostitution in the figure of Aunt Esther in *Mary Barton* (1848), her story 'Lizzie Leigh', which appeared in *Household Words* in 1850, and at full novel length in *Ruth* (1853). The figure of Martha in *David Copperfield* (1849–50) is narrowly rescued from the same fate as the subject of Hood's poem. Leading mid-century painters picked up the theme: G.F. Watts in *Found Drowned* (1850), Spenser Stanhope in *Thoughts of the Past* (1852), Millais in *Virtue and Vice* (1853), and Rossetti in his unfinished

Found, begun in 1853. Other well-known paintings – Ford Madox Brown's *Take Your Son, Sir* (1851) and Holman Hunt's *The Awakened Conscience* (1853), for example – have an obvious bearing on this subject as well. Another important source and symptom of this interest was Mayhew's writing on prostitution, particularly in his work for the *Morning Chronicle*. His revelations about prostitution among needlewomen which appeared in 1849 had caused a sensation.[17]

These sketchy outlines are an attempt to give some sense of the context within which *Aurora Leigh* was produced and read. They should not, however, be seen as mere 'background', any more than *Aurora Leigh* should be regarded as some merely superstructural efflorescence. Published in 1856, it inevitably became part of wider political and social debate about the status of women, their position in mid nineteenth-century society, and the implications of re-emergent feminism for the family and the social structure in general. Certainly, it was perceived in this way by the periodical press. The review of *Aurora Leigh* in *The National Magazine* was sandwiched between a hostile rejoinder to Caroline Norton's claim for mothers to have custody rights, and a piece entitled 'London Children', which contrasted the paradise of the countryside with the purgatory of the city, and was heavy with the fear of prostitution, although the subject itself was never made explicit. This was followed by the magazine's regular feature 'The Home', a lengthy column of advice on domestic economy.[18] The layout of the magazine connected the literary text *Aurora Leigh* with adjacent and connected areas of social and political practice. *The North British Review* article on the employment of women, referred to above, appeared in the same issue as Patmore's review of *Aurora Leigh*, and the author cited the poem in the discussion of prostitution, adding that more use would have been made of the work if there had not been a separate article devoted to it. And as *Aurora Leigh* was being reviewed by most of the leading periodicals, the Divorce and Married Women's Property Bills were being hotly debated in their pages.[19] In this way we can begin to see how the literary text *Aurora Leigh* was part of a broader ideological clash. It was not simply that *Aurora Leigh* mirrored many of these conflicts but that, as Terry Eagleton has argued in relation to *Clarissa*, it was a material part of these struggles, an agent rather than an account.[20] The work *Aurora Leigh* was not just a literary text, nor was Aurora herself merely a fictional character.

The work itself was immensely popular. It had gone through twenty editions by 1887 and was reprinted regularly until the end of the century. The letters of leading writers of the period give a sharp impression of the interest and controversy it provoked. Its most ardent admirer was Ruskin who gave the work his imprimatur in *The Elements of Drawing* which appeared just after *Aurora Leigh* had been published:

'Mrs Browning's *Aurora Leigh* is, as far as I know, the greatest poem which the century has produced in any language.'[21] The poem spoke to and out of the heart of mid-century British culture, provoking a wide range of response and generating an unusually large body of written comment which took it well beyond the confines of literary circles and out into the public world. This process was assisted by the translation of Aurora Leigh into other cultural forms. 'She' appeared at the Royal Academy exhibition in 1860 in a painting by William Maw Egley, best known for his scenes of contemporary life such as *Omnibus Life in London*.[22] In the same year the Pre-Raphaelite painter Arthur Hughes completed his oil *Aurora Leigh's Dismissal of Romney (The Tryst)* now owned by the Tate Gallery. Nina Auerbach has commented on the way in which Victorian characters, especially female ones, escaped their originating condition – the text – and stepped out into new and transforming contexts. Dickens's characters are an obvious example of this process. Auerbach includes among her examples Mary Cowden Clarke's *The Girlhood of Shakespeare's Heroines* (1850), which invented childhood histories for Shakespeare's women characters, and she also discusses the Victorian practice of making paintings of literary characters.[23] *Aurora Leigh* is a good example of this process whereby the individual literary text was transformed into a cultural event.

The complexity of this process of reception and translation needs to be emphasized, however. Ruskin's admiration was not necessarily more benign than the hostility of the *Blackwoods'* reviewer. Reading *Aurora Leigh* made no difference to his views on the position of women in Victorian society, and within a few lines of celebrating the work he was able to describe Patmore's *The Angel in the House* as 'the sweetest analysis we possess of quiet modern domestic feeling'.[24] Many of the apparently generous responses to *Aurora Leigh* involved a neutralizing of its more radical elements by a process of assimilation and incorporation. Eagleton has described Richardson's novels as organizing forces of the bourgeois public sphere, assisting in the process of carving out a space for the eighteenth-century middle class in the domain of public discourse.[25] If, following Eagleton, *Aurora Leigh* is understood as carving out a space in public discourse for mid nineteenth-century women, and as one of many organizing forces of an emergent female public sphere, it must be added that no sooner was this space won than it was invaded.

The obvious but crucial difference between Richardson and Barrett Browning is that of gender. By comparison with the eighteenth-century middle class, women in mid-nineteenth-century England had hardly begun to construct a public discourse of their own. This meant that *Aurora Leigh* was more exposed and vulnerable to assimilation than *Clarissa*. Eagleton shows how Richardson as a master printer was at the centre of an ideological network – 'the nub of a whole discursive formation'.[26] Barrett Browning, by contrast, spent years reading and writing in a darkened room, sending messages (poems, letters, reviews) out into a world from which she was cut off. The collective, open-ended, revisionary mode of production which Eagleton emphasizes in Richardson[27] had its Victorian equivalents, Dickens for example, but was not available to women writers forced to operate within a more private sphere.

With the advantage of hindsight it is probably true that in the nineteenth century writing was the form of public discourse most open to women. It cannot always have seemed so to women writers at the time, even when reassured to the contrary. The author of the *North British Review* essay on women and work could write, 'There is no injustice done to women here. The road is open. The race is fair. If woman be the fleeter, she wins. ... Women who can write, do write.'[28] But as Barrett Browning had made clear in her criticism of *The Princess*, serious women writers did not see themselves as running the same race as men. They were seeking their own track, their own pace, their own language, and it was precisely here that their difficulties were greatest. Barrett Browning wrote of this to her friend and fellow writer Mary Russell Mitford: 'you, who are a woman and a man in one, will judge if it isn't a hard and difficult process for a woman to get forgiven for her strength by her grace. You who have accomplished this, know it is hard – and every woman of letters knows it is hard.'[29] It is a bitter phrase, 'to get forgiven for her strength by her grace', and still a relevant one. The Greenham Common women who have cast off conventional notions of 'grace' have been all the more virulently attacked for their strength. The requirement that female grace compensate for '(wo)manly' strength was a powerful strategy for resisting the emergence of a female public sphere with its own forms, ideologies and language. Every contemporary review of *Aurora Leigh* I have read criticized it for lapses of taste, by which, it is clear, was meant a fall from 'feminine grace' – strength exposed rather than veiled.

There is nevertheless considerable relevance to Barrett Browning and *Aurora Leigh* in Eagleton's description of Richardson's method of production as sustaining a constant circulation of discourse, generating further texts and converting the process of his art into an act of ideological solidarity.[30] There were special difficulties for the woman writer of this period in transforming literary production into effective social practice. However, the ways in which Barrett Browning drew on women's texts, argued with male texts, won a hearing for a woman's voice on the woman question, and prompted further writing by women was an act of ideological solidarity whereby seemingly private literary production became social practice. [...]

In the introduction to a new edition of *Aurora Leigh* in 1898, Swinburne wrote 'there is not a dead line in it', but few, it seems, still agreed. Soon after the turn of the century the stream of editions dried up. There were no new editions between 1905 and 1978. By 1932, when Virginia Woolf wrote of Elizabeth Barrett Browning, 'Nobody reads her, nobody discusses her, nobody troubles to put her in her place', the work seems almost to have slipped out of sight. As Woolf continued, one takes *Aurora Leigh* from the shelf 'not so much in order to read it as to muse with kindly condescension over this token of bygone fiction, as we toy with the fringes of our grandmothers' mantles and muse over the alabaster models of the Taj Mahal which once adorned their drawing-room tables'.[31]

There is something curious about this disappearance of *Aurora Leigh* just as the next major wave of feminism was breaking. It was not, apparently, a text that spoke to the era of the Women's Social and Political Union. One obvious reason for this is that *Aurora Leigh's* politics are consistently hostile to socialism. By the mid nineteenth century the earlier, mainly Owenite, alignment of feminism and working-class radicalism had disappeared. Sex oppression and class exploitation had become separate objects of separate struggles, and the new feminism of the 1850s was middle-class and free of any taint of socialism or atheism.[32] Romney's phalanstery – his socialist experiment with an extended communal family of the kind found in Owenite communities – is rejected much more sharply than the bourgeois family, notwithstanding the poem's sustained critique of patriarchal power. *Aurora Leigh's* main ideological affinity is with the more pragmatic middle-class feminism of the 1850s and 1860s, and the poem is not at all concerned with women gaining political power through the ballot box.

Yet the sexual politics of *Aurora Leigh* has remained of central importance to feminism, and there must be a further reason for its disappearance in the early years of this century. This, I think, lies in its status as a Victorian classic. The reception and reputation of a work inevitably affects the ways in which it is read and understood, becoming an important determinant of its meanings. The reviewers, the Royal Academicians, the moderate reformism of the High Victorian period, and all those other determinants of how *Aurora Leigh* was received and understood, were largely successful in neutralizing its more radical feminist elements. Barrett Browning's relatively early death and her canonization as England's female laureate assisted in this. *Aurora Leigh* was not available to early twentieth-century feminists as a feminist text; effectively, it had been rewritten.

However, neither the originating moment of a text nor the immediate determinants of its meanings can limit its later identities. Raymond

Williams, in arguing that literary studies should be concerned with exploring the social conditions of production of literary texts, has emphasized that these conditions of production include the conditions of making a text contemporary: 'All the forces which keep the text current are among its conditions of production.'[33] Subsequent determinations 'remake' the text, which is itself no passive spectator of its own fate. Virginia Woolf saw *Aurora Leigh* as a Victorian curio, but acknowledged that it remained, 'with all its imperfections, a book that still lives and breathes and has its being'.[34] These traces of life discerned in the Victorian corpse of *Aurora Leigh* by the leading woman writer of her age helped its resuscitation in our own time. The new feminist presses have given the kiss of life to many apparently dead texts, and the successful republication of *Aurora Leigh* by the Women's Press is a leading example of this. It has been made available to us in a new way, and is therefore a different text from the one which was left to hibernate earlier in this century.

As *Aurora Leigh* has been brought into a freshly relevant relationship to our time, it has once again shown that potential for translation which marked its early history. It has been dramatized by Michelene Wandor and performed by feminist theatre groups. Michelene Wandor also adapted it for radio.[35] In 1979 an article in *Time Out* described *Aurora Leigh* as 'a Victorian female voice speaking acutely of the relationships between gender, art and politics'.[36] Barrett Browning would have recognized this description. Lost meanings have been rediscovered in the text as well as new meanings created.

Notes

1. See ALETHEA HAYTER, *Mrs Browning: A Poet's Work and Its Setting* (London: Faber & Faber, 1962), p. 151; CORA KAPLAN, Introduction to *Aurora Leigh and Other Poems* (London: The Women's Press, 1978) – all references to the text are to this edition; ELLEN MOERS, *Literary Women* (London: The Women's Press, 1978); PATRICIA THOMSON, *George Sand and the Victorians* (New York: Columbia University Press, 1977).
2. KAPLAN, p. 8.
3. BARBARA HARDY, 'Gossip made permanent', *Times Literary Supplement*, 1 July 1983.
4. 'The Lady Novelists', *Westminster Review*, July 1852: 129.
5. *North British Review*, February 1857: 454.
6. *Blackwoods' Edinburgh Magazine*, January–June 1857: 33.
7. Ibid., p. 34.
8. *Westminster Review*, October 1857: 401.
9. W.M. ROSSETTI (ed.), *Ruskin: Rossetti: Pre-Raphaelitism* (London: G. Allen, 1890), p. 147.
10. KAPLAN, p. 30.

11. This summary has come mainly from MARY LYNDON SHANLEY, ' "One Must Ride Behind": married women's rights and the Divorce Act of 1857', *Victorian Studies*, 25 (3).

12. This summary has come from CYNTHIA FANSLER BEHRMAN, 'The Annual Blister: A sidelight on Victorian social and parliamentary history', *Victorian Studies*, 11 (4).

13. KATHLEEN TILLOTSON, *Novels of the Eighteen-Forties* (Oxford: Oxford University Press, 1962), p. 15.

14. J.A. BANKS and OLIVE BANKS, *Feminism and Family Planning in Victorian England* (Liverpool: Liverpool University Press, 1965), pp. 27–9.

15. RAY STRACHEY, *The Cause: A Short History of the Women's Movement in Great Britain* (London: G. Bell & Sons, 1928), pp. 91–4.

16. *North British Review*, February 1857.

17. E.P. THOMPSON and EILEEN YEO (eds), *The Unknown Mayhew* (Harmondsworth: Penguin, 1973), pp. 25–34.

18. *The National Magazine*, Vol. 1 (1857). The subject of this particular column was the Condensed Air-Bath.

19. E.g. *Edinburgh Review*, January 1857; *Quarterly Review*, July 1857; *North British Review*, August 1857.

20. TERRY EAGLETON, *The Rape of Clarissa* (Oxford: Basil Blackwell, 1982), pp. 4ff.

21. E.T. COOK and ALEXANDER WEDDERBURN (eds), *The Works of John Ruskin* (London: George Allen, 1904), Vol. 15, p. 227.

22. ALGERNON GRAVES, *The Royal Academy of Arts: A Complete Dictionary of Contributors and their Work from its Foundation in 1769 to 1904* (Wakefield: S.R. Publications, 1970), Vol. 2, p. 34.

23. NINA AUERBACH, *Woman and the Demon: The Life of a Victorian Myth* (Cambridge and London: Harvard University Press, 1982), pp. 191–219.

24. COOK and WEDDERBURN, p. 227.

25. EAGLETON, p. 6.

26. Ibid., p. 7.

27. Ibid., pp. 10–13.

28. *North British Review*, February 1857: 328–9.

29. BARBARA HARDY.

30. EAGLETON, p. 12.

31. VIRGINIA WOOLF, '*Aurora Leigh*', *Collected Essays* (London: Hogarth Press, 1971), Vol. 1, pp. 209–10.

32. BARBARA TAYLOR, *Eve and the New Jerusalem* (London: Virago, 1983), pp. 263–4, 276ff.

33. RAYMOND WILLIAMS, *Politics and Letters* (London: New Left Books, 1979), Chapter 5, especially pp. 328–9, 344–5. See also TONY BENNETT, 'Text and History', in P. Widdowson (ed.), *Re-Reading English* (London: Methuen, 1982).

34. WOOLF, p. 218.

35. This was broadcast on BBC Radio 3 in 1981 and rebroadcast the following year.

36. *Time Out*, August–September 1979.

Part Three
Christina Rossetti

8 The Aesthetics of Renunciation*

SANDRA GILBERT and SUSAN GUBAR

Like Homans (Chapter 1), Gilbert and Gubar are here concerned with explaining the dearth of women poets. In their reading, nineteenth-century culture, in the comments of 'masculinist' critics, and in the internalised self-images of women poets, presents poetry as an immodest and inappropriate activity for women. In particular, the selflessness required of women contrasts with the assertive 'I' of lyric poetry. Some women, like Rossetti, were however able to make poetry out of the very renunciation demanded of them – as for Homans, the poems are *about* the woman poet's silencing. Male muses (the goblins) also play a part here, enticing women into the dangerous and forbidden masculine realm of art and imagination. Rossetti is not silenced by these muses, as Brontë was, but performs a self-silencing through the agency of the super-ego, Lizzie, who enforces proper womanly behaviour. Just as Kaplan (Chapter 1) sets out the parameters for future discussion of *Aurora Leigh*, so Gilbert and Gubar here do the same for *Goblin Market*. They note the possibility of a reading in which an Amazonian Lizzie is the feminist heroine, rescuing Laura for a world of sisterly solidarity and separatism, before opting instead for Laura as the feminist heroine, the suppressed and repressed woman writer. They deploy Freudian theory, and a reading of the nineteenth-century literary tradition to make their argument. Subsequent critics make use of psychoanalytic and/or historicist theories to argue for repressive or resistant readings of the poem.

If the extraordinary difficulty of conceiving and sustaining living poetry in a woman's body is made clear when we read the pronouncements of 'masculinist' critics, it is made even clearer when we compare the

* Reprinted from SANDRA GILBERT and SUSAN GUBAR, *The Madwoman in the Attic* (New Haven and London: Yale University Press, 1979), pp. 549–54 and 564–75.

self-images of the women who did manage to become poets with those of similarly situated male poets. At the age of nineteen, Christina Rossetti wrote a prose narrative that is extremely interesting in this connection, a semi-autobiographical novella entitled *Maude*, into which she set a number of her most accomplished verses. Rossetti's protagonist, fifteen-year-old Maude Foster, is certainly a surrogate self: she is a precocious poet who would have been 'very pretty' except for 'a fixed paleness, and an expression . . . languid and preoccupied to a painful degree'. Perhaps, however (or so Rossetti implies), this expression of anxiety is caused by Maude's knowledge that 'people thought her clever, and that her little copies of verses were handed about and admired', even though 'it was the amazement of every one what could make her poetry so broken-hearted as was mostly the case'.[1]

Certainly a number of Maude's poems *are* broken-hearted – mysteriously so, it seems at first. In some the girl longs for death or sleep, in others she admonishes lilies and roses to fade, and in still others she rebukes herself for 'vanity' or 'wrath'. In fact, Maude produces only one comparatively cheerful verse in the whole novella, this as part of a *bouts rimés* sonnet contest with her cousin Agnes and Agnes's friend Magdalen, the predetermined *bouts rimés* end words being given by her other cousin Mary. Yet cheerful though it is, this sonnet is also a peculiarly hostile piece:

> Some ladies dress in muslin full and white,
> Some gentlemen in cloth succinct and black;
> Some patronize a dog-cart, some a hack,
> Some think a painted clarence only right.
> Youth is not always such a pleasing sight,
> Witness a man with tassels on his back;
> Or woman in a great-coat like a sack
> Towering above her sex with horrid height.
> If all the world were water fit to drown
> There are some whom you would not teach to swim,
> Rather enjoying if you saw them sink;
> Certain old ladies dressed in girlish pink,
> With roses and geraniums on their own: –
> Go to the Bason, poke them o'er the rim. –[2]

Could Maude's comical desire to drown 'certain old ladies dressed in girlish pink' be somehow associated with her perpetual and otherwise inexplicable melancholy? What about her cringing dislike of that grotesque woman 'towering above her sex with horrid height'? Of course all participants concede that she has won the *bouts rimés* contest, though her competitors' verses have also been notably revealing. Her cousin Agnes produces a sonnet whose gist is that its author would do anything – freeze, drown, be transformed into a donkey or a turnip or a 'miserable hack / Dragging a cab from left to right', even wear 'a hideous yellow satin gown' – rather than have to write another sonnet. Agnes's more spiritual friend Magdalen, on the other hand, writes a dutifully spiritual poem, declaring that 'I fancy the good fairies dressed in white . . . To foster embryo life.'[3]

Plainly, the very act of poetic assertion, with its challenge to attempt self-definition or at least self-confrontation, elicits evasions, anxieties, hostilities, in brief 'painful preoccupation', from all competitors, so that the jolly poetry game paradoxically contains the germ of just that gloom it seems designed to dispel. Later in the story Maude's gloom thickens, and broadens too, to threaten also the innocently unpoetic Agnes, Mary and Magdalen. That these girls are all doubles or alternative selves for Maude is indicated in a number of poems, including one of Rossetti's better-known early works, 'She sat and sang alway', in which two girls act out the complementary anxieties of female adolescence:

> She sat and sang alway
> By the green margin of a stream,
> Watching the fishes leap and play
> Beneath the glad sun-beam.
>
> I sat and wept alway
> Beneath the moon's most shadowy beam,
> Watching the blossoms of the may
> Weep leaves into the stream.
>
> I wept for memory;
> She sang for hope that is so fair; –
> My tears were swallowed by the sea;
> Her songs died on the air.[4]

'Her songs died on the air': what Maude evidently sees, and what evidently 'breaks her heart', is that there will not or cannot be any real blossoming for her talent. Her songs are doomed to die on the air.

But why? As the story unfolds and each girl meets with her symbolic fate, we begin to understand. Mary gets married and becomes wholly, humiliatingly absorbed in her new husband. Magdalen enters a convent and gives 'all for this Cross I bear'. Serious-minded Agnes seems destined to become a sensible and useful spinster, perhaps one of the gentle sisterhood Ransom so admired. And Maude, unable to love or pray, suddenly refuses to go to church, explaining that she is incorrigibly wicked – for 'No one will say that I cannot avoid putting myself forward and displaying my verses.'[5] Then, on her way to Mary's wedding, she is severely injured in a strange cab accident: 'She had been overturned; and, though no limb was broken, had neither stirred nor spoken since.' Obviously the catastrophe of *overturning* is psychically necessary, as much for Rossetti herself as for her young poet, and our sense of this is reinforced by Maude's death, which comes calmly but inexorably, three weeks later. She appoints her anti-literary and superego-like cousin Agnes as her literary executrix, enigmatically instructing her to 'destroy what I evidently never intended to be seen', and Agnes has no trouble carrying out these vague directions. She instantly consigns Maude's locked workbook/journal, unopened, to the girl's coffin, and then, though she is 'astonished at the variety of Maude's compositions ... piece after piece she commit[s] them to the flames, fearful lest any should be preserved which were not intended for general perusal: but it cost[s] her a pang to do so; and to see how small a number remained for [Maude's mother]'.[6]

As several commentators have observed, the moral of this story is that the Maude in Christina Rossetti – the ambitious, competitive, self-absorbed and self-assertive poet – must die, and be replaced by either the wife, the nun, or, most likely, the kindly useful spinster. Rossetti says of Maude that 'Whatever might employ her tongue and to a certain extent her mind, had always an undercurrent of thought intent upon herself',[7] and here is the worst, the most unforgivable sin, the ultimate female sin of vanity. Whether literally or figuratively, a woman must never become enamored of her own image in nature or art. On the contrary, as Rossetti demonstrated in her Lewis Carroll-esque children's story *Speaking Likenesses*, and as she wrote in a much later poem,

> All things that pass
>   Are woman's looking-glass;
> They show her how her bloom must fade,
>   And she herself be laid
> With withered roses in the shade;
> Unlovely, out of reach
>   Of summer joy that was.[8]

After all this, it hardly seems necessary to point out that when John Keats (whom Rossetti and both her brothers much admired) was nineteen years old, he had already committed himself seriously and passionately to his own artistic career. By the time he was twenty-one, in fact, he had planned a formidable program of self-development: 'O for ten years, that I may overwhelm / Myself in poesy; so I may do the deed / That my own soul has to itself decreed.'[9] Significantly, the image of self-immolation suggested by the word *overwhelm* is balanced here by the fiercely assertive and 'masculine' notion of verse-writing or 'soul-making' as a 'deed'. Of course Keats understood the need for proper modesty, even humility. How else, after all, could truly effective self-education proceed? At the same time, however, he saw even his ignorance as ambiguously 'giant',[10] and he did not hesitate to declare his intuitive sense that he might be 'among the English poets' after his death; no considerations of 'vanity' appear to have troubled him in this self-appraisal. Like Maude, he entered a verse-writing contest (with Leigh Hunt, in 1816) and like her, too, he projected his deepest concerns into the sonnet he wrote swiftly, jovially, on a set theme. 'The poetry of earth is never dead' was his opening sentence (as opposed to Maude's 'Some ladies dress in muslin full and white'), and the health and joy of his certainty that poetry was everywhere, in him as in all of nature, must have been at least in part made possible by his masculine certainty that he was a lord of creation. By contrast, Maude/Rossetti obviously sees herself as a fragile, vainly costumed lady, no ruler of nature at all but a tormented servant.

Like Rossetti's heroine, too, Keats died at an absurdly early age. Where Maude was inexplicably 'overturned' by her anxious author, however, Keats – despite Byron's jests and Shelley's suspicions – was killed by no force more inimical than his own heredity. Though Maude dies willingly, Keats struggled hard against extinction, fighting even his own pained half-love for 'easeful death'. When he died, to be sure, his friends buried several letters from his fianceé, Fanny Brawne, with his body, but they certainly did not destroy a single word *he* had written. That Rossetti may have gotten from Keats the idea of burying Maude's own journal with the dead writer herself suggests, then, just how masochistically a woman poet may transform male metaphors into female images of anxiety or guilt.[11]

Finally, where Maude's last poem stresses her vanity and her need for the constraining cross inflicted by a patriarchal God who 'Knoweth when thou art weak, and will control / The powers of darkness' (and presumably vanity) so 'that thou needst not fear', Keats's bitter epitaph – 'Here lies one whose name was writ in water' – ironically emphasizes the poet's passionate commitment to himself, to his art, and thus to what he believes should rightly be the immortality of his name. In fact, in an early sonnet entitled 'On Keats', Rossetti herself quoted this epitaph precisely so that she might refute it by declaring that unto this 'strong man' a 'goodly lot / Hath fallen in fertile ground; there thorns are not, / But his own daisies', and 'His name, in every humble heart that sings, / Shall be a fountain of love, verily.'[12] But of course Keats also refuted his own disingenuous epitaph, for the poem generally thought to be his last reaches with raging, masterful passion even from beyond the grave:

This living hand, now warm and capable
Of earnest grasping, would, if it were cold
And in the icy silence of the tomb,
So haunt thy days and chill thy dreaming nights
That thou wouldst wish thine own heart dry of blood
So in my veins red life might stream again,
And thou be conscience-calmed – see here it is –
I hold it towards you.

While Maude lies passively, angelically, dutifully dead – and the living Christina Rossetti takes up her pen to spend a lifetime writing 'Amen for us all' – dead John Keats refuses to die, shaking an angry fist at the living world that threatens to forget him. More genially but only half-mockingly, he confesses in the last sentence of his last letter that he is impolite: he hesitates to leave the warm room of life because 'I always made an awkward bow.'[13] [. . .]

Given the maze of societal constraints by which women poets have been surrounded since Anne Finch's day, it is no wonder that some of the finest of these writers have made whole poetic careers out of the virtue of necessity. We might define this virtue as, at its most intensely articulated, a passionate renunciation of the self-assertion lyric poetry traditionally demands, and at its most ironic a seemingly demure resignation to poetic isolation or obscurity. [Emily] Dickinson, of course, wrote many poems praising the paradoxical pleasures of such painful renunciation – so many, indeed, that a number of readers (Richard Wilbur, for instance) have seen 'Sumptuous Destitution' as the key motif of her art.[14] And certainly it is *one* key motif in her verse, as it also is in the verse of Emily Brontë and George Eliot. But at the same time that she is an inebriate of *air* – or perhaps because she is an *inebriate* of air – Dickinson is greedy, angry, secretly or openly self-assertive, as we shall see. The very phrase *'sumptuous* destitution' expresses the ambivalently affirmed sensuality she is determined to indulge even in her poverty. By comparison, Christina Rossetti and, to a lesser extent, Elizabeth Barrett Browning build their art on a willing acceptance of passionate or demure destitution. They and not Dickinson are the great nineteenth-century women singers of renunciation as necessity's highest and noblest virtue.

Rossetti's *Maude* was an early attempt at exploring the landscape of destitution in which a ladylike fifteen-year-old poet ought (the writer implies) to condemn herself to dwell. But besides being exaggerated and self-pitying, it was cast in a form uncongenial to Rossetti, who was never very good at sustaining extended story lines or explaining complex plots. Her extraordinary *Goblin Market*, however, was written

ten years later at the height of her powers, and it is a triumphant revision of *Maude*, an impassioned hymn of praise to necessity's virtue.

Like *Maude*, *Goblin Market* (1859) depicts multiple heroines, each representing alternative possibilities of selfhood for women. Where *Maude*'s options were divided rather bewilderingly among Agnes, Mary, Magdalen, and Maude herself, however, *Goblin Market* offers just the twinlike sisters Lizzie and Laura (together with Laura's shadowy precursor Jeanie) who live in a sort of surrealistic fairytale cottage by the side of a 'restless brook' and not far from a sinister glen. Every morning and evening, so the story goes, scuttling, furry, animal-like goblins ('One had a cat's face, / One whisked a tail, / One tramped at a rat's pace, / One crawled like a snail') emerge from the glen to peddle magically delicious fruits that 'Men sell not . . . in any town' – 'Bloom-down-cheeked peaches, / Swart-headed mulberries, / Wild free-born cranberries', and so forth.[15] Of course the two girls know that 'We must not look at goblin men, / We must not buy their fruits: / Who knows upon what soil they fed / Their hungry thirsty roots?' But of course, nevertheless, one of the two – Laura – does purchase the goblin fruit, significantly with 'a lock of her golden hair', and sucks and sucks upon the sweet food 'until her lips [are] sore'.

The rest of the poem deals with the dreadful consequences of Laura's act, and with her ultimate redemption. To begin with, as soon as she has eaten the goblin fruit, the disobedient girl no longer hears the cry of the tiny 'brisk fruit-merchant men', though her more dutiful sister does continue to hear their 'sugar-baited words'. Then, as time goes by, Laura sickens, dwindles, and ages unnaturally: her hair grows 'thin and grey', she weeps, dreams of melons, and does none of the housework she had shared with Lizzie in the old fruitless days when they were both 'neat like bees, as sweet and busy'. Finally, Lizzie resolves to save her sister by purchasing some fruit from the goblin peddlers, who still do appear to her. When she does this, however, they insist that she herself eat their wares on the spot, and when she refuses, standing motionless and silent like 'a lily in a flood' or 'a beacon left alone / In a hoary roaring sea', they assault her with the fruit, smearing her all over with its pulp. The result is that when she goes home to her sick sister she is able to offer herself to the girl as almost a sacramental meal: 'Eat me, drink me, love me . . . make much of me.' But when Laura kisses her sister hungrily, she finds that the juice is 'wormwood to her tongue, / She loathed the feast; / Writhing as one possessed she leaped and sung.' Finally she falls into a swoon. When she wakens, she is her old, girlish self again: 'Her gleaming locks showed not one thread of gray, / Her breath was sweet as May.' In after years, when she and her sister, now happy wives and mothers, are warning their own daughters about the fruit-merchant men, she tells them the tale of 'how her sister stood / In deadly peril to do her good. . . . "For there is no friend like a sister, / In calm or stormy weather; / To cheer one on the tedious way, / To fetch one if one goes astray, / To lift one if one totters down, / To strengthen whilst one stands." '

Obviously the conscious or semi-conscious allegorical intention of this narrative poem is sexual/religious. Wicked men offer Laura forbidden fruits, a garden of sensual delights, in exchange for the golden treasure that, like any young girl, she keeps in her 'purse', or for permission to 'rape' a lock of her hair. Once she has lost her virginity, however, she is literally valueless and therefore not worth even further seduction. Her exaggerated fall has, in fact, intensified the processes of time which, for all humanity, began with Eve's eating of the forbidden fruit, when our primordial parents entered the realm of generation. Thus Laura goes into a conventional Victorian decline, then further shrinks and grays, metamorphosing into a witchlike old woman. But at this point, just as Christ intervened to save mankind by offering his body and blood as bread and wine for general spiritual consumption, so Laura's 'good' sister Lizzie, like a female Saviour, negotiates with the goblins (as Christ did with Satan) and offers herself to be eaten and drunk in a womanly holy communion. And just as Christ redeemed mankind from Original Sin, restoring at least the possibility of heaven to Eve's erring descendents, so Lizzie rehabilitates Laura, changing her back from a lost witch to a virginal bride and ultimately leading her into a heaven of innocent domesticity.

Beyond such didacticism, however, *Goblin Market* seems to have a tantalizing number of other levels of meaning – meanings about and for women in particular – so that it has recently begun to be something of a textual crux for feminist critics. To such readers, certainly, the indomitable Lizzie, standing like a lily, a rock, a beacon, a 'fruit-crowned orange tree' or 'a royal virgin town / Topped with gilded dome and spire', may well seem almost a Victorian Amazon, a nineteenth-century reminder that 'sisterhood is powerful'. Certainly, too, from one feminist perspective *Goblin Market*, with its evil and mercantile little men and its innocent, high-minded women, suggests that men *hurt* while women redeem. Significantly, indeed, there are no men in the poem other than the unpleasant goblins; even when Laura and Lizzie become 'wives and mothers' their husbands never appear, and they evidently have no sons. Rossetti does, then, seem to be dreamily positing an effectively matrilineal and matriarchal world, perhaps even, considering the strikingly sexual redemption scene between the sisters, a covertly (if ambivalently) lesbian world.

At the same time, however, what are we to think when the redeemed Eden into which Lizzie leads Laura turns out to be a heaven of domesticity? Awakening from her consumptive trance, Laura laughs 'in the innocent old way', but in fact, like Blake's Thel withdrawing from the pit of Experience, she has retreated to a psychic stage prior even to the one she was in when the poem began. Living in a virginal female world and rejecting any notions of sexuality, of self-assertion, of personal pleasure (for men are beasts, as the animal-like goblins proved), she devotes herself now entirely to guarding the 'tender lives' of her daughters from dangers no doubt equivalent to the one with which the fruit-merchants threatened her. For her, however, the world no longer contains such dangers, and a note of nostalgia steals into Rossetti's verse as she describes Laura's reminiscences of 'Those pleasant days long gone / Of not-returning time', the days of the 'haunted glen' and the 'wicked quaint fruit-merchant men'. Like Lizzie, Laura has become a true Victorian angel-in-the-house – selfless and smiling – so naturally (we intuitively feel the logic of this) the 'haunted glen' and the 'quaint' goblins have disappeared.

But why is it natural that the glen with its merchants should vanish when Laura becomes angelically selfless? Do the goblins incarnate anything besides beastly and exploitative male sexuality? Does their fruit signify something more than fleshly delight? Answers to these questions may be embedded in the very Miltonic imagery Rossetti exploits. In *Paradise Lost*, we should remember, the Satanic serpent persuades Eve to eat the apple not because it is delicious but because it has brought about a 'Strange alteration' in him, adding both 'Reason' and 'Speech' to his 'inward Powers'. But, he argues, if he, a mere animal, has been so transformed by this 'Sacred, Wise, and Wisdom-giving Plant', the fruit will surely make Eve, a human being, 'as Gods', presumably in speech as in other powers.[16] Rossetti's goblin men, more enigmatic than Milton's snake, make no such promises to Laura, but *Goblin Market*'s fruit-eating scene parallels the *Paradise Lost* scene in so many other ways that there may well be a submerged parallel here too.

Certainly Eve, devouring the garden's 'intellectual food', acts just like her descendent Laura. 'Intent now wholly on her taste', she regards 'naught else', for 'such delight till then . . . In Fruit she never tasted . . . Greedily she ingorg'd without restraint', until at last she is 'hight'n'd as with Wine, jocund and boon'.[17] But though she is pleasuring herself physically, Eve's true goal is intellectual divinity, equality with or superiority to Adam (and God), pure self-assertion. Her first resolve, when she is finally 'Satiate', is to worship the Tree daily, 'Not without Song'. Given this Miltonic context, it seems quite possible that Laura too – sucking on the goblin fruit, asserting and indulging her own desires 'without restraint' – is enacting an affirmation of intellectual (or poetic) as well as sexual selfhood. There is a sense, after all, in which she is metaphorically eating *words* and enjoying the taste of *power*, just

137

as Eve before her did. 'A Word made Flesh is seldom / And tremblingly partook / Nor then perhaps reported', wrote Emily Dickinson. She might have been commenting on *Goblin Market*'s central symbolism, for she added, as if to illuminate the dynamics of Laura's Satanically unholy Communion,

> But have I not mistook
> Each one of us has tasted
> With ecstasies of stealth
> The very food debated
> To our specific strength.[18]

Both the taste and the 'Philology' of power are steeped in guilt, she seems to be saying. And as we have seen, for women like Eve and Laura (and Rossetti herself), they can only be partaken 'with ecstasies of stealth'.

Such connections between female pleasure and female power, between assertive female sexuality and assertive female speech, have been traditional ones. Both the story of Eve and Dickinson's poem make such links plain, as do the kinds of attacks that were leveled against iconoclastic feminists like Mary Wollstonecraft – the accusation, for instance, that *The Rights of Woman* was 'a scripture archly fram'd for propagating whores'.[19] (Richard Polwhele, one of Wollstonecraft's most virulent critics, even associated 'bliss botanic' with the 'imperious mien' and 'proud defiance' of Wollstonecraft's 'unsex'd' female followers.)[20] We should remember, too, that Barrett Browning was praised for her blameless sexual life, since 'the lives of women of genius have so frequently been sullied by sin . . . that their intellectual gifts are [usually] a curse rather than a blessing'. In this last remark, indeed, the relationship between sexuality and female genius becomes virtually causal: female genius triggers uncontrollable sexual desires, and perhaps, conversely, uncontrollable sexual desires even cause the disease of female genius.

That genius and sexuality *are* diseases in women, diseases akin to madness, is implied in *Goblin Market* both by Laura's illness and by the monitory story of Jeanie, 'who should have been a bride; / But who for joys brides hope to have / Fell sick and died / In her gay prime'. For though Rossetti's allusion to bridal joys does seem to reinforce our first notion that the forbidden goblin fruit simply signifies forbidden sexuality, an earlier reference to Jeanie renders the fruit symbolism in her case just as ambiguous as it is in Laura's. Jeanie, Lizzie reminds Laura, met the goblin men 'in the moonlight, / Took their gifts both choice and many, / Ate their fruits and wore their flowers / Plucked from bowers / Where summer ripens at all hours'. In other words, wandering in the moonlight and trafficking with these strange creatures from the glen, Jeanie became a witch or madwoman, yielding herself entirely to an 'unnatural' or at least unfeminine life of dream and inspiration. Her punishment, therefore, was that decline which was essentially an outer sign of her inner disease.[21]

That the goblins' fruits and flowers are unnatural and out-of-season, however, associates them further with works of art – the fruits of the mind – as well as with sinful sexuality. More, that they do not reproduce themselves in the ordinary sense and even seem to hinder the reproduction of ordinary vegetation reinforces our sense of their curious and guilty artificiality. Jeanie and Laura are both cursed with physical barrenness, unlike most Victorian fallen women, who almost always (like Eliot's Hetty Sorel or Barrett Browning's Marian Erle) bear bastard children to denote their shame. But not even daisies will grow on Jeanie's grave, and the kernelstone Laura has saved refuses to produce a new plant. Sickening and pining, both Jeanie and Laura are thus detached not only from their own healthful, child-oriented female sexuality, but also from their socially ordained roles as 'modest maidens'. The day after her visit to the goblin men Laura still helps Lizzie milk, sweep, sew, knead, and churn, but while Lizzie is content, Laura is already 'Sick in part', pining for the fruits of the haunted glen, and eventually, like Jeanie, she refuses to participate in the tasks of domesticity.

Finally, while the haunted glen itself is on one level a female sexual symbol, it becomes increasingly clear that on another, equally significant level it represents a chasm in the mind, analogous to that enchanted romantic chasm Coleridge wrote of in 'Kubla Khan', to the symbolic Red Deeps George Eliot described in *The Mill on the Floss*, or to the mental chasms Dickinson defined in numerous poems. When we realize this we can more thoroughly understand the dis-ease – the strange weeping, the dreamy lassitude, the sexual barrenness, and witchlike physical deformity – that afflicts both Laura and Jeanie. The goblin men were not, after all, real human-sized, sexually charismatic men. Indeed, at every point Rossetti distinguishes them from the *real* men who never do appear in the poem. Instead, they are – were all along – the desirous little creatures so many women writers have recorded encountering in the haunted glens of their own minds, hurrying scurrying furry ratlike *its* or *ids*, inescapable *incubi*. 'Cunning' as animal-like Bertha Rochester, 'bad' as that 'rat' or 'bad cat' the nine-year-old Jane Eyre, they remind us too of the 'it' goblin-dark Heathcliff was to Catherine Earnshaw, and the 'it' Dickinson sometimes saw herself becoming, the 'sweet wolf' she said 'we all have inside us'. Out of an enchanted but earthly chasm in the self, a mossy cave of the unconscious, these it-like inner selves, 'mopping and mowing' with masculine assertiveness, arise to offer Jeanie, Laura, Lizzie and Rossetti herself the unnatural but honey-sweet fruit of art, fruit that is analogous to (or identical with) the luscious fruit of self-gratifying sensual pleasure.

As *Maude* predicted, however, either Rossetti or one of the surrogate selves into whom she projected her literary anxieties would have to reject the goblin fruit of art. With its attendant invitation to such solipsistic luxuries as vanity and self-assertion, such fruit has 'hungry thirsty roots' that have fed on suspicious soil indeed. 'From House to Home', one of Rossetti's other major poems of renunciation, was written in the same year as *Goblin Market*, and it makes the point more directly. She had inhabited, the poet-speaker confides, 'a pleasure-place within my soul; / An earthly paradise supremely fair'.[22] But her inner Eden 'lured me from the goal'. Merely 'a tissue of hugged lies', this paradise is complete with a castle of 'white transparent glass', woods full of 'songs and flowers and fruit', and a muse-like male spirit who has eyes 'like flames of fire . . . Fulfilling my desire'. Rossetti's 'pleasure-place' is thus quite clearly a paradise of self-gratifying art, a paradise in which the lures of *Goblin Market*'s masculine fruit-merchants are anticipated by the seductions of the male muse, and the sensual delights of the goblin fruit are embodied in an artfully arranged microcosmos of happy natural creatures. Precisely because this inner Eden *is* a 'pleasure-place', however, it soon becomes a realm of banishment in which the poet–speaker, punitively abandoned by her muse, is condemned to freeze, starve and age, like Laura and Jeanie. For again like Laura and Jeanie, Rossetti must learn to suffer and renounce the self-gratifications of art and sensuality.

As a representative female poet–speaker, moreover, Rossetti believes she must learn to sing selflessly, despite pain, rather than selfishly, in celebration of pleasure. A key passage in 'From House to Home' describes an extraordinary, masochistic vision which strikingly illuminates the moral aesthetic on which *Goblin Market* is also based.

> I saw a vision of a woman, where
>   Night and new morning strive for domination;
> Incomparably pale, and almost fair,
>   And sad beyond expression.
>   . . .
>
>
> I stood upon the outer barren ground,
>   She stood on inner ground that budded flowers;
> While circling in their never-slackening round
>   Danced by the mystic hours.

140

But every flower was lifted on a thorn,
    And every thorn shot upright from its sands
To gall her feet; hoarse laughter pealed in scorn
    With cruel clapping hands.

She bled and wept, yet did not shrink; her strength
    Was strung up until daybreak of delight:
She measured measureless sorrow toward its length,
    And breadth, and depth, and height.

Then marked I how a chain sustained her form,
    A chain of living links not made nor riven:
It stretched sheer up through lightning, wind, and storm,
    And anchored fast in heaven.

One cried: 'How long? Yet founded on the Rock
    She shall do battle, suffer, and attain.' –
One answered: 'Faith quakes in the tempest shock:
    Strengthen her soul again.'

I saw a cup sent down and come to her
    Brimful of loathing and of bitterness:
She drank with livid lips that seemed to stir
    The depth, not make it less.

But as she drank I spied a hand distil
    New wine and virgin honey; making it
First bitter-sweet, then sweet indeed, until
    She tasted only sweet.

Her lips and cheeks waxed rosy-fresh and young;
    Drinking she sang: 'My soul shall nothing want';
And drank anew: while soft a song was sung,
    A mystical slow chant.

What the female poet–speaker must discover, this passage suggests, is that for the woman poet only renunciation, even anguish, can be a suitable source of song. Bruised and tortured, the Christ-like poet of Rossetti's vision drinks the bitterness of self-abnegation, and *then* sings. For the pure sweetness of the early 'pleasure-place', Rossetti implies, is merely a 'tissue of lies'. The woman artist can be strengthened 'to live' only through doses of paradoxically bittersweet pain.

Like the sweet 'pleasaunce' of 'From House to Home', the fruit of *Goblin Market* has fed on the desirous substrata of the psyche, the childishly self-gratifying fantasies of the imagination. Superegoistic Lizzie, therefore, is the agent of necessity and necessity's 'white and golden' virtue, repression. When Laura returns from eating the forbidden fruit, Lizzie meets her 'at the gate / Full of wise upbraidings: "Dear, you should not stay so late, / Twilight is not good for maidens; / Should not loiter in the glen / In the haunts of goblin men."' Although, as we noted earlier, the goblin men are not 'real' men, they are of course integrally associated with masculinity's prerogatives of self-assertion, so that what Lizzie is telling Laura (and what Rossetti is telling herself) is that the risks and gratifications of art are 'not good for maidens', a moral Laura must literally assimilate here just as the poet–speaker had to learn it in 'From House to Home'. Young ladies like Laura, Maude, and Christina Rossetti should not loiter in the glen of imagination, which is the haunt of goblin men like Keats and Tennyson – or like Dante Gabriel Rossetti and his compatriots of the Pre-Raphaelite Brotherhood.

Later, becoming a eucharistic Messiah, a female version of the patriarchal (rather than Satanic) Word made flesh, Lizzie insists that Laura must devour her – must, that is, ingest her bitter repressive wisdom, the wisdom of necessity's virtue, in order to be redeemed. And indeed, when Laura does feast on Lizzie, the goblin juice on her repressive sister's skin is 'wormwood to the tongue'. As in 'From House to Home', the aesthetic of pleasure has been transformed by censorious morality into an aesthetic of pain. And, again, just as in 'From House to Home' the female hero bleeds, weeps, and *sings* because she suffers, so in *Goblin Market* Laura does at last begin to leap and sing 'like a caged thing freed' at the moment in which she learns the lesson of renunciation. At this moment, in other words, she reaches what Rossetti considers the height of a woman poet's art, and here, therefore, she is truly Rossetti's surrogate. Later, she will lapse into childlike domesticity, forgoing all feasts, but here, for a brief interval of ecstatic agony, she 'stems the light / Straight toward the sun' and gorges 'on bitterness without a name', a masochistic version of what Dickinson called 'the banquet of abstemiousness'. Then, having assimilated her repressive but sisterly superego, she dies utterly to her old poetic/sexual life of self-assertion.

Once again a comparison with Keats seems appropriate, for just as he was continually obsessed with the same poetic apprenticeship that concerned Rossetti in *Maude*, he too wrote a resonantly symbolic poem about the relationship of poetry and starvation to an encounter with interior otherness incarnated in a magical being of the opposite sex. Like Rossetti's goblin men, Keats's 'belle dame' fed his vulnerable knight mysterious but luscious food – 'roots of relish sweet, / And honey-wild, and manna dew –' and, cementing the connection between

142

food and speech, she told him 'in language strange ... "I love thee
true."' Like Rossetti's Laura (and like the speaker of 'From House to
Home'), Keats's knight was also inexplicably deserted by the muse-like
lady whom he had met in the meads and wooed in an eerie 'elfin grot'
analogous to the goblin's haunted glen, once she had had her will of
him. Like Laura, too, he pined, starved and sickened on the cold
hillside of reality where his *anima* and his author abandoned him. Yet
in Keats's case, unlike Rossetti's, we cannot help feeling that the poet's
abandonment is only temporary, no matter what the knight's fate might
be. Where her betrayal by goblin men (and the distinction between a
beautiful queen and rat-faced goblin men is relevant here too)
persuades Laura/Rossetti that her original desire to eat the forbidden
fruit of art was a vain and criminal impulse, the knight's abandonment
simply enhances our sense of his tragic grandeur.

Art, Keats says, is ultimately worth any risk, even the risk of
alienation or desolation. The ecstasy of the beautiful lady's 'kisses
sweet' and 'language strange' is more than worth the starvation and
agony to come. Indeed, the ecstasy of the kisses, deceptive though they
are, itself constitutes the only redemption possible for both Keats and
his knight. Certainly any redemption of the kind Lizzie offers Laura,
though it might return the knight to the fat land where 'the squirrel's
granary is full', would destroy what is truly valuable to him – his
memory of the elfin grot, the fairy's song, the 'honey wild' – just as
Laura's memory of the haunted glen and the 'fruits like honey to the
throat' is ultimately destroyed by her ritual consumption of repressive
domesticity. And that *Goblin Market* is not just an observation of the
lives of other women but an accurate account of the aesthetics Rossetti
worked out for herself helps finally to explain why, although Keats can
imagine asserting himself from beyond the grave, Rossetti, banqueting
on bitterness, must bury herself alive in a coffin of renunciation.

Notes

1. *Maude: Prose and Verse*, edited and with an introduction by R.W. Crump
   (Hamden, Conn.: Archon Books, 1976), pp. 30–1.
2. Ibid., p. 37.
3. Ibid., pp. 35–6.
4. Ibid., p. 41.
5. Ibid., p. 53.
6. Ibid., p. 72.
7. Ibid., p. 32.
8. 'Passing and Glassing', in *The Poetical Works of Christina G. Rossetti*, ed.
   William Michael Rossetti (London: Macmillan, 1904), 2, p. 115.

9. 'Sleep and Poetry', ll. 96, 98.
10. See 'To Homer', which begins 'Standing aloof in giant ignorance, / Of thee I hear and of the Cyclades . . . .'
11. It is worth remembering here that twelve years after his sister wrote *Maude*, Dante Gabriel Rossetti, perhaps influenced by her story, perhaps by the Keats episode, buried his own poems in his wife's coffin. But the renunciation Christina imagines for her female poet did not prove viable for an ambitious male poet: within seven years Rossetti had his wife's body exhumed so that he could recover his poems for publication. For further details see OSWALD DOUGHTY, *A Victorian Romantic: Dante Gabriel Rossetti* (London: Frederick Muller, 1949), pp. 412–19.
12. *Maude*, p. 75. 'On Keats', in *New Poems*, ed. W.M. Rossetti (1896), pp. 22–3.
13. To Charles Brown, 30 November 1820.
14. See RICHARD WILBUR, 'Sumptuous Destitution', in Richard B. Sewell (ed.), *Emily Dickinson: A Collection of Critical Essays* (Englewood Cliffs, NJ: Prentice Hall, 1963), pp. 127–36.
15. 'Goblin Market', *The Poetical Works of Christina G. Rossetti*, 1, pp. 3–22.
16. *Paradise Lost*, IX, 599, 600, 679.
17. Ibid., IX, 790–800.
18. *The Poems of Emily Dickinson*, ed. Thomas Johnson, 3 vols (Cambridge, Mass.: The Bellknap Press, 1955), poem no. 1651.
19. See RALPH WARDLE, *Mary Wollstonecraft* (Lincoln: University of Nebraska Press, 1951), p. 322.
20. RICHARD POLWHELE, *The Unsex'd Females: A Poem* (New York: Garland, 1974; first published 1798), pp. 6–9. Polwhele complained in a footnote that 'Botany has lately become a fashionable amusement with the ladies. But how the study of the sexual system of plants can accord with female modesty, I am not able to comprehend.' And in his diatribe against Wollstonecraft he wrote that 'I shudder at the new unpictur'd scene, / Where unsex'd woman vaunts the imperious mien; Where girls . . . With bliss botanic as their bosoms heave, / Still pluck forbidden fruit, with mother Eve, / For puberty in sighing florets pant, / Or point the prostitution of a plant; / Dissect its organ of unhallow'd lust, / And fondly gaze the titillating dust.' He felt, in other words, that botanizing literally accompanied sexual and political self-assertion, as a sign of female depravity.
21. The dynamics of Jeanie's (and Laura's) disease are further illuminated by Rossetti's sonnet 'The World'. Here the speaker describes 'The World' as a woman who is beautiful by day, offering 'Ripe fruits, sweet flowers, and full satiety', but who becomes 'a very monster void of love and prayer' by night. Thus 'By day she stands a lie: by night she stands, / In all the naked horror of the truth, / With pushing horns and clawed and clutching hands.' Clearly Rossetti has converted the traditional allegorical threesome of 'the world, the flesh, and the devil' into a single terrifying figure who incarnates, among other things, her deep anxieties about female ambition, inspiration, and self-assertion. (See *Poetical Works*, 1, p. 96.)
22. 'From House to Home', ibid., pp. 103–12.

9 Heroic Sisterhood in *Goblin Market**
Dorothy Mermin

Mermin takes up, restates and defends the optimistic feminist reading of *Goblin Market* that Gilbert and Gubar (previous chapter) mention only to discard. To do so, she has first to reject the 'psychosexual' interpretations that allegorise the sisters as the two halves of one self – much as Gilbert and Gubar do, in reading Lizzie as the oppressive super-ego. By reading the sisters as two separate people, a message of sisterly solidarity is restored to the poem, and it can be set in its Victorian social world. Mermin relates the poem to the positions available to women in the Pre-Raphaelite movement (as for many critics, the goblin 'brothers' recall the Pre-Raphaelite Brotherhood), to the Anglican sisterhoods, and to Rossetti's work with 'fallen women'. While Gilbert and Gubar present their women writers as victims of a monolithic patriarchal ideology, here we begin to get a sense of oppositional or resistant positions for women. While Rossetti accepts her 'inferior' status as a woman, within the dominant ideology she discovers strong female positions: the mother, the nun, the woman-only community. In the 'tale' Laura tells her daughters at the end of the poem, Mermin sees female artistic expression – the poem is not about the suppression of women's poetic voice. Here she has the advantage of Gilbert and Gubar (Chapter 8) and Homans (Chapter 1), all of whom point to substantial poetic outputs as the expression of women's silencing.

Goblin Market is usually read as an allegory of the poet's self-division that shows, in Lionel Stevenson's representative summary, the conflict between 'the two sides of Christina's own character, the sensuous and the ascetic', and demonstrates 'the evil of self-indulgence, the fraudulence of sensuous beauty, and the supreme duty of renunciation'.[1] Readings of this sort even when they are not reductively biographical

---

* Reprinted from *Victorian Poetry*, 21 (1983): 107–18.

(as Stevenson's is not) do not allow for the openness and multiplicity of meanings that we acknowledge in such predecessor poems as Coleridge's *The Ancient Mariner* or Keats's 'La Belle Dame Sans Merci'. They usually assume that the poem welled up spontaneously and artlessly from Rossetti's unconscious and press towards exclusively psychosexual interpretations. By turning the two sisters into parts of one person, they minimize or distort the central action in which one sister saves the other; they shy away from the powerful image of Lizzie as Christ saying, '"Eat me, drink me, love me"' (l. 471);[2] they ignore the energy, triumph and joy of the poem; and they give insufficient weight to the ending. Recent readings have suggested other dimensions to the poem: that it is about art as well as sex, and that it represents the development of female autonomy in a largely female world.[3] An inclusive reading will demonstrate what is evident from the sensuousness, luxuriance, cheerfulness, and energy of the poem and from the serenity of the ending: that it is not a poem of bitter repression but rather a fantasy of feminine freedom, heroism, and self-sufficiency and a celebration of sisterly and maternal love. It is a dream or a vision of the Pre-Raphaelite world from a woman's point of view.

The goblins represent the temptations of sexual desire, but of a highly imaginative kind.[4] Jeanie 'for joys brides hope to have / Fell sick and died' (ll. 314–15). This sexuality is without marriage or issue: no grass grows on Jeanie's grave and the kernel Laura brings back does not sprout. As in much of Rossetti's poetry and that of others in the Pre-Raphaelite circle, desire here has no end or final object. The goblins are like odd, furry, cuddly little animals of the sort Rossetti loved, sometimes childlike and charming, purveyors of desire but not its object. The fruits are not the real object either, since they feed the appetite instead of satisfying it; once tasted, they have served their purpose and cannot be found again. They are unreal even in the fairy-tale world of the poem – 'Men sell not such in any town' (ll. 101, 556) – seeming to come from a paradise 'Where summer ripens at all hours' (l. 152) but where no one ever goes. They represent desire for a paradise of the imagination that does not exist and therefore can be only desired, never obtained. The conflation of erotic and imaginative significance in a story about non-human objects of desire which exist outside of time recalls La Belle Dame Sans Merci, whose victims eat strange fruit in fairyland and then loiter, turn pale, starve and waste away, and also Tennyson's 'Tithonus' and (proleptically) 'The Holy Grail'. In Tennyson's poem the Grail quest begins with a nun who starves herself to a shadow after her love has been thwarted; the quest leads Percivale through a world of shadows and into a monastery and gives (as in *Goblin Market*) a framework of explicitly Christian meaning to a deeply ambiguous story. In all these poems the sexualized imaginative world is infinitely attractive but sterile and destructive, and those who commit themselves to longing for it waste away in gloom and frustration, cut off from natural human life.

Rossetti's knowledge of the lives and art of the Pre-Raphaelites, especially her brother Gabriel's, as well as the idea of Keats that was current at mid century would have enforced the association between imaginary worlds, sexuality and art. In her story 'The Lost Titian' (1856) she describes a party at Titian's studio that resembles both a glorified version of Gabriel's house and the goblins' feast:

> The studio was elegant with clusters of flowers, sumptuous with crimson, gold-bordered hangings, and luxurious with cushions and perfumes. From the walls peeped pictured fruit and fruit-like faces. ... On the table were silver dishes, filled with leaves and choice fruits; wonderful vessels of Venetian glass, containing rare wines and iced waters; and footless goblets, which allowed the guest no choice but to drain his bumper.[5]

The fruit both attracts and frightens Laura by suggesting a combination of sensuous richness, moral irresponsibility, and sinister eroticism that is frequent in Pre-Raphaelite art. 'Who knows upon what soil they fed / Their hungry thirsty roots?' (ll. 44–5), she warns; but then: 'How fair the vine must grow. ... How warm the wind must blow / Thro' those fruit bushes' (ll. 60–3). The fruit seems to her to offer access to a paradise of art; she herself, moreover, is described in terms that suggest that she belongs in a Pre-Raphaelite picture. She 'stretched her gleaming neck' like a swan, a lily, 'a moonlit poplar branch' (ll. 81–4) – or like the long-necked women in Gabriel's paintings – and finally like a 'vessel' (l. 85) about to break free, an association of woman and drifting boat that recalls a favorite Pre-Raphaelite subject, the Lady of Shalott. The other extended description of Laura refers to the most notable attribute of Pre-Raphaelite women, long loosened hair (ll. 500–6).

Laura sounds, in fact, like Lizzie Siddal, with her long neck and fabulously luxuriant red-gold hair[6] – Laura's hair 'streamed' like a 'torch' (l. 500) even though it had turned 'thin and gray' (l. 277). Elizabeth Siddal, Dante Gabriel Rossetti's model and eventually his wife, was a painter and a poet too; she was reclusive, thin and unhealthy, and took large quantities of laudanum, dying of an overdose shortly before *Goblin Market* was published. The goblins, 'Brother with queer brother' (l. 94), suggest the Pre-Raphaelite brotherhood with their queer lives and also, perhaps, childhood memories and fantasies of Rossetti's own two brothers; as Ellen Moers points out, the goblins seem to reflect 'fantasies derived from the night side of the Victorian nursery'.[7] They call Lizzie 'proud, / Cross-grained, uncivil' (ll. 394–5) – terms that Rossetti could well have imagined applied to herself by the Brotherhood, among whom she was often both sharp-tongued and reserved.[8] She was cool to Lizzie Siddal; nor did she get on well later with her other sister-in-law, Lucy (a name fortuitously apposite in sound to *Goblin Market*), the daughter of Ford Madox Brown, whom William Rossetti married in 1874. On the simplest biographical level, the poem seems to describe possible lives for women among the Pre-Raphaelites and to imagine a sisterly feeling among them that did not, so far as Christina Rossetti was concerned, actually exist.

In narrative terms the story is a transformation of a traditional fairy tale.[9] The sisters live alone in a cosy little house. Asleep, they are compared to blossoms, snow, 'wands of ivory / Tipped with gold for awful kings' (ll. 188–91). Their sleep is protected as if by enchantment: 'Wind sang to them lullaby, / Lumbering owls forebore to fly, / Not a bat flapped' (ll. 193–5). A verbal ambiguity makes them seem imprisoned: 'Cheek to cheek and breast to breast / Locked together in one nest' (ll. 197–8) like sleeping princesses waiting for princes (or 'awful kings') to rescue them. But this is a fairy tale that Rossetti usually tells with a difference. Her princes are dilatory and lovers seldom come to those who wait. (They are more likely to come to women who are doing something: making music in 'Maiden-Song', getting married in 'Love from the North'.) Once Laura yields to desire she becomes that central figure in Rossetti's poems and stories, the woman 'Grown old before [her] time' ('Song: Oh roses for the flush of youth', l. 4), doomed to pine away like the princess in *The Prince's Progress* who dies before her lover gets there. Laura is cured, however, by discovering that what she pined for is not really desirable. Rossetti tells the same story again in 'Commonplace' (1870), in which Lucy (again, a name fit for *Goblin Market*) learns that the man she loved has married someone else. Immediately she ages, fades, and withdraws from her family and the world. Then she meets him again, sees that he's not worth pining for, regains her health, looks, and cheerfulness, and marries a nicer man. Similarly, the goblins show their evil nature when Lizzie resists them and the juice she brings back tastes bitter. Knowing the bitterness is the 'fiery antidote' (l. 559) to Laura's yearning. She is cured not because her fairy prince comes but because she ceases to want him.

Since the goblin fruit has explicitly sexual connotations, however, and since in the moral logic of poetry desire and deed blur together, Laura is in effect a 'fallen woman' – an object that fascinated Victorians from the Pre-Raphaelites up the social and moral scale to Gladstone. Several of Rossetti's poems deal with women who have been seduced and abandoned. Like *Goblin Market*, these poems are remarkably uncensorious, particularly in contrast to the sentimental cruelty of works like Dante Gabriel Rossetti's painting 'Found' or his poem 'Jenny', to which the name 'Jeanie' in *Goblin Market* may allude. Rossetti treats such women sympathetically, reserving her scorn for the men. Thus in 'The Iniquity of the Fathers Upon the Children' the speaker forgives the mother who does not dare to acknowledge her and blames her unknown father, and in 'Cousin Kate' and 'Light Love' illegitimate children cause their mothers more pride than shame. The speaker in 'Jenny' compares the prostitute to 'a rose shut in a book / In which pure women may not look' and contrasts her with his virtuous cousin:

> Of the same lump (as it is said)
> For honour and dishonour made,
> Two sister vessels. Here is one.

> It makes a goblin of the sun.[10]

'Sister', 'vessels', and 'goblin' all suggest *Goblin Market*. For Christina Rossetti, however, sin does not necessarily cancel sisterhood, and she thought like Barrett Browning that women should know and write about such things. In the 1860s she spent a considerable amount of time at a 'Home for Fallen Women',[11] a form of social welfare work that allowed respectable middle-class women to read in the 'book' that Gabriel's 'Jenny' says 'pure women' may not look into. So Lizzie, emboldened by love for her sister, 'for the first time in her life / Began to listen and look' (ll. 327–8); and what she sees does not, in the end, hurt her. Laura's heated imagination inhabits the erotic world of Pre-Raphaelite art, while Lizzie's imagination leads her towards – if not actually into – a realistic, socially responsible moral world like Barrett Browning's. Rossetti's defense of 'The Iniquity of the Fathers' against Gabriel's disapproval can serve as a reply to 'Jenny' and an explanation of *Goblin Market*:

> Whilst I endorse your opinion of the unavoidable and indeed much-to-be-desired unreality of women's work on many social matters, I yet incline to include within female range such an attempt as this: where the certainly possible circumstances are merely indicated as it were in skeleton. . . . Moreover the sketch only gives the girl's own deductions, feelings . . . and whilst it may truly be urged that unless white could be black and Heaven Hell my experience (thank God) precludes me from hers, I yet don't see why 'the Poet mind' should be less able to construct her from its own inner consciousness than a hundred other unknown quantities.[12]

Lizzie's rescue of Laura, the main action of the poem, has several aspects. As in *The Ancient Mariner* redemption comes – thirst is sated – through imaginative identification analogous to the poet's own. Primarily, however, it is an heroic exploit. Lizzie stands firm under attack like a large, substantial object, mixing male and female qualities: a lily, a rock, a beacon, an orange-tree, a beleaguered town (ll. 409–21). It is a triumph of cleverness and daring: she would not open her mouth, she made no bargain, she 'laughed in heart' (l. 433) while the goblins attacked her. She outwits them like a folktale heroine, getting their treasure without paying their price; the 'bounce' of her unspent penny in her purse is 'music to her ear' (l. 454), an image as much simply economic as sexual. She runs home in the sheer physical pleasure of strength and freedom, impelled not by fear (l. 460) but by joy and filled again with 'inward laughter' (l. 463). As her laughter indicates, her story has to do not with temptation resisted – neither the goblins nor their fruit attract her, and what she is resisting is attempted rape – but with danger braved and overcome, an heroic deed accomplished.

She brings the 'fiery antidote' (l. 559) and she *is* the antidote. She brings proof that the goblin fruit is bitter, and she offers as an alternative both a gift of love and an example of a better way of life. She brings back 'the fruit forbidden' (l. 479) without tasting it herself – that is, she shows that it is possible in erotic and artistic matters, if not in Genesis, to know good and evil and not succumb to evil. 'Eat me, drink me, love me' (l. 471): like Christ, she saves both by her self-sacrifice and by her example. 'The next Christ will perhaps be a female Christ', Florence Nightingale wrote in *Cassandra*; 'at last there shall arise a woman, who will resume, in his own soul, all the sufferings of her race, and that woman will be the Saviour of her race.'[13] The speaker in Rossetti's 'From House to Home', written shortly before *Goblin Market*, is saved from despair after losing her paradise of love by a vision of a woman suffering torment like the crucifixion. In simpler terms, the moral is a good Victorian one, familiar from many novels: moral and emotional salvation comes from a loving response to selfless love.

'Hug me, kiss me, suck my juices', cries Lizzie (l. 468), and Laura 'kissed and kissed her with a hungry mouth' (l. 492). The eroticism troubles many readers; we are more nervous about manifestations of affection between women than Victorians were, and we find it hard to allow a nineteenth-century religious poet the conflation of spiritual and erotic intensity that we accept without question in Crashaw or Donne.[14] Calmer traditional images of eating and drinking are used to exemplify the relation of Christ to mankind in several of the devotional poems published with *Goblin Market* ('The Love of Christ Which Passeth

Knowledge', ll. 9–12; 'A Bruised Reed Shall He Not Break', l. 4; 'A Better Resurrection', ll. 17–24; 'Advent', ll. 31–2). Embodying this symbolic relationship in two women evokes strange overtones. But there is nothing erotic in Lizzie's jubilant shouts of triumph, heroic boasting even: 'Laura, make much of me: / For your sake I have braved the glen' (ll. 472–3). Laura's reaction is excessive, but the excess here as in her gluttonous sucking at the fruit is part of the evil as well as its cure. She falls into a highly stylized, rather biblical frenzy that is like a ritual of exorcism:

> Writhing as one possessed she leaped and sung,
> Rent all her robe, and wrung
> Her hands in lamentable haste,
> And beat her breast.
>
> (ll. 496–9)

Then, 'Pleasure past and anguish past' (l. 522) – the mixture of pleasure and pain, poison and delight characteristic of Pre-Raphaelite formulations of alluring, evil love – she falls senseless, almost dies, and is reborn at dawn into the natural cycle of life: chirping birds, reapers, dewy grass and buds, and moderate behavior. She 'Hugged Lizzie but not twice or thrice' (l. 539).

The full meaning of the story, however, is seen in its consequences. 'Afterwards, when both were wives' (l. 544), Laura would tell their children about the goblins and how her sister 'stood / In deadly peril to do her good' (ll. 557–8), and then,

> joining hands to little hands
> Would bid them cling together,
> 'For there is no friend like a sister.'
>
> (ll. 560–2)

The story thus completed is clear and simple in its essential structure: two girls live alone; they encounter goblin men; they have children. Except for the word 'wives', which legitimizes the children, there is no mention of any men but the goblins, who are explicitly male. The children are apparently all girls and are exhorted to keep the female circle closed and complete. This is a world in which men serve only the purpose of impregnation. Once both sisters have gone to the goblins and acquired the juices of their fruits, they have no further need of them.

Many of Rossetti's poems and stories suggest that the fantasy of such a world might well attract her. *Sing-Song*, for instance, is filled with a yearning for children that is so intense as to be painful:

Motherless baby and babyless mother,
Bring them together to love one another.

My baby has a mottled fist,
    My baby has a neck in creases;
My baby kisses and is kissed.[15]

In 'Commonplace' childlessness is regarded as a terrible sorrow, and the
death of children, a recurrent motif in her writings, is the worst of
calamities (see 'Eve', 'Vanna's Twins', and much of *Sing-Song*).
Relationships between mothers and babies and between women, usually
sisters, are central to her poems and stories, whereas men are generally
peripheral or absent; often the relationship is the darker side of the
sisterly coin, competitiveness and envy, but even then it is a source of
dramatic excitement and energy. Marriage is seldom depicted as
wholly desirable. 'A Triad' gives the most negative view, telling of
three women:

One shamed herself in love; one temperately
    Grew gross in soulless love, a sluggish wife;
One famished died for love.

(ll. 9–11)

In 'Maude Clare' the speaker denounces her lover, who is marrying
another woman; he quakes inarticulately with shame, but Nell (the
name, perhaps significantly, of the virtuous cousin in Gabriel's 'Jenny')
answers her:

'Yea, tho' you're taller by the head,
    More wise, and much more fair;
I'll love him till he loves me best.'

(ll. 45–7)

Maude Clare is strong, proud, and bold, while a good wife is humble,
unambitious, uncensorious, and loving, like Nell: virtues that most of
Rossetti's speakers find almost impossible to attain and hard even to
praise, although admitting that in fact they lead to happiness. The
speaker in 'The Lowest Room' who reads Homer and is restless with
her 'aimless life' (l. 81) ends up unmarried, bitterly envious of her
sister's cosy family – which a woman who is not content with a
woman's lot cannot, evidently, hope for. But such discontent is a
strong and persistent undercurrent in Rossetti's poems, and a good deal
of poetic and moral energy goes into resisting it. She was encouraged

to resist it, too: her brother Gabriel saw in 'The Lowest Room' a 'taint' of 'falsetto muscularity' which he attributed to the influence of Barrett Browning and thought 'utterly foreign' to his sister's 'primary impulses'.[16]

As in *Goblin Market*, however, Rossetti sometimes imagines other alternatives than soft domesticity, resentful loneliness, and 'falsetto muscularity'. In *Maude* (written in 1850) the only mode of life the heroine admires is that of a friend who joins an Anglican sisterhood and is seen just once more 'walking with some poor children', 'thoughtful, but very calm and happy';[17] like Laura and Lizzie, she has both sisterhood and children. Rossetti was much attracted to sisterhoods; her work with fallen women made her an 'Associate' of one, and in 1873 her older sister Maria became an Anglican nun, as she had long wanted to do – and thereby (as Lona Mosk Packer points out, p. 304) left the seclusion and limited sphere of home and entered a wider and busier world. The Anglican sisterhoods, like the central fantasy of *Goblin Market*, satisfied the need that haunts *Maude* and such poems as 'The Lowest Room', 'A Royal Princess', and 'Maggie a Lady': the need for a sphere of significant activity, combined with emotional fulfillment, within the limits of women's traditional roles. In 1854 Rossetti wanted to join Florence Nightingale in her Crimean venture – that apotheosis of a traditionally feminine activity into strenuous, serious, public deeds – but was rejected as too young. She thought that motherhood, too, could confer heroic strength and even masculine status: 'I do think if anything ever does sweep away the barrier of sex, and make the female not a giantess or a heroine but at once and full grown a hero and giant, it is that mighty maternal love which makes little birds and little beasts as well as little women matches for very big adversaries.'[18] Unwed mothers, furthermore, are among the strongest figures in her poetry ('Cousin Kate', 'Light Love'), and female strength often goes with rejecting a man, as in 'Maude Clare' and 'No, Thank You, John' (in which Gabriel found the objectionable Barrett Browning 'taint' recurring).[19] Virgin saints also offered a model of female independence. In *Time Flies*, Rossetti tells of St Etheldreda, who remained virgin through two marriages and 'after twelve years of successful contest, ended strife by separating from her enamoured husband'. 'Thus she fought the battle of life', Rossetti comments, carrying out the martial image, 'thus she triumphed'. Having escaped from husbands, Etheldreda founded and ruled 'a monastery for men and women'.[20] She is evidently one of Rossetti's favorite saints.

A world of female potency and exclusively female happiness appears in Rossetti's works only covertly, as fantasy, and in clearly unrealistic modes: ballads, fairy-tales, and legends of saints. Her lyrics generally keep to conventional lyric themes, and when women in her narrative poems lose or leave their lovers, religion is usually their only solace. She accepted these limitations, writing with some wryness to her brother Gabriel in 1870:

It is impossible to go on singing out-loud to one's one-stringed lyre. It is not in me, and therefore it will never come out of me, to turn to politics or philanthropy with Mrs Browning: such many-sidedness I leave to a greater than I, and, having said my say, may well sit silent. . . . Here is a great discovery, 'Women are not Men.' and you must not expect me to possess a tithe of your capacities, though I humbly – or proudly – lay claim to family-likeness.[21]

Religious belief both curbed her ambition and offered escape from the restrictions imposed by her sex. Her didactic and devotional works assert women's inferiority with relentless stringency and with an undertone of rebellion and pain that she finds hard to subdue; but part of the comfort she finds in religion is the promise that in the soul's relation to Christ gender, finally, does not matter. She says in *Seek and Find*: 'if our proud waves will after all . . . not be allayed (for stayed they must be) by the limit of God's ordinance concerning our sex, one final consolation yet remains to careful and troubled hearts: in Christ there is neither male nor female, for we are all one'.[22]

The optimistic plot of *Goblin Market* reappears, however, in *Speaking Likenesses* (1874), an unpretentious little book of three fairy-tales told in one narrative frame by a very prim aunt to her nieces. In the first story a little girl finds herself at a fantastic party with terrible children who torment her as the goblins do Lizzie and whose marvellously tempting food she does not eat; from this she learns to put up with the normally unpleasant children at her birthday party. In the second a little girl goes into the woods and tries unsuccessfully, with the help of friendly but ineffectual animals, to boil a kettle for tea; she learns that she cannot manage to live alone. In the third story a little girl walking through the woods on a generous errand refuses to join the terrible children's party, to feed or eat with a monstrous boy whose face has only a huge mouth, or to fall asleep with a band of gypsies. The way is cold and difficult and the recipients of her generosity are ungrateful, but she completes her errands. Apparently as a reward, she finds a pigeon, a kitten, and a puppy which she brings back to her cosy house and loving grandmother. As in *Goblin Market*, resistance to male figures which attract some sympathy and yet repel and refusal to eat their food or join their dreams are parts of a painful and strenuous quest that frees the heroine both from a disagreeable social world of males and females together (as in the first story) and from helplessness (as in the second), and leaves two women self-sufficient and happy with baby creatures to care for. The frame is conventional, repressive and moralistic, but the unstated theme is not.

Much of Rossetti's poetry presents frustrated, unhappy women yearning for love. *Goblin Market*, in contrast, shows women testing the allurements of male sexuality and exploring the imaginative world that male eroticism has created. By entering but finally rejecting that world, they discover that a woman can be strong, bold, and clever, Christ-like in active self-sacrifice as well as in silent endurance, and that sisters and daughters can live happy lives together. For Rossetti this may have been as unrealizable a dream as the variously uninhabitable realms of art imagined by Keats and his Victorian followers; but it was a dream that sought to integrate passion and art into life and not, as critics often say, merely to reject or repress them. Sexuality is not repressed in the poem – it is quite evidently and undisguisedly there – but its proper function is shown to be the generation of children and literary works. Laura turns the encounter with the goblins into a tale told and retold as a ritual to bind the children together, and the moral she draws from it is not that girls should avoid goblins – the sisters seem to remember them, in fact, with some pleasure – but that 'there is no friend like a sister' (l. 562). Similarly, the imaginative experience of the goblin world appears to generate the poem that includes and goes beyond it. Rossetti's sense of poetical possibilities was restricted by Pre-Raphaelite assumptions about the subjects, moods and tones appropriate to art, but in *Goblin Market* she shows that the erotic and imaginative intensity cultivated by the Brotherhood need not be self-enclosing, all-engrossing, or male. The energy, freedom and easy control of the fluent irregular meter (which seems to have shocked Ruskin with its apparent waywardness)[23] reflect Rossetti's triumphant appropriation of Pre-Raphaelite materials for her own purposes. She uses a literary form, furthermore, that purports to be nothing more serious than a tale told by a woman to amuse and instruct children; the form, like the content, seems to betray an assumption that women can only be grown-up, independent, productive, and active in a life without men.

Notes

1. *The Pre-Raphaelite Poets* (University of North Carolina Press, 1972), p. 105. WINSTON WEATHERS gives the fullest explication of the sisters as two halves of one self in 'Christina Rossetti: The Sisterhood of Self', *Victorian Poetry* (*VP*), 3 (1965): 81–9.
2. Citations from the poems unless otherwise specified are from *The Complete Poems of Christina Rossetti: A Variorum Edition*, ed. R.W. Crump (Louisiana State University Press, 1979), 1.

3. A.A. DE VITIS sees the sisters as two halves of an artist in '*Goblin Market*: Fairy Tale and Reality', *Journal of Popular Culture* (*JPC*), 1 (1967), 418–26. The poem is read as showing, in part, growth into adulthood and the development of female autonomy by MARTINE WATSON BROWNLEY in 'Love and Sensuality in Christina Rossetti's *Goblin Market*', *Essays in Literature* (*ELWIU*), 6 (1979): 179–86; ELLEN GOLUB in 'Untying Goblin Apron Strings: A Psychoanalytic Reading of *Goblin Market*', *Literature and Psychology* (*L&P*), 25 (1975): 158–65; and MIRIAM SAGAN in 'Christina Rossetti's *Goblin Market* and Feminist Literary Criticism', *Journal of Pre-Raphaelite Studies* (*PRR*), 3 (1980): 66–76. SANDRA M. GILBERT and SUSAN GUBAR find hints of 'an effectively matrilineal and matriarchal world' as well as 'bitter repressive wisdom' in *The Madwoman in the Attic: The Woman Writer and the Nineteenth-Century Literary Imagination* (Yale University, Press, 1979), pp. 567, 573. WILLIAM T. GOING shows that the poem draws significantly on the life of the Pre-Raphaelite Brotherhood in '*Goblin Market* and the Pre-Raphaelite Brotherhood', *PRR*, 3 (1979): 1–11, and JEROME J. McGANN analyses it as an enactment of the sisters' discovery that they need not be emotionally dependent on goblin men in 'Christina Rossetti's Poems: A New Edition and a Revaluation', *Victorian Studies* (*VS*), 23 (1980): 237–54.

4. WEATHERS says that the goblins tempt to 'a kind of imaginative, fanciful, visionary – even hallucinatory – state of mind' (p. 82), and LONA MOSK PACKER sees it as (in Rossetti's own words) 'the seduction of imaginative emotion' (*Christina Rossetti*: University of California Press, 1963, p. 145). GILBERT and GUBAR suggest that the fruits are works of art (pp. 568–70).

5. *Commonplace, and Other Short Stories* (London, 1870), p. 149.

6. In her edition of *Goblin Market* (New York, 1975), GERMAINE GREER notes the likeness and makes it more impressive by calling Laura and Lizzie by each other's names (p. xxxi and passim). Violet Hunt associates Lizzie with Maria Rossetti and Laura with Christina herself. The story she tells is highly implausible (that Maria kept Christina from eloping by crouching for several nights on the door mat), but some general allusion to Maria, to whom the poem is dedicated, seems likely. See VIOLET HUNT, *The Wife of Rossetti: Her Life and Death* (New York, 1932), p. xiii.

7. *Literary Women* (Garden City, NY, 1976), p. 105.

8. VIOLET HUNT's characterization of her suggests that such opinions were held by some Pre-Raphaelites; see *The Wife of Rossetti*, pp. xii–xiii, 45, 58.

9. THOMAS BURNETT SWANN points out that they are like fairytale princesses in *Wonder and Whimsy: The Fantastic World of Christina Rossetti* (Francestown, New Hampshire, 1960), pp. 103, 105. Readings of the fairytale element in terms of repressed eroticism are given by STEPHEN PRICKETT in *Victorian Fantasy* (Indiana University Press, 1979), pp. 103–6, and MAUREEN DUFFY in *The Erotic World of Faery* (London, 1972), pp. 288–91.

10. 'Jenny', *The Works of Dante Gabriel Rossetti*, ed. William M. Rossetti (London, 1911).

11. PACKER notes the connection between *Goblin Market* and this welfare work, p. 154.

12. *Three Rossetis: Unpublished Letters to and from Dante Gabriel, Christina, William*, ed. Janet Camp Troxell (Harvard University Press, 1937), p. 143.

13. *Cassandra*, ed. Myra Stark (Old Westbury, 1979), pp. 53, 50. *Cassandra* was written in 1852.

14. GREER finds the poem 'deeply perverse' (p. xxxvi). BROWNLEY says, 'Her sexual fall requires a sexual redemption' (p. 183). CORA KAPLAN finds the poem 'an exploration of women's sexual fantasy which includes suggestions

of masochism, homoeroticism, rape or incest' ('The Indefinite Disclosed: Christina Rossetti and Emily Dickinson', in *Women Writing and Writing About Women*, ed. Mary Jacobus (London, 1979), p. 69). None of these critics thinks that Rossetti knew what she was doing when she wrote passages like this.

15. *Sing-Song, Speaking Likenesses, Goblin Market*, ed. R. Loring Taylor (New York, 1976), pp. 125, 23.

16. *Letters of Dante Gabriel Rossetti*, ed. Oswald Doughty and John Robert Wahl (Oxford, 1967), III, p. 1380.

17. *Maude: Prose & Verse* (Chicago, 1897), p. 83.

18. MACKENZIE BELL, *Christina Rossetti: A Biographical and Critical Study* (Boston, 1898), p. 124.

19. *Letters*, III, p. 1380.

20. *Time Flies: A Reading Diary* (Boston, 1886), p. 244. As a child Rossetti would have read the legend in HONE's *Every-Day Book*.

21. *The Family Letters of Christina Georgina Rossetti*, ed. William Michael Rossetti (London, 1908), p. 31.

22. *Seek and Find: A Double Series of Short Studies of the Benedicite* (New York, 1897), p. 32.

23. See WILLIAM MICHAEL ROSSETTI (ed.), *Ruskin: Rossetti: Pre-Raphaelitism: Papers 1854 to 1862* (London, 1899), pp. 258–9.

10 Christina Rossetti – Diary of a Feminist Reading*

ISOBEL ARMSTRONG

Armstrong's essay departs delightfully from the conventions of the academic article. She introduces autobiography and uncertainty into the form, refusing to pretend to the usual objectivity and 'mastery'. As the word 'mastery' suggests, this disruption of form can be seen as part of a feminist project. 'Objectivity' has also been seen as a cover for male bias by feminist critics. Armstrong's descriptions of her different readings of Rossetti over time historicises her interpretations – one of the most useful parts of the essay is the account of the unquestioned New Critical and Leavisite orthodoxies in which she was educated, and which excluded any serious consideration of Rossetti's poetry. Armstrong also articulates an initially resistant and still evolving encounter with feminist criticism: her project emerges as an effort to combine the sensitivity to language of her early training with a feminist awareness of politics. Pursuing this aim, she tries out some deconstructive and psychoanalytic theory in an exploration of the linguistic subtlety of Rossetti's poetry – but also does not want to lose sight either of historicised readings, or the agency of the woman poet in 'experimenting' with predetermined forms. The dialogic theory of Volosinov suggests a way of theorising these negotiations, in an historical context. The essay as a whole is a beautiful example of readings 'informed by' a number of theoretical approaches, rather than 'using' any one theory to argue for a single interpretation.

'That's it.' I said, or probably felt, this when I was nine and reading Christina Rossetti's 'Who Has Seen the Wind?' for the first time. I was looking for something I called 'real' poetry, which seemed to be very rare. I would not have used the quotation marks which a knowing

---

* Reprinted from *Women Reading Women's Writing*, ed. Sue Roe (Brighton: Harvester Press, 1987), pp. 117–37.

maturity makes me place round 'real'. This experience, 'That's it', is fused with the smell of a peculiarly sour disinfectant used in country primary schools after the war, when the caretaker spread a kind of disinfected meal of sawdust over the unpolished wood floor, and swept it up again. It comes together with the worn green cloth boards of a poetry anthology, probably some variant of the Child's Golden Treasury, and the tedium, suddenly changed, of silent reading in a hot room.

There were no illustrated paperbacks like Penguin's *Voices* to search through. I was exasperated by class readings of 'The Owl and the Pussy Cat' which was taught to us (we drew pictures of the pea-green boat), as far as I can see, because it was funny, and wasn't poetry. It wasn't funny as well as not being poetry. It never occurred to us to think of homonyms for 'pea'. It was the kind of thing grown-ups and teachers liked, as I did when I became both. Christina Rossetti's poem was quite different. It is a sparse two stanzas long and hauntingly lucid and mysterious all at once. An intransigently impersonal reserve releases intense lyricism. Its directness of address – 'Who has seen the wind? /Neither I nor you' – gives access to a rush of questioning which 'you' are invited to initiate. Who has *seen* the wind? Who *has* seen the wind? Nobody? It was written for children in a volume of poems called *Sing Song*. It is playful without being condescending because it has a serious respect for the metaphysical, and certainly epistemological, questions it presents with such economy and through such ordinary words. How do we know the wind when we see it only by its effects on other things, trembling leaves and bowed branches? The concord is reduced to the relations between seen, familiar movement and the source of movement. Or is it concord? She does not mention the obvious, sound, which is present only in the 'passing' syllables of the poem itself – 'The wind is passing by'. Such evanescence must make one wonder on what basis the confident and familiar connections of cognitive life are made. A subtle disturbance is effected.

How far these questions were known to me in the energy of discovery and delight (the same delight people later called jouissance?) is inevitably lost. But I now guess that I must have known at some level that this crystal, limpid simplicity did not infantilise. It never occurred to me to question, of course, where I got the idea of 'real' poetry from, or who 'I' was, and what status the 'I' of the poem had in relation to my 'I'. The poem might be subtly questioning assumptions about the solidity of 'I' and 'you', but the primal certainty of 'That's it' was consolidating. That we, the writer and myself, were both women, certainly did not occur to me, let alone that the term 'woman' was a category needing some investigation. There were 'men' and 'women' in the world just as certainly as 'I' and 'you'. Much later a colleague was collecting a gathering of quotations about the 'wind' of inspiration for a light-hearted lecture – Joyce's gross collic, Wordsworth's 'motions of the wind / Embodied in the mystery of words'. I suggested Christina Rossetti's poem but he had not heard of it. Now I think of that poem in the context of feminism and this produces further readings. It is a curiously proud yet self-effacing lyric about the masterful romantic idea of inspiration. Seen, but not heard, to tremble and bow down the head: what is happening to the woman's voice? How guardedly the wind of inspiration, prerogative of male poets, is considered. The tree, trembling in obedience to the wind, may be a root-bound Daphne subjected and unable to flee from Apollo's powerful lyre, but the poem is deeply sceptical of an authoritative relation between wind and lyre.

The excitement about Christina Rossetti's poems, however, was buried for easily twenty years. My resistance to feminist criticism lasted for about the same time.

I had forgotten Christina Rossetti so thoroughly that I asked a graduate student once why he was interested in editing the work of a minor poet.

During public examinations and throughout my undergraduate career no single poem by Christina Rossetti was put before us for close reading. No essays were set on her work. Or, if poems of hers were discussed, I forgot them, which is equally significant. It was as if she and real poetry had never been. Instead there was the effort of discussing Marvell ('The tough reasonableness beneath the lyric grace' (T.S. Eliot): Discuss) and finding an analytical strategy for looking at poetry. T.S. Eliot, I.A. Richards, William Empson, F.R. Leavis, these were the people I learned from. I am not setting up an antithesis between the male analysis of these critics and 'female' intuition. But what amazes me is the narrow understanding of what analysis was, and its extraordinary exclusiveness. I am even more amazed by our unquestioning acceptance of the institution of criticism, its canon and criteria.

We struggled with the Pelican *Guides*, half realising the contradictions of those curious volumes, with their preliminary chapters on 'Background' and subsequent essays on individual authors which never mentioned 'background' once. The Pelican *Guides* were then effecting their revolution in poetry criticism by insisting on what was conceived of as a lost tradition of intellect and cerebral power to be found in seventeenth-century poetry and an account of 'wit' as the play with paradox, ambiguity and logical complexity. The artificial category, 'the metaphysical poets', invented by Grierson, was consolidated. It was not for some years that I realised that the metaphysical poets did not call themselves this. This tradition was allied with an entirely discrepant neo-romantic belief in 'vividness', 'immediacy', 'intensity', 'range' (F.N. Lees on Hopkins, Pelican *Guide*, 6). I did not see this discrepancy at the time, probably because the seventeenth-century poets were assumed to be in possession of a 'unified sensibility' (an invention of T.S. Eliot's) in which feeling and thought were fused. And it was assumed we knew, and could distinguish, feeling from thought in a poem.

Above all, the *Guides* asserted the need for authoritative tradition as an ethical imperative, an élite tradition based on 'rigorous standards' (General Introduction): 'Which authors matter most?' 'Where does the strength of the period lie?' The confident judgmental assumptions behind the questions (you *had* to judge, you *had* to choose) dictate the form of the answers required.

Oddly, nineteenth-century poetry coincided with none of the criteria required, as the title of the sixth volume implies – *From Dickens to Hardy* (1958). The authors who 'mattered' most were the novelists, and another 'tradition' (but note the singular) to support them – a tradition which was entirely separate from the one to which the best poetry was supposed to belong – was invoked. It did not occur to me to ask how genuinely historical the tradition was, or how far it was an invention. Other people have looked at the elementary and depoliticised notions of culture and the tradition behind these choices, and at the covert political choices being made in disguise. A tradition guaranteed stability and authenticated one's choice of writer as if it were a pre-given matter which required no investigation. Leavis himself could be a very fine historical critic, but the Pelican *Guides* simplified his positions, as they simplified the account of poetic language explored by Empson and Richards. Novels in particular could always be redescribed in terms of universal values and ethical imperatives which did not move into the sphere of the social or engage with the questions of politics. At the very most, nineteenth-century novelists turned out to endorse Fabian socialism. If they did not, like the Brontës, they were thought of as passionate and *psychologically* wayward. This was, of course, a male-created tradition and consisted mainly of male authors. What is interesting is that Christina Rossetti, with the double disadvantage of being a woman and a Victorian poet, should have featured in this critical context. She did, and her work was actually discussed much more fully than that of Elizabeth Barrett Browning. But her poetry is described with an uneasiness I have only noticed recently.

She is frequently called 'Christina', and compared to her detriment with the 'wit' of Herbert and the force of Hopkins. But it is the uncertainty of the critical language and its collapse into a paucity of vocabulary which is interesting. It is subtly denigrating *praise* which is most striking. All the 'tough' criteria of 'wit', cerebral complexity and logical analysis are abandoned when she is discussed. I take repeated phrases from the work of the two sophisticated critics quoted below. Her work is found to be depressing but praised because it is 'simple

161

and modest'. The strenuous work on the nature of poetic language undertaken by I.A. Richards and Empson which, for all its aestheticised and excessive preoccupation with the trope of ambiguity, was supremely intelligent and impressive, seems to collapse. Nevertheless, both critics are trying very hard to be fair.

> Christina Rossetti (1830–94) is in some ways a more interesting and considerable poet than either [Dante Gabriel or William Morris]. Christina continues to attract the modern reader by the general *simplicity* and *delicacy* of her language ... by her *simplicity* ... she bears a resemblance to her American contemporary Emily Dickinson (1830–86) ... ambiguousness of effect disturbs but also rather oddly deepens her work ... (and there is a significance too in the narrowly missed failure or success of her poems) ... her *modest* attempts to write ... her *Poems for Children* contain too much talk of death and transience to be useful in the nursery.
>
> (E.D. Klingopulos, *Pelican Guide*, 6, pp. 88–9, emphasis added)

> It is significant that one finds oneself appraising her work in these *negative* terms ... an extensive reading of it is *depressing* ... *exquisite good taste* and spiritual *good manners* ... The distinctiveness and *limitation* of Christina Rossetti's talent ... the *shy reserve, tenderness* and *wistfulness* of the speaker are presented *simply* and *truthfully*, and our acceptance of her truthfulness is bound up with our recognition of her authentic speaking voice ... its *modest* acceptance of very *limited pretension* which makes it seem if not mawkish, a little *mièvre* ... If we pay Christina Rossetti the archaic compliment of calling her a *lady*, this will be understood to have *no implication of snobbery* ... *touchingly sincere* and disinterested ...
>
> (W.W. Robson, *Pelican Guide*, 6, pp. 364–7, emphasis added)

The snobbery referred to is social not sexual snobbery, as Robson makes clear when describing the 'embarrassing intimacy' of Mrs Browning. I do not offer these assessments to 'overturn' them in the interests of 'revaluing' Christina Rossetti (as Maud Ellmann has said, you only value something when you want to sell it). That would be to collude with the competitive techniques of male dressage operating in the work of so many critics, whether in the straight fights of Leavis or the Oedipal struggle of Bloom. Gubar and Gilbert in *Madwoman in the Attic* make a great mistake in reinstating the female tradition in terms of power.[1] What is important here is that Christina Rossetti can only be praised for qualities in which the 'tradition' is not really interested. Or is it? Simplicity, modesty, delicacy, good taste, good manners, shy reserve, tenderness, truthfulness, limited pretensions, touching sincerity, ladylikeness – all these epithets are in effect coercive. The magisterial 'we' of Robson's piece assumes a consensus from which no reader will dissent. This is what women, and women's poetry, should be like. Better modesty and simplicity than 'embarrassing intimacy'. The term 'simplicity' closes discussion rather than opens it. That something important might be going on in the 'simple' lyrics of Blake and Christina Rossetti was vaguely understood, but this criticism had no categories for dealing with 'simplicity'. Christina Rossetti, who as a violent child slashed her arm with scissors, who as an adult wrote *Goblin Market* (not discussed in the *Guide*), a poem so scandalous that it could only be read by children, does not consort easily with these descriptions. Looking back I consider that if intelligent male critics of the late 1950s could read her work so inattentively and with such expectations, how hard it must have been for women to read her work, and how hard it must have been for women trying to write poetry then. It certainly did not occur to us to ask such questions then. We accepted this, just as we accepted being told not to wear trousers in lectures.

I was taught with meticulous care and seriousness in a Department of English which had one very remarkable woman on its staff. Two-thirds of the students were women but it never occurred to us to consider why most of our teachers were men. This was the impercipient, apolitical time described in A.S. Byatt's novel, *Still Life* (1985). The scrupulous and thorough teaching we received was informed with Arnoldian values and an Arnoldian view of culture. We were being given something, the best that had been thought and said in the world, a life-giving tradition of thought and feeling and moral values which could somehow contribute to the sum of human goodness. And we ourselves would pass this on. It was a noble enterprise of high seriousness. Its strength was that the Leavisian assumptions were grafted on to an older syllabus with the tradition of literary history and philology behind it. I would never wish to have been in another context. (I'm glad I did not go to Oxbridge.) I still feel deeply disturbed when I read Terry Eagleton's demolition of English Studies in *Critical Theory*, for instance. That the category of literature and culture itself, which Foucault thinks of as appearing at the end of the eighteenth century, was a social construction, was not a conceivable possibility for us then. Raymond Williams's *Culture and Society* came out in 1958, the year of the sixth volume of the Pelican *Guide* which I have mentioned. That literature is all the more important for study just *because* it is a social construct, and must therefore be of critical importance in our history, is an argument I would not have been in possession of. Part of my enterprise in writing this piece is to see where feminist criticism can enable us to stand, both in relation to traditional criticism and to literary theory.

I am frequently asked why I teach 'theory' to students. I always do so with considerable hesitation. But my answer is partly that there are many theories, and that feminist criticism intensifies the questions we should be asking anyway. The questions of consciousness, ideology, history, language, raised in different theoretical debates, will not go away, just as their instigators, Marx, Freud and Nietszche, will not disappear. We have a commitment to our students to show as lucidly and responsibly as we can where debates in the subject are at. The historical movement from practical criticism to critical practice is one in which we and they are formatively involved and to withdraw from the effort of providing students with a framework for dealing with these problems is to disable us both. Founding texts by the authors I have mentioned should surely be discussed. I am convinced that it is possible to engage a range of students with debate. And that is the very reverse of giving them formulas to 'apply'. Our education system encourages the belief that only a minority of students can deal with concepts. Of course we are responsible if a 'weak' feminist student writes naïvely of patriarchy, but I wonder if this is not any less preferable (at least the notion of patriarchy has some historical base) to our own confident handling of that phantasm, 'the dissolution of sensibility'? All teaching is full of danger because of the power of the teacher, but it can nevertheless help to unbind one from the power of ideology. It is said that an education into concepts is dangerous because of the narrower range of reading undertaken by students now. Is it that narrow? And if so, is it not more necessary, rather than less, to have a framework to read in? *Lear*, Milton, the metaphysicals, George Eliot, isn't that canon as restricting as any? I read Dickens after taking my degree. We can recognise that questions of power enter into the teaching situation, but this is a way to liberate oneself from being controlled by them. That is why feminism needs to evolve a criticism which will recognise but not collude with a power relationship.

'That's it', came again many years later when I came across Christina Rossetti's 'Winter: my secret'. I was amazed by the coldness, almost frigidity of the poem's reserve and by its flagrant coquetry. 'I tell my secret? No indeed not I.' Once you have said there is a secret you have betrayed it. But what it may be is kept provocatively in abeyance throughout the poem. 'It' may be a secret passion, or no secret at all, the poet's virginity, which is paradoxically a hidden and an 'open' secret. 'I wear my mask for warmth.' The mask is a fragile protection which is both disguise and representation. The poem came to seem about a troubled negotiation with accounts of women's sexuality, the devious path of female identity which Freud thinks of as circuitous and mysterious. When 'That's it' came for the second time I was looking out from the fourteenth floor of a tower block, which housed the English Department, on to an informal path plotted by students across the path to the university. It looked like a hair-parting from the height I observed it. The alternative route seemed like the poem, which manoeuvres in narrow space, and the route one had to make through traditional criticism and feminist criticism as well.

When you have decided on a feminist reading, what then? I will pass over my reluctant response to feminist criticism, but this reluctance obviously shaped my approach. I shall write about successive readings of 'Winter Rain' for the rest of this essay, because it poses the problems I experienced more sharply than 'Winter: my secret'.

Winter Rain

Every valley drinks,
   Every dell and hollow:
Where the kind rain sinks and sinks,
   Green of Spring will follow.

Yet a lapse of weeks
   Buds will burst their edges,
Strip their wool-coats, glue-coats, streaks,
   In the woods and hedges;

Weave a bower of love
   For birds to meet each other,
Weave a canopy above
   Nest and egg and mother.

But for fattening rain
   We should have no flowers,
Never a bud or leaf again
   But for soaking showers;

Never a mated bird
   In the rocking tree-tops,
Never indeed a flock or herd
   To graze upon the lea-crops.

Lambs so woolly white,
   Sheep the sun-bright leas on,
They could have no grass to bite
   But for rain in season.

We should find no moss
   In the shadiest places,
Find no waving meadow grass
   Pied with broad-eyed daisies:

But miles of barren sand,
  With never a son or daughter,
Not a lily on the land,
  Or lily on the water.

To begin with, the poem does not have an overtly 'female' content. I
was dissatisfied with restricting myself to poems which could be
literalised as accounts of women's experience because this circumscribes
and isolates women as special cases, culturally and psychologically.
What was I permitted to say? It is significant that an oppressive sense
of what was 'allowed' hung over me. The sort of individualist feminist
criticism I knew then (Kate Millett) pointed to the ideological repression
of women expressed in female texts. Barbara Hardy had shaken me by
the scruff of the neck with Millett a few years before but I did not want
to resolve the poem into a sexual politics of this kind. It seemed to
lead me to rage and anger (though I reflect that a little of this would
have been useful in confronting my earlier education). It seemed to be
a 'vulgar' feminism, like vulgar Marxism. People were beginning to
describe women's writing in terms of its claims to an independent
tradition. Though I liked the work of Cora Kaplan and Dolores
Rosenblum I was tentative – too much so – about making these claims.
Like the cruder feminist individualism it seemed to make women
special cases of oppression. But if you do not take this route, how do
you prevent yourself from falling into a stodgy impartiality which is not
impartiality at all?

I read biography avidly, trying to find out what Christina Rossetti
read. If she belonged to a network of texts one could find one's way
back to a set of cultural relationships, relationships with some 'central'
discourse, which did not trap her into isolation. But in trying to do this
I discovered the extraordinary passionate and traumatic story of her
love for William Bell Scott and his casually brutal treatment of her,
which is proposed in Lona Moske Packer's biography. I noticed that
Geoffrey Grigson's review of the first volume of R.W. Crump's edition
(1979) of Rossetti's work in the *Times Literary Supplement* simply ignores
Packer's hypotheses. Did he know of them? He prefers a more
credible account of her life which is actually more tortuously ingenious.
Was I 'allowed' to deal with this agony, and if so, how? My feeling
that the biography was important did not seem to match with any form
I could write in.

It is interesting that the sense that I was able or 'permitted' to say
some things and not others remained as some undefined coercion even
in a feminist reading. I believed, and still believe, that one must talk
about a politics and simultaneously about language, but how? The
politics must be in the form and in the language, I decided, because

that frees one to think of structures which must belong to cultural patterns. And since poetry does not simply reproduce, but creates and becomes the materials of cultural forms themselves, this reciprocity seemed promising for the way out of the impasse which makes women the passive object of a special or marginalised experience. It makes the woman poet an agent.

'Winter Rain' is conjured out of rigorous repetition and the iteration of negations. '*Every valley* drinks, / *Every dell* and *hollow*: / Where the kind rain *sinks* and *sinks* . . .'. It is one of those pastoral lyrics so familiar in English writing that the form is virtually sourceless, speaking out of an idiom so generalised that it comes from everywhere and nowhere. The voice speaks from conventions which are both hidden and obvious. One meets this simultaneous sharing and not sharing in Christina Rossetti's poetry constantly. It is a scrupulous way of marking community with and dissociation from the pastoral tradition which is after all a male preserve. The action of 'fattening' rain appears to follow a conventional course, as it irrigates the concavities of dell and hollow, bursting buds, creating a natural environment for fertility, though the pregnant solidity of 'fattening' works oddly with the diffusing nature of rain. But then comes a systematic deviation into the denial of negatives – 'But for . . . But for . . . no . . . never . . . never . . . no . . . no . . . no . . . never . . . not.' Without rain the natural processes of birth and propagation would cease, the poem says in its 'simplicity'. The frightful matching sterility of land and water, which would not be water but desert, is the final negation. The simple statement of lack goes much further however, questioning expectations about the teleological necessity of recurrence and regularity. What is 'natural' when this is denied?

It seemed that much could be understood when I got to this point. If the teleological order and the 'natural' is being questioned, so implicitly is the cultural. If the 'natural' order which exists in interdependence with the teleological order turns out to be neither natural nor ordered, then a great deal has been said about the coercive force of accepted assumptions. The constant action of doubling, repetition, iteration and duplication seemed to me to create an intransigently restricting order which the poem disrupts by using the processes of order themselves. It was tempting to think in terms of Kristéva's antithesis between the semiotic and the symbolic. The subversive, semiotic freedom of 'fattening' rain, which keels over from the sheer physicality of organic growth to the idea of fattening for slaughter, is in opposition, perhaps, to the repressive abstract patterns of symbolic 'masculine' syntax and repetition. But I was not happy with this. The 'repressive' pattern, if it was that, was overwhelmingly dominant and seemed to be tested in its capacity to sustain itself by showing that it collapsed of itself. There seemed to be a play in and with pattern which made order both restricting *and enabling*. Thus the antithesis between semiotic and symbolic maintained by Kristéva was not sustained, in this poem at least.

The idea that an order could be restricting *and* enabling took me some way for I saw that one could regard the dominant Victorian poetics of expression in a parallel way that seemed both psychoanalytically and politically important. Victorian poetics (Keble is an obvious example) assumes that expression occurs when the barrier of the customary restraints of consciousness is broken. Emotion breaks out of the self into representation. But by the same token, though this is never consciously theorised, the barrier constitutes repression. Each needs, and is predicated on, the other. Though there are significant differences, this does not seem far away from Freud's account of repression as effecting a continual displacement and indeed, creation of energy. I did not wish to use Freud at that time because the two sets of theories don't converge in very important ways, but I am bolder now. We can bring the two theories together. After all, without Freud one would not conceptualise any form of repression. Victorian poetics could be seen as a paradigm for both sexual and political life. I saw that in playing so daringly with the barrier of the symbolic and in recognising the interdependence of expression and repression, Christina Rossetti was both confirming and questioning the limits of both.

Goblin Market, where the 'good' Lizzie smears the goblins' forbidden fruit on the face of the 'bad' Laura, who had been denied the fruit she once bought with a piece of herself, her own hair, took on a new meaning. That there is a market price for the glory of Laura's experience which is paid for with one's identity is one gross fact. But we are not asked to 'choose' between a bad and a good girl because there is in reality no *moral* opposition here. The play of desire and restriction, Laura and Lizzie, create one another and the play of opposition is enabling. But Christina Rossetti chooses to distort and intensify the opposition between Laura and Lizzie in this poem because she sees that the play of desire and repression is subjected to a fierce economic and ethical code in their world. The dripping fruit crushed against the faces of both girls, one resisting, one rejoicing, becomes both outrage and orgy, a deliberate demonstration that what is literally 'expressed' here can only be so in the context of violation, abuse, scatological fury and aggression. For a structural condition has been turned into a moral order. The morbid aspect of Victorian culture is in this poem, but, it seems to say, can these facts ever be 'neutral'?

This is something I felt I 'could' say. I took a lecture to America on the problems of full-frontal feminism and its preoccupation with content at the expense of language and form. Elaine Showalter rose in majestic disagreement. She argued that I was colluding with a central academic discourse which always assimilated women to men's concerns. I was too ready to show that Christina Rossetti was part of a dominant Victorian aesthetics of expression. I was not making claims for a feminine tradition. After a long argument I said, 'But *I* want to write poetry which men will read.' 'Ah', said Elaine. She was right to feel that I had not used the sanctions of feminist criticism powerfully. But there is a problem. What can be said about Christina Rossetti ought to be relevant to Tennyson, Browning and Hopkins.

Back again, I read more Kristéva, the French feminists, Derrida, the English translators of Lacan, Juliet Mitchell and Jacqueline Rose, *m/f*. I also read Bachelard in the hope that he might provide a new and more free way of writing which women could use to break out of conventional criticism. This is a telescoped account of reading which took place over a period. What I read sifted a series of questions. I did not read this in order to 'use' it, and often did not see the relevance of what I read for some time. This should make us beware of asking students to 'use' theory. In the end it was Christina Rossetti herself who helped, through the Preface to 'Monna Innominata'. Klingopulos reminds his readers in 1958 that Christina Rossetti there talks about the happy condition of Mrs Browning as against her own depressive art. However, he did not see that the Victorian euphemism for the spinster is to call her *unhappy* in contradistinction to the 'happy' married woman. In that Preface Christina Rossetti is boldly describing herself as an unmarried woman, i.e. an 'unhappy' spinster who writes of sexual as well as religious feeling under all the constraints of her society. Such poetry, she writes, must be 'less dignified' when it is written by a woman. So much for Robson's ladylike poetess and Elizabeth Barrett Browning's 'embarrassing intimacy'. If it was clear that Christina Rossetti was fully aware of her position as a woman poet, her boldness must make her readers as bold.

What could one do, then? Going back to 'Winter Rain', the dells and hollows where the generative principle of rain 'sinks and sinks' seemed more emphatically female declivities. I could never see what writing the female body was really about, whether literally or figuratively, but the sexuality of this and the bursting buds with their viscous gluey coats, seemed more insistent. Certainly the infinitely sinking rain could seem like the flow of the female body described by Madelaine Gagnon, but this seemed altogether too literal, and anyhow didn't collaborate with the logic of the poem. The poem rests upon dysymmetry, on the principle of subtraction, a world 'without'. Take one element, the flow of water, from the precarious hierarchical harmony of nest and egg and *mother*, mated birds, lambs and sheep, the protecting and the dependent, allow rain to 'sink and sink' *away*, and an empty world will follow as

169

inexorably as spring once followed winter. But the scepticism also
hovers round the idea of rain 'in season'. Rain out of season is as
devastating as none at all, leading equally to a sterile world all 'water'.
The cold strategy of denial begins to investigate itself further in the last
stanza.

The poem ends when the logic of denial, with its successive
hypotheses of a world of lack, supersedes all else, and the consequential
shifts become progressively enormous. The lack is total.

> But miles of barren sand,
>   With never a son or daughter.
> Not a lily on the land,
>   Or lily on the water.

I began to understand that the poem was about, not denial, not the
repressive withdrawal of the principle of fertility, but the logical
consequences of *seeing* the world in terms of lack and negation. That is
why 'Winter Rain' is in the subjunctive – 'But for' – to denote the
hypothetical, as so many of the poems are. Ultimately the 'barren sand'
of negation will not even produce the hierarchical order of 'sons and
daughters' which is founded on the principle of denial and upon which
it itself is founded. It will simply produce itself. That the definition of
lack might be the product of a masculine order – think of Derrida's
account of woman as 'non-identity, appearance, simulacrum' – is
nowhere to be found in the poem. That is one of its strengths. It is the
principle of negation which is important rather than its origin. But the
sudden appearance in the last stanza of 'sons and daughters', human
progeny and the taboos of sexual difference, prompts a reading which
pays attention to gender if only because of the traditional identity of lily
and virginity. Both sons and daughters are caught up in the principle
of negation. It differentiates at the same time as it includes them in its
anxieties. The world of lack is delicately and searchingly generalised.
It is grossly clumsy to literalise a reading in terms of the phallic lack of
Freud's subsequent Oedipal theory. But castration theory, defining both
sons and daughters as 'without', but giving the daughter no way to
surmount this, does help here. Part of the difficulty of writing this
piece has been to introduce these ideas in a way which is faithful to the
poem's lyric 'simplicity' and austerity. They are not there as literal
presences but as buried, subliminal *structures*. I hope that the poem's
bare, overwhelming understanding of emptiness overwhelms a facile
reading. I cannot sneak Freud and Lacan into a footnote, as I might in
a more conventional piece of criticism. Nor can I take it for granted
that everyone knows them. 'Lack' for some people indicates the notion

of the Oedipal 'without'. For some people it does not. I am reduced to this clumsy expedient by the need not to seem arcane. At the same time I run the risk of making these ideas literal presences in the poem.

The final deprivation, the last stanza, refuses a facile reading. The mirror image of the lily on the land, the lily on the water, is not an image of anything because the lily is only phantasmally conjured by its absence. There is a consummate shift of the male Narcissus myth here. Lilies grow on land and in water: they are also reflected in water. But here the absent lily faces the absent, illusory lily. The water is a mirror without a reflection, or a desert without a reflective surface. 'The woman does not exist', Lacan said. It follows that a nothing cannot be reflected and find an identity. The lily cannot be in love with itself or discover its being through self-reflection. But it also follows, as the poem pursues an inexorable logic, that the virginity of which the lily is a symbol may also be an illusory thing. It may cease to exist and cease to be necessary in another alternative order. After all, the strict reflective concordance and perfect equalisation arranged in the final stanza is fallacious. It is a representation in language of a condition which is not 'true'. And here the poem's virtuosity achieves another turn out of the negation it describes by following its own logic. If the lily of virginity is illusory, the double lily *has* been represented in language, even if paradoxically through the language of negation. The virginity of the double lily is a verbal artefact, just as the proposition that rain could be systematically absent from the economy of nature is a hypothetical fiction, the representation of an alternative world. It depends on a contract between poem and reader to sustain a logic which seems on the face of it contrary to experience. The deconstructive movement, however, opens up two further possibilities both of which 'follow', but which are antithetical to one another. One possibility is that if this world of intransigent negation, the 'non' or 'nom' of the father as the Lacanian pun has it, is an order constructed in language it must be possible to redefine, reconstrue and shift these rigid negations. It must be possible to construct another order of language through language even at the cost, or gain, of seeing all orders as constructs.

The beauty of the poem's logic is that it defines the world of 'non', not as a norm but as an aberrant artifice, deviating from what we know of experience. The entire absence of rain is not a norm, though it is thinkable. But, on the other hand, the second consequence of regarding the world of 'non' as an alternative world is in opposition to the first possibility I have described, and not so consoling. What is it alternative to? Is there an unalterable world beyond language from which the self-referring processes of words deviate at their cost? After all, we 'know' rain does not disappear. Is that unalterable world 'the bower of love'

171

described at the start of the poem? The bower of love, where birds 'meet each other', as the non-reflected lilies do not, is a seductive and enticing world of pastoral concord and security. But it is nonetheless fixed in repetitive cycles in which all things occur 'in season'. The pattern can never be changed. Or, as the pastoral convention of conscious artifice may denote, is this a fiction, too? The pastoral may simply be the reverse side of the order of 'non', an enclosed world on which the economy of negation is predicated. The *soaking, fattening rain*, the bitten grass, are curiously threatening. The poem's pursuit of the possibilities which 'follow' from its premises is so complex that I have had to resort to the clumsy forms of 'But', 'And yet', 'On the other hand', 'both . . . and . . .', in order to describe the shifting dialectic it both sustains and stands aloof from. There is both boundlessness and limit in this last stanza as it moves through self-created cycles of endless hope and despair, neither of which can be decisive. To have experimented so resiliently with these endless questions in such a fragile form by taking the idea of limit to the limit is remarkable. The poem seems to perform structurally what Derrida calls the 'operation' of the woman, or the idea of woman. The idea of woman is a function, not a content and disrupts because it suspends 'decidable oppositions', as this poem does. But we should not forget that there *is* a content to the decidable oppositions themselves, something that an abstract Derridean reading too often forgets.

A good many things worry me about this discussion. I did not want to simply dump the Lacanian idea of lack in the poem in an unhistorical way: the Lacanian idea is far more specific than anything in the poem. It can only be invoked as a marker. His and Derrida's are descriptive formulas which can make every poem the same. I do not like the idea of 'applying' theory to texts in some technological way, for the form in which theory and texts relate is subtle and indirect. But Lacan and Derrida seemed to illuminate the poem's questions. I do not think my early training in ambiguity could have got me here. My reading, I hope, is informed by, but does not 'apply' their work. But what I found fascinating was the poem's resistance to their very essentialist strategy and the integrity with which it considers the possibility of the coercive 'non'. The world of 'non' is intransigent and yet, conceivably, alterable. Christina Rossetti seems to go round behind Lacanian determinism. I would like to think further about Victorian patriarchy to embody this reading in history. All this must have repercussions for Christina Rossetti's religious poetry, but that is a discussion for somewhere else. Certainly it helps one to see the force of the coda to *Goblin Market*. Laura and Lizzie bury their experiences, which are transmitted in terms of an admonitory fable to their children. They are absorbed into a cultural order of marriage and the family which allows them to interpret their experiences by limiting them to the moral; they fall to one side of a decidable opposition.

Other worries concern language. Though it seems to me that the poem understands oppression in language very well, I do not want to settle for the politically dangerous notion of a female language which circumvents phallogocentrism by separatism. The strength of the poem is that it negotiates directly with the power of repressive language, using pastoral in a way which recognises that pastoral conventions can be both liberating and coercive. Again, for the first time in my criticism I have talked of deconstruction. It seems to me that wrongful Derridean readings revolve on their own axis round the perpetual abstract sameness of the nature of the sign, of absence and presence, just as the Lacanian postulates of lack can be abstracted. Christina Rossetti's opening up of endless and very particular interrogations is not like this at all. The poem has a deconstructive movement because it reveals contradictions by putting pressure on its own logic. It seems to me that 'real' Derridean readings are deeply inward. Because they must deal with particular complexities of contradiction in a particular way, the unique form in which questions are asked in any text must be controlled by 'the process of its own becoming', to think for a moment in the Hegelian terms to which deconstruction is heir. Perhaps my formative days in 'traditional' criticism, which I have often talked about with Gillian Beer, have persuaded me towards this reading. If so, so much the better. There is no need for a feminist deconstruction to collapse into sterile negations and abstractions. Derrida's thinking on the suspension of 'decidable opposition' is interesting for feminist criticism in repudiating power, but Derrida is so provocative and ingeniously evasive as a writer that I am not certain about this. His game with power reintroduces it.

I am still struggling with Kristéva's work on abjection and with new layers of reading, or changed readings, of 'Winter Rain'. Kristéva's exploration of abjection as 'the recognition of the fundamental *lack* of all being, meaning, language and desire',[2] as a constant dissolution and creation of limits which must therefore provoke a 'narcissistic crisis' because it disrupts the self-sufficient order of self-reflection, must bear upon this poem and those doubled but non-existent lilies. Her association of the incommensurable of abjection with religious constructions may well be a way into Christina Rossetti's religious poetry and back from that to the other poems. It is not proper to sever her religious poems from the rest of the work. Kristéva's association of abjection with 'the rite of impurity' deepens the cultural and psychological implications of defilement in *Goblin Market*, the pulped fruit smeared on the women's faces. And yet I am worried by Kristéva because the notion of abjection does without history. One would have to wonder about Victorian abjection, perhaps Carlyle's 'everlasting No' in *Sartor Resartus*, before exploring what relation her work might have to Christina Rossetti's work. The same worry pursues Derrida's cunning conceptualisation of woman in terms of disruption through suspension of decidable oppositions. And I still wonder if you can say this only if you are a man.

Where does the alternative hairline path lead now? It still seems to me that women's criticism has to think more deeply about language and politics. If we are in dialogue with a male discourse, this will be different in different historical periods, or patriarchy would be of the same order as the universals of traditional criticism. Voloshinov's account of language in terms of an ideological struggle for the sign in *Marxism and the Philosophy of Language* is surely suggestive for feminist criticism.[3] Its dialogic project can be extended into intertextual dialogue. The politics of Christina Rossetti's language would become far clearer if we read her against the work of other women poets – Landon, Hemans, Greenwell, Ingelow. The discourses of male-produced theology, the language of the social theories which clustered round Christina Rossetti's work with fallen women, the evolutionary discourse of Darwin and above all, the men she must have been perpetually in dialogue with, her brother and the Pre-Raphaelite brotherhood, all these would enable us to read her relation to Victorian ideology and culture. And this is also a way of rereading the relations of biography and culture.

Does this intertextual project look too much like 'ordinary' criticism? In that case, feminist criticism subsumes ordinary criticism, not the other way round, because ordinary criticism is too often blind to questions of gender. Does that mean that men will write feminist criticism? Yes. We can never become post-feminists. I began by saying that the idea of literature as a 'new' cultural construct was unknown to my early education, but that does not make it disappear. Literature, Laura Marcus said in conversation, seems to be the marked off area where the writer is both deeply and unconsciously coerced by the hardened forms and discourses he or she finds in experience and is strangely enabled to experiment with them and with language. The idea of experiment gets us out of the discourse of power because it suggests that experiment can be free from oppression. Feminist criticism can move freely among these experiments with hardened form on the understanding that its interest in gender must make it part of the experiment. It can put pressure on inflexible and petrifying assumptions and, whether they are unconsciously held or not, test out the conventions of criticism itself.

I have used the word coerce too much, but I do so unapologetically. My reading of Christina Rossetti makes me aware of the degree to which I have colluded with coercion. This diary form with its holiday from footnotes and references to friends is a way of expressing my tentativeness by escaping from conceptions of the legitimate form for literary essays. It also tries to escape from accepting the notion of criticism both as mastery and as disinterested discussion. One hidden censorship is a silent injunction against exploring a theory of emotions in reading and writing. Barthes's 'jouissance' was an attempt to reinstate and theorise a (masculine?) theory of pleasure. Women's criticism should take this further. Perhaps we need a gendered account of pleasure. One need not return to naïve expressive and psychological theories or to a doctrine of sincerity or to a simplified conception of the text and consciousness to do this. The task is infinitely complex. But in order to undertake it, it will be necessary to be bold – and probably un-'dignified'.

Notes

1. Sandra M. Gilbert and Susan Gubar, *The Madwoman in the Attic: The Woman Writer and the Nineteenth-century Literary Imagination* (New Haven: Yale University Press, 1979).
2. *Oxford Literary Review*, 5 (1982): 128.
3. V.N. Voloshinov, *Marxism and the Philosophy of Language* (Seminar Press, 1973; repr. Harvard University Press, 1986).

11 Intertextuality: Dante, Petrarch and Christina Rossetti*

ANTONY HARRISON

Many of the extracts in this book show an interest in intertextuality, if it is not always identified by that term. They trace the interconnections between Victorian women's poetry and contemporary texts or poetic traditions, to show either revisions, or inescapable influence. Harrison here takes Rossetti's intertextuality as his main theme, in a more rigorously theorised and detailed study of the *Monna Innominata* sonnet sequence, and its relations to the Petrarchian and Dantean traditions. The theorists he uses see intertextuality as a process going on in a purely textual world, whether historicised or not. Harrison differs by reading Rossetti's revisions of the tradition as relating also to social reality: an assumption basic to all the feminist critics who use intertextual comparisons. The same discourses that prevail in the texts construct social relations. Harrison is also able to draw on a theory of parody, to show how Rossetti's revisions of the love-sonnet work to critique the tradition. Here, his notion of the woman poet's relationship to an inimical tradition is more flexible than Homans's (Chapter 1), whose ideas (in another article) he attacks. Homans claims that the love-sonnet tradition, much like the Romantic tradition, casts the woman inescapably as the silent object of desire. But Harrison shows how Rossetti contests that position, insisting on copious speech before a final silence which works not against the woman poet, but against the 'bankrupt tradition' she writes in.

Thomas Sebeok has recently described the concept of intertextuality as 'Janus-faced', working 'as much prospectively as . . . in retrograde scape'. Extending Bakhtin's 'hardly precise formulation of heteroglossia, dialogism, and polyphony', Sebeok emphasizes the ways in which

---

* Reprinted from *Christina Rossetti in Context* (Chapel Hill and London: University of North Carolina Press, 1988), pp. 148–63.

'works of art – especially literature – are produced in response not to social reality but to previous works of art and the codes and conventions governing them'. For him the concept of intertextuality helps us to understand all that is most *ahistorical* about a work of art: to the degree that it is intertextual, a novel, poem, or film 'becomes distorted, opaque even, a darkly specular reflection of actuality – as, for instance, a myth. It becomes a lattice of signposts, regressing into, effectively, infinity, and thus capable of sustaining many alternative interpretations.'[1]

In opposition to Sebeok, Claus Uhlig perceives the intertextual dimensions of a literary work as a precise barometer of the text's self-conscious historicity:

> It is exactly in the intertext [as palimpsest] . . . that historically conditioned tensions come to the fore: tensions not only between calendar time and intraliterary time but also between the author's intention and the relative autonomy of a text, or between the old and the new in general. What in this way contradicts the obsolete aesthetic ideal of an organically structured work of art appears from the literary historian's point of view as a necessary consequence of that history within the text the palimpsest preserves. . . . Any text will the more inevitably take on the characteristics of a palimpsest the more openly it allows the voices of the dead to speak, thus . . . bringing about a consciousness of the presentness of the past.[2]

Such speculation brings Uhlig to the startling and problematic conclusion that many literary works, because of their deliberate intertextuality, concern themselves pre-eminently with their own histories or genealogies. 'It is doubtlessly true, and all the more so since the Romantic era', he insists, 'that the aging of poetic forms and genres constantly increases their self-consciousness as knowledge of their own historicity. Through this progressive self-reflection, whose sphere is intertextuality, literature is in the end transformed into metaliterature, mere references to its own history.'[3] The intriguing difference between the positions of Sebeok and Uhlig – for those who study the evolution of literary forms in their relations with cultural value systems, that is, with ideology – is that Sebeok assumes an absolutist view of history and Uhlig sustains a relational concept of history. Whereas Sebeok is what Hayden White would describe as an 'historicist', Uhlig is a 'radical relativist'.[4] Both critics agree, however, that self-consciously intertextual literary works usually have little concern with 'social reality'. As is evident in her intertextual uses of Dante, Christina Rossetti proves an exception to this rule and employs parodic reworkings of literary palimpsests, their forms and themes, precisely in order to present a critique of particular deficiencies and false values basic to the social reality of Victorian England.

Sebeok and Uhlig also agree that views of history and of the self in relation to history – especially our creations or works in relation to past works – are deeply ideological.[5] Yet the preoccupation with such relations might be said to have begun only in the nineteenth century. It was during the nineteenth century that 'the modern discipline of history first came fully into its own as a truly rigorous inquiry into the past'.[6] Ultimately, however, because of 'the very success of scientific history at reconstituting the past', the powerful awareness of the past itself became 'burdensome and intimidating . . . revealing – in Tennyson's metaphor – all the models that could not be remodeled'. In fact, the apocalyptic aims of the Romantic poets early in the century reflected 'the idea that history, simply by existing, exhausts possibilities, leaving its readers with a despairing sense of their own belatedness and impotence. And this despair in turn leads to anxious quests for novelty, to a hectic avant-gardism, and in the end to an inescapable *fin de siècle* ennui.'[7]

As self-appointed heirs of the Romantics, the Pre-Raphaelite poets, including Christina Rossetti, display in their works an extraordinary degree of historical self-consciousness. As we have seen, with Rossetti such historical self-awareness can be either elided or explicit, as is the case in the *Monna Innominata* sonnets. When Rossetti's work operates openly and directly in the sphere of literary historical relations – that is, of intertextuality – it becomes deliberately parodic in the full and true sense of the term. Moreover, when her poetry functions parodically it can simultaneously accomplish solipsistic, aestheticist effects on the one hand, and the aims of a cultural critique on the other.

Some especially useful theoretical discussion of parody has appeared in recent years in the writing of Roland Barthes, Gerard Genette, Michael Riffaterre, and Mikhail Bakhtin. But these theorists have done work that serves, finally, to marginalize, bracket, or in other ways delimit and deflate parody both as a literary genre (or subgenre) and as a medium for self-conscious ideological discourse. Linda Hutcheon's recent book, *A Theory of Parody*, however, largely succeeds in rehabilitating parody by cogently redefining it as a specific mode of discourse and by enlarging our notions of what constitutes parody and what literary parody can accomplish.[8] In doing so, she forcefully demonstrates the interrelations between parody and some central issues that emerge in recent semiotic, formalist, and new historical approaches to literature and literary theory.

According to Hutcheon,

a parodic text [is] defined as a formal synthesis, an incorporation of a backgrounded text into itself. But the textual doubling of parody (unlike pastiche, allusion, quotation, and so on) functions to mark difference. . . . [O]n a pragmatic level parody is not limited to producing a ridiculous effect (*para* as 'counter' or 'against'), but . . . the equally strong suggestion of complicity and accord (*para* as 'beside') allow[s] for an opening up of the range of parody.

(Hutcheon, p. 54)

Thus there exist 'both comic and serious types of parody'. Indeed, as Hutcheon points out, 'even in the nineteenth century, when the ridiculing definition of parody was most current . . . reverence was often perceived as underlying the intention of parody' (Hutcheon, p. 57). Further, parody 'is never a mode of parasitic symbiosis. On the formal level, it is always a paradoxical structure of contrasting synthesis, a kind of differential dependence of one text upon another.' Parody, moreover, can involve a whole ethos or set of conventions rather than a single text; paradoxically, 'parody's transgressions [or transvaluations of a text or a set of conventions] ultimately [are] authorized by the very norm it seeks to subvert. . . . In formal terms, it inscribes the mocked conventions onto itself thereby guaranteeing their continued existence.' But of course, 'this paradox of legalized though unofficial subversion . . . posits, as a prerequisite to its very existence, a certain aesthetic institutionalization which entails the acknowledgement of recognizable, stable forms and conventions' (Hutcheon, p. 75).

But the texts, conventions, traditions, or institutions encoded by an author in his or her parodic text often require a sophisticated reader to recognize them and to decode the text, that is, to perceive the work at hand as parodic and dialogic, as transcontextual and transvaluative. Most works thus understood are also perceived finally as avant-garde. They engage in a form of what Barthes termed 'double-directed' discourse, often 'rework[ing] those discourses whose weight has become tyrannical'. For Christina Rossetti, as well as her brother Dante Gabriel and A.C. Swinburne, one of the most important among such 'discourses' is found in the tradition of Dante.

Swinburne, who greatly admired the *Monna Innominata*, had since 1866 sent Christina Rossetti copies of nearly all his volumes of poetry.[9] In his poems and prose he had written copiously on the subject of literary inheritance and its influence on the poetic imagination. Many of his poems are richly and complexly intertextual and parodic (in Hutcheon's sense of the term). Such is the case with 'Ave Atque Vale', his Dantean elegy on the death of Charles Baudelaire (himself greatly influenced by Dante), and with his 'Prelude' to *Tristram of Lyonesse* (a volume Christina Rossetti described as 'a valued gift').[10] In the 'Prelude' he specifically alludes to Dante and Dante's career as emblematic of the poetic vocation and activity. As he is about to launch into his epic poem on the well-worn subject of the love between Tristram and Iseult, Swinburne, like Rossetti at the beginning of her *Monna Innominata*, is careful to place his imaginative enterprise in its full and proper historical context. In doing so he identifies himself with all great lover-poets, and specifically with Dante. Re-envisioning Dante's image of Tristram and Iseult that appears in the *Inferno*, Swinburne asserts that 'these my lovers', at the moment of their encounter with the poet,

> Saw Dante, saw God visible by pain,
> With lips that thundered and with feet that trod
> Before men's eyes incognisable God;
> Saw love and wrath and light and night and fire
> Live with one life and at one mouth respire.[11]

Commenting on this passage, Jerome McGann has elucidated Swinburne's point that, like every great poet, 'Dante created the world anew.... Therefore, Swinburne has been called to explain a fuller significance for Dante's own creation, just as Blake knew himself called to explain the "true" meaning of the Bible and Milton.'[12] At the end of his 'Prelude' Swinburne explains his own vocation, identifiable metaphorically as an intense and essential impulse, or 'heart'. He questions his motives for (and implicitly the value of) writing yet another grand love poem based upon the myth of Tristram and Iseult:

> So many and many of old have given my twain
> Love and live song and honey-hearted pain,
> Whose root is sweetness and whose fruit is sweet,
> So many and with such joy have tracked their feet,
> What should I do to follow? yet I too,
> I have the heart to follow, many or few
> Be the feet gone before me.[13]

Christina Rossetti invokes precisely this pattern of self-justification in her writing of the *Monna Innominata* sonnets, as her preface and epigraphs make clear. At work in her awareness of literary precedents (and in Swinburne's) is a phenomenon more complex than mere 'anxiety of influence' or the inescapable activity of interpretation (though both of those are involved in Rossetti's endeavors).

In her preface to the *Monna Innominata* Rossetti lays claim to an already intertextual tradition that her sonnets appropriate, extend and transvalue for her own particular historical moment. Discussing the nineteenth-century love lyric as the 'successor to the Petrarchan love lyric', Margaret Homans has acknowledged that 'women writers did not often choose to write romantic lyrics, for to do so was either to repeat the traditional quest plot, in linguistic drag, or to take up the position of the silent object [of desire] and attempt to speak from there'.[14] Rossetti, she insists, in the *Monna Innominata*

> provides an example of the challenges and pitfalls of the second of these strategies. In her self-consciously anti-Petrarchan sonnet sequence . . . she writes love lyrics from the position of the silent object in the complete awareness that she is attempting to reverse centuries of tradition when she does so, but in the end tradition writes her perhaps as much as she rewrites tradition.
>
> (Homans, p. 574)

A brief overview of the structure and the 'plot of desire' in Rossetti's sonnet sequence will help demonstrate some important oversights in Homans's critique, however, and will help elucidate the work's true historical relations and value.

The thematic structure of the *Monna Innominata* is at first difficult to discern, and once perceived, it includes a good deal of repetition and variation. However, like her brother's *House of Life*, the structure of this sequence echoes that of the Petrarchan sonnet itself.[15] Four discrete thematic units appear within this 'sonnet of sonnets', or macrosonnet.[16] These roughly correspond to the first and second quatrains of the octave within a Petrarchan sonnet and the two triplets of the sestet. The first sonnet of the series establishes the aesthetic context (sustained through all fourteen sonnets) identifying 'song' with 'love'; it also strikes the dominant thematic note for the first four sonnets – the desire for fulfillment of erotic passion. The first sonnet states the need for the beloved's physical presence. The second expresses a poignant wish to generate memories of the lovers' first meeting. The third acknowledges that, at present, perfect union between the lovers occurs only in the speaker's dreams. And in sonnet 4 the desires expressed in sonnets 1 and 2 and the fantasies of sonnet 3 are abruptly realized. The lovers are apparently together, their respective feelings of love for each other at first in open competition but finally yielding unity between them. Such union has been achieved, as far as the reader can tell, exclusively through the exercise of the poetic imagination, in an operation reminiscent of Keats's comparison of that faculty's workings to Adam's dream: 'He awoke and found it truth.'

The focus in the second quatrain of sonnets (5 through 8) is the role of God in the speaker's secular love relationship. In sonnet 5 (analogous to the first line of the macrosonnet's second quatrain) the speaker renounces the service proffered by her lover in favor of his granting it to God. This psychological turn occurs as abruptly as the realization of unity between the lovers in sonnet 4. Sonnet 6, however, tempers the renunciation that precedes it and reasserts the indissoluble unity of the lovers. It also asserts an absolute dependency of the speaker's love for her innominate earthly lover upon her love of God. The tension between earthly and religious devotions culminates in sonnet 7 with a vision of relief from this tension and a perfect union between the lovers 'as happy equals' in the afterlife. Sonnet 8 perplexingly reinforces the speaker's hope for such a union by prefacing a prayer for God's sanction of her earthly love with an elaborately sensualized rendition of the book of Esther.

In the first triplet of the macrosonnet's sestet (sonnets 9 through 11), the speaker now fully resigns herself to renouncing any earthly fulfillment of her love. Yet she retains hope for a preferable fulfillment in the afterlife. Sonnets 12 and 13 reassert the speaker's inexorable belief in her feelings of union with the beloved whether she renounces him in this world in favor of another woman (12) or God (13). Sonnet 14 reinforces the themes of renunciation and resignation but introduces a new emphasis on the speaker's melancholy awareness of mutability. Despite the dolorous tone of this sonnet, its extended implications for the macrosonnet's themes are salubrious, for without mutability, the wished-for heavenly reunion of the lovers could not take place. The sequence concludes with a description of the same 'longing . . . heart pent up forlorn' that began the sequence but which now, having explored possible routes for the release and fulfillment of its longing, adopts the silent pose of 'love that cannot sing again'.

With this overview of the *Monna Innominata*'s structure in mind, we can observe that the sequence self-consciously uses for experimental purposes the guise of an unrequited poet–lover and the tradition of song as a medium of release for such a figure. The sequence is an experiment in aesthetic and psychological exploration that also tests the boundaries of literary and religious traditions, especially as these appear to conflict and to intersect with each other. Optimistic about the power of song and imagination early in the sonnets, the speaker is apparently pessimistic by the end. Neither one alone nor both in combination have sufficed to relieve the speaker's pent-up longing heart or satisfy her passion, whether intended by the author to appear real, fictionalized, or a psychologically realized fiction. The reader can envision, through the aesthetic enterprise of the sequence, an author steeped in Dantean and Petrarchan tradition, the poetry of Keats and biblical texts, and the literature of confession and renunciation trying in verse to work out the problem of love. The origins of the author's Romantic endeavor and of the speaker's romantic expectations appear to include both literature and social reality because of the extent to which actual Victorian patterns of behavior in love (especially among the Pre-Raphaelites) were conditioned more radically than our own by literary paradigms. We are reminded of this fact by the focus in the symmetrical framing sonnets on 'song', on the value (or lack of it) of the poetic mode as a medium for filling 'love's capacity'.

For the Victorian 'poetess' who speaks in the sequence, however, the Petrarchan paradigm fails to yield satisfaction, exposing the social, moral, and spiritual inadequacies of the tradition itself and of her own historical moment. The sonnets conclude with her resignation to unfulfillment, with

> The longing of a heart pent up forlorn,
>   A silent heart whose silence loves and longs;
>   The silence of a heart which sang its songs
> While youth and beauty made a summer morn,
> Silence of love that cannot sing again.
>
> > (*Poems*, 2, p. 93)

Yet this voice has, of course, already sung, and done so eloquently, in a radical, avant-garde fashion. This conclusion to the *Monna Innominata* follows thirteen sonnets that powerfully and with unconventional assertiveness articulate a female poet–lover's commitment to her passion and her struggle to overcome all temptation to mere earthly fulfillments of love. The posture of silence she assumes at the end is, therefore, not one whereby the speaker simply relapses into the role of the silent object of desire, but one in which she deliberately defies that role as traditionally conceived, having not only renounced the typical patterns and expectations of experience found in ritual Petrarchan love lyrics, but having also instructed her traditionalist lover to yield to such conventions if he must: in sonnet 12 she unjealously 'commends' him to any woman with 'nobler grace, / And readier wit than mine'. In sonnet 4 she has asserted their equality: 'With separate "I" and "thou" free love has done, / For one is both and both are one in love'; and in sonnet 7 she envisions transcendent fulfillment of passion, when the two shall 'stand / As happy equals in the flowering land / Of love.' Rossetti thus subverts the post-Dantean values and expectations of her genre while defiantly resisting the conventional role of silent object and overturning the gender relations usually accepted in Petrarchan sonnet sequences.

Margaret Homans thus ignores at least two important implications of Rossetti's preface to the *Monna Innominata* that become increasingly significant as we read through this sequence of sonnets, which moves from desire to transient union with the beloved to the female speaker's renunciation of him in this world. The first implication is that, for Rossetti, Laura and Beatrice are 'resplendent with charms but . . . scant of attractiveness' precisely *because* they are silent objects of desire, powerless to respond to their lovers. When Rossetti gives the *donna innominata* a voice, she also gives her a *character* rather than the merely idealized 'charms' traditionally projected upon such female objects of desire. Rossetti's speaker subverts Petrarchan tradition, however, not only by becoming a personality and abjuring all expected courtly compliments from her beloved, but also by assuming the role of an equal (rather than a subordinate and powerless idol) in the relationship. Yet she goes further than this, taking full control of the relationship after sonnet 9; in order to preserve the integrity of her love, she repudiates all possibility of the sort of earthly fulfillment often desperately sought by male love poets after Petrarch. As a final gesture, she abjures even the literary form in which such fulfillment has been traditionally sought. Her sequence thus serves to expose the corrupt and fraudulent ideology the form itself has come to represent.

Such a strategy is made clearer still by the immediate historical context Rossetti invokes in her preface. She refers explicitly to the 'Great Poetess of our own day and nation' as a prospective writer of these sonnets had she 'only been unhappy instead of happy' in love. With this curious invocation Rossetti announces further parodic dimensions of her work, inviting the reader to compare and contrast her sonnets of renounced love with Elizabeth Barrett Browning's *Sonnets from the Portuguese,* which speak of fulfilled love and do so with inferior craft in more than thrice the number of poems.[17] Unlike Rossetti's sequence, Browning's surrenders entirely to tradition. As all readers of her sonnets are aware, Browning's speaker repeatedly embraces her subordinate role in the relationship with her beloved.

Accepting the traditional 'charms' and courtly compliments projected upon *donne innominate* (as well as ritual conventions such as the exchange of locks of hair in such relationships), Browning's speaker fully identifies with the tradition she employs. She thus lacks genuine character as an individual. Whereas Rossetti's speaker insists upon equality and refuses to be objectified as a 'charming' idol, Browning's implicitly adopts this conventional role by reciprocating the discourse of courtly compliment and embracing its economy of artifices, one that claims to worship women while disempowering them in praxis:

> I should not love withal, unless that thou
> Hadst set me an example, shown me how,
> When first thine earnest eyes with mine were crossed.[18]

Browning's emphasis upon her speaker's subordinate and protected position runs as a dominant motif throughout her sequence: 'Thou art more noble and like a king, / Thou canst prevail against my fears and fling / Thy purple round me' (Browning, p. 217). By further contrast with Rossetti's heroine, who loves 'God the most' – her love being such that 'I cannot love you if I love not Him' (*Poems*, 2, p. 89) – Browning's speaker, 'who looked for only God' but 'found *thee*', is content with her earthly lover and the baggage of conventional Petrarchan desires, expectations, and fulfillment that accompany him: 'I find thee; I am safe, and strong, and glad' (Browning, p. 220). Unlike Browning's poet–lover in another way, Rossetti's speaks characteristically in imperatives, ultimately renouncing all the modes of fulfillment and happiness to which traditional Petrarchan sonneteers aspire.

In this sense, once again, the intertextual qualities of Rossetti's poem function as a corrective to the lapsed Dantean tradition that she recovers by a process Jerome Bump has termed metalepsis; it is 'the attempt to establish priority over the precursor by being more true to the precursor's own sources of inspiration'.[19] Reconstituting and purifying the love-lyric tradition, whose most eminent practitioner, for Rossetti, was Dante, her speaker becomes, unlike Browning's complacent poetess, a genuine type of Beatrice leading her beloved to salvation and their relationship ultimately to a transcendent, rather than an earthly, level of fulfillment. At the same time, Rossetti – the poet behind the fictitious 'poetess' of the sonnet sequence – represents herself obliquely as a cultural critic whose special concern is with the presently corrupt relations, not only between men and women, but also between love and religion, especially as those relations are expressed in a particular artistic tradition.

Within the projected action of the sonnets themselves, however, any direct cultural criticism is elided. In repudiating the values of love as they are typically enacted in 'the world', the speaker attains an aestheticist and solipsistic distance from the amatory issues the sequence raises. The poems she generates succeed in the forceful expression of a yearning – indeed, a passion – for death, peace, and an amorphous but ideally fulfilling afterlife in 'the flowering land' where 'all is love'. At the same time, however, art itself (as the process of creation) demonstrably provides a psychological and imaginative space in which a kind of fulfillment – as redemption from intense, unsatisfied longings – takes place, even while it expresses and reinforces the desire for fulfillment. Describing a frustrated passion for the ideal in a sense achieves that ideal, for it is exclusively in the tension between longing and a vision of fulfillment that the ideal exists. And art gives that tension palpable form.

For Rossetti's speaker, as for Dante in Rossetti's own reading of him (and in that of other, more modern critics of Dante), art thus attains a unique primacy and autonomy. It becomes a mode of redemption, a simultaneously aesthetic, spiritual and emotional pursuit. As Franco Ferrucci explains,

Dante's genius lies in his deep-rooted conviction that heaven is attainable through a poetic masterpiece, and his profound faith rests upon the vast expressive possibilities that the Christian hereafter offers to his imagination. Spiritual evolution can never be separated from its representation. *To believe is to represent,* and vice versa; consequently, spiritual flowering cannot be separated from creative rebirth.[20]

In this sense, then, 'heaven' becomes the embodiment of an imaginative ideal in the real world and can be attained only in art.

In its complex relations with the text of the *Monna Innominata,* the literary genealogy that prefaces the poem illuminates the values, patterns of meaning, and origins of many poems by Christina Rossetti. The preceding analysis of the preface – as it bears upon the generalized action, the themes, and literary form of the poem – helps us also more fully to understand how Rossetti's poetry operates within its special Pre-Raphaelite contexts, as well as the larger contexts of formal and thematic developments in canonical Victorian poetry.

Because Christina Rossetti appears in her poetry to be an 'orthodox' devotee of both amatory and religious literary traditions that dominate the Victorian scene, her works are more fascinating than those of her brother or Swinburne or Morris, all of whose poems are often overtly subversive of accepted ideologies. Christina Rossetti's poems reflect an historically more complex set of cultural tensions than do the works of the other Pre-Raphaelites. Her works, in fact, simultaneously illustrate two of the three dominant post-Romantic directions in nineteenth-century literature for social, cultural and (ultimately) spiritual amelioration. The central direction, which Rossetti generally eschews in her poetry, is found in the realistic and topical, often openly didactic, literature of the Victorians, which can be seen as a reaction against the potential solipsism of the Romantics. Another direction is visible in the early literature of aestheticism, which (as it is fully realized in Pater and the decadents) accepts – indeed revels in – the solipsism so feared by the Romantic poets themselves. The final direction appears in the ascetic withdrawal advocated by participants in the Oxford Movement. While the aesthetes focus their attention on secular passions or empirical beauties and the religious writers focus on love of God, both groups ultimately move toward withdrawal and transcendence of the phenomenal world. In that sense the art of both is generally self-reflexive and self-sustaining, rather than mimetic or topical.

Christina Rossetti's poetry, as we have seen, combines characteristics visible in aesthetic as well as Tractarian poetry. It is in every sense

idealistic, has largely literary origins, and forcefully delineates
struggle between the ascetic and aesthetic alternatives while at
time synthesizing them. Yet the effect of such a synthesis in Rc
work is, finally, to distance her poetry from its immediate historical
contexts and by doing so – paradoxically, it would seem – to present a
forceful ideological critique of those contexts. Her work's focus on
broad cultural issues and traditions – religious, amatory, philosophical –
draws attention to the inadequacies, hypocrisies and false values of her
society as well as the literary work that has preceded her and that
proceeds around her.

In accomplishing this goal she finds her purest precursor in Dante.
Looking at Christina Rossetti's love poems, many of which either
explicitly or implicitly extend Dantean tradition, one might say about
the exemplary value of these traditions for Rossetti what she said about
the symbolic value of Beatrice for Dante: 'either [they] literally, or else
that occult something which [the poetry they produced] was employed
at once to express and to veil, must apparently have gone far to mold
[her] . . . ; to make [her] what [she] was, to withhold [her] from
becoming such as [she] became not'.[21] Ultimately, it is the Dantean
contexts for Rossetti's poetry that allow us to arrive at some holistic
view of her work, which seems, at the superficial level, to be divided
into secular and religious categories. Those contexts enable us, as well,
to understand the full and complex relations between Rossetti's project
as a writer and the work of the other Pre-Raphaelites on the one hand;
and, on the other, between her project and the directions and ideologies
of other major Victorian poets.

In the *Monna Innominata* Rossetti operates at a self-consciously
intertextual level, as we have seen. She succeeds in integrating not only
Dantean, but also troubadour, Petrarchan, and biblical tradition in a
fashion similar to that which Claude Lévi-Strauss originally defined as
bricolage. This method is common also in her brother's work (and that
of his subsequent imitators). Ron Bannerjee has described the results of
bricolage, for instance, in discussing T.S. Eliot's allusions in 'La Figlia che
piange' (1917) to D.G. Rossetti's 'The Blessed Damozel'. In Eliot's poem
'a new system of myths not only reorganizes the fragments of the
preceding system, but . . . the "ends" of that system become its "means".
. . . What looks like reorganization is also a process of transvaluation.'
Rossetti generated a purely aesthetic mythology that Eliot wished to
supersede with his own. But clearly such an effect is also accomplished
in Christina Rossetti's own uses of Dante. Although the effect of
bricolage in the *Monna Innominata* sonnets is different from that achieved
by Eliot and by Dante Rossetti, the method itself is certainly at work in
Christina Rossetti's poem. It involves

the ambivalence, indirection, synthesis of heterogeneous elements, the quality of myth embodying repetition. Multiple analogues are functional in the same way as exemplary universality of myth is. . . . Allusions serve as myths, not to control the poem, but to define its boundaries of suggestion.[22]

Thus, assembled in the *Monna Innominata* – along with direct allusions to Dante, to troubadour tradition, and to Petrarch – are biblical echoes, evocations of Shelleyan Platonism and of some eighteenth-century treatments of love (we are reminded powerfully here of Pope's *Eloisa*), and an atmosphere and language familiar from gothic and sentimental nineteenth-century fiction. Although the poem's most wrenching emotional effects may come simply from the speaker's personality and her final tone of loss and discouragement, the poem's total effect upon the reader results in large part from its yoking together of only partially compatible traditions, which it attempts simultaneously to revive, sustain and critique. Ultimately, the framework of literary allusions that surrounds the speaker reinforces her eclectic Victorian voice.

That voice seems intensely Victorian, in part because of the standard of taste implied by its ornamental but weighty literary *bricolage*, but also because of its sentimentality that depends upon the use of commonplace – especially religious – allusions, language and images. Such a procedure, though fairly rare in Rossetti's secular poetry, is typical in her devotional verse with its many subjectively employed biblical allusions, and it reflects a pervasive tendency in much Victorian art to use such images and diction as code words. This procedure dominates Rossetti's prose works, especially *Seek and Find* and *The Face of the Deep*, but it also characterizes the *Monna Innominata* sequence. In sonnet 6, for instance, the speaker describes herself as 'the sorriest sheep Christ shepherds with His crook'. Earlier, in sonnet 5, the speaker with a loose biblical allusion compares her love, which will extend from this life into the next, to 'the Jordan at his flood', which 'sweeps either shore'. And in sonnet 9, she alludes to the story of Jacob wrestling with God's angel (Genesis 3: 2). Transvaluing for spiritual purposes images that are at once economic and sexual, the speaker compares Jacob's struggle to the conflict within her between love of God and the passion she feels for her earthly beloved:

> . . . love may toil all night,
> But take at morning, wrestle till the break
>   Of day, but then wield power with God and man: –
>   So take I heart of grace as best I can
> Ready to spend and be spent for your sake.

(Poems, 2, p. 91)

Sonnet 11 provides us with an example of yet another peculiarly Victorian element of the *Monna Innominata* sequence: its free, almost reckless adaptation of the medieval traditions of poetry concerning obstacled love. Rossetti's female troubadour focuses upon her 'love and parting in exceeding pain / Of parting hopeless here to meet again, / Hopeless on earth, and heaven is out of view.' Yet her love 'foregoes you but to claim anew / Beyond this passage of the gate of death, / . . . at the judgment' (*Poems*, 2: 91–2). Rossetti's procedure here reflects a characteristic more specific to the Pre-Raphaelites than the general tendency among Victorian writers to take liberties with medieval values and tradition.[23] Dante Rossetti, Morris and Swinburne in their poems repeatedly project upon this tradition their own compulsions to sublimate sexual energies and redirect them as aesthetic or spiritual (often mystical) aspirations.[24] Just as Morris appropriates Malory and Froissart in his *Defence of Guenevere* volume, as Dante Rossetti exploits Dante for aesthetic effects and psychological backgrounds in much of his verse, and as Swinburne uses for his own purposes Romantic and various medieval literary sources and precedents, so in the *Monna Innominata* Christina Rossetti projects an imagined psychological resonance with troubadour and Dantean tradition. She is manifestly enamored of this special literary tradition, and the poet-speaker she depicts as born of it craves union with a fantasy lover. Yet the speaker finally feels compelled to sublimate the psychological reality of her love to religious aspirations that conflict with it; and she does so in a manner represented as true to the originary Dantean tradition, which is at once amatory, literary and religious.

Dante and his early successors were able, in their art, to build upon and enhance erotic impulses so as to translate them finally into all-pervading and all-encompassing spiritual passions. While Rossetti attempts to parody and thus recover the fundamental ideological values of that art, her brother, Morris and Swinburne generally allude to medieval tradition in order to flaunt or sublimate erotic impulses. In the latter case, the result can be either an unsatisfactory conflation of erotic and spiritual yearnings, or an ultimately unsuccessful attempt to redirect erotic passions in vaguely spiritual directions, or (more rarely) an ineffective and seemingly affected attempt to disguise *eros* as *agapē*. Because troubadour and Dantean cultural values are psychologically irrecoverable in Christina Rossetti's positivist and post-Romantic era, however, her own Victorian poet-lover's attempted reconstitution of Dantean tradition in the *Monna Innominata* is doomed to fail. She, too, appears merely to conflate the erotic and the spiritual, or to sublimate passion, or to place supreme value on an art that is generated by the insatiable 'craving heart'. But *her* failure constitutes *Rossetti's* avant-garde exposé of a spiritually bankrupt culture. Thus Rossetti's Dantean works, like her other amatory poems, function as a cultural critique, simultaneously idealizing and lamenting a lost age of spiritual opportunity and unified, rather than fragmented, sensibilities. These works, like love poems by the other Pre-Raphaelites, most often culminate in pathos and aestheticism, but for different reasons. Moreover, although the radical appropriation of literary tradition upon which Rossetti's poems depend for such effects is – like that strategy in the work of the other Pre-Raphaelites – virtually unique in her era, the resulting *mood* of her amatory poetry (and theirs) is in many respects typically Victorian.

The speaker's voice in the *Monna Innominata* sonnets would therefore have seemed comfortably familiar to Christina Rossetti's contemporary readers. In its spirit of melancholy resignation, it resembles the voices we find in Meredith's *Modern Love*, Dante Rossetti's *The House of Life*, and even Arnold's 'Marguerite' poems. The *Monna Innominata*, like these love poems, seems characteristically Victorian in its false starts, its equivocations, and its dominant tone of frustration. Ultimately Rossetti's sonnet sequence exposes its speaker's immobility in the quest for fulfillment and transcendence. Wandering between two worlds, she pursues an archaic, no longer functional set of ideals, to which she is, nonetheless, wholly committed. Thus, rather than shoring up the fragments of tradition against her ruin, the speaker's adherence to traditional ideologies and the poetic forms used to express them ensures her psychological ruin and finally her spiritual malaise. As a result, the poem reflects at a highly generalized level the Victorian poet's typical condition: torn between past ideals, primal (that is, universal) emotional, spiritual and intellectual needs, and modern scientific and social realities that subvert those ideals and threaten the satisfaction of those needs.

At this level the *Monna Innominata* may appear to be an historically inevitable poem. Yet Christina Rossetti differs significantly from most other important Victorian poets in the value system that underlies her work and belies the apparent similarities between her poetry and theirs. The others are perpetually questing for alternative ideals to those discovered in the traditional literature they most admired. The alternatives they generate, however, yield only partial fulfillment or the promise of it. For Arnold, religion and the literary culture associated with it in providing a sustaining system of beliefs and ideals must be replaced with a more monolithic 'culture', whose heart is poetry. For Tennyson – in a more limited, personal way – fame, the laureateship and the Victorian prophet's podium appear to have allowed some compensation for lost ideals. For Morris (and Ruskin), art and its power for social amelioration promised hope. And – more radically but in the same direction – for Dante Rossetti and for Swinburne, art and devotion to beauty itself became an ultimately melancholy substitute for the less limited (and limiting) spiritual and emotional values of the writers they viewed as their own precursors. More conservative, finally, than any of these writers, Christina Rossetti returned with fierce determination to the no longer functional religious and amatory ideals of her literary fathers, especially those of Dante.

Notes

1. SEBEOK, 'Enter Textuality', pp. 657–8.
2. UHLIG, 'Literature as Textual Palingenesis', p. 502.
3. Ibid., p. 503.
4. WHITE, 'Historical Pluralism', pp. 482–6.
5. On this topic in connection with nineteenth-century literary studies, see the recent work of Jerome J. McGann and Hayden White, as well as that of Marilyn Butler, Terry Eagleton, Fredric Jameson, and Jane Tompkins.
6. GILBERT, 'Female King', p. 866. Also see CULLER, *Victorian Mirror of History*, and DALE, *Victorian Critic and the Idea of History*.
7. GILBERT, 'Female King', p. 866.
8. HUTCHEON, *Theory of Parody*. Hereafter cited in the text as Hutcheon.
9. In a letter to his sister dated 7 September 1881, Dante Rossetti describes Swinburne's reaction to *A Pageant and Other Poems*, in which *Monna Innominata* first appeared: 'Swinburne's delight with the [volume] amounted to a dancing and screaming ecstasy' (DOUGHTY and WALL, *Letters of D.G. Rossetti*, 4: 1920). It is clear that Christina read Swinburne's poetry with some care. See *The Family Letters of Christina Georgina Rossetti*, ed. William Michael Rossetti (New York: Scribners, 1908), p. 120, and PACKER, *Christina Rossetti*, p. 353.
10. PACKER, *Christina Rossetti*, p. 353.
11. SWINBURNE, *Poems*, 4, p. 11.
12. McGANN, *Swinburne*, p. 140.
13. SWINBURNE, *Poems*, 4, p. 12.
14. HOMANS, '"Syllables of Velvet"', p. 574. Hereafter cited in the text as Homans.
15. For a similar argument regarding Dante Rossetti's sonnet sequence, *The House of Life*, see WILLIAM FREDEMAN's now classic discussion, 'Rossetti's "In Memoriam"'.
16. Hereafter I have adopted the 'macro' designation when discussing the structure of the sequence, as opposed to its thematic and psychological movements.
17. Joan Rees has convincingly demonstrated the superiority of Rossetti's craft in the *Monna Innominata*. REES insists that Rossetti exercises 'the utmost economy and simplicity of statement' in the sequence, while exhibiting 'tautness' and 'firm intellectual control' (*Poetry of Dante Gabriel Rossetti*, pp. 146–60).
18. BROWNING, *Poetical Works*, p. 217. Hereafter cited in the text as Browning.
19. See BUMP, 'Hopkins, Metalepsis, and the Metaphysicals'.
20. FERRUCCI, *Poetics of Disguise*, p. 121.

21. CHRISTINA ROSSETTI, 'Dante. The Poet Illustrated out of the Poem', p. 571.
22. BANNERJEE, 'Dante through the Looking Glass', p. 148.
23. For a full discussion of this topic, see GIROUARD, *Return to Camelot*.
24. For a comprehensive commentary on Swinburne's debt to this complex tradition, see HARRISON, *Swinburne's Medievalism*. For discussions of Morris and medieval romantic tradition, see SILVER, *Romance of William Morris*, and RIEDE, 'Morris, Modernism, and Romance'.

References

BANNERJEE, RON, 'Dante through the Looking Glass': Rossetti, Pound and Eliot', *Comparative Literature*, 24 (1972): 136–49.

BROWNING, ELIZABETH BARRETT, *The Poetical Works of Elizabeth Barrett Browning* (Boston: Houghton Mifflin, 1974).

BUMP, JEROME H. (ed.), *The Pre-Raphaelites* (New York: Modern Library, 1968).

BUTLER, MARILYN, 'Against Tradition: The Case for a Particularized Historical Method', *Historical Studies and Literary Criticism*, ed. Jerome J. McGann (Madison: University of Wisconsin Press, 1985), pp. 25–47.

CULLER, A. DWIGHT, *The Victorian Mirror of History* (New Haven: Yale University Press, 1985).

DALE, PETER ALLEN, *The Victorian Critic and the Idea of History: Carlyle, Arnold, Pater* (Cambridge, Mass.: Harvard University Press, 1977).

DOUGHTY, OSWALD, and JOHN R. WAHL (eds), *The Letters of D.G. Rossetti*, 4 vols (Oxford: Clarendon Press, 1967).

FERRUCCI, FRANCO, *The Poetics of Disguise*, trans. Ann Dunnigan (Ithaca: Cornell University Press, 1980).

FREDEMAN, WILLIAM, 'Rossetti's "In Memoriam": An Elegaic Reading of *The House of Life*', *Bulletin of the John Rylands Library*, 47 (1965): 298–341.

GILBERT, ELLIOT, 'The Female King: Tennyson's Arthurian Apocalypse', *PMLA (Publications of the Modern Language Association of America)*, 48 (1963): 863–78.

GIROUARD, MARK, *The Return to Camelot* (New Haven: Yale University Press, 1981).

HARRISON, ANTONY, *Swinburne's Medievalism: A Study in Victorian Love Poetry* (Baton Rouge: Louisiana State University Press, 1988).

HOMANS, MARGARET, '"Syllables of Velvet": Dickinson, Rossetti and the Rhetorics of Sexuality', *Feminist Studies*, 11 (1985): 569–93.

HUTCHEON, LINDA, *A Theory of Parody* (London: Methuen, 1985).

McGANN, JEROME J., *The Beauty of Inflections: Literary Investigations in Historical Method and Theory* (Oxford: Clarendon Press, 1985).

PACKER, LONA MOSK, *Christina Rossetti* (Berkeley: University of California Press, 1963).

REES, JOAN, *The Poetry of Dante Gabriel Rossetti: Modes of Self-Expression* (Cambridge: Cambridge University Press, 1981).

RIEDE, DAVID, 'Morris, Modernism, and Romance', *ELH*, 51 (1984): 85–106.

ROSSETTI, CHRISTINA, 'Dante. The Poet Illustrated out of the Poem', *The Century* (February 1884): 566–73.

SEBEOK, THOMAS, 'Enter Textuality: Echoes from the Extra-Terrestrial', *Poetics Today*, 6 (1985): 657–63.

SILVER, CAROLE, *The Romance of William Morris* (Athens: Ohio State University Press, 1982).

SWINBURNE, ALGERNON CHARLES, *The Poems of Algernon Charles Swinburne*, 6 vols (London: Chatto & Windus, 1904).

UHLIG, CLAUS, 'Literature as Textual Palingenesis: On Some Principles of Literary History', *New Literary History*, 16 (1985): 481–513.

WHITE, HAYDEN 'Historical Pluralism', *Critical Inquiry*, 12 (1986): 480–93.

12 'Men Sell Not Such in Any Town': Exchange in *Goblin Market**

TERRENCE HOLT

Holt presents his argument as mediating between the irreconcilable interpretations of Gilbert and Gubar, and Mermin (Chapters 8 and 9). To do so, he usefully points to an area of the poem that has been relatively neglected in the feminist concentration on Laura and Lizzie's relationship: the economic language of the 'market'. Using mainly Foucault and Lacan, he reads this 'market' as a system of inescapably phallogocentric power-relations. A close attention to the language of the poem allows him to demonstrate the failure of its attempt to separate the utopian world of the sisters, and the contaminating 'market' of the goblins. He therefore dismisses Mermin's conclusion as an impossibly utopian fantasy. He is nearer to Gilbert and Gubar in seeing male-centred systems of power and of representation as inescapable – but he points to the paradox of the evident *existence* of Rossetti's poetry, and prefers to see the poem as embodying a difficult and unresolved struggle to find a female voice. It may be, however, that Rossetti's use of language works in more subtle, parodic, or revisionary ways than he proposes – as Armstrong and Harrison suggest in the two previous extracts. We do not know by what devious strategies Lizzie acquired her 'penny'; and Laura's recovery of 'innocence' may be questioning taken-for-granted ideas about virginity, instead of being a hopeless attempt to deny them. Here Holt could be seen as imposing his theoretical framework on the poem, without letting it answer back on the same level.

Goblin Market has been read as a nursery-tale, as a portrait of a divided self, as a fantasy about sexuality, and, most recently, as a parable about sisterhood.[1] The emphasis in all of these readings has been on the goblins, and the issues of gender and sexuality they seem to represent,

---

* Reprinted from *Victorian Poetry*, 28 (1990): 51–67.

while the 'market' of the title has received little attention. A reading of the poem's economics, however, helps to resolve some of the issues that have troubled readings focusing on gender. Seen in terms of the economic, sexual, and linguistic exchange incorporated in it, the poem becomes a parable not only about gender relations, but about power relations as well.[2] *Goblin Market* attempts to imagine a position for women outside systems of power, but its language, which cannot escape from gender, undoes the attempt: the autonomy is an illusion.

In *The Madwoman in the Attic*, Sandra Gilbert and Susan Gubar observe that Christina Rossetti's *Goblin Market* has become a 'textual crux for feminist critics' (p. 566). Gilbert and Gubar themselves see in it a bitter renunciation of literature – of an art, they argue, that is (and perhaps can only be) male.[3] More recently, Dorothy Mermin has described *Goblin Market* as an assertion of women's literary power. The two readings seem impossibly opposed, suggesting that another, unacknowledged, force is at work within the text, a force that neither reading sees whole.

One such force within *Goblin Market* is economic. Economic language and metaphors, terms of finance and commerce ('buy', 'offer', 'merchant', 'stock', 'money', 'golden', 'precious', 'sell', 'fee', 'hawking', 'coin', 'rich', etc.) permeate the poem, which opens with an extended invitation to the market: 'Morning and evening / Maids heard the goblins cry: / "Come buy our orchard fruits, / Come buy, come buy".'[4] The phrase 'come buy' echoes throughout the poem, its iteration stressed by the description of it as the goblins' 'shrill repeated cry' (l. 89), their 'customary cry, / "Come buy, come buy", / With its iterated jingle / Of sugar-baited words' (ll. 231–4). Economic metaphors inhabit apparently innocent words: the cry is 'customary' because it solicits the custom of Lizzie and Laura; the words 'jingle' not only because of their iteration,[5] but because they evoke the jingle of coin (cf. ll. 452–3). That the goblins are costermongers, economic creatures as well as sexual ones, suggests that sexual and economic systems of relation may intersect in other ways as well.[6]

Despite the pervasiveness of the goblins' cry, however, the ostensible function of this discourse of the marketplace is to stress the difference between maidens and goblins. Exchange, *Goblin Market* claims, is the province of goblins, not of girls. Indeed, Lizzie and Laura seem to know instinctively that 'We must not look at goblin men, / We must not buy their fruits' (ll. 42–3). The market is dangerous to maids, who belong safely at home. This emphasis on difference is of course partly a matter of sexual difference. But this is not so much an interest in the prurient possibilities of difference as an attempt at keeping the sexes apart. A separation between maidens and goblins must be preserved, the poem warns, because commerce with goblins is dangerous to maids.

The goblins' glen is 'haunted' (l. 552), and has caused the death already of one maid (ll. 147–61). Lizzie's virtuous horror of the place (ll. 242–52) alludes to a nameless threat, but her delicate evasion only pretends to conceal the obvious: the threat is the proverbial fate worse than death.

The sexual threat in the glen touches as well on another concern in *Goblin Market*, the place of women in the literary world. The glen echoes with a literary tradition that has used women as sexual scapegoats. The 'bowers' (l. 151) from which these fruits are plucked parody a similar snare in Spenser, the Bower of Bliss; Laura's reaction to this low, swampy place (ll. 226–7) suggests its affinity with the Slough of Despond in *The Pilgrim's Progress*.[7] A woman who enters the glen, especially a woman writer, places herself in a historical context that assigns her a negative value on the literary exchange.

A difference between maidens and goblins must be preserved, furthermore, because commerce with the goblins is also potentially infectious: the threat in the goblins' glen is not only that one may be attacked by them, but that one may become like them. Their victims become as 'restless' (l. 53) as the brook that whispers there, a restlessness like the 'Helter skelter, hurry skurry' (l. 344) activity that typifies the goblins. Lizzie, counseling her sister to keep away, assumes that separation can enforce difference, an assumption echoed in the two passages that introduce us to the sisters' home.

Home in *Goblin Market* seems the opposite of the goblins' glen, isolated from the world of commerce. The first scene in the home (ll. 184–98) stresses the sisters' isolation, in implicit contrast to the goblins' prolific trade. The home is also a scene of busy industry, wherein the sisters produce healthful foods independently of the marketplace, foods that differ pointedly from the goblins' exotic fruits:

> Early in the morning
> When the first cock crowed his warning,
> Neat like bees, as sweet and busy,
> Laura rose with Lizzie:
> Fetched in honey, milked the cows,
> Aired and set to rights the house,
> Kneaded cakes of whitest wheat,
> Cakes for dainty mouths to eat,
> Next churned butter, whipped up cream,
> Fed their poultry, sat and sewed;
> Talked as modest maidens should:
> Lizzie with an open heart,
> Laura in an absent dream,
> One content, one sick in part;

One warbling for the mere bright day's delight,
One longing for the night.

(ll. 199–214)

The sisters produce foods for their own consumption, enacting on an economic level the hermeticism of their domestic scene. The description of the sisters as they set to work compares them to bees, and the simile is peculiarly apt: they are bee-like not only in the quiet hum of their industry, but especially in their self-sufficiency, producing with their own labor the food that sustains them.

The sisters themselves glean from nature the raw materials of food they produce at home, and have no need to resort to the market to trade for someone else's wares. By contrast, the goblins' wares may not even have been, originally, their own. Lizzie's question about their fruit – 'Who knows upon what soil they fed / Their hungry thirsty roots?' (ll. 44–5) – questions the root-origins of those fruits; the goblins have the look of middlemen, and their fruits, coming from a tropic distance, seem far from their native soil. This goblin capital is thus doubly alienated, an alienation that makes the sisters' apparently uncomplicated and direct nourishment by the land yet another sign of their difference from the commercial goblins.

The repeated journeyings back and forth between market and home make this difference literal, defining a physical distance between them. The two are separated by an extensive waste (l. 325), a steep bank (l. 227), and a gate (l. 141). The goblins themselves stress the difference between the two places in their conversation with Lizzie, who wants to take some of their fruit back to succor her dying sister: 'Such fruits as these / No man can carry; / Half their bloom would fly' (ll. 375–7), they tell her. Indeed, the failure of the 'kernel-stone' to grow goblin-fruit at the sisters' home (ll. 281–5) reinforces their message. The two places belong to different biological (and moral) orders, a difference that, despite Laura's despair, is ultimately consoling: if that kernel had grown, what havoc might its fruit have wrought in the sisters' domestic haven?

But the repeated distinctions between the glen and the home, which seem intended to assert the sisters' independence from goblin economics, are not as absolute as they seem. The home is inescapably involved in economics – as the word's Greek root, *oikonomia* ('management of a household'), suggests. The domestic is historically a scene of economic exploitation, prison and workhouse as much as haven.[8] *Goblin Market* expresses the potential involvement of the home in exchange in part by the very strength of its attempt to evade such involvement.[9]

The insistence on the separation between the two realms cannot

197

conceal the home's contamination by exchange. Even in our first view of it, Laura already keeps house in an 'absent dream', 'sick in part' and 'longing for the night' (ll. 211–14). She only seems like a modest maiden; inside, the goblin's poison is working in her veins. The honey they gather is tainted: it has appeared already in the poem, literally in a goblin's mouth. 'In tones as smooth as honey' (l. 108), the goblins hawk their wares to the sisters. The honey not only sustains the home but is at the same time an inducement to go outside it, to partake in the system of exchange that invades and undoes that world.

Another sign of that undoing is one of the more peculiar rhetorical features of the poem, the use of parenthesis.[10] The parenthetical phrase '(Men sell not such in any town)' is, like the goblins' 'come buy', a characteristic iteration, characteristic not of the goblins, but of the poem itself. As a figure, parenthesis tropes the attempt of the poem to bracket off the sisters from the surrounding world of exchange. But this parenthesis seems to exempt 'men' from the goblins' world of exchange. The apparent oddness of this claim reminds us that parenthesis, rather than existing outside of the discourse it interrupts, speaks (as in the dramatic convention of the aside)[11] to the heart of the matter. The bracketing off of a parenthetical phrase does not exclude it, so much as clear for it a privileged space. The rhetorical form of parenthesis, even as it figures the bracketing off of the sisters from the dangers of the marketplace, also points to the paradox undermining that strategy: we know that in terms of rhetoric what we seem to set aside is actually not separate from, but centrally involved in, the discourse it interrupts.

The content of this particular parenthesis, '(Men sell not such in any town)', by exempting men while neglecting the women we would expect to find exempted, suggests another problem. The claim that 'men sell not' seems to distract us from the possibility that women might be involved in exchange. The phrase appears twice: first when the poetic speaker describes the goblins in the act of laying out their wares (ll. 97–104), and second when Laura repeats the description to her children (ll. 552–6). Each time, the speaker and Laura lay great stress on the allure of the fruit, enticing their audiences – Lizzie or us – to come and participate either (as buyer) in the goblins' market or (as reader) in *Goblin Market*.[12] The poem raises its seemingly irrelevant question as to what men do or do not sell at just those moments when the sisters' separation from the world of marketing threatens to collapse.

Human (not goblin) men are invoked here, introducing *ad hoc* a 'real' set of distinctions between men and women, because the fantastic structure of domestic maiden and merchant goblin threatens to break down. But instead of obfuscating the question of who is involved in the market and who is not, the introduction of 'men' only reveals the goblins as scapegoats for the sisters' involvement in exchange. The mention of human men reminds us that the opposition between maidens and goblins is an artificial one, that the goblins are literary constructs, and it begs the question of their function: either to stand for men in a transparent allegory, or to stand for someone else. But 'men sell not', and the only someone else remaining is the sisters themselves. This brings us to a recognition of the specular relationship between community and scapegoat, projector and projection, sister and 'queer brother'.

Strategies of exclusion elsewhere in the poem tend to follow this same self-defeating logic, by which excluded material returns to the domestic fold in the inevitable return of the repressed. Laura's fall and redemption is paradigmatic: intended to assert the sisters' essential difference from the goblins, it leads instead to a collapse of distinctions. Although Laura wants what the goblins have to sell, she cannot buy it, precisely because of her difference from them. The sisters' domestic retreat is distinguished from the goblins' world of exchange by the reiterated fact that their retreat has no money. Laura tells the goblins:

> Good folk, I have no coin;
> To take were to purloin:
> I have no copper in my purse,
> I have no silver either,
> And all my gold is on the furze
> That shakes in windy weather.

(ll. 116–20)

Laura's paradise of unalienated labor has no need for money, and no means of getting it. But her attraction to the world of exchange, her powerlessness within it, and most of all the nature of the exchange she makes there suggest that her lack of a coin stands for fears that what a woman really lacks is a privileged term of gender.

The goblins' response puts this essentialist logic into motion, equating her body with her value within a gendered system of exchange. Laura does have gold to exchange: '"You have much gold upon your head", / They answered all together: / "Buy from us with a golden curl"' (ll. 123–5). The clipping of her lock, the crucial act in the drama of exchange in the poem, is sexually problematic. As the allusion to Pope hints,[13] and what follows seems to confirm, the scene is in many ways a rape. But any attempt to read it in this way must take into account Laura's complicity: Laura enters into this exchange with her eyes literally wide open (ll. 50–4). The similarity of the goblin feast to a rape disguises something worse. Especially in its erotically charged context, the shearing of something long from a woman's body is powerfully suggestive of castration.[14]

Such a reading is complicated, however, by an equally crucial paradox. Although Laura seems to castrate herself as the condition of entering into intercourse with the goblins, this act only confirms her in a condition already hers. She has already told them that she has 'no coin', that her 'purse' is empty (ll. 116, 118). Moreover, she has been described from her first appearance in terms of her desire for the goblins' fruit, her felt lack of what those 'fruit globes fair or red' (l. 128) represent. The goblins' bargain is a cheat, requiring that she give up precisely what she desires. Worse, in figuring women as castrated men, the gesture denies the essential difference between maidens and men. Worst of all, in shearing her own lock, Laura collaborates in this construction of her within a male order.

The implications of the sisters' construction within a phallocentric conception of gender are fended off by projecting those implications onto the goblins. As half-animal, half-human monsters, the goblins displace the burden of anatomical deformity. Each 'merchant man' possesses an animal attribute – cat's face, tail, rat's pace, snail's foot (ll. 71–6). In differing so strangely from their essential, human form, they seem to possess no integrity of body or of character. Varying not only from each other, but from themselves – 'Leering at each other, / Brother with queer brother; / Signalling each other, / Brother with sly brother' (ll. 93–6) – the goblins are marked off from themselves. The iterated 'brothers' are estranged by the intervening modifiers, and the modifiers themselves, 'queer' and 'sly', add to the goblins' duplicity. The sisters suffer no such self-division: their sameness is emphasized both by the description of them (ll. 184–90), and by the contrast to the goblins' unruly variety.

But this attempt to reverse the traditional hierarchies of sexual privilege also fails. The sisters' saving sameness is characterized in figures that culminate in 'wands of ivory . . . for awful kings' (ll. 190–1). The sisters, too, differ from their essential qualities of femininity and sameness. The 'wands' are not only phallic, but also 'tipped with gold': value and the phallic coincide, repeating the pervasive assumption that whatever the goblins have is worth having. Worse, these wands are *'for* awful kings'. The sisters, even in the heart of their sanctuary, are figuratively in service of a male system of power. Rather than reversing traditional hierarchies, the figurative language restates them.

There are other attempts to reverse traditional valuations of male and female in other ways as well, most notably by figuring the goblins as parasitical users of language, associated with mimicry, mockery, and theft.[15] 'One parrot-voiced and jolly / Cried "Pretty Goblin" still for "Pretty Polly"' (ll. 112–13): the substitution of 'Goblin' for 'Polly' is typical, as a goblin displaces a woman as the one whose speech is supplementary to an original voice. 'Chuckling, clapping, crowing, /

Clucking and gobbling' (ll. 334–5), the goblins approach Lizzie 'Chattering like magpies' (l. 345), thieves not only of shiny objects (such as a maiden's penny) but of speech itself.[16] Their theft of speech is not only parasitic but deficient: their stolen speech is merely animal noise, 'Barking, mewing, hissing, mocking' (l. 402), meaningless parody that in its half-animal departure from sense echoes the goblins' bodily difference from the sisters' physical integrity.

But this attempt to ascribe to the goblins the deficiency traditionally associated both with women's bodies and with women's writing succumbs to the same internal contradictions that thwart other such attempts in the poem. Through their mockeries, the goblins succeed in compromising the very bodily integrity the sisters must preserve. At the climax of their violence against Lizzie, they 'Scratched her, pinched her black as ink, / Kicked and knocked her, / Mauled and mocked her, /Lizzie uttered not a word' (ll. 427–30). The lines associate goblin sexual violence with writing, and although it attempts to render that writing deficient, claiming that the goblins fail in their assault on her virginity, the imagery of ink contradicts the claim: Lizzie leaves the market marked by goblin pens. Lizzie's stained, disheveled appearance as she leaves the market confirms what the poem has already told us when the goblins 'Twitched her hair out by the roots' (l. 404).

As if to dispel the implications of this loss, the raucous goblins disappear 'without a sound' (l. 445), taking on the obdurate silence that has been Lizzie's only defense. Here, again, the poem differs with itself: if Lizzie's silence is her strength, to silence the goblins strengthens them; and if unspotted virtue is what such silence is supposed to buy, Lizzie's traffic with the goblins has hardly been the sharp trading the poem goes on to declare it.

The malign influence of the goblins' fruit follows the same vexed logic of projection. 'In an absent dream . . . sick in part', and 'longing', Laura shows all the symptoms of the disease of sexuality that the poem has attempted to make the goblins' problem. Blaming it on the goblins makes Laura's problem something external, not (as one might fear) something essentially and inescapably female: this is only *a* curse, not *the* curse. But such essentialist fears about gender resist repression in *Goblin Market*: Laura's illness goes deep, and its effect is pervasive. 'Gone deaf and blind' (l. 259), she sinks farther from any proficiency with language, becoming capable only of watching 'in vain / In sullen silence of exceeding pain' (ll. 270–1). Unlike Lizzie's heroic silence in the face of the goblins' assault, Laura's silence signifies her weakness: 'Her tree of life drooped from the root: / She said not one word in her heart's sore ache' (ll. 260–1). She 'dwindles' (l. 278) into a comparison with the waning moon, another emblem of changefulness traditionally associated with women.

As the similarity of Lizzie's tactics of silence to Laura's symptom of silence suggests, and the identity of the means of Laura's fall and of her deliverance reveals, the magic used to counter the goblins is the same as the goblin magic itself.[17] Magic is traditionally a practice of fetishism, and the magic in *Goblin Market*, with its stress on deracinated fruits and uprooted hair, is no different.[18] The most important fetish that the sisters enlist in their commerce with the goblins is the penny that Lizzie takes to purchase Laura's salvation. Arming Lizzie with a coin is for the poem an act of apotropaeia, but the attempt is foredoomed because the coin, once used to supplement an assumed deficiency, represents a tacit acceptance of that assumption.[19]

Lizzie needs the coin to fill the void that might otherwise ordain the sisters' powerlessness, but her possession of that coin transgresses the economic logic that divides the world of *Goblin Market* into goblin and maiden, have and have-not. Unlike Laura, Lizzie is not penniless. She 'put[s] a silver penny in her purse' (l. 324) and goes off to save Laura. In light of Laura's poverty, Lizzie's access to cash here is so unproblematic that it begs the question of how she came by the coin. Their only gold, we know, is 'furze' (l. 120) (which the *OED* tells us is of no economic value), and everything else we have learned about them confirms them in their innocence of exchange, not only their pennilessness but their complete lack of anything (beside their bodies) that they might convert to coin. The very self-sufficiency of their *oikonomia* makes that penny a wildly unlikely object for Lizzie to produce at this moment.

So has Lizzie, too, sold herself in the market? Of course she has: by figuring the sisters' only exchangeable goods as their bodies, the poem makes that penny nothing but a sign of sexual experience. The kind of freedom from exchange that the poem has attempted to imagine for these sisters is impossible, whether we look to the historical context within which *Goblin Market* was composed, or within the poem itself, where so many disturbing traces of goblin activity appear in the heart of its ostensibly excluded zones. The penny appears in Lizzie's hands as yet another sign of an inescapable taint, an original guilt as well as an originary lack. Moreover, that it can only magically supply her with a penny confirms that she can not really have one, and tacitly accepts and asserts the goblins' valorization (which is actually a disvaluation) of women's bodies, a valorization predicated on women's lack of these arbitrary symbols of power.

Another issue vexing Lizzie's use of the penny is that exchange also functions in *Goblin Market* as a kind of scription, in which attempts at fixing distinctions, at determining meaning or value, unleash instead a runaway, inflationary spiral of desire.[20] As Laura eats, more and more fruit does not satisfy. 'She sucked and sucked and sucked the more'

(l. 134), but her hunger only sharpens. As her disease grows, it fixes on no object of desire; the signifying elements of her exchange do not arrive at any final referent: they only iterate, and Laura is left with 'emptied rinds' (l. 137), dreaming

> of melons, as a traveller sees
> False waves in desert drouth
> With shade of leaf-crowned trees,
> And burns the thirstier in the sandful breeze.
>
> (ll. 289–92)

The iteration of empty signs strikes no root into the real, and leaves Laura finally a victim of mirages, seeing only 'false waves' repeating the iterative structure of signification. These lines seem to represent the dead end of Laura's descent: from here on until her miraculous cure, she appears only in terms of what she does not, will not, or can not do (ll. 293–8, 309, 320–1). No wonder the thing she wants will not cloy with use: its uses her more than she uses it; her inscription within desire seems to render her incapable of activity in the world of things, and a victim – not the master – of the world of signs.

Implicit in Laura's deficiency is a belief that men – goblin or human – are empowered; just as that assumption of deficiency disvalues women's bodies, it values men's. The central figure for value in *Goblin Market* is actually not the penny, but what it buys – the goblins' fruit, the object of Laura's desire. The fruit is not only the goblins' property, it is the prop of their power within exchange, the sign of their construction as male, putative possessors of both the phallus and power. The identification between power and the phallic goes beyond the goblins' mastery over Laura, or Lizzie's problematic possession of that penny. As Lizzie resists the goblin onslaught, she appears

> Like a beacon left alone
> In a hoary roaring sea
> Sending up a golden fire, –
> Like a fruit-crowned orange-tree
> Sore beset by wasp and bee, –
> Like a royal virgin town
> Topped with gilded dome and spire
> Close beleaguered by a fleet
> Mad to tug her standard down.
>
> (ll. 412–21)

Laura, too, as the cure works in her, is described as a 'watch-tower', a 'mast', a 'tree', even a 'foam-topped waterspout'. When the sisters

achieve power, these figures for triumph retain their goblin trait, calling
into question their function as figures of a total victory for women. The
fantasy collapses, as if under its own weight: the watch-tower is
shattered by an earthquake (ll. 513–15), the mast struck by lightning
(l. 516), the tree uprooted (l. 517), and the waterspout 'cast down
headlong' (l. 520). And to the extent that these images repeat the heroic
images of Lizzie's resistance, Laura's fall is the collapse of Lizzie's
power as well.

Mastery of language and literature seems to compensate the women
for their powerlessness in other realms. After Lizzie's triumph, as she
runs back to her sister, she 'heard her penny jingle / Bouncing in her
purse, / Its bounce was music to her ear' (ll. 452–4). She gets back her
penny, compensating her loss of all that penny stands for. Its jingle is
similarly consoling: it appropriates the 'iterated jingle' of the goblins'
cry. As the poem moves toward its conclusion, music, song and poetry
burst forth from Lizzie and Laura. Laura in particular is compensated
for her former powerlessness within language: her 'sullen silence of
exceeding pain' (l. 271) is redeemed as she becomes the chief user of
language in the closing lines of the poem. The ending of the poem, in
which Laura appears as a story-teller, confirms this reassuring control.
Just as the goblins call the sisters at the beginning of the poem, Laura
in its closing lines calls another audience to come to *Goblin Market*:

> Laura would call the little ones
> And tell them of her early prime,
> Those pleasant days long gone
> Of not-returning time:
> Would talk about the haunted glen,
> The wicked, quaint fruit-merchant men,
> Their fruits like honey to the throat
> But poison in the blood;
> (Men sell not such in any town:).
>
> (ll. 548–56)

Within her retelling of the tale she must repeat the goblins' fruit-cry:
thus Laura expropriates the goblins' mercantile cry, seeming to
recapture the honey they have expropriated. But more than taking over
the goblins' marketing words, Laura takes over the words of *Goblin
Market* itself: the tale she tells is, presumably, the tale we have been
reading. Incorporating the text into her tale, Laura seems to bring the
entire system of exchange – the goblin market, and the poem
disseminating it – with all its disquieting iterations, under her control.

But the containment this gesture at closure seems to establish is, like
other such attempts at enclosure within the poem, of mixed success. As

closure, this ending only signals the start of yet another telling of the story. The evident nostalgia of Laura's retelling of her adventures,[21] the enjoyment and complicity implicit in her assumption of the goblins' role of caller or crier, story-teller or -seller, leave us with a world not purged of goblin marketing, but bound together by incitements to exchange. The poem ends with an assertion of women's power over that world, but to the extent that such a claim only contradicts doubts raised elsewhere in the poem, the claim leaves the issue of women's power unresolved. The question left open might be, 'Can women actually profit in a market so dominated by goblins.' Or, to put it in literary terms, 'Can women find poetic voices in a world where the structures of representation are male?' The enduring value of *Goblin Market*, finally, is that it does not offer a simple resolution to an insoluble dilemma. It does not evidence any despair of answering the question affirmatively, as Gilbert and Gubar claim, nor does it really represent a wishful utopian fantasy of success. Rather, it ends not with the resolution of the question, but with the definition of a long, uphill struggle.

Goblin Market does not end in despair of the possibilities of a woman's literature. That its closing lines portray a woman as an effective story-teller says as much. But couching such a proclamation in a fairy-tale context (Laura literally becomes a teller of fairy [or goblin] tales, a marginal purveyor of old wives' romances rather than a modern, realist poet such as Elizabeth Barrett Browning envisions in *Aurora Leigh*) also expresses a fear that women may not achieve such power so readily in the real world. The poem ultimately, if indirectly, brings us to recognize that utopian fantasies of a separate women's culture are just that: fantasies of an impossible utopia.

Although Lizzie returns in triumph to her sister, her joy is not alone the full story. The complete passage reads:

> She heard her penny jingle
> Bouncing in her purse,
> Its bounce was music to her ear.
> She ran and ran
> As if she feared some goblin man
> Dogged her with some gibe or curse
> Or something worse:
> But not one goblin skurried after
> Nor was she pricked by fear.

(ll. 452–60)

The fear that dogs Lizzie's footsteps as she runs home to her sister qualifies her triumph. The passage concludes with an unconvincing claim that she runs only because her 'kind heart made her windy-paced' (l. 461). But the 'gibe or curse' that Lizzie fears – the words that might 'prick' her – still echo with 'something worse', something that the lines do not name, and whose effects the poem as a whole denies. Certainly Lizzie's explanation makes sense: she runs to aid her dying sister. But it is just as certainly only half the story: if there is no fear (and we have seen much demonstrating that there is something to fear), why mention it?

The unnameable threat is the very power to name. Such a power is, in the world of *Goblin Market*, essentially goblin. In the goblins' and sisters' struggle to construct each other as essentially deficient, a goblin gibe has the power of a curse because language itself favors the goblins. Throughout the poem, although the sisters are implicated in goblin speech, the goblins appear as the more powerful users of language, able to determine the terms of a bargain or of a discourse of gender. The central element in Laura's enslavement, in fact, is her acceptance of the goblins' use of figural language. Troping the gold she lacks with the gold on her head, the goblins lead her to accept their construction of her within their gendered system of exchange: she bargains on their terms. This is the 'gibe or curse' that dogs Lizzie's steps, the 'something worse' that cannot be named: the power of the goblins to determine her significance, to name her price within their system. The goblins' systems of exchange, including language, are constructed in terms of what the sisters lack – it surfaces as the 'prick' even within these lines[22] – and in those terms the sisters will always be found at a loss for words.

Both the fear of goblin pricking and the sisterly denial define the logic of the closing scenes of the poem, as one stratagem after another is deployed to conceal the fear that would, if acknowledged, render the sisters as mute in their home as in the company of the goblins. Laura's recovery, bringing 'Life out of death' (l. 524), demands impossible reversals, just as the establishment of their women's utopia requires impossible dispensations from the laws of exchange. Chief among these exceptions and reversals, of course, is that mysterious penny and its return, but others obtrude here as well: the disappearance of gray from Laura's hair (l. 540), and especially the recovery of her 'innocent old way' (l. 538). If, as the poem so broadly hints, Laura's transgression was sexual, such a recovery is physically impossible: time, as we read a few lines later, is 'not-returning' (l. 551). Grey hairs do not turn gold; sexually experienced women do not become virgins; death comes after life: a bargain is a bargain.

'Life out of death' is a familiar Christian paradox. In such terms, it marks a crux, both a turning point for Laura and the sign of her redemption through Lizzie's Christ-like passion. This redeeming turn is structurally apocalyptic, offering a discontinuous transition from the conditions of life or history into a realm where the ills of the world are healed by effacing that world, its laws, and all its material concerns. In one set of terms from current critical theory, such a redemption offers a consoling fantasy of the subject's escape from power relations – an impossible exemption, in other words, from the very forces that give the subject existence.[23] The consolation of what follows in *Goblin Market* is plain, but the wishful, fantastic nature of this consolation – its historical discontinuousness and the impossibility of its realization in Rossetti's world – are equally apparent, as repressed threats return in the closing passages of the poem.

The most important repression to return is implicit in the families that the sisters raise, 'Afterwards, when both were wives' (l. 544). 'Wives' suggest husbands, bringing up once again the question raised elsewhere by the parenthetical mention of men and their role in the world of exchange – where are the men? Such questions arise inevitably in an androcentric world, and coming up at the conclusion of *Goblin Market* direct our attention away from the sisters to the inescapable male subject. In *Goblin Market*, 'sisters' become 'wives' – become defined not in relation to other women but in relation to men. The outcome of the sisters' tale seems to assume this change, as if such were the only natural, the inevitable event. Well it might: the change in nomenclature once more concedes on the linguistic level the androcentrism the sisters have fought so hard against and points to the reason for their ultimate defeat in that struggle. The verbal ground they fight on – the language literally constructing them – is already lost. Although 'wife', the *OED* tells us, is ultimately 'of obscure origin', it defines the term unhesitatingly: 'A woman joined to a man by marriage. . . . Correlative of Husband . . . (the ordinary current sense).' This is the second definition. The first definition, 'A woman', merely confirms what the derivation of 'woman' from the Old English *wif-man* already tells us: her origins obscure, woman takes her definition in relation to 'man' (a term the *OED* defines by the etymologically tautological 'A human being'). The control that the mercantile goblins exert in this poem, the extension of their law throughout the world of *Goblin Market*, simply gives mercantile expression to an underlying verbal law.

The answer to the implied question about the husbands is obvious: the goblins are the husbands, of course,[24] and in that relation to these 'wives' they overcome the sisters' attempt to escape them. Through their progeny, the goblins supply the audience for the literary creations of the women. Laura, appearing at the end of the poem as the story-teller in the center of the children's circle, takes up once more the position she occupied earlier in the poem, where she appears surrounded by goblins (ll. 91–6), the object of their gaze.[25] This reminder of that earlier scene calls into question her command of the situation at the end. To be in the middle of an audience is not necessarily a position of authority: perhaps, the ending suggests, to achieve a voice as a woman is no escape from the gendering of representation. And the goblins do not merely surround, they occupy these literary creations as well, displacing the sisters from their own story: this is *Goblin Market*, not 'Laura and Lizzie', or whatever name that unwritten, other poem might have had.

The networks of power binding *Goblin Market* more than occupy the scene of poetic exchange that closes the poem: they overrun the confines of the poem, including us as well in a final dissemination that asserts the pervasiveness of such relations. We, as readers, become goblins too: as audience, in answering Laura's call to come hear the story of *Goblin Market* we share the place of the goblin children. Our stance throughout the poem as voyeurs of sexual exchange recalls that earlier, 'leering' circle of goblins. Ending with its own beginning, the poem describes an endless cycle of iterations in which, by reading the poem, we readers have become embroiled. But our involvement actually aligns us with both sides of the binary structure of the poem in yet another collapse of such distinctions. Doubling the audience within the poem, we become part of the subject of the story. Caught up in its repetition-compulsions, we are held in a situation of compelled audition not unlike Laura's addiction to the goblin fruit: once we have gone to 'Goblin Market', our independence is also in doubt.

The poem brings us to question our own exemption from the systems of power it has revealed. Here, finally, is how Rossetti does not escape but redefines the glass coffin that Gilbert and Gubar see as one fate of women's writing. By refusing to allow the reader to remain complacently on the outside of the poem, by insisting on our implication in systems of power to which we are also subject, Rossetti transforms *Goblin Market* from a fairy tale to a cautionary parable about the difficulty of achieving freedom. This glass coffin is not, finally, only a woman's problem: we are all interred within our separate ideologies, whether of gender, politics, or literature, blind to the very assumptions that seem so transparently true – and thus imprison us.

In imagining women as castrated and in that castration different from men, the reader of *Goblin Market* encounters the full implications of a male strategy that denies male fears by projecting them on to women. Perhaps this is why *Goblin Market* can be read, as Gilbert and Gubar do, as a renunciation of the literary tradition. The androcentric construction of gender seems to have had enormous implications for Rossetti in her own career. If that construction influenced Rossetti's perception of her own literary liabilities, she could well have concluded that the only position she could occupy in the literary world was on the margins: an attitude of abject self-denial; the stance adopted, in fact, in the bulk of her work, the religious poems which in their self-denial and barely tempered despair deny *Goblin Market*'s song of triumph.

Whatever Rossetti's own beliefs, conscious or unconscious, about her own abilities, if we as readers also arrive at such a conclusion about *Goblin Market*, we do her an injustice, and risk relegating the bulk of her work to the same dusty shelf it has occupied for so many years. The flaw in such a conclusion, of course, is that there is a volume – not an inconsiderable one – on that shelf in the first place. Writing is never self-denial. Although unflinching in its assessment of the difficulty of life, especially the life of a single woman, a woman not the 'correlative of a husband', Rossetti's verse yet celebrates endurance, uphill struggle even though the road may be uphill until its end. And so *Goblin Market*, far from rejecting women's literature, as Gilbert and Gubar conclude, makes our desire for such a literature, even while we recognize that wish as utopic, all the more important in the ways it forces us to acknowledge – and even to try to open up – our inscription within oppressively gendered systems of relation. Perhaps this is why the poem ends as it does, emphasizing not triumph achieved and strength attained, but unending struggle. For men and women both, struggling to free themselves from misprisions of the self, there is indeed 'no friend like a sister . . . To strengthen whilst one stands' (ll. 562–7).

Notes

1. Contemporary study of *Goblin Market* begins with WINSTON WEATHERS' 'Christina Rossetti: The Sisterhood of Self', *Victorian Poetry* (*VP*), 3 (1968): 81–9. See also LIONEL STEVENSON, *The Pre-Raphaelite Poets* (Chapel Hill, 1972), pp. 105–7; GERMAINE GREER, 'Introduction', *Goblin Market*, ed. Germaine Greer (Cambridge, Massachusetts, 1975), pp. vii–xxxvi; ELLEN GOLUB, 'Untying Goblin Apron Strings: A Psychoanalytic Reading of *Goblin Market*', *Literature and Psychology* (*L&P*), 25 (1975): 158–65; ELLEN MOERS, *Literary Women: The Great Writers* (Oxford, 1976), pp. 100–7; SANDRA M. GILBERT and SUSAN GUBAR, *The Madwoman in the Attic: The Woman Writer and the Nineteenth-Century Literary Imagination* (New Haven, 1979), pp. 564–75; MIRIAM SAGAN, 'Christina Rossetti's *Goblin Market* and Feminist Literary Criticism', *Journal of Pre-Raphaelite Studies* (*PRR*), 3 (1980): 66–76; JEROME J. MCGANN, 'Christina Rossetti's Poems: A New Edition and a Revaluation', *Victorian Studies* (*VS*), 23 (1980): 237–54; GEORGINA BATTISCOMBE, *Christina Rossetti: A Divided Life* (New York, 1981), pp. 102–13; STEVEN CONNOR, '"Speaking Likenesses": Language and Repetition in Christina Rossetti's *Goblin Market*', *VP*, 22 (1984): 439–48; and DOROTHY MERMIN, 'Heroic Sisterhood in *Goblin Market*', *VP*, 21 (1985): 107–18.

2. For the theory of power relations, see MICHEL FOUCAULT, *Discipline and Punish: The Birth of the Prison*, trans. Alan Sheridan (New York, 1979), and 'The Subject and Power', *Critical Inquiry (CritI)*, 8 (1982): 777–95; BIDDY MARTIN, 'Feminism, Criticism, and Foucault', *New German Critique (NGC)*, 27 (1982): 3–30.

3. GILBERT and GUBAR, p. 575. For phallogocentrism see JACQUES LACAN, *Ecrits: A Selection*, trans. Alan Sheridan (New York, 1977), pp. 281–91; JANE GALLOP, *Reading Lacan* (Ithaca, 1985), pp. 133–56; LUCE IRIGARAY, *Speculum of the Other Woman*, trans. Gillian C. Gill (Ithaca, 1985), pp. 13–129; SHOSHANA FELMAN, 'Women and Madness: The Critical Phallacy', *Diacritics*, 5, no. 4 (1975): 2–10, and 'Rereading Femininity', *Yale French Studies (YFS)*, 62 (1981): 19–44; and MARY JACOBUS, *Reading Woman* (New York, 1986), pp. 83–196, especially pp. 110–36.

4. CHRISTINA ROSSETTI, *Goblin Market*, in *The Complete Poems of Christina Rossetti*, ed. R.W. Crump (Baton Rouge, 1979), I: 11–26, ll. 1–4. All further quotations from this edition appear parenthetically by line number within the text.

5. For the role of iterability in linguistic circulation, see JONATHAN CULLER, *On Deconstruction: Theory and Criticism after Structuralism* (Ithaca, 1982), p. 102.

6. See CATHERINE GALLAGHER, 'More about "Medusa's Head"', *Representations*, 4 (Fall, 1983): 55–7, for discussion of costermongers as emblems of eighteenth- and nineteenth-century anxieties about economic and gender roles.

7. Spenser's villainesses typify the monstrous-feminine as defined in JULIA KRISTEVA, *Powers of Horror: An Essay on Abjection*, trans. Leon S. Roudiez (New York, 1982), pp. 1–31; the rhetoric of scum, filth, and blood in Bunyan's description of Christian's family as well as the Slough draws heavily on the religious vocabulary Kristeva also identifies (pp. 56–89) with the 'holy abject'.

8. GILBERT and GUBAR, p. 570; see also pp. 122–6, 134–7, 171–80, 289–91, 381–2, 545, 558–9, and MARY POOVEY, *The Proper Lady and the Woman Writer: Ideology as Style in the Writings of Mary Wollstonecraft, Mary Shelley, and Jane Austen* (Chicago, 1984), pp. 3–47.

9. For discussion of the futility of such evasions see: SIGMUND FREUD, 'The Uncanny', in *The Standard Edition of the Complete Psychological Works of Sigmund Freud* (London, 1953–74), 17, pp. 219–52; JACQUES DERRIDA, 'The Law of Genres', *Glyph*, 7 (1980): 202–32; and MICHEL FOUCAULT, *History of Sexuality* (New York, 1980), 1: 1–50.

10. Parenthesis, we may recall, is a figure in formal rhetoric. The *OED* defines it as 'a grammatical or rhetorical figure', a 'word, clause or sentence inserted into a passage with which it has not necessarily any grammatical connexion'. The term has been recognized in English rhetoric since 1577 at least, when HENRY PEACHAM's *The Garden of Eloquence* (Menston, England, 1971) defined parenthesis specifically in terms of its supplementary relation to the grammar of the sentence (a relation Derrida explores in depth in *Of Grammatology*; see note 15 below for full citation).

11. The function of the aside, for instance, is 'to allow the inner feelings of the character to be made known to the audience' (C. HUGH HOLMAN, *A Handbook to Literature* (New York, 1972), p. 46).

12. Although in both instances the speakers are ostensibly quoting the goblins, recent theoretical discussion argues that distinctions between citation and use are not so distinct as we would like to believe. See CULLER, pp. 110–25.

13. GILBERT and GUBAR note this allusion in passing, p. 566.

14. Locks of hair are, as FREUD points out, a common phallic symbol. See 'Medusa's Head', The Standard Edition, 18, pp. 273–4.

15. For the standard critique of such strategies, see JACQUES DERRIDA, Of Grammatology, trans. Gayatri Chakravorty Spivak (Baltimore, 1976), pp. 141–64.

16. STEVEN CONNOR also notes the 'furious variegation' of the goblins' speech as characteristic, reading it as a part of their function as tempters into the 'verbal promiscuity' of language (p. 444).

17. For the identity and futility of the strategies of resistance available to the subject constructed in terms of the phallus (strategies strikingly similar to the responses of Lizzie and Laura) see JULIA KRISTEVA, Desire in Language: A Semiotic Approach to Literature and Art, ed. Leon S. Roudiez, trans. Thomas Gora, Alice Jardine, and Leon S. Roudiez (New York, 1980), p. 191.

18. For fetishism and its relation to castration see SIGMUND FREUD, 'Fetishism', in The Standard Edition, 22, pp. 152–7.

19. The self-defeating logic of the apotropaic gesture is also described by FREUD in 'Medusa's Head'.

20. 'Scription' is Julia Kristeva's term for language that aspires to root itself in the world of things. For discussion see KRISTEVA, Desire in Language, especially pp. 115–21.

21. A quality DOROTHY MERMIN also notes ('Heroic Sisterhood', p. 117).

22. The OED finds this sense of 'prick' current as early as 1592.

23. The terms are, of course, FOUCAULT's and find their fullest exposition in his Discipline and Punish and 'The Subject and Power'.

24. As DOROTHY MERMIN observes, the mystery of paternity in Goblin Market is no mystery. The poem 'is clear and simple in its essential structure: two girls live alone; they encounter goblin men; they have children' ('Heroic Sisterhood', pp. 113–14).

25. For discussion of the male identification of the audience and its relation to the gaze see the references in note 3 above, LAURA MULVEY, 'Visual Pleasure and the Narrative Cinema', Screen 16, no. 3 (1975): 6–18, and JACQUES LACAN, The Four Fundamental Concepts of Psycho-Analysis, trans. Alan Sheridan (New York, 1981), pp. 67–119. Whether that structure is actually in Rossetti's text and our culture or whether it is merely projection of my own is a question I am not, for a variety of structural reasons, in a position to settle. The charges of essentialism leveled at Lacanian theory may be answered, however, by a reminder that gender – those qualities and expectations we attach to biology – is a matter of convention, not of anatomy. But the tendency in some contemporary theory, especially that influenced by Foucault, to move from a proclamation of the inescapability of a (male) system of power to an attempt to subsume feminism is disturbing and gives this writer pause; for discussion of this (probably intractable) question, see LAURIE LANGBAUER, 'Women in White, Men in Feminism', Yale Journal of Criticism, 2, no. 2 (1989); 219–43.

13 'Eat Me, Drink Me, Love Me': The Consumable Female Body in Christina Rossetti's *Goblin Market**

MARY WILSON CARPENTER

Carpenter's article is in some ways a direct response to the preceding
extract by Holt (see her note 15). She diversifies his ideological framework by pointing to the possibilities of a feminocentric discourse in
the texts of the Anglican sisterhoods with which Rossetti was involved.
Here, she takes up an idea of Mermin's (Chapter 9), but instead of
seeing Rossetti's work with 'fallen' women as a personal biographical influence on the poem, she places it in a wider discursive context
which allows her to argue against Holt's monolithic phallocentrism.
Both she and Holt see the poem as determined by available discourses,
rather than produced by the conscious intention or unconscious expression of the poet. In the language of the sisterhoods, Carpenter
finds the possibility of an inter-female gaze that undercuts the
Lacanian suppositions of Holt's approach (this move recalls Chapter
5), a gaze that is repeated in the homoerotic encounter between Lizzie
and Laura. Lesbian desire also undercuts the male-centred sexual
economy, and frees female bodies from control. By putting the
poem into historical context – rather as Edmond did for *Aurora Leigh*
(Chapter 7) – Carpenter can specifiy its particular relations with contemporary discourses of imperialism, consumerism and gender. By
contrasting it with the imperialist discourse of 'The Round Tower at
Jhansi', Carpenter shows the way it elides differences of class and
race. Her article manifests the growing feminist preoccupation with
ideas of difference – class, race, sexual orientation – that puts in doubt
'women' as a unified category.

When Alice falls down the rabbit-hole she behaves, as Nancy Armstrong
has pointed out, like a typical shopper – picking out and then putting
back a jar of orange marmalade from the shelves of the rabbit-hole.[1]

---

* Reprinted from *Victorian Poetry*, 29 (1991): 415–35.

Later, she discovers that objects in Wonderland tend to come inscribed with such unsubtle advertising ploys as 'eat me' or 'drink me'. Noting that all Alice's troubles seem to 'begin and end with her mouth', Armstrong relates Alice's dilemma to 'a new moment in the history of desire', a moment when the burgeoning 'consumer culture' based on British imperialism changed the nature of middle-class English femininity (p. 17). *Alice in Wonderland* (1865) demonstrates the logic that links the colonial venture to the appetite of a little girl through the image of a 'double-bodied woman' – a conflation of non-European women with European prostitutes and madwomen, all three of which were thought to exhibit the same features of face and genitals and, more crucially, to display the disfiguring results of unrestrained 'appetite'.[2] Victorian consumer culture both produced objects of desire and dictated that little Alices must learn to control their desires, in imagined contrast to women of the 'dark continents' and prostitutes on the dark streets of their own cities.

So runs Armstrong's persuasive reading of a Victorian 'children's' classic known to as many adults as children. Christina Rossetti's poem, *Goblin Market*, first published in 1862, suggests its location in the same intersection of imperialist culture and consumer capitalism that Armstrong elucidates for *Alice in Wonderland*.[3] Opening with the sensuous advertisement of exotic fruits hawked by goblin men to innocent young women, Rossetti's poem presents an explicitly articulated image of a marketplace in which female 'appetite' is at stake. But whereas in Carroll's narrative, according to Armstrong's reading of it, '*all possibility for pleasure splits off from appetite and attaches itself to self-control*', in Rossetti's poem female appetite is simply redirected toward another female figure, where it is provoked, encouraged, and satiated in the undeniably homoerotic text of the poem (p. 20; Armstrong's emphasis). Lizzie urges Laura to 'Hug me, kiss me, suck my juices' as well as to 'Eat me, drink me, love me' (ll. 468, 471). While Laura is said to loathe this 'feast' proffered on her sister's body, it makes her leap and sing 'like a caged thing freed' (l. 505). The result of Laura's totally unrestrained, orgiastic consumption of the 'juices' on her sister's body is her restoration to life and health and, I will argue, to desire. The female body in the poem is subject to 'consumption' as a commodity – as Laura's near-fatal experience demonstrates – but it is also 'consumable' as a regenerative and self-propagating 'fruit', as Lizzie's example shows us.

If *Alice in Wonderland* is structured on the 'problem' of female desire in the imperialist marketplace, then Christina Rossetti's *Goblin Market* presents a startlingly different assessment of female sexual appetite. Yet the drive to evoke and regulate female appetite is not unique to the Revd Charles Dodgson's children's story or even to children's literature conceived by Victorian clergymen. Charles Bernheimer argues that for nineteenth-century French male artists and novelists, the image of the prostitute stimulated representational strategies to control and dispel the fantasmatic threat of female 'sexual ferment'.[4] These artists associated the female body with 'animality, disease, castration, excrement, and decay' (p. 2). Bernheimer acknowledges that in writing his book he 'had to confront powerful expressions of disgust for female sexuality' (p. 4). As the nineteenth century progressed, the fear of 'contamination' by the prostitute's unrestricted sexuality was given medical justification in France by 'theories of degenerate heredity and syphilitic infection' (p. 2). Similarly, as Judith R. Walkowitz shows, the passage of the Contagious Diseases Acts in England in the 1860s suggests that prostitution was increasingly perceived there also as a dangerously contaminating form of sexual activity, one 'whose boundaries had to be controlled and defined by the state'.[5]

Even closer to Christina Rossetti's artistic context was her brother Dante Gabriel Rossetti's poem about a prostitute, 'Jenny', which articulates a typical construction of female sexuality as diseased and contagious appetite:

> For is there hue or shape defin'd
> In Jenny's desecrated mind,
> Where all contagious currents meet,
> A Lethe of the middle street?[6]

If, as Armstrong argues, the 1860s represent a new moment in the history of desire in which consumer culture changed the nature of middle-class English femininity, both producing the desire for objects and structuring femininity in relation to that desire, then what accounts for the radically different representation of female appetite in *Goblin Market*? How was it possible for Christina Rossetti, devout Victorian practitioner of what Jerome McGann has called a 'severe Christianity', to produce a poem in which fear of the contagion of the female body is radically disavowed?[7] And is it nonetheless possible to locate a 'deviant counterpart' – the 'double-bodied' figure of the prostitute-cum-African or -Asian woman – as a structuring figure repressed from *Goblin Market*?

D.M.R. Bentley has recently speculated that Christina Rossetti may have written *Goblin Market* with the intention of reading it not to children but to the inmates – 'fallen women' or prostitutes – of the St Mary Magdalene Home, Highgate, where she is known to have volunteered during the 1860s.[8] However much this possibility may alter our perception of the poem, Rossetti's intentions are not my concern here. Rather, I would propose that the foundation of Anglican

Sisterhoods associated directly with the two churches which Rossetti is known to have attended, and the work of those Sisterhoods with homeless, destitute and fallen women, gave the poet access to a uniquely feminocentric view of women's sexuality and simultaneously opened her eyes to its problematic position in Victorian culture. In particular, her immediate experience with the interaction between prostitutes and women's religious communities may have constructed Rossetti's representation of a 'marketplace' in which 'appetite' puts a woman at risk, but where her salvation is to be found not in controlling her appetite but in turning to another woman.

Like the other 'fruits of empire', women's bodies were vended in the streets surrounding the churches, and zealous churchwomen like Christina Rossetti went out to 'buy' them back. But these shoppers were themselves commodified by the market in which they bargained, their own bodies and appetites implicated in the exploitative sexual economy they sought to resist and evade. In this scene of 'compulsory heterosexuality', *Goblin Market* suggests that female erotic pleasure cannot be imagined without pain, yet the poem not only affirms the female body and its appetites but constructs 'sisterhood' as a saving female homoerotic bond.[9]

While *Goblin Market* pushes the normative realm of heterosexual marriage to the margins of its narrative – invoking husbands only by implication in the final lines of the poem – that normative realm with its inscription of gender, class, and racial hierarchies is nevertheless exhibited in the poem which followed *Goblin Market* in its 1862 edition (Crump, I, p. 26).[10] In that little-discussed poem, 'In the Round Tower at Jhansi', I find a final comment on what *Goblin Market* is, and is not, about.

Sisterhoods and the female gaze

The extraordinary homoerotic energies of *Goblin Market* seem particularly unaccountable in relation to the familiar assessment of Christina Rossetti as a devout Anglo-Catholic spinster who lived out her entire life with her mother, sister, and elderly aunts. William Rossetti described her as a 'devotee', instancing her 'perpetual church-going and communions, her prayers and fasts, her submission to clerical direction, her oblations, her practice of confession' – a catalogue that suggests a religious practice stripped of much social interaction and certainly of all pleasure.[11] Yet the histories of Christ Church, Albany Street, and All Saints Margaret Street, and of the Sisterhoods founded at these two churches, produce a very different reading of the Oxford Movement that constructed both Rossetti's religious practice and her poetic texts. Far from McGann's conception of a 'severe Christianity', the 'Church' as represented in these histories appears to have been a hotbed of social reforms and sexual tensions generated by those reforms. The work of the newly formed Anglican Sisterhoods proved to be inseparable from the 'work' of 'fallen women', producing an unprecedented mingling of 'pure' and 'tainted' women. Moreover, as Martha Vicinus has noted, the Anglican Sisterhoods empowered women, validating their work and values.[12] The feminism and intense homoeroticism of *Goblin Market* are fully accountable when read intertextually with this unconventional 'social text' of the Victorian Anglican Church.

In speaking of the homoeroticism of the poem as 'accountable', I am assuming, as Mary Poovey states, that 'the representation of biological sexuality, the definition of sexual difference, and the social organization of sexual relations are social, not natural, phenomena'.[13] Rather than reading *Goblin Market* as 'expressing' by virtue of the poet's creative genius an 'inner' and unaccountable desire – a reading which might be called a humanist Freudian interpretation – I look for the 'origins' of Rossetti's representation of female sexual desire in the complex interactions between the social institutions and texts of her culture. Thus, I will argue that the characteristics of the historical institution of 'sisterhood' unique to Christina Rossetti's churches constituted a social and discursive matrix which enabled the production of a radical subjectivity in *Goblin Market*: that is, a female speaker or subject of discourse which does not take up the conventional phallocentric position, in which the female body is the object of a male gaze.[14] In a text exemplary of the Oxford Movement's 'women's mission to women', as I will show, the female body is represented as the object of a female gaze, and in *Goblin Market* we find a similarly radical female subjectivity.

What I will be arguing here is that the writer, though determined by the ideological structuring of her society, may also be emancipated in some degree by exposure to unconventional or disruptive ideological discourses. Such 'uneven developments', as Poovey says, result from the different positioning of individuals within the social formation, and from the different articulation of the ideological formulation by different institutions, discourses, and practices (p. 3). While Marxist or materialist readings may position the writer as the 'simple' subject of the dominant ideology, subjectivities are constituted at the intersection of multiple and competing discourses.[15] This multiplicity accounts for such 'uneven developments' as a powerfully feminist and homoerotic text written by a devout Victorian lady poet.

Previous attempts to link *Goblin Market* with Rossetti's associations with 'sisters' and 'fallen women' have focused on her involvement with the institution at Highgate, despite William Rossetti's recollection that this work did not begin until 1860, while the manuscript of *Goblin Market* is dated 27 April 1859. So little is known about the 1850s in Christina Rossetti's life that they have been described as the 'grey years'.[16] Scholars have relied largely on William's reminiscences, but these are often vague and spotty and may also be inaccurate, as demonstrated in his comments to Mackenzie Bell about Christina's church-related work:

> She was (I rather think) an outer Sister – but in no sort of way professed – of the Convent which Maria afterwards joined – Also at one time (1860–70) she used pretty often to go to an Institution at Highgate for redeeming 'Fallen Women' – It seems to me that at one time they wanted to make her a sort of superintendent there, but she declined – In her own neighbourhood, Albany Street, she did a deal of district visiting and the like.[17]

William's use of the term 'Convent', which suggests an enclosed community of women, to refer to the All Saints' Sisterhood which Maria joined in 1873 shows how unacquainted he must have been with the Sisterhood and its activities, for it was primarily a nursing order which occupied an ever-increasing number of buildings adjacent to All Saints Church and administered various institutions both in London and outside it. The headnote, 'House of Charity', which Christina penciled in on her poem, 'From Sunset to Star Rise', and which William thought referred to the Highgate institution, may have referred to the All Saints' Home run by these Sisters, since the Revd W. Upton Richards described it as an institution entirely dependent on voluntary gifts and commended to the 'Christian charity of all'.[18]

William's statement that Christina did district visiting in 'her own neighbourhood, Albany Street' may also be misleading, as this implies that she did this kind of work only after March 1854, when the Rossetti family moved to 45 Upper Albany Street. Since the Rossetti women began attending Christ Church in 1843, it seems probable that Christina participated in its social work and reform efforts well before 1854 (Battiscombe, p. 30). Built in 1837 at the instigation of William Dodsworth, a fiery young preacher who was then the incumbent at the Margaret Street Chapel (whose remaining parishioners went on to build All Saints' Church), Christ Church was characterized by 'zeal' for social reform from its beginnings.[19] According to Canon Burrows, who became the incumbent in 1851, Christ Church became 'the leading church in the [Oxford] movement', and the scene of sermons by such well-known preachers as Archdeacon Manning, Dr Pusey, and Dr Hook

(Burrows, p. 14). Doubtless much more important to Christina Rossetti and her sister Maria was the fact that the first Anglican Sisterhood since the Reformation was founded there.

Pusey seems to have been the guiding force for the formation of this Sisterhood, which some thought might 'save' certain Anglican members from converting to Roman Catholicism while others despaired that it would only further encourage such 'Romanising'.[20] Pusey's desires for the Sisterhood, however, appear to have been intimately linked with his grief for his own daughter, who died tragically on the very day of the meeting which decided to establish such a community (Cameron, p. 31). Pusey thought that for a Bishop to have anything to do with the Sisterhood, which should consist simply of a few young women living together, would be to violate 'the sacredness of domestic charity and devotion' (Cameron, p. 32). His close and even tender relationship with the Sisters began on 26 March 1845, when the first two aspirants arrived. As Pusey later wrote to Keble, 'We (i.e. Dodsworth and myself) had a little service with them on Wednesday; they were in floods of tears, but in joy' (Cameron, p. 33).

If Pusey imagined a sanctified domestic enclave of perpetual daughters, others – particularly the women who either entered or founded such Sisterhoods – seem to have had quite a different vision. Far from seeking out an ecclesiastical version of the patriarchal families most of them were leaving, they saw themselves as embarking on a new and independent existence in which they would undertake useful, important work. The Park Village Sisters are reported to have immediately begun to visit the 'low Irish people' and the brothels in their district (Williams and Campbell, p. 23).[21] Before founding the All Saints' Sisterhood, Harriet Brownlow Byron took a nursing course.[22] She then began the work of this Sisterhood by taking homeless women and orphan girls right into the house where the Sisters lived, the All Saints' Home. By 1862 this 'Home' occupied four buildings on Margaret Street, and the Sisters' various enterprises eventually occupied every building on Margaret Street as far as Great Titchfield Street. By 1866 they were conducting an asylum for aged women, an industrial school for girls, an orphanage, a home for incurables, two convalescent homes, and the nursing service for the entire University College Hospital, in addition to teaching in the district night-school and nursing the sick poor in their own homes.[23]

Unlike the more successful All Saints' Sisterhood, the Park Village Sisterhood encountered many difficulties, finding itself at the center of fierce religious controversy in Christ Church.[24] Throughout the years of 1849 and 1850 Dodsworth – increasingly convinced that he should convert to Catholicism – was preaching sermons at Christ Church of such a nature that Pusey said 'he wished he could induce the sisters to read their Bibles during his sermons or shut their ears'.[25] One of the Sisters was actually kidnapped by a 'Miss White' and taken to a Roman Catholic convent. She was eventually released, only to be assailed and accused of 'apostasy' the following Sunday as she tried to enter the door of Christ Church (Williams and Campbell, pp. 81–2). Christina Rossetti could hardly have escaped involvement in the parish turmoil. She was at this time engaged to James Collinson, who had converted from the Roman Catholic to the Anglican Church to further his courtship of Christina. During the early months of 1850, Collinson decided that he must rejoin the Catholic Church, and upon hearing this, Christina decided to end their engagement. The Revd Mr Dodsworth 'romanized' on the last day of 1850.[26]

Despite such disruptions, both Christ Church and the Sisterhood moved ahead vigorously with new plans for ministering to the poor. A second church was to be built at the south end of the parish near 'the notoriously evil York Square', where brothels flourished because of the nearby Cumberland Barracks (Coombs, pp. 9–12). On 15 July 1849, the laying of the foundation stone for 'St Mary Magdalene' was planned, with the congregation to make a procession from Christ Church to the site.[27] John Keble, who preached the sermon, hinted that troublemakers might be encountered and begged the congregation to 'go reverently . . . as we pass through the streets of Babylon'. The 'long tramping procession' accordingly wound its way silently through the 'sordid district' (Coombs, p. 13). A little over a year later, in September 1850, Pusey laid the foundation stone for the 'House of Religion', which was to be occupied by the Sisters of Park Village but was also intended to accommodate fourteen homeless women, forty orphan girls, and fourteen 'ladies' (Coombs, p. 15). This building was very near the site for the new St Mary Magdalene Church (and therefore near the brothels). On All Saints' Day (1 November) in 1850, Pusey also laid the foundation-stone for what would become the extravagantly beautiful All Saints Church, built on the site of the old Margaret Street Chapel.

Christina Rossetti, her sister Maria, her mother Frances, and her aunts could all have been a part of that unprecedented outdoor procession through the neighboring 'red-light' district to the site chosen for the new church.[28] That Christina and one of her aunts were very much caught up in the new fervor for women's work with the needy is known from the fact that they were among some 'ladies of the [Christ Church] congregation' who joined the Park Village Sisters and others in volunteering to go with Florence Nightingale to the Crimea in December, 1854.[29] Nightingale rejected Christina on the grounds that she was too young, but her aunt was accepted.

Neither the Park Village nor the All Saints' Sisters had a mandate for working with 'fallen women', but their work with 'homeless women' and 'orphan girls' would in fact have been inseparable from work with 'fallen women'.[30]   Other Anglican Sisterhoods which were newly forming at this time, however, displayed a predominant interest in work with prostitutes. The first Sister at St Mary's, Wantage, felt called to penitentiary work and founded a penitentiary there in 1850, despite the distress of the Vicar, who had wanted this Sisterhood to be dedicated to educational work. The Clewer Sisterhood was formed because three women moved into a 'House of Mercy' in 1851, simultaneously undertaking the religious life and the work of the 'penitentiary'.[31] This 'House of Mercy' had been founded two years earlier by a Mrs Tennant, a laywoman living in the village of Clewer who offered to take the 'abandoned women' of the parish into her own home. She was said to have an unparalleled ability to control the 'most undisciplined and impassioned natures' of these women and to attach them to herself 'in a marvellous manner' (Cameron, pp. 58–9).

Such enthusiasm for work with prostitutes and willingness to share living-quarters with them was not confined to religious sisterhoods. Josephine Butler, who led the Ladies' National Association in its campaign against the Contagious Diseases Acts, began her career by taking women from the workhouses, jails and streets of Liverpool into her own home, where she devotedly nursed them herself. Walkowitz reports that by 1878 the LNA leadership had actually grown wary of the 'rescue impulse', recognizing by then that there were 'a "hundred women" who would engage in rescue work for the "one" who would bravely enter the political arena to combat the acts' (Walkowitz, p. 133).

The St Mary Magdalene Home at which Christina Rossetti worked in the 1860s may have been staffed by lay 'sisters' who committed themselves to the work but took no permanent religious vows. According to its Annual Reports, St Mary's 'sisters' were to be divided into two groups, 'approved sisters' and 'sisters under probation', either of whom were to be free to resign at any time.[32] Christina Rossetti's work at St Mary's in the 1860s appears to have been only a continuation of her involvement with the 'rescue work' which had appealed to the desires of British women in general, and Anglican Sisterhoods in particular, including the two Sisterhoods associated with the churches attended by the Rossetti women. *Goblin Market*, written sometime during the late 1850s, is inscribed by the turbulent history of 'women's mission to women' in the Oxford Movement during this period. In this ecclesiastical 'female world of love and ritual', how was the female body and its 'appetite' represented?[33]

I would like to begin by noting that ecclesiastical discourse constituted saving 'sisters' and 'fallen women' together, as if part of a unitary entity. In a preface to two sermons on penitentiary work, W.J. Butler, Vicar of Wantage, wrote that, 'so soon as the evil [prostitution] was fairly faced . . . nothing could quell it so much as purity and tender love, that these would foster habits of prayer and industry and faith in virtue and goodness, . . . the lack of which had occasioned so fearful a moral wreck'.[34] The Sisters' 'purity and tender love' are defined by the 'moral wreck' so in need of them.

Like the discourses of nineteenth-century male artists, the discourses of the Oxford Movement also reveal a fear of 'contamination'. But while the male artists' imagery suggests a fear of physical and moral pollution from the prostitute's body, male clerics appear to have feared that the sisters would be contaminated by the attractions of the 'fallen women' and their way of life. In a sermon preached at St Mary's Home, Wantage, in 1861, Samuel Wilberforce, the Bishop of Oxford, displays this anxiety by taking as his opening subject the prevailing notion that those who work to reform the corrupted are themselves liable to be corrupted. He also labors to disprove the idea that institutions such as St Mary's tended to 'discredit homely virtue and to throw a gloss over vice' (*On Penitentiary Work*, p. 5). In a second sermon preached on the same occasion, Henry Parry Liddon indicates that the 'decay' of prostitution begins with a woman's 'act of rebellion', and that this first act of rebellion is generally followed by a second and a third, such that 'you find yourself in the presence of a new and formidable force – the force of habit' (p. 19). This habit of rebellion, he suggests, must be met by 'a counter-habit of purity' (p. 20).

These sermons thus articulate a fear that, far from 'experiencing 'disgust for female sexuality' or 'sexual repulsion', the sisters who worked with fallen women might themselves be 'corrupted' by these living examples of active female sexuality and 'rebellion'. In an 1867 sermon to the Parochial Mission-Women Association, Canon Burrows' text fairly resonates with the fear that rescue work might encourage the development of an unwomanly sense of authority, and that after going into the streets, mission women might not return exactly as they had been before. Noting uneasily at the outset that he was not often called upon to 'address a body so largely composed of women' and that there were many 'Managers and Superintendents here today', he takes as his theme the imperative of maintaining a proper sense of humility amidst the heady excitement of this mission work: 'Many of you, Mission Women, must be tempted to think . . . when you find yourselves associated with rank and talent, the clergy co-operating, congregations applauding, and all men speaking well of you, that surely success is certain; but you come together today to the House of God, to humble yourselves.'[35] Commenting that 'yours is woman's work, and a true woman's best work is modest, retiring, humble, self-sacrificing', Burrows reminds his feminine audience of 'the special deference to authority' involved in their 'constitution' and urges his hearers to be always

willing to 'take the lowest place' and to be 'persistent' in humility
(pp. 7, 9, 11). He mentions that these mission women not only have no
house or institution, no official dress, but that they almost always work
singly. They go out on the streets and bring women in to the Mission
room, the School, the Church. They must never forget, he concludes,
that they should be 'the servant of all' (p. 11).

Although always organized hierarchically and on the assumption that
class differences were part of God's plan and not to be interfered with,
the Oxford Movement actually fostered associations between middle-
class church women and working-class women on the belief that the
former could help prevent the latter from 'falling'. In 1856 Upton
Richards founded an organization called the All Saints Confraternity for
Girls and Young Women.[36] According to the 1866 Manual, the
association was intended for the 'mutual help and encouragement of
Girls and Young Women wishing to lead a Christian life amidst the
difficulties and temptations of the world'. The Objects of the
Confraternity further specified that the organization was to help
'carefully brought up' and pious girls retain their beliefs and good
behavior after they were sent out into the world to earn a living.[37]

These objectives obviously suggest another possibility for an intended
audience for *Goblin Market*, which certainly can be read as a cautionary
tale for girls and young women wishing to lead a Christian life amidst
the temptations of the 'world', for which read the streets of London.
Again, however, my interest is not to speculate on an 'intended'
audience but rather to examine certain texts produced by or for the
Confraternity which I believe are paradigmatic of female relations in the
Oxford Movement, and to read in them a construction of the female
gaze that I think is highly pertinent to the reading of *Goblin Market*. In
this construction of the female gaze we may find a 'look' exchanged
between women that constitutes an unorthodox (feminine) subjectivity.

Class difference and hierarchy clearly structured the Confraternity,
like all of the Sisterhood enterprises. In 1866 its membership consisted
of sixty 'members' and twenty 'Lady-Associates', headed by a 'Superior-
General' or the Revd Upton Richards, and a 'Sister-Superior', who was
one of the All Saints Sisters.[38] But these rigid demarcations of class and
authority do not appear in the Confraternity hymns to the Virgin
Mother, or to the Virgin's mother, St Anne. In a hymn to St Anne I
find a particularly significant revision of Jacques Lacan's construction of
the 'mirror stage' as the moment when the infant first perceives itself as
a coherent image. In Lacan's theorization of this moment, the infant is
constituted by its perception of this mirrored image, an image which
the mother who holds the infant only 'guarantees'. In short, the infant,
not the mother, is the subject here.[39]

If we take the Confraternity hymn to St Anne as textual exemplar, we read in it instead an egalitarian exchange of gazes between the Virgin's mother and the future Virgin Mother:

Blest among women shall thy daughter be!
  Yes, highly favoured above every other;
The little one reposing on thy knee,
  (Believe, and fear not) shall be GOD's own Mother.

The clear, grave eyes that now look up to thine,
  In the calm faith that sheds its radiance o'er her,
Thus shall they gaze upon the form divine
  Of God's bright Angel, as he stands before her.

                                 (*Manual*, pp. 65–6)

There are several important points here. For one, it is the gaze of the infant daughter which is represented as guaranteeing the mother's subjectivity. The Virgin's mother looks down on the 'little one reposing' on her knee, and in the infant's mirroring gaze sees the promise of a future divine motherhood. Rather than beginning (and ending) with the infant and ignoring the mother as anything but 'guarantee', it starts (though it does not end) with the mother.

Another interesting difference is the hymn's explicit construction of the gaze between two feminine subjects. The hymn virtually excludes males from this female exchange, and what is male appears only as prophetic image that grants permission to the mother's gaze: the female child can be taken as 'object' because she is validated by the divine form of the angel who will announce that she is a virgin mother. The hymn thus authorizes the female gaze to take a feminine object as its focus.

The infant daughter here, however, obviously functions as subject herself: her look 'up' to the mother's look is already a gaze upon a future 'form divine' that is in turn a guarantee of her subjectivity. As such, I think the exchange can be said to undo the hierarchy of mother and daughter as it does of infant and 'mirror'. How shall we describe the relationship constructed by such an exchange of looks between female subjects? As 'sisterhood' – a 'sisterhood' which represses hierarchical differences and permits the female gaze to feast on the female form.

Goblin Market and feminine guessiness

Criticism of *Goblin Market* can be divided into two camps in the reading of Lizzie and Laura: one camp assumes that Laura represents the 'fallen woman' and Lizzie the 'pure woman', or that Laura is a type of Eve and Lizzie a type of Mary; the other camp asserts that the poem does not construct either sister as morally superior and that Lizzie is as much 'redeemed' by her confrontation with the goblins as Laura is by ingesting Lizzie's 'antidote'.[40]

I take my stance very much in this second camp, for it seems to me the poem quite deliberately denies any suggestion of categorical differences between the two women. That is, the text excludes any suggestion of sexual, racial, class, or any other kind of hierarchical difference between the two women – or girls, since the difference between sexual maturity and childish innocence also seems to be blurred. We cannot find in the text of this poem or in the illustration Dante Gabriel designed for it of the two 'golden heads' any suggestion of Armstrong's 'double-bodied woman'. On the contrary, even after Laura has eaten of the goblin fruits – an act many readers regard as synonymous with a 'fall' – the poem constructs them in what Jerome McGann appropriately calls 'unspeakably beautiful litanies' of identical innocence (p. 253):

Like two blossoms on one stem,
Like two flakes of new-fall'n snow,
Like two wands of ivory.

(ll. 188–98)

I would like to suggest that the poem excludes difference between the two girls or women in order to focus on women's common plight as commodities in the linked capitalist and sexual economies. By erasing categorical differences between Laura and Lizzie, the poem can construct those various characterological differences among women which make them vulnerable to the market, on the one hand, but which the poem, on the other hand, argues 'sisters' can also capitalize upon in order to rescue each other from exploitation.

Christina Rossetti's own reflective interpretation of Eve and her 'fall' in an 1882 work of biblical commentary, Letter and Spirit, is relevant here:

It is in no degree at variance with the Sacred Record to picture to ourselves Eve, that first and typical woman, as indulging quite innocently sundry refined tastes and aspirations, a castle-building spirit (if so it may be called), a feminine boldness and directness of aim combined with a no less feminine guessiness as to means. Her very virtues may have opened the door to temptation.[41]

So it appears with Laura in Goblin Market – her very virtues open the door to temptation. She combines a 'feminine boldness and directness

of aim' with 'sundry refined tastes and aspirations'. She exhibits a
'castle-building spirit', if so we may read the heroic similes which
describe her as stretching her 'gleaming neck' and being like a 'moonlit
poplar branch', or a 'vessel at the launch / When its last restraint is
gone' (ll. 81–6).

But she also exhibits a 'feminine guessiness as to means'. Untutored
in the deceptive strategies employed in the goblin market, she gets
herself in for more than she bargained for. Although her desire to
indulge 'refined tastes' for the exotic and delicious fruits hawked by the
goblin men is nowhere condemned in the poem, Laura finds that in
consuming those fruits a part of herself has also been 'consumed'.
What has been stolen from her in this shady transaction is her 'desire'
itself, a desire which far exceeds that for real fruits, however exotic.

Yet we should not fail to notice how infinitely more potent as locus
of desire these 'fruits' are than that pathetically domesticated jar of
marmalade that is supposed to tempt Alice. The very words for these
fruits are quite literally mouth-filling and sensuously delectable, but they
are also packed with metaphorical and associational meanings. Both a
woman and the product of her womb may be called a 'fruit', but with
what different valances! And 'fruits' can refer to the profits of any kind
of enterprise – economic, spiritual, or sexual.

The poem, moreover, specifically links the fruits to 'the fruits of
empire': these are not just common, home-grown English apples and
cherries, but also a rich variety of gourmet fruits imported from foreign
climes – pomegranates, dates, figs, lemons and oranges, 'citrons from
the South'. These are luxury fruits that appeal to 'sundry refined tastes'
such as have been cultivated by Britain's colonial empire. That Rossetti
associated the availability of such luxuries with the capitalistic
exploitation of the poor is clearly indicated in her 1892 commentary on
the Book of Revelation, *The Face of the Deep*, where she identifies her
country with the apocalyptic Babylon and assails it with prophetic
wrath: 'Alas England full of luxuries and thronged by stinted poor,
whose merchants are princes and whose dealings crooked, whose
packed storehouses stand amid bare homes, whose gorgeous array has
rags for neighbours!'[42]

Amidst this market with its packed storehouses and gorgeous array,
Laura, who has not a single 'copper' in her purse, is taken in by the
crooked dealings of the goblin men. When they tell her she does not
need any money because they will be happy with a 'golden curl', she
hands over this emblem of her virginity with only a single tear. Her
'feminine guessiness as to means' – her *naïveté* about the marketplace –
has condemned her to a loss far greater than she knows.

So far it would almost be permissible to read the poem as a sort of
feminist guide to shopping: watch out for those so-called bargains,

sister, especially the ones offered by the funny little men – you'll be taken for a lot more than you know. But to read it as such a sororal cautionary tale is to neglect what the poem has to say about the importance of looking. While one can get into trouble by satisfying the desire to look and listen, the trouble is precisely the loss of that desire. Christina Rossetti herself wanted to name the poem, 'A Peep at the Goblins', but when her brother Dante Gabriel suggested 'Goblin Market', Christina accepted this as a 'greatly improved title'.[43] Yet while the poem is certainly about the 'traffic in women', it also seems to be about the desire to 'peep'. Even more interestingly, the poem does not appear to condemn this voyeuristic desire in itself but rather to represent its risks in the goblin market.

Thus, Laura at first warns Lizzie, 'We must not look at goblin men', as well as 'We must not buy their fruits.' But apparently sensing her sister's weakening control, Lizzie responds, 'Laura, Laura, / You should not peep at goblin men' (ll. 42, 43, 48, 49). Lizzie sticks her fingers in her ears and shuts her eyes, but Laura lingers and looks, 'Wondering at each merchant man'.[44]

When she returns after having made her unwittingly disastrous bargain, and 'sucked and sucked and sucked' the goblin fruit until her lips were sore, Lizzie meets her 'at the gate / Full of wise upbraidings' (ll. 141–2). 'Dear, you should not stay so late, / Twilight is not good for maidens', she reminds her sister primly, and now already too late tells her the sad tale of Jeanie who 'lies low' because she loitered so (ll. 143–63). But when Laura first suffers agonies because of the frustration of her 'baulked desire', and then, like her 'kernel-stone', begins to dry up, dwindle, and face the prospect of a 'sandful' sterility (how painful that 'sandful' is!), Lizzie is jarred out of her maidenly correctness by her sister's 'cankerous care'. After taking the prudent precaution of supplying herself with a silver penny, Lizzie ventures out, 'And for the first time in her life / Began to listen and look' (ll. 327–8).

The narrative thus clearly affirms woman's listening and looking – Lizzie needs to listen and look, the line suggests, or she will remain merely a happy little bird in her closed domestic cage. The decision to confront the goblins of the twilight, to open her eyes and unstop her ears, is as crucial to Lizzie as the recovery of desire will be to Laura. So long as Lizzie remains safely behind her garden gate, she will never know desire or taste its fulfillment and she will be no better off – though her case will be different – than her sister, whose desire has been stolen from her. The sisters represent women's double plight in the Victorian sexual economy: either risk becoming a commodity yourself, or risk never tasting desire, never letting yourself 'peep'.

The poem demonstrates for us how listening may be as seductive as looking: the goblins laugh when they spy Lizzie 'peeping', and they

slither towards her in a fascinating cacophony of sounds that fills the
ear just as the earlier listing of fruits fills the mouth. These sounds are
full of sinister, sexual, spell-binding implications – snake-like, we might
say.

But looking and listening are not enough to accomplish the poem's
desire for Lizzie here. She must also suffer, putting up at first with
name-calling, then with what we would call sexual harassment and
physical abuse. The goblins push her and jostle her, rip her dress, tear
out her hair, and step on her feet. Finally, they try to force their 'fruits'
into her mouth. Under this treatment, Lizzie is transformed into a
heroic and unviolated figure. The list of similes here interestingly refers
both to colonial and sexual economies: she's like a 'fruit-crowned
orange tree' beset by wasps and bees, or like 'a royal virgin town'
beleaguered by a fleet 'Mad to tug her standard down'. Laughing in
her heart, Lizzie gleefully lets the goblins 'syrup' her face with their
juices, but she keeps her mouth shut. The goblins are unable to
penetrate her. When she leaves the glen, the penny jingling in her
purse is testimony that she got what she wanted for a smaller price
than she thought she might have to pay. The price was only 'a smart,
ache, tingle' – not so bad, under the circumstances.

Ecstatically, she offers Laura the 'juices' of her sexual knowledge,
spread over the surface of her bruised body:

> She cried 'Laura', up the garden,
> 'Did you miss me?
> Come and kiss me.
> Never mind my bruises,
> Hug me, kiss me, suck my juices
> Squeezed from goblin fruits for you,
> Goblin pulp and goblin dew.
> Eat me, drink me, love me;
> Laura, make much of me:
> For your sake I have braved the glen
> And had to do with goblin merchant men.'
>
> (ll. 464–74)

Laura clings about her sister, 'kissed and kissed and kissed her', and
is transformed in her turn. Though the juice is 'wormwood' to her
tongue, and she 'loathes' the feast, she appears to experience a
masochistic orgy – writhing like one possessed, leaping and singing,
and beating her breast. In simile, she streams upward like an eagle
toward the sun, like a caged thing freed, like a flying flag when armies
run. And then she falls – falls like a mast struck by lightning, like a

tree uprooted by the wind, like a waterspout that falls into the sea. She falls, 'pleasure past and anguish past', into a deep sleep, from which she awakens as innocent as ever, and quite healthy.

Lizzie appears to have restored her sister by recirculating the erotic energies first set into motion by the goblin market. Inviting her sister to feast on her instead of on the goblin fruits produces a saving satisfaction. But all such exchanges involve the paying of some price, and here the price is pain – a pain which seems always to originate from the 'goblin merchant men'. However, the pain does not seem to be part of a sadistic–masochistic pairing. Rather, the pain which accompanies the women's erotic pleasure appears to be the inevitable effect of that dimly glimpsed other world that frames and constructs the sisters' relationship to each other. Nevertheless, within their own sphere, sisters can do a lot for each other. Or, as Laura teaches the little ones to sing, 'there is no friend like a sister'.

In the end, however, we must acknowledge that the poem accomplishes this transformative sisterhood by pushing the heterosexual world to its margins – husbands are not completely excluded, they are implied in the last paragraph – and by wiping out all reference to class or racial differences as if they did not exist. That they did exist, and that they determine the vision in *Goblin Market* of non-hierarchical sisterhood, is demonstrated by the poem which has been placed immediately after *Goblin Market* in the 1862 volume. This poem, 'In the Round Tower at Jhansi, June 8, 1857,' carries in its title the specific reference to time and place, and to empire and colony, that has been excluded from *Goblin Market*.

The title of the poem refers to an incident in what was called the 'Indian Mutiny' but was actually part of the Indian rebellion against the British Empire, an incident in which a young white officer reportedly shot first his wife and then himself in order to protect her from the threat of rape by 'The swarming howling wretches below'. These 'wretches below' are, presumably, the Indian troops. In this poem, then, we find the traces of the imperialist discourse missing from the preceding poem: the purity of the (English) female body here is constituted by its absolute difference from 'The swarming howling wretches below'. Lizzie's consumable body is, after all, offered to an equally blond sister – those 'wretches below' on the London streets have not been invited to the saving feast.

I have suggested that *Goblin Market* constructs a radically different view of the female body and its appetites, and that the poet's access to the social and discursive matrix of the Oxford Movement's 'women's mission to women' accounts for this radical discourse. Read in this context, the poem articulates women's common vulnerability to sexual and economic exploitation while affirming the bodies and appetites that

'Eat Me, Drink Me, Love Me'

are implicated in that exploitation. But 'In the Round Tower at Jhansi' demonstrates that *Goblin Market* achieves this seemingly radical vision of women's bodies through its deliberate exclusion of racial and class differences. Like that first and typical woman, Christina Rossetti's work is still limited by a 'feminine guessiness as to means'.

Notes

1. NANCY ARMSTRONG, 'The Occidental Alice', *Differences*, 2 (Summer 1990): 3–40.
2. Ibid., p. 9. On the 'double-bodied image', see also SANDER GILMAN, 'Black Bodies, White Bodies: Toward an Iconography of Female Sexuality in Late Nineteenth-Century Art, Medicine, and Literature', in Henry Louis Gates, Jr (ed.), *'Race', Writing, and Difference* (Chicago, 1985), pp. 223–61.
3. All references to *Goblin Market* are to *The Complete Poems of Christina Rossetti*, ed. R.W. Crump (Baton Rouge, 1979), vol. I, pp. 11–26. Perhaps the 'eat me' and 'drink me' labels in *Wonderland* are already a more restrained and heterosexually-oriented version of Lizzie's 'eat me, drink me, love me', for 'Lewis Carroll' (Revd Charles Dodgson) not only knew Rossetti well but was extremely enamored of little girls and very likely to have been intrigued by *Goblin Market*. See *The Annotated Alice*, ed. Martin Gardner (Harmondsworth, England, 1960), pp. 11–13, and U.C. KNOEPFLMACHER's 'Avenging Alice: Christina Rossetti and Lewis Carroll', *Nineteenth-Century Literature (NCL)*, 41 (1986): 302, 311.
4. CHARLES BERNHEIMER, *Figures of Ill Repute: Representing Prostitution in Nineteenth-Century France* (Cambridge, Mass., 1989), p. 2.
5. JUDITH R. WALKOWITZ, *Prostitution and Victorian Society: Women, Class and the State* (Cambridge, 1980), p. 3.
6. *The Poetical Works of Dante Gabriel Rossetti*, ed. William M. Rossetti (London, 1911), p. 39. D.M.R. BENTLEY points out that Dante Gabriel turned 'intensively to the fallen-woman theme between 1853 and 1858', and that William Rossetti stated that 'Jenny' was finished toward 1858, though revised in 1869 ('The Meretricious and the Meritorious in *Goblin Market*: A Conjecture and an Analysis', in David A. Kent (ed.), *The Achievement of Christina Rossetti* (Ithaca, 1987), p. 60). *Goblin Market*, dated 27 April 1859, would appear to have been written in roughly the same period as 'Jenny'.
7. JEROME J. McGANN, 'Christina Rossetti's Poems: A New Edition and a Revaluation', *Victorian Studies (VS)*, 23 (1980): 254.
8. 'The Meretricious and the Meritorious in *Goblin Market*', p. 58.
9. See ADRIENNE RICH's foundational analysis of the strategies universally employed by cultures to make heterosexuality compulsory by discouraging and even punishing homosexuality, thus coercing women into 'choosing' heterosexuality. Rich theorizes that all women remain more attached to their mothers than men do, and that all women are therefore part of a 'lesbian continuum'. See 'Compulsory Heterosexuality and Lesbian Existence' in Ann Snitow, Christine Stansell, and Sharon Thompson (eds), *Powers of Desire: The Politics of Sexuality* (New York, 1983), pp. 177–205.
10. As DOROTHY MERMIN comments, 'This is a world in which men serve only

the purpose of impregnation' ('Heroic Sisterhood in *Goblin Market'*, *Victorian Poetry* (*VP*), 21 (1983): 114).

11. *The Poetical Works of Christina Georgina Rossetti,* with memoir and notes by William Michael Rossetti (London, 1924), p. lv.

12. MARTHA VICINUS, *Independent Women: Work and Community for Single Women, 1850–1920* (Chicago, 1985), p. 83.

13. MARY POOVEY, *Uneven Developments: The Ideological Work of Gender in Mid-Victorian England* (Chicago, 1988), p. 2.

14. LAURA MULVEY, referring to Jacques Lacan's theory, explains how 'the unconscious of patriarchal society' structures Western narrative so that woman is the object of the male gaze ('Visual Pleasure and Narrative Cinema', reprinted in Constance Penley (ed.), *Feminism and Film Theory* (New York, 1988), pp. 57–68).

15. TERRENCE HOLT's otherwise insightful reading of sexual and economic exchange in *Goblin Market,* for example, is limited by its reading of the language of the poem exclusively in relation to a dominant phallocentrism. Not surprisingly, Holt ignores the female homoeroticism of the poem. See '"Men sell not such in any town"': Exchange in *Goblin Market'*, *VP*, 28 (1990): 51–67.

16. GEORGINA BATTISCOMBE, *Christina Rossetti: A Divided Life* (New York, 1981), p. 76.

17. MACKENZIE BELL, *Christina Rossetti: A Biographical and Critical Study* (Boston, 1898), p. 60. Interestingly, William's letter goes on to document the interaction between Christina's church-related social work and the consumer culture of her day. One thing which occupied Christina 'to an extent one would hardly credit', William writes,

> was the making-up of scrapbooks for Hospital patients or children – This may possibly have begun before she removed to Torrington Sq[uare]: was certainly in very active exercise for several years ensuing – say up to 1885. When I called to see her and my mother it was 9 chances out of 10 that I found her thus occupied – I daresay she may have made up at least 50 biggish scrapbooks of this kind – taking some pains in adapting borderings to the pages etc. etc.

These scrapbooks, no longer extant but presumably compiled from popular magazines and newspapers, suggest the poet's interest in popular culture.

18. *Poetical Works,* p. 485. DIANE D'AMICO, in 'Christina Rossetti's "From Sunset to Star Rise": A New Reading' (*VP*, 27 (1989): 95–100) has also pointed out that William was probably mistaken in this surmise, not only because 'House of Charity' is never used in the records for this institution, but because an Anglican institution for the 'fallen' was much more usually referred to as a 'House of Mercy'. Concluding that Christina's note, 'House of Charity', probably refers to some other institution – perhaps the House of Charity in Soho – D'Amico suggests that the poet probably worked in more than one charitable institution.

19. Canon Burrows described its foundation as 'a time of fervour and revival of church principles'. By January, 1839, only a year and a half after its founding, for example, the congregation had set up schools in which no fewer than 871 district children were enrolled. See HENRY W. BURROWS, *The Half-Century of Christ Church, Albany Street, St Pancras* (London, 1887), pp. 12–14.

20. ALLAN T. CAMERON, *The Religious Communities of the Church of England* (London, 1918), pp. 28–34.

21. THOMAS JAY WILLIAMS and ALLAN WALTER CAMPBELL, *The Park Village Sisterhood* (London, 1965), p. 23.
22. Pitkin Guide, *All Saints Margaret Street* (London, 1990), p. 18.
23. *All Saints' Church, Margaret Street*. Reprinted from *The Orchestra* (London, 1866).
24. The Park Village Sisterhood merged with the Devonport Sisterhood in 1856. See Chapter 12 in WILLIAMS and CAMPBELL, *The Park Village Sisterhood*, pp. 112–17.
25. JOYCE COOMBS, *One Aim: Edward Stuart, 1820–1877* (London, 1975), p. 11.
26. BATTISCOMBE, *Christina Rossetti*, pp. 55–7. BURROWS, *Half-Century of Christ Church*, p. 22.
27. So far as I have been able to determine, there was no connection between this church and the St Mary Magdalene institution at Highgate.
28. Christina visited Collinson's family (James Collinson himself was not there) at Pleasley Hill during August 1849, but there is no evidence that she was not in London during July 1849. See *The Family-Letters of Christina Georgina Rossetti*, ed. William Michael Rossetti (London, 1908), pp. 5–8; also LONA MOSK PACKER, *Christina Rossetti* (Berkeley, 1963), p. 35.
29. JANET GALLIGANI CASEY, in 'The Potential of Sisterhood: Christina Rossetti's Goblin Market', *VP*, 29 (1991): 63–78, also gives an account of Rossetti's interest in Nightingale and the 'sisterhood movement', but argues that 'sisterhood' in the poem 'potentially includes the experience of both sexes' (p. 63).
30. WALKOWITZ notes that women who moved into prostitution were most often girls in their late teens, living outside the family, in fact often half or full orphan, and frequently having previously been casual maids of all work. See *Prostitution and Victorian Society*, p. 19.
31. CAMERON, *Religious Communities*, pp. 43, 59. Interestingly, these two Sisterhoods which took work with prostitutes as their primary focus grew to be two of the largest Anglican communities (VICINUS, *Independent Women*, p. 72).
32. First organized under a council formed by the Bishop of London in 1854, this 'penitentiary' at Highgate was known originally as 'Park House' but called 'St Mary Magdalene's' in order to give it a 'distinctive name'. See Deed to the London Diocesan Penitentiary, St Mary Magdalene, London Guildhall Library, MS 18532 and the Annual Reports of the London Diocesan Penitentiary, St Mary Magdalene's, London Guildhall Library, MS 18535. The institution is not listed among those institutions supervised by the All Saints' Sisterhood, nor is it mentioned in accounts of the Park Village Sisters. CAMERON notes that 'The House of Mercy', North Hill, Highgate, was taken over by the Clewer Sisters in 1901 (*Half-Century of Christ Church*, p. 65).
33. CARROLL SMITH-ROSENBERG, 'The Female World of Love and Ritual' in *Disorderly Conduct: Visions of Gender in Victorian America* (New York, 1985), pp. 53–76.
34. *On Penitentiary Work . . . Two Sermons Preached At the Opening of the Chapel of St Mary's Home, Wantage, July 30, 1861, by Samuel [Wilberforce], Lord Bishop of Oxford, and Henry Parry Liddon, M.A., with a Short Preface on Sisterhoods, by W.J. Butler, M.A., Vicar of Wantage* (Oxford and London, 1861), pp. iv–v.
35. *Parochial Mission-Women Association*. A Sermon Preached at St James's, Westminster, on June 20th, 1867, by the Rev. H.W. Burrows, B.D., Perpetual Curate of Christ Church, St Pancras (Oxford and London, 1867), pp. 4–5.
36. Although there is no evidence that Christina Rossetti was a member of this

particular organization, a Young Women's Friendly Society was organized at Christ Church for the benefit of servant girls. Tea, bible lessons, and other 'religious recreations' were offered on Sunday afternoons (BURROWS, *Half-Century of Christ Church*, p. 34). Maria Rossetti not only worked with this society but wrote a series of letters (dated 1860–61) to the young women in it, published as *Letters to My Bible Class on Thirty-Nine Sundays* (London, 1872).

37. *The Manual of the Confraternity of All Saints, for Girls and Young Women*, in connection with the All Saints' Home, 82, Margaret Street, Cavendish Square, 2nd edn (London, 1866), p. 1.

38. In a notice to the public, the Superior of the All Saints' Home stated that 'women of a superior class are received to be trained for Nursing the Sick Poor in Hospitals; and for Private Nursing in the Families of the rich' ('Nurses for the Sick, in Private Families', All Saints' Home, 82, Margaret Street, Cavendish Square, 1862). VICINUS comments on the 'upper-class character' of the All Saints' and Clewer Sisterhoods and notes that both were known as 'fashionable' (*Independent Women*, pp. 55–6).

39. JACQUES LACAN, 'The mirror stage as formative of the function of the I as revealed in psychoanalytic experience', in *Écrits: A Selection*, trans. Alan Sheridan (New York, 1977), pp. 1–7. As JANE GALLOP notes, 'In Lacanian models she [the mother] is the prohibited object of desire; in object-relations she is the mirror where the infant can find his or her subjectivity. In either case her only role is to complement the infant's subjectivity; in neither story is she ever a subject' ('Reading the Mother Tongue: Psychoanalytic Feminist Criticism', *Critical Inquiry* (*CritI*), 13 (1987): p. 324).

40. HELENA MICHIE, for example, speaks of Laura and Lizzie as representing a culturally constructed difference between sisters, in which one sister is the 'fallen' and the other the 'unfallen', one the 'sexual' and the other the 'pure woman', in '"There is No Friend Like a Sister": Sisterhood as Sexual Difference', *ELH*, 56 (1989): p. 404. JEROME McGANN typifies the other reading which argues that without Laura's 'precipitous act the women would have remained forever in a condition of childlike innocence' and that 'Lizzie's timidity is by no means condemned, but its limitations are very clear', in 'Christina Rossetti's Poems', p. 250.

41. CHRISTINA ROSSETTI, *Letter and Spirit* (London, 1882), p. 17.

42. *The Face of the Deep: A Devotional Commentary* (London, 1892), p. 422.

43. *Poetical Works*, p. 459: CRUMP, I, p. 234.

44. We should not overlook the fact that 'merchant man' also refers to a cargo-carrying ship.

References

BATTISCOMBE, GEORGINA, *Christina Rossetti: A Divided Life* (New York, 1981).

BURROWS, HENRY W., *The Half-Century of Christ Church, Albany Street, St Pancras* (London, 1981).

CAMERON, ALLAN T., *The Religious Communities of the Church of England* (London, 1981).

COOMBS, JOYCE, *One Aim: Edward Stuart, 1820–1877* (London, 1975).

CRUMP, R.W. (ed.), *The Complete Poems of Christina Rossetti* (Baton Rouge, 1979).

McGANN, JEROME J., 'Christina Rossetti's Poems: A New Edition and a Revaluation', *Victorian Studies*, 23 (1980): 254.

WALKOWITZ, JUDITH R., *Prostitution and Victorian Society: Women, Class and the State* (Cambridge, 1980).

WILLIAMS, THOMAS JAY, and CAMPBELL, ALLAN WALTER, *The Park Village Sisterhood* (London, 1965).

Part Four
Other Poets

14 Michael Field*

ANGELA LEIGHTON

'Michael Field' was the pseudonym of two women poets, Katherine Bradley and Edith Cooper, aunt and niece, and probably lovers. The first part of Leighton's chapter, leading up to this extract, is largely biographical, including an account of the poets' conversion to Catholicism. In the extract, Leighton finds their best poetry in their pre-Catholic, 'pagan' phase. More information about the poets, and an argument for their lesbianism, can be found in Christine White's article. Leighton's inclusion of Michael Field in her book, along with poets such as Augusta Webster amd Charlotte Mew, continues the feminist expansion of the canon, and may be influenced by the efforts of lesbian critics to discover a lesbian tradition. For Leighton, the poets' lesbianism puts them in a special relationship to the female tradition she has been tracing. They are freed from having to engage with the passivity and suffering allocated to women in a heterosexual tradition. Here, we could compare their love poetry with the convoluted, parodic love sonnets of Rossetti as analysed by Harrison (Chapter 11). Their nature poetry too is exceptional: they evade the problems Homans (Chapter 1) finds for women in the Romantic tradition, and adopt their own form of Darwinism. Leighton compares them also to their 'decadent' male contemporaries: their paganism is without the self-advertising sense of sin of Swinburne. They thus escape into an amoral, erotic world outside the ideologies of their time. As for Carpenter (Chapter 13), lesbianism allows a way round or behind an oppressive discursive framework.

* Reprinted from *Victorian Women Poets* (New York and London: Harvester Wheatsheaf, 1992), pp. 225–43.

When a girl becomes a lover

Michael Field's best poems are love poems. Throughout their lives, Katherine and Edith wrote verses about and to each other, celebrating their love as a sensual and sexual end in itself. Strikingly free of the morbid penalties and self-denying mischances of much Victorian women's love poetry, they write in a voice which is forthright, requited and relaxed. The exhibited melancholy of sentimentalism, the scarlets and whites of Christian morality and the coins of the socio-sexual market are all missing from their verses. It is as if these poems exist in an atmosphere altogether outside the moral and ideological structures of the age. Idiomatic, witty and informal, they are cheerfully defiant both of the literary heritage of the heart and of the heterosexual bargains of the fall. They thus open up a pagan subtext which has lain in 'reserve' in much previous women's poetry, and make it freely and unproblematically accessible. It is true that their poetry therefore lacks, like [Augusta] Webster's, though for different reasons, the imaginative advantages of that 'reserve' – the sense of a residual depth of metaphor which plays against the poem's moral and narrative patterns and, therefore, the sense of language itself as a forbidden fruit snatched from the world of punishing experience. This is a poetry which altogether misses that stress of truth against pleasure, conscience against desire, which constitutes the main tension of other Victorian women poets.

A short, untitled verse from the early volume *Underneath the Bough* (1893) expresses the underlying principle of this new-found freedom:

> How sweeter far it is to give
> Than just to rest in the receiving,
> Sweeter to sigh than be sighed over,
> Sweeter to deal the blow than bear the grieving,
> That girl will learn who dares become a lover.
>
> The songs she sings will have the glee,
> The laughter of the wind that looses
> Wing and breaks from a forest cover;
> Freedom of stream that slips its icy nooses
> Will be her freedom who becomes a lover.

(UB: pp. 131–2)

Christina Rossetti also pleaded for passion in, for instance, 'The heart knoweth its own bitterness':

> To give, to give, not to receive,
> I long to pour myself, my soul,

Not to keep back or count or leave
But king with king to give the whole . . .

(*CP*: III, pp. 265–6, ll. 25–8)

However, where Rossetti's register remains open-endedly teleological,
duplicating heavenly and earthly desire, even though at cross-purposes,
Michael Field's is sturdily, if less musically, literal. The girl, here, must
not just 'pour' her love, with all its emblematic significance, but, more
practically and strategically, 'become a lover'. As in 'Prologue', the
word 'lover' carries a startlingly secular and anti-romantic charge.
Where Rossetti craves reciprocity, Field craves self-assertion; where
Rossetti waits, like a 'fountain sealed' (p. 44), for the other lover who
may come, Field advocates free-flowing 'songs' and 'laughter', whether
he comes or not. The explosive self-repression of the one is in strong
contrast to the relaxed self-expression of the other. It is not surprising
that Edith was nonplussed by Christina's life of 'prayer and denial', and
by the rumour that she was determined to be 'Love's Martyr for [Dante
Gabriel's] sake' (*WD*: pp. 115–16). By comparison with Rossetti's
tormented depths of meaning and evasive cross-purposes, Field's poems
seem light and obvious. They assert a connection between creativity
and sexual pleasure, art and laughter, which Rossetti buries deep in the
tactical ambiguities of metaphor. In Michael Field those connections are
embraced as the very public manifesto of their inspiration. The woman
poet who 'dares become a lover', and does not merely hope, wait, yearn
or call for one, is the poet who has freed her imagination from the 'icy
nooses' of faithful expectation and repressed desire, and who can thus
speak with the free-spirited, careless 'laughter of the wind'. As
Adrienne Rich puts it, in relation to a much later lesbian poet, Judy
Grahn: 'The word *lover*, purged of romantic–sentimental associations,
becomes a name for what human beings might mean to each other in a
world where each person held both power and responsibility' (1980:
p. 251). The girl, in the nineteenth century, 'who dares become a lover'
dares, paradoxically, to be also free of love, in a world where too much
love is woman's one compensation for having no 'power and
responsibility'.

This carefree passionateness runs through the Sapphic verses in *Long
Ago*, 'a little collection of poems by a great genius' (1985: p. 95), as
Robert Browning called it. When, during the early 1890s, Katherine and
Edith were feeling especially aggrieved by the critical silence which met
their work, and felt that their publisher was pushing younger poets
ahead of them, they may have been thinking in particular of Dollie
Radford. John Lane's edition of her *Songs and Other Verses* was
published in 1895, and it shows the extent to which minor women's
poetry continued to fit the sentimentalist model. Although Radford

wrote some comical feminist poems, like 'A Novice' (to her cigarette) and 'From Our Emancipated Aunt in Town', these are categorically headed 'Other Verses', while the 'Songs' themselves fall into a disappointingly familiar rote of rhymed lyricism. The frontispiece drives home the message of the whole collection: it shows the woman poet in a state of improvising abandon under her large lyre. The poems themselves then coyly insist on this epithetical imagery in mournful set-pieces:

> The little songs which come and go,
> In tender measures, to and fro,
> Whene'er the day brings you to me,
> Keep my heart full of melody.
>
> But on my lute I strive in vain
> To play the music o'er again,
> And you, dear love, will never know
> The little songs which come and go.

> (1895: p. 20)

By comparison with this furtive, miniaturist passion, blandly addressed to the observing reader, Michael Field's poems in *Long Ago* sound daringly assertive and specific. Their Sappho is not the old sad lutanist of death, but an urgently prosaic speaker, whose love poems to her girls, as well as to gods and men, are free of any morality of faithfulness or idealism. This Sappho is not tied to one object, but sings variously of desire, jealousy, maternal love and friendship. Even when, at the end, she leaps from her cliff (an event for which Wharton expressly finds no 'firm historical basis': 1895: p. 15), she thinks as much of 'Damophyla, the lovely-haired' and of 'Eros' (*LA*: p. 127) her goal, as of Phaon, the betrayer. Meanwhile, the many poems addressed to girls: Anactoria, Gorgo, Atthis, Mnasidica, Gyrinna, Erinna, Dica, bring into English poetry a homosexual strain which, at least in women's poetry, is quite new.

For instance, poem XXXV in *Long Ago* is addressed by Sappho to another woman who has been distracted from real pleasure by a ring. The original fragment consists merely of the line: '*Foolish woman, pride not thyself on a ring*' (Wharton: p. 93). Around this tantalising hint, Michael Field develops a flirtatiously suggestive little scene:

> Come, Gorgo, put the rug in place,
>   And passionate recline;
> I love to see thee in thy grace,
>   Dark, virulent, divine.

But wherefore thus thy proud eyes fix
  Upon a jewelled band?
Art thou so glad the sardonyx
  Becomes thy shapely hand?

Bethink thee! 'Tis for such as thou
  Zeus leaves his lofty seat;
'Tis at thy beauty's bidding how
  Man's mortal life shall fleet;
Those fairest hands – dost thou forget
  Their power to thrill and cling?
O foolish woman, dost thou set
  Thy pride upon a ring?

(LA: p. 56)

The causal, homely voyeurism of 'Come, Gorgo, put the rug in place, /
And passionate recline'[1] shows none of the self-appreciating poses of
the older Sapphos. This one has indeed become a lover, able to
appreciate a body which is not her own and which is not hysterically
traumatised by death. The poem is not a plea for sexual attention from
some disembodied male eye, whether the reader's or the imagined
unfaithful lover's, but an attentive, half-playful, half-erotic verbal caress,
with no ulterior motives of reciprocity, rings or religious idealism.
Furthermore, Michael Field's description of love between women has
none of the allure of disease and sin which made it fashionable among
the decadents. By comparison with this clarity of passion and style,
Swinburne's steamy sensationalism in his lesbian poems seems oddly
artificial. 'Anactoria', for instance, becomes yet another unspecifically
aggressive fantasy of pain:

I would my love could kill thee; I am satiated
With seeing thee live, and fain would have thee dead.
I would earth had thy body as fruit to eat,
And no mouth but some serpent's found thee sweet.
I would find grievous ways to have thee slain,
Intense device, and superflux of pain . . .

(1904: I, p. 58)

This decadent's Sappho is as much a self-indulgently unnatural
invention as the sentimentalist's.[2] In fact, the one is very much the
reverse side of the other. Both insist on an extremity of feeling which
only betrays its own failure to feel.

By comparison, Michael Field's Sappho has an authentically light-
hearted, classical intensity. Around the fragment '*To you, fair maids, my*

241

mind changes not' (Wharton: p. 80), for instance, they elaborate the stanzas:

> Maids, not to you my mind doth change,
> Men I defy, allure, estrange,
> Prostrate, make bond or free:
> Soft as the stream beneath the plane
> To you I sing my love's refrain;
> Between us is no thought of pain,
> > Peril, satiety.
>
> Soon doth a lover's patience tire,
> But ye to manifold desire
> Can yield response, ye know
> When for long, museful days I pine,
> The presage at my heart divine;
> To you I never breathe a sign
> Of inward want or woe.
>
> When injuries my spirit bruise,
> Allaying virtue ye infuse
> With unobtrusive skill:
> And if care frets ye come to me
> As fresh as nymph from stream or tree,
> And with your soft vitality
> > My weary bosom fill.

(*LA*: pp. 52–3)

This Sappho is no masochistic martyr to love. The verbs are active, 'I defy, allure, estrange', 'I sing', and the gender difference between men and maids knowledgeably sexual. 'Soft as the stream beneath the plane' is a description of an unhampered woman-to-woman's language as suggestively labial as any Irigarayan writing of the body ('When our lips speak together', *Signs*, 6 (1980): 69–79). By contrast to the changeable power games of her love for men, this Sappho acknowledges the other 'refrain' of her tender and consoling love for women, with its gratifications of much more 'manifold desire'. The sheer colloquial lucidity of these verses, with their forthright invitations and their plurality of love objects, is in striking contrast to the possessive, fixated idealism of both the courtly and the decadent modes. The register shifts easily from the lustful to the protective, the sexual to the maternal, thus projecting an innocence of purpose which half disguises the subject matter. Unlike Swinburne's swampy declarations of sadistic passion, the naturalness of Michael Field disarms censorship from the start. Their verse shows up the extent to which decadence relies on an endemic and even loudly advertised sense of sin. Without that sin, it loses much of its effect. By contrast, their poetry is genuinely 'Indifferent to heaven and hell'; its Pateresque paganism never a bogey for frightening the philistines. Furthermore, by being simply not interested in sin, they seem to have escaped the scandalised disapproval Swinburne is eager to court.

Evidently, then, so long as Browning's 'two dear Greek women' did not seem to combat 'social conventions' (*WD*: p. 8) in any obvious way, they caused no offence. His admiration for the poems in *Long Ago* suggests that such conventions are rigidly defined ideas, which cannot be recognised unless they appear, precisely, in conventional forms. The Victorian imagination was, perhaps, singularly free *not* to imagine, at least until Freud named them or the law incriminated them, areas of experience not 'conventionally' immoralised. Although terms like 'Sapphism' and 'lesbian' were current in France at least since the 1840s, they only started to appear in English in specialised medical dictionaries at the beginning of the 1890s (Hallett, 1979: p. 451). The theory of lesbianism found its permitted expression, in France, in the language of decadent aesthetics, but in England, in the much more regulatory language of psychology. When, in 1883, J.A. Symonds published his essay, *A Problem in Greek Ethics*, ten years after it was written, he dared print only ten private copies. Even in 1908 the work, which contains a most tactful account of Greek sexual mores, was only published privately. Symonds glances passingly at 'feminine homosexual passions', and then only to affirm their social invisibility: they 'were never worked into the social system' (1908: p. 70), he explains. The difference between Michael Field's uninhibited life and writings and Charlotte Mew's anxious reticence may have had as much to do with the two ages' different conventions of naming and not naming, ignoring and illegalising, as with the poets' own different temperaments.

In general, then, this is a love poetry which focuses on physical desire as an enlightened, innocent end in itself. Such desire has no metaphysical or moral goals. It is not a metaphor for some other drama of salvation or inspiration, neither is it an exquisitely managed hedonism which, like the far-fetched pleasures of the decadents, substitutes sexual artifice for art, pain for passion, sin for love. When Katherine and Edith agreed with Wilde that 'the whole problem of life turns on pleasure' (*WD*: p. 136), they were speaking as eager novices rather than as weary *cognoscenti*. For them, the idea of pleasure involves an exhilarating recall of woman's subjectivity from the moribund misery of the old Sapphos, as well as a new and explicit demand for real sexual experience in a girl's life.

The poem, 'A Girl' (1893), which was almost certainly written by

Katherine for Edith, is, like 'Prologue', a personal testament to their union. In some ways, it recalls one of the two complete poems by Sappho to survive the ravages of time and the deliberate book burnings of the Middle Ages (see Foster, 1958: p. 21): 'To a Girl' or 'To Brochea'. Its description of female passion as a physical response of blushing, sweating and being tongue-tied was much translated and imitated, notably by Tennyson, though, of course, he radically alters the meaning of the original by writing as the observing male, not as the female lover herself. Although Michael Field's verse does not reproduce Sappho's description of physical passion, its subject draws on this literary tradition of love-addresses to girls, while subtly reintroducing the original homosexual context which had been lost:

> A girl,
>   Her soul a deep-wave pearl
> Dim, lucent of all lovely mysteries;
>   A face flowered for heart's ease,
>   A brow's grace soft as seas
>   Seen through faint forest-trees:
>   A mouth, the lips apart,
> Like aspen-leaflets trembling in the breeze
>   From her tempestuous heart.
>   Such: and our souls so knit,
>   I leave a page half-writ –
>   The work begun
>   Will be to heaven's conception done,
>   If she come to it.

(UB: pp. 68–9)

The wave effect of the metre here subtly reproduces the very tentative outline of the girl herself, who is seen, as if underwater, like a creature still finding shape. Each specific feature, her face, brow, mouth and lips, is described in such a way that it blurs into distantly imagined prospects of the landscape. 'A face flowered for heart's ease' hovers between its two meanings, of easing the heart and of being, itself, like a pansy, 'heart's ease'. The idea of her brow then opens into another hazy vista, of distant seas shadowed by trees. Far from being a list of the coy mistress's attributes or even a list of the dying woman's wasted attractions, these details capture the sense of unknown potential in the girl, of far possibilities not yet clearly envisaged, of an identity still fluid and shifting. Like some Venus emerging from 'the deep-wave pearl' of seas, she takes shape in a language still, as it were, rippling with the uncertainty of her reality in the speaker's life. Half a love poem and half a poem almost, it feels, of verbally giving birth – ' "I speak as a mother; mothers of some sort we must all become"', Katherine once stated – it catches the fathomless and free quality of the girl's very nature in the wavering rhythms of its lines. This poem of coming to birth and to consciousness keeps the tone of ambiguous desire and motherliness of Sappho's poems. Michael Field's pagan imagination is not at odds with anything, any system of man or God, but inhabits another land, 'in the open air of nature'. At the end, the invitation to the girl to 'come to it' remains like a delicate, open-ended *double entendre* of love and poetry together.

Such a love poem, like many others by Michael Field, simply avoids the literary figures which, since the Middle Ages, had dictated the terms of love. While Barrett Browning re-appropriates that courtly imagery, though making it as foreign a language to the woman's heart as any 'Portuguese', and while Rossetti re-animates it, in her own quizzical way, by being always, at the last minute, dead, Michael Field has no truck with any of its suing and pleading, buying and denying. All the courtly clutter of desire: gloves, curls, rings, flowers, lutes and letters, has gone, and instead the intonations of real speech come cleared of the dust of literary self-reference:

> I love you with my life – 'tis so I love you;
> > I give you as a ring
> The cycle of my days till death:
> > I worship with the breath
> That keeps me in the world with you and spring:
> And God may dwell behind, but not above you.
>
> Mine, in the dark, before the world's beginning:
> > The claim of every sense,
> > Secret and source of every need;
> > The goal to which I speed,
> And at my heart a vigour more immense
> Than will itself to urge me to its winning.

(WH: p. 71)

Instead of that bookish and rather dusty exchange of goods, which the courtly model substitutes for desire, the natural imagery of Michael Field's love poetry insists on an alternative perspective. The motivation for love is a force which pushes darkly from 'before the world's beginning'. The superstructures of desire are thus reduced to a basic life-force, which has no ulterior 'goal' beyond the 'claim of every sense'. Vigorous rather than hurt, 'winning' rather than to be won, the 'heart', here, is not a trembling instrument of sensibility, waiting to be struck, but part of an anonymous compulsion of lusts and needs. There is no

wrangle for this 'ring' of love because it has no marketable, social value;
it is simply the 'cycle of my days till death'. On the one hand, this
natural imagery seems unengaged with the complex myths and
ideologies of the real world; but on the other hand, its very remoteness
is a challenge to those myths. Where Rossetti goblinised them from
within and Barrett Browning and Webster boldly mocked them from
without, Michael Field has moved out of their range altogether. By
taking human love out of the context of courtship and marriage, as they
naturally do, and putting it in the context of life's ancient, evolutionary
forces, they strip it of all but its own inner rationale of 'sense' and
'need'. In some ways, this is not an escape from the contemporary
world, but another kind of engagement with it. In the place of
sentimentalism, Michael Field offers a kind of literal, elemental
Darwinism of the heart.

The language of this unsocialised love draws especially on the active
'drive' of verbs:

> The love that breeds
>   In my heart for thee!
> As the iris is full, brimful of seeds,
> And all that it flowered for among the reeds
> Is packed in a thousand vermilion-beads
> That push, and riot, and squeeze, and clip,
> Till they burst the sides of the silver scrip,
> And at last we see
> What the bloom, with its tremulous, bowery fold
> Of zephyr-petal at heart did hold . . .

(UB: pp. 77–8)

Such reproductive imagery packs the poem with a Keatsian sense of
elemental reality. 'That push, and riot, and squeeze, and clip' turns the
heart, not into a vessel of outpouring tears, but into a crammed and
seedy flower head, bursting with new life. Elsewhere, the verbs seem
even more sexually assertive:

> I love her with the seasons, with the winds,
> As the stars worship, as anemones
> Shudder in secret for the sun, as bees
> Buzz round an open flower: in all kinds
> My love is perfect, and in each she finds
> Herself the goal . . .

(WH: p. 173)

Once again, love is an activity not an abstraction, a deed not a religion,
a matter of lovers rather than of loving to death.

Other love poems, however, show a streak of fantastical wit. The quirky sonnet, 'The Mummy Invokes his Soul' (1908), for instance, which obviously derives from an idea in the Egyptian *Book of the Dead*, is addressed by the trapped, mummified body to its own free soul. But the direction in the poem, unlike its original, is far from spiritual and transcendent:

> Down to me quickly, down! I am such dust,
> Baked, pressed together; let my flesh be fanned
> With thy fresh breath; come from thy reedy land
> Voiceful with birds; divert me, for I lust
> To break, to crumble – prick with pores this crust! –
> And fall apart, delicious, loosening sand.
> Oh, joy, I feel thy breath, I feel thy hand
> That searches for my heart, and trembles just
> Where once it beat. How light thy touch, thy frame!
> Surely thou perchest on the summer trees . . .
> And the garden that we loved? Soul, take thine ease,
> I am content, so thou enjoy the same
> Sweet terraces and founts, content, for thee,
> To burn in this immense torpidity.

> (WH: p. 88)

The poem evidently has its roots deep in Katherine's past when, at the age of twenty-one, she worried over the theological doctrine of soul sleep, and wrote in her diary: 'it seems to me a strange almost ghastly notion, – that of our Lord having dominion over thousands of torpid souls – Of the buried centuries, that he could quicken with a breath'.[3] Unlike the early 'Trompetenruf', however, 'The Mummy Invokes his Soul' has shed all its Christian anxieties about salvation, and turns the idea of interminable death into a conceit for heightened sexual desire. The positioning of phrases like 'I lust', 'I feel thy hand', 'and trembles just', lets the meaning hang, suggestively, in undecided expectation of the pleasure to come. In spite of the incongruity of the mouldering mummy quickening with new desires, the poem enacts, in its language, the barely disguised climax of physical pleasure. The 'come to me' motif carries no theological promise; only the sheer delight of a touch which rifles the mummy's hard-baked dust for the 'heart' which is touched as literally as by a 'hand': 'Oh, joy, I feel thy breath, I feel thy hand / That searches for my heart . . .' Such rummaging for the heart, in this reductively literal-minded context of a dead body, seems grotesque, a grim mockery of all the emblematically bared hearts of other, more soulful lovers. Yet, the rising excitement of the phrases also metonymises the heart into a more practically responsive organ of desire. The anatomical specificity of 'flesh', 'breath', 'hand' and 'heart' allow the airy soul and the dusty mummy to consummate, at least in the mummy's imagination, the pleasures of their long-dead senses.

The poem is a nonsense, but it is also a prolonged joke against the metaphysical or merely macabre connotations of the title. For all the Neoplatonic imagery of the soul as a bird in the 'trees', this is a love poem of the body, which invokes its soul, not as a principle of spiritual freedom or new life, but as the lost pleasure principle of its own material reality. Bound in mummy cloth, this absurdly passionate, dry-as-dust lover never seeks anything else than the hand to move its heart. In the end, however, with generous forbearance, it grants the soul 'ease' and enjoyment in the pleasure gardens of the afterlife, while it continues to burn in the 'immense torpidity' of lustful sleep and heat which are its eternal lot. No trumpet of the resurrection or bird of artistic immortality ever diverts the poem from its eccentrically insistent physical invitation. Out of the unresurrected tomb comes a posthumous consciousness still obsessed with its physical, fleshly life.

Another burial poem, 'Embalmment', similarly explodes the traditional motifs which it seems to invoke:

Let not a star suspect the mystery!
A cave that haunts thee in the dreams of night
Keep me as treasure hidden from thy sight,
And only thine while thou dost covet me!
As the Asmonaean queen perpetually
Embalmed in honey, cold to thy delight,
Cold to thy touch, a sleeping eremite,
Beside thee never sleeping I would be.

Or thou might'st lay me in a sepulchre,
And every line of life will keep its bloom,
Long as thou seal'st me from the common air.
Speak not, reveal not . . . There will be
In the unchallenged dark a mystery,
And golden hair sprung rapid in a tomb.

(WH: p. 26)

This queer conceit of being embalmed beside her lover, cold and chaste and perpetually awake, is imagined by the speaker as a figure, not of repression and self-denial, as in much women's poetry, but as a figure for being perpetually desired. The origin of the conceit comes from the story of Mariamne, the 'Asmonaean queen', who was Herod's first wife and whom, suspecting her of adultery, he had executed and embalmed in honey. However, nothing of the (heterosexual) horror of that story remains in Michael Field's poem. Instead, the embalmment (perhaps by way of the notion that mummia was an aphrodisiac, as in a nearly contemporary poem by Rupert Brooke)[4] serves as a figure for an entirely responsive and accessible sexual desire. The speaker asks to be buried where she will remain invisible except when actively coveted. Death is invoked, not as a state of cold-hearted abstraction from the world or of punishing inaccessibility to the lover, but as a perpetual, unfailing physical attentiveness: 'Beside thee never sleeping'.

In the second part, this metaphysical conceit is extended even more elaborately and absurdly. If sealed 'in a sepulchre' the lover will not fade or pale, but remain, in that air-tight atmosphere, as if freshly loved and cherished. Furthermore, in such a sealed place she will even thrive, like any 'mystery' that is 'unchallenged' in the 'dark'. The last line then invokes an idea which runs through Victorian literature, and which, in 1869, became a real-life legend. One of the observers at Lizzie Siddal's exhumation spread the rumour, which haunted a whole generation of writers, that her hair had continued to grow after her death and had filled the coffin with its gold. Dante Gabriel Rossetti refers to the event in the last lines of his sonnet 'Life-in-Love': "'Mid change the changeless night environeth, / Lies all that golden hair undimmed in death' (1913: p. 115). In 'Embalmment', all the controlled, delayed expectancy of the speaker's wish to be preserved in her lover's dreams suddenly climaxes in that disconcertingly lively image of 'golden hair sprung rapid in a tomb'. It is as if Michael Field has taken a figure for woman's repressed sexuality – a sexuality which flowers only in the grave – and turned it into a figure of comically prompt, live and 'rapid' responsiveness.

The Rossettian myth of burial is thus turned into a fantastical, mock-heroic simile of which the tone of secret mystery-mongering: 'Let not a star suspect the mystery!' 'Speak not, reveal not', is only part of a long-drawn-out strategy of seduction, audibly culminating in that flowering hair. Such an image is no more than a far-fetched, shared joke, and a 'mystery' only if it remains in 'the unchallenged dark' of innumerable airless Gothic vaults of desire. Ultimately, 'Embalmment' mocks its own macabre conceit of love, and challenges the very unenlightened morbidity of the Pre-Raphaelite myth which it has enjoyed. With a certain tasteless but witty exuberance, the poem takes the figure of the dead woman, embalmed and mummified, and brings her energetically back to life as a figure of speech for the unwilled, uncontrolled pleasure of sexual love.

The fascination with mummies in *fin-de-siècle* literature was partly encouraged by accounts of real archaeological excavations at the time. During the 1890s, the *Athenaeum* carried regular features on the discoveries of new tombs and cemeteries in Egypt, not so much for their own interest, but because they were rich sources of classical writings. The papyri which were used as mummy wrappings were frequently covered in classical texts, many of them new. One of the most important finds was at Oxyrhynchus where, among other things, new fragments of Sappho's poems were brought to light, and these explicitly proved the female sex of many of her lovers (Foster, 1958: pp. 19–20). In 1894, Pierre Louÿs published his *Chansons de Bilitis*, a set of mildly pornographic verses, allegedly written by one of Sappho's girl lovers, which he claimed to have discovered in Bilitis' real tomb in Egypt (1949: p. 21). The connection, which Louÿs exploited, between mummies and Sapphic love poetry may lie bedded deep in the 'cryptic' (Stimpson, in Abel, 1982: p. 21) imagery of Michael Field's own sonnet. Out of the crypt of women's repression and morbidity they bring, not a dead Lizzie with such hair, but a real, live lover who has only been waiting her time: at some level, another Sappho, 'sprung rapid' from the mummy cloths of sealed tombs.

Such, then, is Michael Field's strange, sometimes excessive and baroque, but also witty and sceptical contribution to the tradition of Victorian women's love poetry. In mockery of all the metaphorical vaults of death and repression as well as of all the spiritual goals of heaven and salvation which haunt their predecessors, they assert their alternative creed of self-justifying physical pleasure. To celebrate such pleasure as a female right – the right of 'a girl' not only to love but to 'become a lover' – is to break one of the most deep-seated silences in nineteenth-century women's poetry. Sappho has finally been recuperated for women as a model of poetry and of love together, with no social or metaphysical (death) penalties to be paid for either.

The ancient law of pleasure

Apart from these love poems to or for women, Michael Field also wrote a number of poems about the law of desire in nature. These bleaker, impersonal verses portray a universe cleared of religious or human purpose, and driven only by the anonymous, evolutionary forces of life itself. It is in these that Michael Field's earlier pagan creed is most movingly and sometimes quite awesomely expressed. Such a creed accepts the harsh realities of the natural world without judgment or sentimentality, and reproduces them in a sparing, depersonalised style which is quite unlike any other contemporary verse. Meredith's Darwinian perspectives, in 'The Woods of Westermain' for instance, are much more long-windedly deliberate and spooky, while Mathilde Blind's, in 'The Ascent of Man', are more philosophical and abstract.

Michael Field's sense of nature, by comparison, is largely free of imported human significance. Neither socially combative nor metaphysically comforting, their best nature poems continue their own creed of looking 'deep into birth and death – unflinchingly' (*WD*: p. 111), and accepting those elemental realities without protest or distortion. Being 'out in the open air of nature' (6) also means, for them, being outside the drawing-room conventions of Victorian women's lives. Their imaginative scepticism is rooted in that ideologically outdoor place.

The sonnet 'Eros' (1908), for instance, searches both the harshness and the scope of this natural law of life:

O Eros of the mountains, of the earth,
One thing I know of thee that thou art old,
Far, sovereign, lonesome tyrant of the dearth
Of chaos, ruler of the primal cold!
None gave thee nurture: chaos' icy rings
Pressed on thy plenitude. O fostering power,
Thine the first voice, first warmth, first golden wings,
First blowing zephyr, earliest opened flower,
Thine the first smile of Time: thou hast no mate,
Thou art alone forever, giving all:
After thine image, Love, thou did'st create
Man to be poor, man to be prodigal;
And thus, O awful god, he is endued
With the raw hungers of thy solitude.

(*WH*: p. 142)

No baby philanderer with bow and arrow, 'Eros', here, is the older, Homeric god of love, associated with the germinating force of life itself. Such love is no more than a tyrannical and lonely 'drive', a lust to live, as ancient as the universe itself. Such a pleasure principle is not benign, discriminating or moral. Neither is it decadent, extravagant and immoral. Man, who is explicitly made in the 'image' of Eros rather than in the image of God, is a creature of both unfulfillable and wasteful desires, of need which is both starved and squandered, both 'poor' and 'prodigal'. In the end, the characteristic of Eros is not a warm ripeness of the senses, but rather 'raw hungers' – a phrase which sharply summarises lust's crude, impersonal, plural appetites. This is the bleak side of Michael Field's creed of pleasure. It is not, like Huysmans', an exquisite, indoor sampling of multiple sensations, but an ancient, universal, almost deterministic law, in which love remains immemorially tied to some essential, ancient hunger of the planet.

Far from being a source of regret, as it is for Tennyson, this vast, pre-historic backdrop to human life is welcomed and celebrated. 'Nests in Elms', for instance, proposes that the very indifference of nature is comforting:

> The rooks are cawing up and down the trees!
> Among their nests they caw. O sound I treasure,
> Ripe as old music is, the summer's measure,
> Sleep at her gossip, sylvan mysteries,
> With prate and clamour to give zest of these –
> In rune I trace the ancient law of pleasure,
> Of love, of all the busy-ness of leisure,
> With dream on dream of never-thwarted ease.
> O homely birds, who know not anything
> Of sea-birds' loneliness, of Procne's strife,
> Rock round me when I die! So sweet it were
> To die by open doors, with you on wing
> Humming the deep security of life.

(WH: p. 62)

The sound of the rooks is a language of the past: 'old music', sleepy 'gossip', 'prate and clamour', strange 'rune' or final 'Humming'; it is a natural ur-language which expresses nothing human, but also, for that very reason, 'nothing sad'. The 'ancient law of pleasure' which is also, inseparably, the law of 'love', is an idea which runs through much of Michael Field's work, and gives to its human purpose the harsh association of nature's post-Darwinian insouciance and age. The paradoxes at the end typically offer no consolations beyond the material facts themselves: the homeliness of the rooks is found through 'open doors'; death is a return to 'the deep security of life'. This nature is no nurse or guardian of human desires, but simply a free, open-doored reality, which continues irrespective of all the living and dying around it. The keening cry of 'sea-birds', with its Anglo-Saxon melancholy, is thus rejected for this cheerfully common 'cawing', which, in its crowded and unliterary homeliness, offers a rough, oblivious sort of home to the imagination. After all, whoever dies under these trees, there will always be more 'Nests in Elms'.

Michael Field's is thus essentially an outdoor aestheticism, sharpened by a Darwinian perspective of life's impersonality. Their best poems have an emotionless detachment and a verbal casualness which is in strong contrast to the sensational, wordy artifices of their contemporary decadents. Something of this almost devastating impersonality of nature is caught in one of the rare poems Michael Field wrote about a contemporary event. 'After Soufrière' (1908) is about the destruction of a town in Guadeloupe by a volcanic eruption. Its tone is in marked contrast to Alice Meynell's poem, published five years later, about the earthquake which destroyed Messina. 'Messina, 1908', in attempting to explain the event as an act of God, sounds both reductive and sickly cruel: 'Lord, Thou hast crushed Thy tender ones, o'erthrown / Thy strong, Thy fair' (*Poems*: p. 111). By contrast, 'After Soufrière' describes the eruption as an act of nature, involving no crime, no retribution and no moral meaning of any kind. The language itself perfectly conveys the catastrophic simplicity of the event:

> It is not grief or pain;
> But like the even dropping of the rain,
> That thou art gone.
> It is not like a grave
> To weep upon;
> But like the rise and falling of a wave
> When the vessel's gone.
>
> It is like the sudden void
> When the city is destroyed,
> Where the sun shone:
> There is neither grief nor pain,
> But the wide waste come again.
>
> (*SP*: p. 31)

The idiomatic simplicity of this is much more expressive of the reality than Meynell's frantically moralising gestures. The human reactions of 'grief or pain' or of weeping on 'a grave' are made irrelevant by this cataclysm of nature which happens as 'naturally' and as meaninglessly as 'the even dropping of the rain' or the 'rise and falling of a wave'. The sheer inhumanity of the event is caught in the emotionless, forgetful quiet of the verse. Nature is heartless and indifferent, its eruptions as ordinary as 'rain' or 'sun', and its destruction of a city simply a return of things to the old order of what was there before: 'the wide waste come again'. The metrical irregularity of the poem, its unexpected rhymes and understating brevity and ease, movingly convey the awesome surprise and effortlessness of nature's own movements.

It is this register of utter clarity which the baroque ingenuity of the later poems, especially the religious poems, misses. Such simplicity seems essentially connected to a world-view which Katherine and Edith held before their conversion: that of a bleak yet bracing paganism, 'Indifferent to heaven and hell', but, in itself, exhilaratingly sensual and pleasure-loving. Furthermore, they can express such a world-view, not regretfully, protestingly or on behalf of some new-age morality of brave atheism, but with an almost shrugging naturalness:

> Death, men say, is like a sea
>> That engulfs mortality,
> Treacherous, dreadful, blindingly
>> Full of storm and terror.
>> . . .
>
> Death's a couch of golden ground,
> Warm, soft, permeable mound,
> Where from even memory's sound
>> We shall have remission.

(UB: pp. 8–9)

During her last illness, Edith was visited by the Indian poet, Rabindranath Tagore. Her rejection of his, as she sees it, sentimental pantheism is interesting for the light it throws on the two poets' own development. 'Pantheism ignores sin, evil, suffering, or vaguely trusts in nature – in sunrises, sunsets, rushing seas, air full of birds and suchlike pleasurable things', she complains. But she does not dismiss pantheism out of hand, even in 1911, four years after her conversion. Instead, she only rejects Tagore's optimistic pantheism, which, as she explains, 'demands passion for nonenity [*sic*] – for, to the heart, to ask it to love a vague all – a Pan, who has never had his Syrinx – is to ask it to love non-entity' (*WD*: p. 318). The comment recalls Michael Field's many poems about Pan, particularly the strange, heavy-aired 'Penetration',[5] which suggestively reworks Barrett Browning's 'A Musical Instrument' by reversing the roles and having Syrinx seduce and penetrate her clumsy, animalesque lover with sweet music:

> I love thee; never dream that I am dumb:
> By day, by night, my tongue besiegeth thee,
> As a bat's voice, set in too fine a key,
> Too tender in its circumstance to come
> To ears beset by havoc and harsh hum
> Of the arraigning world; yet secretly
> I may attain . . .

(WH: p. 13)

In the journal, then, Edith is not repudiating, but reasserting the basic aesthetic of their own verse: Pan must have his Syrinx, or rather, Syrinx her Pan. Sexual desire is the main, motivating impulse of the imagination as it is the impulse of life itself. The law of life, like the 'law of pleasure', is not separate from hunger, destruction and suffering, and, indeed, in the best of Michael Field, the pantheism is neither rosy-coloured nor God-scaped. Instead, it is harsh and exact. Even if such poetry does not always speak overtly for the cause of woman, it always speaks, 'secretly', in a woman's voice which, like Syrinx's, penetrates by its different 'key'. As the poets once protested in their journal:

> And here is the *Athenaeum* saying that women only have sentimental experiences – & that they cannot approach the fires of Eros, they who are his priestesses by fate & experience, if only rarely in song . . . but [they conclude triumphantly] Sappho has sung her sensations, and Christina Rossetti her suffering.[6]

In one short poem, placed towards the end of the *Wild Honey* volume, Michael Field seems finally to acknowledge the strength of their 'old accents' of pagan freedom, and the comparative weakness of their 'new right way of singing'. 'A Palimpsest' describes two writings, old and new. In their journal, Edith had described their conversion to Catholicism as a dethroning of the old gods: 'Demeter and Dionysus (our lord Bacchus) yield themselves up as victims to the great Host' (*WD*: p. 273). However, the poem tells a different story:

> . . . The rest
> Of our life must be a palimpsest –
> The old writing written there the best.
>
> In the parchment hoary
> Lies a golden story,
> As 'mid secret feather of a dove,
> As 'mid moonbeams shifted through a cloud:
>
> Let us write it over,
> O my lover,
> For the far Time to discover,
> As 'mid secret feathers of a dove,
> As 'mid moonbeams shifted through a cloud!

(WH: p. 180)

The act of writing 'it over' is, paradoxically,' also a way of preserving the 'golden story' of the past. The overlay of truth keeps the fiction 'secret', a thing obscured, like clouded moonlight. But the relation between the two is not, as the journal version suggests, one of simple supersession, but of palimpsestic doubleness. The new writing may be more true, but the 'old writing' was certainly 'the best'. The new gods may sigh for the cost and pain of salvation, but the old gods had the advantage in always being able to 'laugh and dream'.

It is that laughter – the imagination's daring and free recognition of woman's sexual pleasure, accepted as an ancient, impersonal law of nature – which inspires the best of Michael Field's poetry. They were right in surmising, sadly but also surely, that it would take 'the far Time' a long time to 'discover' it.

Notes

1. CHRISTINE WHITE suggests that this is 'no sexless romance between friends, but rather a dangerous eroticism' ('"Poets and lovers evermore": interpreting female love in the poetry and journals of Michael Field', *Textual Practice*, 4 (1990): 199). In my view, there is more playfulness than danger in the poem.
2. I disagree, here, with JOYCE ZONANA's claim that Swinburne's identification of Sappho as a Muse helps to recuperate 'female creativity and female sexuality' ('Swinburne's Sappho: The Muse as Sister-Goddess', in *Victorian Poetry*, 28 (1990): 48). By comparison with Michael Field, Swinburne violently and sadistically appropriates the voice of Sappho for his own fantasies.
3. Bodleian Library MS Eng. misc. e. 33b, fol. 24.
4. As those of old drank mummia
    To fire their limbs of lead,
  Making dead kings from Africa
    Stand pandar to their bed;

  Drunk on the dead, and medicined
    With spiced imperial dust,
  In a short night they reeled to find
    Ten centuries of lust.
            (Brooke, 1918: 70)

5. In his *Selection from the Poems of Michael Field* (London: The Poetry Bookshop, 1923), T. STURGE MOORE has almost certainly correctly subtitled this sonnet 'Syrinx to Pan' (p. 59).
6. British Library Add. MS 46783, fol. 151b.

References

ABEL, ELIZABETH (ed.) (1982), *Writing and Sexual Difference* (Hemel Hempstead: Harvester Wheatsheaf).

BROOKE, RUPERT (1918), *The Collected Poems of Rupert Brooke* (London: Sidgewick & Jackson).

BROWNING, ROBERT (1985), *More Than Friend: The Letters of Robert Browning to Katharine de Kay Bronson*, ed. Michael Meredith (Winfield, Kans.: Wedgestone Press).

FOSTER, JEANETTE H. (1958), *Sex-Variant Women in Literature* (London: Frederick Muller).

HALLETT, JUDITH P. (1979), 'Sappho and Her Social Context: sense and sensuality', *Signs*, 4 (1979): 447–64.

HUYSMANS, J.K. (1884; 1959), *Against Nature*, trans. Robert Baldick (Harmondsworth: Penguin).

IRIGARAY, LUCE (1980), 'When Our Lips Speak Together', trans. Carolyn Burke, *Signs*, 6 (1980): 69–79.

LOUŸS, PIERRE (1894; 1949), *Les Chansons de Bilitis* (Paris).

RADFORD, DOLLIE (1895), *Songs and Other Verses* (London).

RICH, ADRIENNE (1980), *On Lies, Secrets and Silence: Selected Prose 1966–1978* (London: Virago).

ROSSETTI, DANTE GABRIEL (1913), *Rossetti: Poems and Translations 1850–1870* (London: Oxford University Press).

SWINBURNE, ALGERNON CHARLES (1904), *The Poems of Algernon Charles Swinburne*, 6 vols (London: Chatto & Windus).

SYMONDS, JOHN ADDINGTON (1883; 1908), *A Problem in Greek Ethics* (London).

WHARTON, HENRY THORNTON (ed.), *Sappho: Memoir, Text, Selected Renderings, and a Literal Translation* (London: John Lane).

Abbreviations

Christina Rossetti

CP *The Complete Poems of Christina Rossetti: A variorum edition*, 3 vols, ed. R.W. Crump (Baton Rouge and London: Louisiana State University Press, 1979–90).

Michael Field

NM *The New Minnesinger* (Arran Leigh) (London, 1875).

LA *Long Ago* (London, 1889).

UB *Underneath the Bough* (London: 1893).

WD *Works and Days: From the Journal of Michael Field*, ed. T. and D.C. Sturge Moore (London: John Murray, 1933).

WH *Wild Honey from Various Thyme* (London: T. Fisher Unwin, 1908).

SP *A Selection from the Poems of Michael Field* (London: The Poetry Bookshop, 1923).

Alice Meynell

Poems *The Poems of Alice Meynell* (London: Oxford University Press, 1940).

15 Precursors*

Isobel Armstrong

In *Victorian Poetry* Armstrong develops some of the ideas she projected in her essay on Rossetti (Chapter 10). In particular, she reads Victorian poetry in terms of its contemporary aesthetic theories; and she pays close and detailed attention to language, rejecting any theory that ignores the specificity of individual poems. So in her chapter on women poets, she identifies their commonality not as a matter of women's oppression, or women's experience, but as a common confinement within nineteenth-century theories of femininity and female poetry – the sentimental, the didactic, the affective. As much as Homans (Chapter 1), she is interested in the contemporary construction of the feminine, within a particular poetic tradition – but unlike Homans, she both identifies a feminine variant of that tradition, and reads a 'doubleness' in the poems as, in different ways, they question and subvert this construction. From this perspective even an old chestnut like 'Casabianca' – forced on generations of children as a simple didactic tale about filial obedience – can be given a surprisingly subversive reading. Leighton, too, in *Victorian Women Poets*, sees the Victorian poets as 'Writing Against the Heart' – struggling within and against a sentimental tradition – but she sets up Hemans and Landon as founders of this tradition, while Armstrong reads them as already questioning its limits. In doing so, they set up themes and techniques useful to the later Victorian women poets, such as the exploration of different cultures, or the dramatic monologue.

The altar, 'tis of death! for there are laid
The sacrifice of all youth's sweetest hopes.
It is a dreadful thing for woman's lip
To swear the heart away;   yet know that heart

* Reprinted from *Victorian Poetry* (London and New York: Routledge, 1993), pp. 318–32.

Annuls the vow while speaking, and shrinks back
From the dark future which it dares not face.
The service read above the open grave
Is far less terrible than that which seals
The vow that binds the victim, not the will:
For in the grave is rest.

(Letitia Landon (L.E.L.))[1]

Swept into limbo is the host
    Of heavenly angels, row on row;
The Father, Son, and Holy Ghost,
    Pale and defeated, rise and go.
The great Jehovah is laid low,
    Vanished his burning bush and rod –
        Say, are we doomed to deeper woe?
        Shall marriage go the way of God?

Monogamous, still at our post,
    Reluctantly we undergo
Domestic round of boiled and roast,
    Yet deem the whole proceeding slow.
Daily the secret murmurs grow;
    We are no more content to plod
Along the beaten paths – and so
    Marriage must go the way of God.

Soon, before all men, each shall toast
    The seven strings unto his bow,
Like beacon fires along the coast,
    The flames of love shall glance and glow.
Nor let nor hindrance man shall know,
    From natal bath to funeral sod;
Perennial shall his pleasures flow
    When marriage goes the way of God.

Grant, in a million years at most,
    Folk shall be neither pairs nor odd –
Alas! we shan't be there to boast
    'Marriage has gone the way of God!'

(Amy Levy, 1915)[2]

It is not difficult to find, from the beginning to the end of the nineteenth century, poems of protest such as those by Letitia Landon, writing early in the century, and Amy Levy, writing towards the end, in which an overt sexual politics addresses the institutions and customs which burden women, including, in Levy's case, the taboo against lesbianism. There is Elizabeth Barrett Browning's outburst against the trivial education which trains women for marriage in *Aurora Leigh* (1856), and which conditions them into acceptability 'As long as they keep quiet by the fire/And never say "no" when the world says "ay"', a statement which perhaps adds another kind of complexity to Robert Browning's 'By the Fire-side' (1855).[3] There is Christina Rossetti's passionate wish to be a 'man',[4] and as one moves later into the century there are, if possible, fiercer expressions of protest in the work of poets such as Augusta Webster and Mathilde Blind. And yet the poems by Landon and Levy are as interesting for their differences as for their common theme. For Landon marriage is a terminal moment which requires the language of sacrifice and victim. For Levy, the end of marriage and the 'law' of God still leaves a patriarchy intact, for it is men who benefit from promiscuity, not women, and the narrow coercions of heterosexual pairing continue. Ironically, a world without marriage still goes 'The way of God' by perpetuating His patriarchal ways informally.

Yet it is too easy to describe the work of these very different women as a women's tradition based on a full frontal attack on oppression. Though such an attack undoubtedly often existed, a concentration on moments of overt protest can extract the content of a direct polemic about women's condition in a way which retrieves the protest, but not the poem. It is sometimes tempting to extrapolate such material from the poems (because they supply it in such abundance), personalising, psychologising or literalising by translating this material back into what is known or constructed as socioeconomic patriarchal history in a univocal way, so that all poems become poems about women's oppression. In this way the nature of the particular language and form of individual poems becomes obliterated by the concentration on a single theme.

Similarly, the same kind of difficulty attends the construction of a women's tradition according to a unique modality of feminine experience. For this would be to accept the distinction between two kinds of gender-based experience, male and female, and leaves uninvestigated a conventional, affective account of the feminine as a nature which occupies a distinct sphere of feeling, sensitivity and emotion quite apart from the sphere of thought and action occupied by men. This *was* a distinction frequently made by women poets themselves and by male critics in the nineteenth century, but it is necessary to be wary of it because, while it gave women's writing a very secure place in literary culture, it amounts to a kind of restrictive practice, confining the writing of women to a particular mode or genre. W.M. Rossetti, for instance, had this to say in his Preface to his edition of the poems of Felicia Hemans:

Her sources of inspiration being genuine, and the tone of her mind being feminine in an intense degree, the product has no lack of sincerity: and yet it leaves a certain artificial impression, rather perhaps through a cloying flow of 'right-minded' perceptions of moral and material beauty than through any other defect. 'Balmy' it may be: but the atmosphere of her verse is by no means bracing. One might sum up the weak points in Mrs Hemans's poetry by saying that it is not only 'feminine' poetry (which under the circumstances can be no imputation, rather an encomium) but also 'female' poetry: besides exhibiting the fineness and charm of womanhood, it has the monotone of mere sex. Mrs Hemans has that love of good and horror of evil which characterize a scrupulous female mind; and which we may most rightly praise without concluding that they favour poetical robustness, or even perfection in literary form. She is a leader in that very modern phalanx of poets who persistently coordinate the impulse of sentiment with the guiding power of morals or religion. Everything must convey its 'lesson', and is indeed set forth for the sake of its lesson: but must at the same time have the emotional gush of a spontaneous sentiment.[5]

'Cloying', 'feminine', 'female', 'sentiment', 'lesson', 'emotional gush': not all this vocabulary is offered in a critical spirit, though it betrays uneasiness, but even the most cursory examination of the language here suggests the qualities attributed to women's poetry – conventional piety, didactic feeling, emotions, sentiment. Coventry Patmore parodies women's religious verse in *The Angel in the House* in a way which attributes the same qualities to their work. Honoria's pious sister entrusts a poem to the hero:

Day after day, until today,
    Imaged the others gone before,
The same dull task, the weary way,
    The weakness pardon'd o'er and o'er.

The thwarted thirst, too faintly felt,
    For joy's well nigh forgotten life,
The restless heart, which, when I knelt,
    Made of my worship barren strife.

Ah, whence today's so sweet release,
    This clearance light of all my care,
This conscience free, this fertile peace,
    These softly folded wings of prayer,

This calm and more than conquering love,
　With which naught evil dares to cope,
This joy that lifts no glance above,
　For faith too sure, too sweet for hope?

O, happy time, too happy change,
　It will not live, though fondly nurst!
Full soon the sun will seem as strange
　As now the cloud which seems dispersed.[6]

Since the hero is courting one of three sisters, this is possibly a cruel parody of one of Anne Brontë's poems, but the conventions of women's writing were sufficiently established for it to be a parody of the work of Letitia Landon (in some moods), Adelaide Anne Procter or Christina Rossetti. What is interesting about it is that it suggests that there *were* recognised conventions established for women's verse by this time in the century (1854). Interestingly, Patmore's carefully regular quatrains pick up a *limited* assent to the sense of limit in neutrally simple religious and psychological language, a self-admonitory withdrawal from protest and a pious but none too easy recognition of the difficulties of transcending limit. His parody responds to pessimism rather than to piety, and even at the level of satire negotiates with more complex elements than the self-abnegation attributed to it by Patmore's hero.

It is probably no exaggeration to say that an account of women's writing as occupying a particular sphere of influence, and as working inside defined moral and religious conventions, helped to make women's poetry and the 'poetess' (as the Victorians termed the woman poet) respected in the nineteenth century as they never have been since. In a survey of poetry early in the century in *Blackwood's Magazine* John Wilson ('Christopher North') wrote enthusiastically of women poets, and a respectful study of British women poets appeared in 1848, *The Female Poets of Great Britain*, selected and edited by Frederic Rowton. At the end of the century Eric Robertson published his *English Poetesses* (1883). Though Robertson was less sympathetic than Rowton to women's poetry, believing that it would never equal the poetry of men, it is clear that the category of the 'poetess' was well established. Men assiduously edited women's work. Laman Blanchard edited Letitia Landon's *Life and Literary Remains* in 1841. W.M. Rossetti edited not only the work of his sister and Mrs Hemans but also Augusta Webster's *Mother and Daughter* sonnet sequence after her death (1895). Arthur Symons edited Mathilde Blind's works in 1900, with a memoir by Richard Garnett. It seems that men both enabled and controlled women's poetic production in a way that was often complex, and which requires more sustained discussion than can be given here. After a literary scandal about her association with a patron (probably William

Maginn), Letitia Landon, in her early twenties, described her complete dependence on male help for the business of publication in moving terms.

> Your own literary pursuits must have taught you how little, in them, a young woman can do without assistance. Place yourself in my situation. Could you have hunted London for a publisher, endured all the alternate hot and cold water thrown on your exertions; bargained for what sum they might be pleased to give; and, after all, canvassed, examined, nay quarrelled over accounts the most intricate in the world? And again, after success had procured money, what was I to do with it? Though ignorant of business I must know I could not lock it up in a box.[7]

Like Mrs Hemans, Letitia Landon relied on her earnings for the support of her family, and so her dependence on men to gain access to the publishing world was of great importance to her.

That middle-class women were hosted by men into the literary world through editions of their work may be one explanation for our lack of knowledge of working-class women poets, who were not edited in this way. Contrary to common understanding there were working-class women poets, and they are still being discovered.[8] Those we know of tend to have survived because they supported conventional morals, such as the anonymous millgirl who wrote eloquently on the Preston lockout in 1862 but connected working-class well-being with temperance. Bamford praised Ann Hawkshaw but she seems to have been an educated poet with strong working-class connections who produced orthodox-seeming work with unusual subtexts. Her *Dionysius the Areopagite* (1842), for instance, is ostensibly about Christian conversion. Quite apart from her vision of an egalitarian heaven, the story is primarily concerned with a relationship between two women. She was an impressively strong and independent writer who wrote a series of sonnets on British history with another subtext concerned with subjugation. Her shorter poems, 'Why am I a Slave?' and 'The Mother to Her Starving Child', are impressive. The slave cannot understand his exclusion from 'the white man's home': 'Who had a right to bind these limbs / And make a slave of me?' The mother is forced to wish her child dead rather than see it starve – and then to go mad with grief. The pun on the 'relief' of madness is sombre, with the ironic social meaning of 'poor relief' shadowing the psychological term.[9] Her work is exceptional. The pastoral didacticism of Louisa Horsfield, a contemporary, contrasts with it. Horsfield retrieves the natural world from the social sins of drunkenness, truancy and immorality in a more conventional way.[10] Ellen Johnston, addressing occasional poems to local bodies and factory workers, moves from awkward heroic poetry to simple ballad and cheerful dialect verse (for instance, in 'The Working Man'). Some of her love poems, particularly 'The Maniac of the Green Wood', are moving, but her work discloses the difficulties of discovering a language in which to address both a total community and a 'literary' audience.[11] Poetry by working-class women could be as didactic as that of middle-class women, if not more so.

If, then, a middle-class women's tradition is constructed by reference to the Victorian notion of what was specifically feminine in poetry, it is likely to be formed not only out of what were predominantly male categories of the female but also out of categories which were regarded as self-evident and unproblematical. This does not enable one to take the analysis of women's poetry in the nineteenth century very far. On the other hand, it is undoubtedly the case that women wrote with a sense of belonging to a particular group defined by their sexuality, and that this sense comprehends political differences and very different kinds of poetic language. Letitia Landon recognised this when she wrote, in her 'Stanzas on the Death of Mrs Hemans', that the poet had made 'A music of thine own'.[12] So it is possible, in spite of the reservations and precautionary remarks expressed above, to consider women poets in terms of a 'music' of their own.

What was the 'music' of the Victorian woman poet? It can be listened to, first, by seeing what the poetry of Letitia Landon and Mrs Hemans could have meant to later writers, for these were the poets to which a number of them looked back as precursors. Even when there seems no direct link between these earlier and later writers it does seem as if they worked within a recognisable tradition understood by them to belong to women. Secondly, this music can be listened to through the dissonances women's poetry created by making problematical the affective conventions and feelings associated with a feminine modality of experience even when, and perhaps particularly when, poets worked within these conventions. Victorian expressive theory later in the century, one of the dominant aesthetic positions of the period, created a discourse which could accommodate a poetics of the feminine. But women poets relate to it in an ambiguous way and interrogate it even while they negotiate and assent to expressive theory. It was this assimilation of an aesthetic of the feminine which enabled the woman poet to revolutionise it from within, by using it to explore the way a female subject comes into being. The doubleness of women's poetry comes from its ostensible adoption of an affective mode, often simple, often pious, often conventional. But those conventions are subjected to investigation, questioned, or used for unexpected purposes. The simpler the surface of the poem, the more likely it is that a second and more difficult poem will exist beneath it.

Letitia Landon, already a prolifically successful poet publishing in periodicals and popular album books, published her first volume of poetry in 1824, *The Improvisatrice*. It was, she wrote,

> an attempt to illustrate that species of inspiration common in Italy, where the mind is warmed from earliest childhood by all that is beautiful in Nature and glorious in Art. The character depicted is entirely Italian, a young female with all the loveliness, vivid feeling, and genius of her own impassioned land. She is supposed to relate her own history; with which are intermixed the tales and episodes which various circumstances call forth.[13]

The Troubadour: Poetical Sketches of Modern Pictures; and Historical Sketches (1825) followed, and her last volume, reiterating the Italian theme, was entitled *The Venetian Bracelet* (1829). The uncollected 'Subjects for Pictures' begins characteristically with a poem on Petrarch and Laura. The movement to Italy is taken up by Elizabeth Barrett Browning in *Aurora Leigh* (1856), and again by Christina Rossetti who in her extraordinary preface to *Monna Innominata*, as will be seen, considers the status of the Petrarchan tradition in relation to modern poetry by women. But perhaps the movement to Italy is less important in itself than the association of women's poetry with an 'impassioned land' or emotional space *outside* the definitions and circumscriptions of the poet's specific culture and nationality. As a child Letitia Landon invented a fantasy country located in Africa (it is the tragic irony of her career that she died there), very much as the Brontës were to do when they constructed Gondal and Angria (Angria was located in Africa), the imaginary lands from which so much of their poetry sprang. Adelaide Anne Procter's narrative poems move to Provence, Switzerland and Belgium. George Eliot's *The Spanish Gypsy* (1868) sends the heroine of the poem from the conflict between Moors and Spaniards to consolidate a Gipsy race in Africa. This need to move beyond cultural boundaries manifests itself in the work of the earlier poets as a form of historical and cultural syncretism which both juxtaposes different cultures and reshapes relationships between them. *The Improvisatrice* unfolds narratives within itself of Moorish and Christian conflict, and of Hindu suttee, for instance, which are juxtaposed. Felicia Hemans brings together British, French, Indian, German, American and Greek narratives from different historical periods in her *Records of Woman* (1828), which ends, in startling contrast to the historicised records, with an elegy on a recently dead poetess, Mary Tighe, taken as a point of reference by Landon in her elegy for Mrs Hemans. The dedication is made in a footnote, however, and the very possibility of a 'record' of woman is thus questioned.

This insistent figuring of movement across and between cultural boundaries, with its emphasis on travel, could be seen as a search for the exotic, an escape from restrictions into the 'other' of bourgeois society. Allied, as it so frequently is, with a metaphor of the prison, or of slavery, it could be seen as an attempt to transcend restrictions in fantasy, or an effort to discover a universal womanhood which transcends cultural differences. But it is rather to be associated with an attempt to discover ways of testing out the account of the feminine experienced in western culture by going outside its prescriptions. The flight across the boundary is often associated with the examination of extreme situations – of imprisonment, suffering, or captivity and slavery – and with an overdetermined emphasis on race and national culture, as if an enquiry is being conducted into the ways in which the feminine can be constituted. Mrs Hemans's elegy appears to emancipate its subject from cultural and historical determinations, but it suggests that we can only think of the poetess in this way when she is dead, and even that is problematical. The elegy has an uncanny aspect of contextlessness which makes it oddly surprising after the very specific 'records' which have preceded it.

The emphasis on the woman as traveller through the imagination can be associated with another aspect of Letitia Landon's account of the *Improvisatrice*. The poem is supposedly the utterance of a persona: it is a mask, a role-playing, a dramatic monologue; it is not to be identified with herself or her own feminine subjectivity. The simplest explanation for this is that, given the difficulties of acceptance experienced by women writers, the dramatic form is used as a disguise, a protection against self-exposure and the exposure of feminine subjectivity. But, given the insistence on speaking in another *woman's* voice, from Mrs Hemans to Augusta Webster and Amy Levy (these last two wrote consciously as dramatic monologuists), it is worth considering further as a phenomenon. The frequent adoption of a dramatised voice by male poets in the Victorian period is, of course, to be connected with dramatic theories of poetry. But Landon's and Hemans's work predates these theories (though not, admittedly, the work of Walter Savage Landor, who might be said to have initiated the dramatic monologue if we are content to think of this as a tradition established by male writers), and it seems that such a mask is peculiarly necessary for women writers. The adoption of the mask appears to involve a displacement of feminine subjectivity, almost a travestying of femininity, in order that it can be made an object of investigation. It is interesting, for instance, that one of Charlotte Brontë's earliest known poems is a monologue by the wife of Pontius Pilate, and that Augusta Webster also wrote a miniature drama between Pilate and his wife, in which the woman's role and moral position is sharply distinguished from association with the husband, as if both are testing out the extent to which it is the woman's function to identify unquestioningly with the husband (and, of course, with orthodox Christianity).[14] A number of poems by women testifying to a refusal to be regarded as an object have been described by feminist critics, but by using a mask a woman writer is in control of her objectification and at the same time anticipates the strategy of objectifying women by being beforehand with it and circumventing masculine representations.[15] This is the theme of Christina Rossetti's poem about masking, 'Winter: My Secret'. It should come as no surprise, then, that it was the women poets who 'invented' the dramatic monologue.

The projection of self into roles is not, as will be seen, really opposed to the axioms of expressive theory which assumes the projection of feeling and emotion onto or into an object, and thus it is not strange to find Letitia Landon speaking of the search for an 'impassioned land', a space for the expression of emotion. Brought up on Hume, she was fascinated by the nature of sensation (often isolating moments of sensation in a narrative), and with the pulsation of sympathy. She uses a metaphor of the responsively vibrating string or chord of feeling which became so common that it could perhaps hardly be said to originate with Hume, but she would certainly have found it in his work, and it recurs in her poetry with an unusual intensity. Allowing as it does of subliminal sexual meaning, it is a thoroughly feminised metaphor for her. In her elegy on Mrs Hemans, for instance, she wrote, 'Wound to a pitch too exquisite, / The soul's fine chords are wrung; / With misery and melody / They are too highly strung.' Such intense vibrations, of course, can kill, as the 'chord' becomes the result of a 'cord' or tightened string which ends sound or strangles even while it produces it. This metaphor was to resonate in women's poetry. Closely allied with it and partly deriving from it is another characteristic figure, the air. An air is a song and by association it is that which is breathed out, exhaled or expressed as breath, an expiration; and by further association it can be that which is breathed in, literally an 'influence', a flowing in, the air of the environment which sustains life; inspiration, a breathing in. All these meanings are present in the elegy, as perfume, breezes, breath or sighs, where they are figured as a responsive, finely organised feminine creativity, receptive to external influence, returning back to the world as music that has flowed in, an exhalation or breath of sound. It is the breath of the body and the breath as spirit. 'So pure, so sweet thy life has been, / So filling earth and air / with odours and with loveliness ... And yet thy song is sorrowful, / Its beauty is not bloom; / The hopes of which it breathes, are hopes / That look beyond the tomb.'[16] Breath can dissipate, a fear peculiarly close to the Victorian woman poet. Expressive theory, as will be seen, tended to endorse and consolidate this figure. The body imprisons breath but involuntarily releases it: this is an apt figure for the release of feeling which cannot find external form.

Letitia Landon and Felicia Hemans each explore the multiplicity of roles and projections which they make available to themselves in different ways, and each takes the affective moment in different directions. A marked feature of Landon's work is the use of tenses in narrative, particularly the historic past, and the present tense used in a succession of discrete phrases to denote successive actions in the past. It is used in such a way that an action is registered, not *as* it happens but when it is either just over or just about to happen. Effects often precede causes. Seen in this way the agent is oddly detached from actions in the slight hiatus when actions are seen but not the agent's acting of them. Such a procedure makes uncertain how far the woman is in responsible control of cause and effect – she seems to *suffer* rather than to act. The woman herself seems to be displaced from action into the psychic experience existing in the gap between actions, and the whole weight of these lyrical narratives is thrown on the temporal space of the affective moment, the emotional space occurring just before or just after something has happened. In 'The Indian Bride', for instance, the girl's prenuptial journey alone on the Ganges is presented in moments which are either over or which precede their causes: 'She has lighted her lamp.... The maiden is weeping. Her lamp has decayed.'[17] The reunion with the lover follows the same syntactic pattern: 'Hark to the ring of the cymeter!... The warfare is over, the battle is won.... And Zaide hath forgotten in Azim's arms / All her so false lamp's falser alarms.' But the lamp is and is not 'false'. The bridegroom dies and she goes deterministically to her death: 'A prayer is muttered, a blessing said, – / Her torch is raised! – she is by the dead. / She has fired the pile.'[18] The tenses both obliterate and sharply question, through this strategy of detachment, by whose agency the girl goes to her death, her own, or the mores of cultural ritual. Before this the narrator has analysed the moment of acute superstitious fear when the girl is on the Ganges without light in tenses which blur the distinction between what does happen and what will happen: 'How the pulses will beat, and the cheek will be dy'd.'[19] This becomes not only a description of the girl's immediate emotional present but also a *prediction* of the future. The affective moment is in the right and the wrong place, describing the girl's immediate fears, proleptically describing the emotions of her death. But the ambiguous status of the tenses proffering the moment of feeling suggests that the girl, or the lamp, was right after all. The irrational affective moment could be trusted, and retrospectively it expands to include her death. The tenses here foreground and investigate a world of intense sensation and emotion and implicitly ask what its place in experience is.

Landon wrote many poems which pictured pictures, freezing women in a static but intense moment just before or just after an event (usually an event of communal significance) has occurred. They become objects whose life is in suspension, waiting for a critical event to occur either through their own or someone else's agency, or else waiting choicelessly. But whether dependent or independent, it is as if emotion and sensation rush in to fill the vacuum of subjectivity. Whether feeling is precipitated by action or whether action is precipitated by feeling seems to be the question such poems raise. Whether consciousness is determined by feeling or action, and what it is when there is no action to be taken at all, and where choice is limited by cultural prescription, is at issue. 'Subjects for Pictures', for instance, considers the woman as subject, often subordinate to men, in innumerable variations on the theme of choice, alternating enclosed environments with open landscapes, moving from history to history, culture to culture, ritual to ritual, myth to myth, marriage, death, murder, revival. These are all studies in the dislocation between consciousness and action, where the subject is placed remorselessly in fixed locations, immobilised by ritual or vigil. In what way the moment of feeling relates to or is determined by the rituals of a culture is a problem which fascinates Landon.

Whether Letitia Landon's figures belong to cultural rituals or place themselves in a transgressive relation to them they are almost always at the mercy of passion. Accused of an excessive preoccupation with love, Landon defended herself by arguing for what is effectively a politics of the affective state: 'A highly cultivated state of society must ever have for concomitant evils, that selfishness, the result of indolent indulgence, and that heartlessness attendant on refinement, which too often hardens while it polishes.'[20] The choice of love as a theme can 'soften' and 'touch' and 'elevate'. 'I can only say, that for a woman, whose influence and whose sphere must be in the affections, what subject can be more fitting than one which it is her peculiar province to refine, to spiritualise, and exalt? . . . making an almost religion of its truth . . . woman, actuated by an attachment as intense as it is true, as pure as it is deep', is more 'admirable' as a heroine. For as she is in art, so she is 'in actual life'.[21] If Landon appears to be completely accepting the sentimental terms in which women were seen, she is turning them to moral and social account and arguing that women's discourse can soften what would now be called the phallocentric hardness and imaginative deficiencies of an overcivilised culture. It is as if she has taken over the melting softness of Burke's category of the 'beautiful', which he saw as an overrefined and 'feminine' principle in contradistinction to the strenuous labour of the 'sublime', and reappropriated it as a moral category which can dissolve overcivilised

269

hardness. Burke associated beauty with nostalgia for a condition which we have 'irretrievably lost'.[22] In particular its nature is questioned and explored when it hovers over that last situation occasioning the last rituals of a culture, death.

Her own early death, which seems to have been the result of an accidental overdose of poison, self-administered to cure a palsy, occasioning scandal and suspicion as her life had done, made her the Keats (or perhaps the Sylvia Plath) of women's poetry. Witty, exuberant and unconventional, and like Mrs Hemans a vigorous and energetic intellectual (just before she died she wrote to ask her brother to send to Africa '"Thiers's History of the Revolution", in French, and all George Sand's works . . . send me also Lamb's works'),[23] she was seen as a seminal figure by later writers.

Rather than exploring what cultural ritual does to the feminine subject, Mrs Hemans figures the flight beyond it, and the condition of extremity and disintegration which occurs when constraints press upon consciousness. Her method is inward and psychological where Landon's is external and classical, but it is just as analytical, turning the expressive moment towards investigation and critique. The heroic rebel and the conformist stand in dialectical relationship to one another in her work, each in dialogue with the other as each is pushed to extremity. The archetypes of her work are represented in the first section of *Records of Woman*, 'Arabella Stuart', and 'Casabianca', a short poem about an episode occurring in the battle of the Nile. 'Arabella Stuart' is a monologue spoken in imprisonment by a woman whose disintegrating mind struggles, and fails, to make the past coherent. The meaning of her history collapses. It is this, as much as the endurance of immediate confinement, which dissolves her reason (though an implicit question here is what 'reason' means). Hers was a political imprisonment (she died in captivity), made at the instigation of James I after a secret marriage and an attempted flight to France. Arabella does not know what has happened to her husband, or whether he has deserted her. The monologue opens with a memory.

'Twas but a dream! I saw the stag leap free,
　　Under the boughs where early birds were singing;
I stood o'ershadowed by the greenwood tree,
　　And heard, it seemed, a sudden bugle ringing
Far through a royal forest. Then the fawn
Shot, like a gleam of light, from grassy lawn
To secret covert; and the smooth turf shook,
And lilies quivered by the glade's lone brook,
And young leaves trembled, as, in fleet career,
A princely band, with horn, and hound, and spear,

Like a rich masque swept forth. I saw the dance
Of their white plumes, that bore a silvery glance
Into the deep wood's heart; and all passed by
Save one – I met the smile of *one* clear eye,
Flashing out joy to mine. Yes, *thou* wert there,
Seymour![24]

A superficial glance at this text will immediately register what appears
to be a slightly mannered Keatsian diction followed by the faintly
absurd address to Seymour. 'Yes, *thou* wert there.' But women's poetry
deliberately risked absurdity, as Christina Rossetti was later to see. In
the extremity of the memory it is precisely important that the lover was
there, as he is *not* in the present moment of the voice speaking from
prison. The diction is used to render the vestigial, uncertain and
discontinuous retrieval by memory of an event which even then may
have been a dream and 'seemed' (there is a double 'seeming', the event
and the memory of it) like a masque. The movement of the eye and of
light is uncertain, the gaze fleeting, as the mere insignia of the helmet
plumes 'glance' into the wood, with a superficial lightness whose pun
on glance/gaze casts doubt on the clear eye which gazes at the woman.
And if Seymour was not 'there', it is not clear 'where' the woman is
either, as her gaze is constantly displaced from stag to fawn to quivering
lilies (aroused *and* fearful sexuality), to huntsmen, plumes and lover.
Though stag and fawn stand as conventionalised proleptic figures of the
hunted woman's condition later in her story (the syntax allows that
both stag and woman are 'Under the boughs'), she is not quite
identified with either, or symbolically split between both, as they escape
to different hiding places. This split condition is a function of her
imprisoned consciousness, but it appears to be just as much a condition
of her freedom: she stood isolated, 'o'ershadowed' by the tree, subject
and metaphorically imprisoned even when her isolation seemed to make
possible the rebellious independence of the secret love affair and
marriage. These are the bitter insights disclosed by a fracturing
consciousness whose mind and history disintegrate simultaneously. The
bitterness, indeed, rests precisely on an awareness that the rebellion was
in fact in conformity with a romantic paradigm which failed to work.
    Like the woman in 'Arabella Stuart' who 'stood' transfixed under the
greenwood tree, the boy in 'Casabianca' 'stood' on the burning deck,
and in both cases the word seems to denote positioning outside the
control of the character. The boy is subject to commands, standing
ground and withstanding the assault of battle in absolute obedience to
the father's orders, responding unquestioningly to the law of the father.
Ostensibly this is a tale of the heroism of simple obedience of son to
father. But in the oedipal fiasco the heroism of absolute obedience is

misplaced, for the dead father, beneath the deck, like the unconscious, is 'Unconscious of his son', and 'His voice no longer heard'.

Consummately, Hemans transposes the terror of a condition of not knowing and hearing to the father, marking the tragic irony of the son's situation, for it is he who rather 'no longer heard' his father's voice, but continues to obey that voice from the past when it no longer sounds in the present. But at a deeper level, the law of the father is founded on its imperviousness to the son's voice, begging for a relaxation of its commands. In the culminating destruction we are enjoined to 'Ask of the winds' (like the boy to his father) which 'strewed the sea' with 'fragments', what became of the son, who is burned and blown to pieces through the act of blind obedience. The voice of the 'natural' elements may, or may not, perhaps, operate with analogous laws as fierce as those of patriarchal imperatives (the voices of the father and the wind are set questioningly against one another), but the natural certainly wreaks as much havoc as the human law, whether they can be differentiated from one another or not. For a frightening moment the 'fragments' seem parts of the boy's body, resolve themselves into mast, helm and pennon 'That well had borne their part', in the final stanza, and then as frighteningly, with all the referential hazardousness of metaphor, become metonymic hints of fragmented phallic parts. The absoluteness of the patriarchal imperative is absolutely ravaging in its violence. There is a kind of exultation in this violent elegy about the way phallic law destroys itself: at the same time the boy's 'heart', both his courage and the centre of his being, the identity bound up with the patriarchal imperatives of heroism, has 'perished'. The remorselessness which separates out 'part' and 'heart' and rhymes them to suggest the way masculine identity is founded, also recognises that this is a law to the death, killing a child on a burning deck. The unmentioned element in this masculine tragedy is the mother, but, with its constant reminder that this is the death of a child (he was thirteen), victim of the crucial Napoleonic battle of the Nile, the voice of the poem is gendered as female and thus brings war and sexual politics together. It is at once a deeply affective lament and a strangely Medaean lyric of castigation – and castration – which takes its revenge on war even as it sees that war takes revenge on itself.

Casabianca

The boy stood on the burning deck
    Whence all but he had fled;
The flame that lit the battle's wreck
    Shone round him o'er the dead.

Yet beautiful and bright he stood,
    As born to rule the storm –
A creature of heroic blood,
    A proud, though child-like form.

The flames rolled on – he would not go
    Without his father's word;
That father, faint in death below,
    His voice no longer heard.

He called aloud: – 'Say, father, say
    If yet my task is done!'
He knew not that the chieftain lay
    Unconscious of his son.

'Speak, father!' once again he cried,
    'If I may yet be gone!'
And but the booming shots replied,
    And fast the flames rolled on.

Upon his brow he felt their breath,
    And in his waving hair,
And looked from that lone post of death
    In still yet brave despair;

And shouted but once more aloud,
    'My father! must I stay?'
While o'er him fast, through sail and shroud,
    The wreathing fires made way.

They wrapt the ship in splendour wild,
    They caught the flag on high,
And streamed above the gallant child
    Like banners in the sky.

There came a burst of thundersound –
    The boy – oh! where was he?
Ask of the winds that far around
    With fragments strewed the sea! –

With mast, and helm, and pennon fair,
    That well had borne their part;
But the noblest thing which perished there
    Was that young faithful heart!²⁵

Notes

1. 'The Marriage Vow', *Life and Literary Remains of L.E.L.*, ed. LAMAN BLANCHARD, 2 vols (London, 1841), II, p. 277.
2. AMY LEVY, *A Ballad of Religion and Marriage* (one of twelve privately printed pamphlets), (British Library catalogue: 1915).
3. ELIZABETH BARRETT BROWNING, *Aurora Leigh and Other Poems*, ed. Cora Kaplan (London, 1978), I, pp. 436–7.
4. 'I wish, and I wish I were a man' ('From the Antique', 1854).
5. *The Poetical Works of Felicia Hemans*, ed. WILLIAM MICHAEL ROSSETTI (London, 1873), Prefatory Notice, p. xxvii.
6. *The Angel in the House*, I, ii, 2, pp. 74–5, *The Poems of Coventry Patmore*, ed. Frederick Page (London, 1949).
7. BLANCHARD, *Life and Literary Remains of L.E.L.*, I, p. 55.
8. See JULIA SWINDELLS, *Victorian Writing and Working Women* (Oxford, 1985). This study retrieves a number of unknown writers.
9. ANN HAWKSHAW, *Dionysius the Areopagite* (London and Manchester, 1842): for the egalitarian heaven see *Dionysius*, pp. 97–9; 'The Mother to Her Starving Child', pp. 170–2: 'Why am I a Slave?', pp. 191–3. Subsequent volumes were *Poems for My Children* (London and Manchester, 1847); *Sonnets on Anglo-Saxon History* (London, 1854).
10. LOUISA HORSFIELD, *The Cottage Lyre*, 2nd edn (London and Leeds, 1862): 'The Truant', pp. 44–7.
11. ELLEN JOHNSTON ('The Factory Girl'), *Autobiography, Poems and Songs* (Glasgow, 1862): 'The Working Man', pp. 79–80; 'The Maniac of the Green Wood', pp. 15–19.
12. BLANCHARD, *Life and Literary Remains of L.E.L.*, II, pp. 245–8: 246.
13. LETITIA LANDON, *Poetical Works*, 2 vols (London, 1850), I, p. xi (Preface to *The Improvisatrice*: 1824).
14. 'Pilate's Wife's Dream', *Poems of Charlotte Brontë*, ed. TOM WINNIFRITH (Oxford, 1984), p. 3.
15. For a description of objectification see DOLORES ROSENBLUM, 'Christina Rossetti: the inward pose', *Shakespeare's Sisters: Feminist Essays on Women Poets*, ed. Sandra Gilbert and Susan Gubar (Bloomington and London, 1979), pp. 82–98.
16. BLANCHARD, *Life and Literary Remains of L.E.L.*, II, pp. 246, 245–6.
17. 'The Indian Bride', *The Improvisatrice, Poetical Works*, I, pp. 28, 30.
18. Ibid., I, p. 31.
19. Ibid., I, p. 29.
20. Preface to *The Venetian Bracelet* (1829), *Poetical Works*, I, p. xiv.
21. Ibid.
22. EDMUND BURKE, *A Philosophical Enquiry into the Origin of Our Ideas of the Sublime and the Beautiful*, ed. James T. Boulton (Notre Dame and London, 1958), p. 51.
23. BLANCHARD, *Life and Literary Remains of L.E.L.*, I, p. 205.
24. ROSSETTI, *Works of Hemans*, *Records of Woman*, Section I, 'Arabella Stuart', p. 144.
25. ROSSETTI, *Works of Hemans*, 'Casabianca', pp. 373–4.

Notes on Authors

Isobel Armstrong is a leading critic of Victorian Poetry. She is Professor in the Department of English Language and Literature at Birkbeck College, London, and author of *Language as Living Form in Nineteenth-Century Poetry* (1982), and *Victorian Poetry: Poetry, Poetics and Politics* (1993). She also writes on feminist theory, and is editor of *New Feminist Discourses: Critical Essays on Theories and Texts* (1992).

Kathryn Burlinson is a Lecturer in English at the University of Southampton. She is researching the work of Victorian Women Poets, including Emily Brontë, Christina Rossetti and Elizabeth Barrett Browning. She is author of ' "What language can utter the feeling": Identity in the Poetry of Emily Brontë', in *Subjectivity and Literature from the Romantics to the Present Day*, ed. Philip Shaw and Peter Stockwell (1991).

Mary Wilson Carpenter is Assistant Professor of English at Queen's University, Kingston, Ontario. She is author of *George Eliot and the Landscape of Time: Narrative Form and Protestant Apocalyptic History* (1986), and is working on a book on 'The Body, the Bible and British Writing in the Nineteenth Century'. She has published articles on Rossetti and Eliot.

Deirdre David is a leading Victorianist feminist critic. She is Professor of English at Temple University, Philadelphia, and author of *Fictions of Resolution in Three Victorian Novels* (1981) and *Intellectual Women and Victorian Patriarchy* (1987). More recently she has published on Victorian imperialism and sexual politics.

Rod Edmond is Senior Lecturer in the Department of English and American Literature at the University of Kent. He is author of *Affairs of the Hearth: Victorian Poetry and Domestic Narrative* (1988), and 'Death Sequences: Patmore, Hardy and the New Domestic Elegy' (*Victorian Poetry*, 1981).

Christine Gallant's interests are in Jungian criticism, and Romanticism. She is Associate Professor of English at Georgia State University, Atlanta. She has edited *Coleridge's Theory of Imagination Today* (1987), and is author of *Shelley's Ambivalence* (1989).

Sandra M. Gilbert and Susan Gubar are among the most influential feminist critics in the field of women's writing. Gilbert is Professor of English at the University of California at Davis; Gubar is Professor of English at Indiana University, Bloomington. Their books include *The Madwoman in the Attic* (1979), *The Norton Anthology of Literature by Women* (1985), and *No Man's Land: The Place of the Woman Writer in the Twentieth Century* (3 vols: 1988, 1991, 1994). Gilbert has also published poetry.

ANTONY HARRISON is an important Rossetti scholar. He is Professor of English at North Carolina State University, and is author of *Swinburne's Medievalism: A Study in Victorian Love Poetry* (1988), *Christina Rossetti in Context* (1988) and *Victorian Poets and Romantic Poems: Intertextuality and Ideology* (1990), and co-editor of *Gender and Discourse in Victorian Literature* (1992). He is editing the collected letters of Christina Rossetti, and is at work on a new book, *Victorian Poetry and the Politics of Culture*.

TERRENCE HOLT was until recently Assistant Professor of English at Rutgers University, New Brunswick. He is at work on a book on the uses of apocalyptic rhetoric in post-Renaissance English literature. He has articles published or forthcoming on Christina Rossetti, Frankenstein, Marxist criticism and New Historicism. He has also published fiction.

MARGARET HOMANS is a leading feminist critic of nineteenth-century women's writing. She is Professor of English at Yale. As well as *Women Writers and Poetic Identity* (1980), she has published *Bearing the Word: Language and Female Experience in Nineteenth-Century Women's Writing* (1989). More recently, she has published on writing by women of colour.

CORA KAPLAN is an influential Marxist-feminist critic. She is Professor of English at Rutgers University, editor of *Salt and Bitter and Good: Three Centuries of English and American Women Poets* (1975), and author of *Sea Changes: Culture and Feminism* (1986), a collection of her most important articles, and *Women and Film* (1987). More recently, she has written articles on feminist theory.

ANGELA LEIGHTON is a leading Barrett Browning critic, and expert on Victorian women poets. She is a Lecturer in the Department of English Language and Literature at the University of Hull, and author of *Elizabeth Barrett Browning* (1986) and *Victorian Women Poets* (1992). An anthology of Victorian women's poetry, edited by her, is forthcoming.

DOROTHY MERMIN is Professor of English at Cornell University, Ithaca. She has published widely on Victorian women poets, including *Elizabeth Barrett Browning: The Origins of a New Poetry* (1989), and *Godiva's Ride: Women of Letters in England, 1830–1880* (1993).

DOLORES ROSENBLUM is an important feminist critic of Rossetti. She taught until recently at the State University of New York, Albany, and at Indiana University. She is beginning a new career in social work. Her work on Rossetti is collected and expanded in her book, *Christina Rossetti: The Poetry of Endurance* (1986).

Further Reading

Emily Brontë

ALLOTT, MIRIAM (ed.), *The Brontës: The Critical Heritage* (London: Routledge & Kegan Paul, 1974) (collection of essays).

CHICHESTER, TEDDI LYNN, ' "Evading Earth's Dungeon Tomb": Emily Bronte, AGA and the Fatally Feminine', *Victorian Poetry*, 29 (1991): 1–15 (on multiple personalities in the Gondal poems).

FRANCIS, EMMA, 'Is Emily Brontë a Woman?: Femininity, Feminism and the Paranoid Critical Subject', in *Subjectivity and Literature from the Romantics to the Present Day*, ed. Philip Shaw and Peter Stockwell (London and New York: Pinter Publishers, 1991) (quite difficult: on Brontë as between genres, genders and periods).

GÉRIN, WINIFRED, *Emily Brontë* (London: Clarendon Press, 1971) (biography).

TAYLOR, IRENE, *Holy Ghosts: The Male Muses of Emily and Charlotte Brontë* (New York and Oxford: Columbia University Press, 1990) (chapter on Brontë's poetry, using object-relations theory, and putting in context of male Romantic poetry and Brontë's biography).

Elizabeth Barrett Browning

FORSTER, MARGARET, *Elizabeth Barrett Browning* (London: Chatto & Windus, 1988) (biography).

GELPI, BARBARA CHARLESWORTH, '*Aurora Leigh*: the Vocation of the Woman Poet', *Victorian Poetry*, 19 (1981): 35–48 (interprets largely in terms of 1980s feminist concerns. Reference to Jungian and object-relations psychology).

GILBERT, SANDRA, 'From *Patria* to *Matria*: Elizabeth Barrett Browning's Risorgimento', *PMLA*, 99 (1984): 194–209 (puts in Italian political context, and tradition of female utopian 'motherlands').

LEIGHTON, ANGELA, *Elizabeth Barrett Browning* (Hemel Hempstead: Harvester Wheatsheaf, 1986) (a critical study, arranged around Barrett Browning's relation to her father).

MERMIN, DOROTHY, *Elizabeth Barrett Browning: The Origins of a New Poetry* (Chicago and London: The University of Chicago Press, 1989) (a biographical and critical study).

STEINMETZ, VIRGINIA V., 'Images of "Mother-Want" in Elizabeth Barrett Browning's *Aurora Leigh*', *Victorian Poetry*, 21 (1983): 351–67 (concentrates on negative mothering imagery in the poem).

Christina Rossetti

CASEY, JANET GALLIGANI, 'The Potential of Sisterhood: Christina Rossetti's *Goblin Market*', *Victorian Poetry*, 29 (1991): 63–78 (like Mermin, sees sisterhood as the message of the poem, but presents this as a state available to either gender).

CHARLES, EDNA KOTIN (ed.), *Christina Rossetti, Critical Perspectives 1862–1982* (London and Toronto: Associated University Press, 1985) (collection of essays).

FOSTER, SHIRLEY, 'Speaking Beyond Patriarchy: The female voice in Emily Dickinson and Christina Rossetti', in *The Body and the Text: Hélène Cixous, Reading and Teaching*, ed. Helen Wilcox, Keith McWatters, Ann Thompson and Linda R. Williams (New York and London: Harvester Wheatsheaf, 1990) (attacking French feminist ideas of a 'women's language').

HOMANS, MARGARET, 'Syllables of Velvet: Dickinson, Rossetti and the Rhetorics of Sexuality', *Feminist Studies*, 11 (1985): 569–93 (expands Homans's argument to other poets).

JONES, KATHLEEN, *Learning Not To Be First: The Life of Christina Rossetti* (Moreton-in-Marsh, Gloucestershire: The Windrush Press, 1991) (biography).

KAPLAN, CORA, 'The Indefinite Disclosed: Christina Rossetti and Emily Dickinson', in *Women Writing and Writing About Women*, ed. Mary Jacobus (London: Croom Helm, 1979), pp. 61–79 (questions the usefulness of these poets to feminism).

KENT, DAVID (ed.), *The Achievement of Christina Rossetti* (Ithaca and London: Cornell University Press, 1987) (collection of essays).

MARSH, JAN, *Christina Rossetti: A Literary Biography* (London: Cape, 1994).

ROSENBLUM, DOLORES, *Christina Rossetti: The Poetry of Endurance* (Carbondale and Edwardsville: Southern Illinois University Press, 1986) (critical study, especially interesting on the idea of the 'mask').

Other Poets

ARMSTRONG, ISOBEL, *Victorian Poetry* (London and New York, Routledge, 1993) (chapter on women poets goes on to look at Victorians).

CLARKE, NORMA, *Ambitious Heights: Writing, Friendship, Love – the Jewsbury Sisters, Felicia Hemans, and Jane Welsh Carlyle* (London and New York:

Routledge, 1990) (Hemans in a context of what was expected of the nineteenth-century woman writer).

HICKOK, KATHLEEN, *Representations of Women: Nineteenth-Century British Women's Poetry* (Westport, Connecticut: Greenwood Press, 1984) (relates representations to contemporary ideologies).

LEIGHTON, ANGELA, *Victorian Women Poets* (New York and London, Harvester Wheatsheaf, 1992) (expands the canon, combining biographical and textual readings).

MELLOR, ANNE, K., *Romanticism and Gender* (New York and London: Routledge 1993) (evolves notions of masculine and feminine Romantic traditions).

MELLOR, ANNE K. (ed.), *Romanticism and Feminism* (Bloomington and Indianapolis: Indiana University Press, 1988) (collection of essays).

ROSS, MARLON B., *The Contours of Masculine Desire* (New York and Oxford: Oxford University Press, 1989) (revalues Hemans and Landon in the Romantic tradition).

WHITE, CHRISTINE, ' "Poets and Lovers Evermore": Interpreting Female Love in the Poetry and Journals of Michael Field', *Textual Practice*, 4 (1990): 197–212 (makes the case for regarding Michael Field as lesbian).

General

ABEL, ELIZABETH (ed.), *Writing and Sexual Difference* (Chicago: Chicago University Press, 1982) (collection of founding feminist literary critical essays).

COSSLETT, TESS, *Woman to Woman: Female Friendship in Victorian Fiction* (London and New York: Harvester and St Martins, 1988) (sections on *Aurora Leigh* and *Goblin Market* in context of contemporary conventions of friendship).

GILBERT, SANDRA and SUSAN GUBAR, *The Madwoman in the Attic: The Woman Writer and the Nineteenth-Century Literary Imagination* (New Haven and London, Yale University Press, 1979) (includes chapters on Barrett Browning, Dickinson and the novelists).

GILBERT, SANDRA and SUSAN GUBAR (eds), *Shakespeare's Sisters: Feminist Essays on Women Poets* (Bloomington: Indiana University Press, 1979).

GREENE, GAYLE and COPPELIA KAHN (eds), *Making a Difference: Feminist Literary Criticism* (London and New York: Methuen, 1985) (collection of essays, including chapters on lesbian and black feminist criticism).

MARKS, ELAINE and ISABELLE DE COURTIVRON (eds), *New French Feminisms: An Anthology* (Amherst, Mass.: The University of Massachusetts Press, 1980) (useful anthology of much-cited essays).

MILLS, SARA, et al., *Feminist Readings/Feminists Reading* (London and New York: Harvester Wheatsheaf, 1989) (helpful account of different critical approaches).

MOI, TORIL, *Sexual/Textual Politics: Feminist Literary Theory* (London and New York: Routledge, 1985) (traces and critiques progress of feminist literary criticism).

MONTEFIORE, JAN, *Feminism and Poetry* (London and New York: Pandora, 1987) (favours a historicised approach).

POOVEY, MARY, *Uneven Developments: The Ideological Work of Gender in Mid-Victorian England* (Chicago: University of Chicago Press, 1988) (relates literature, non-literary texts and ideology).

PRATT, ANNIS, *Archetypal Patterns in Women's Fiction* (Brighton: Harvester, 1982) (Jungian approach).

SHOWALTER, ELAINE, *A Literature of their Own: British Women Novelists from Brontë to Lessing* (London: Virago, 1978) (on novelists, expanding the canon).

WOLFE, SUSAN J. and JULIA PENELOPE (eds), *Sexual Practice, Textual Theory: Lesbian Cultural Criticism* (on lesbian approaches).

Index

Note on the Index: Individual poems and collections are listed by title with author following. Source writers quoted in the text and listed in the notes are omitted.

Index

Index